To the Memory of My Parents

FIFTH EDITION

Presidential Elections & American Politics

VOTERS, CANDIDATES, AND CAMPAIGNS SINCE 1952

Herbert B. Asher

The Ohio State University

Harcourt Brace College Publishers

Fort Worth   Philadelphia   San Diego
New York   Orlando   Austin   San Antonio
Toronto   Montreal   London   Sydney   Tokyo

Copyright © 1992 by Harcourt Brace & Company

All rights reserved. No part of this publication may be reproduced or transmitted in any form or by any means, electronic or mechanical, including photocopy, recording, or any information storage and retrieval system, without permission in writing from the publisher.
Requests for permission to make copies of any part of the work should be mailed to: Permissions Department, Harcourt Brace & Company, 6277 Sea Harbor Drive, Orlando, Florida 32887-6777.
Portions of this work were printed in previous editions.
Printed in the United States of America
ISBN 0-534-16926-0

6 7 8 9 0 1 2 3 4 5 039 9 8 7 6 5 4 3 2 1

Library of Congress Cataloging in Publication Data
Asher, Herbert B.
   Presidential elections and American politics : voters, candidates, and campaigns since 1952 / Herbert B. Asher. — 5th ed.
      p. cm.
   Includes bibliographical references and index.
   ISBN 0-534-16926-0
   1. Presidents—United States—Election. 2. Electioneering—United States. 3. United States—Politics and government—1945–
I. Title.
JK1965.A83 1991
324.973′092—dc20   91-17325
                                                          CIP

Sponsoring Editor *Cynthia C. Stormer*
Editorial Associate *Cathleen S. Collins*
Production Editor *Kay Mikel*
Manuscript Editor *Bob Baker*
Permissions Editor *Carline Haga*
Interior and Cover Design *Lisa Thompson*
Art Coordinator *Lisa Torri*
Interior Illustration *Lotus Art*
Typesetting *Omegatype Typography*
Cover Printing *Phoenix Color Corporation*
Printing and Binding *R. R. Donnelley & Sons Company*

Credits
We have made every effort to trace the ownership of all copyrighted material and to secure permission from copyright holders. In the event of any question arising as to the use of any material, we will be pleased to make the necessary corrections in future printings.

Excerpts on **page 6** from Kellerman, Donald S.; Kohut, Andrew; and Bowman, Carol. "The Age of Indifference: A Study of Young Americans And How They View The News," *Times Mirror Center for the People & The Press*, June 28, 1990. Excerpt on **page 24** from *Party Politics in America*, 2nd Ed., by Frank J. Sorauf, copyright © 1972. Reprinted by permission of HarperCollins Publishers. Excerpts on **pages 44, 45, and 94–97** from *The American Voter*, by Angus Campbell et al. © 1960 by John Wiley & Sons. Excerpt on **page 137** from *Report of the County Chairman* by James A. Michener. Copyright (c) 1961 by James A. Michener. Reprinted by permission of Random House, Inc. Excerpt on **pages 151–152** from "Mr. Nixon and the Arts of Evasion," by James Reston, in *The New York Times*, October 2, 1968. (c) 1968 by The New York Times Company. Reprinted by permission. Excerpt on **page 259** from *The New York Times*, October 26, 1980. (c) by 1980 The New York Times Company. Reprinted by permission. Excerpt on **pages 263–264** from " 'Expectations' the Big Foe," by Bill Peterson and Kathy Sawyer, *The Washington Post*, February 21, 1984, p. A1. (c) 1984, The Washington Post. Reprinted with permission. Excerpt on **page 265** from *Washington Journalism Review*, July–August, 1980, p. 21. Reprinted by permission.

FIFTH EDITION

Presidential Elections & American Politics

VOTERS, CANDIDATES, AND CAMPAIGNS SINCE 1952

Herb Asher is a professor of political science at The Ohio State University. He is the author of numerous articles and books on legislative politics, electoral politics, and political methodology, including *Polling and the Public, Causal Modeling, Theory Building and Data Analysis in the Social Sciences* (coedited with Herb Weisberg), and *Comparative Political Participation* (coauthored with Brad Richardson and Herb Weisberg). Professor Asher received his B.S. degree from Bucknell University and his M.A. and Ph.D. degrees from the University of Michigan.

This book analyzes presidential elections from the dual perspectives of the candidate seeking support from the electorate and the citizen choosing among competing candidates. Elections are viewed as the interplay between citizens and candidates, with each imposing constraints upon the behavior of the other. Hence, the book is organized into two major parts, the first focusing on factors that influence citizens' voting choices and the second on conditions that affect candidates' strategic choices.

Too often students believe that politics began with their own political maturity. Therefore, change is a major theme throughout the book, reflecting my concern that students learn that political arrangements and behavior are not immutable. The first part of the book (chapters 2 through 6) emphasizes trends and developments in citizens' voting preferences that have given shape to the electoral politics of the early 1990s. Chapters 5 and 6 combine the analytical work of political scientists with the descriptive efforts of political journalists to give the student some sense of the issues and candidates that have dominated presidential elections since 1952.

The second part of the book (chapters 7 through 11) also incorporates change as a central theme. Wherever possible, the most recent developments in campaign financing reforms and delegate selection procedures have been included. Chapter 9 focuses on the role of the media in the presidential selection process, reflecting my belief that the media play a much more active role in presidential politics than simply reporting the news.

This book reflects my belief that academic political scientists have much to say to students about the practical world of presidential politics. The presentation of the results of empirical political science research is straightforward; figures and percentage tables are the most common modes of presenting data. After examining the finished product, I feel quite confident that students will find the more quantitative sections readily understandable. Sections of chapter 3, on party identification, and chapter 4, on the issue-voting controversy, may go into greater depth than is needed for some courses. Thus the instructor might selectively assign sections of these chapters.

Acknowledgments

For each edition of the book, I owe a large debt to many people for their assistance. For this fifth edition, Karen Snyder and David Sweasey provided invaluable aid in data analysis; Michelle Blackman and Keith Ronczka helped with manuscript preparation; and Sally Healy and Rosalee Clawson helped on chapters 9 and 11. Thanks are also due to the reviewers of the book for their thoughtful comments and suggestions: Victoria Armstrong, University of Detroit, Michigan; Ted Jelen, Georgetown University, Washington, D.C.; Harvey Lieber, The American University, Washington, D.C.; Andrew McNitt, Eastern Illinois University, Charleston; Helmut Norpoth, SUNY–Stony Brook, New York; Ann G. Quinley, University of Massachusetts, Amherst; David Robinson, University of Houston–Downtown, Texas; and Kay Schlozman, Boston College, Chestnut Hill, Massachusetts. The Department of Political Science and the Office of the President of The Ohio State University provided many resources (some unbeknownst to them). Finally, in all five editions I relied heavily on the national election studies conducted by the Center for Political Studies at the University of Michigan. These studies and others were made available by the Inter-University Consortium for Political and Social Research, which, of course, bears no responsibility for any of the analyses and interpretations presented herein.

Herbert B. Asher

CONTENTS

6   *The Carter, Reagan, and Bush Elections—1976 to 1988* *164*

7   *Elections: From Citizens to Candidates* *199*

CHAPTER 1

Presidential Elections and the American Political System

An Overview of the Presidential Selection Process

Domestic and international political events between 1988 and early 1991 showed how swiftly political tides can turn. On the international front, the rapidity of change in Eastern Europe and the Soviet Union was breathtaking. Whereas Ronald Reagan talked of the "evil empire" in the 1980s, by 1990 American policy makers, including President Bush himself, praised Soviet President Mikhail Gorbachev for the remarkable transformation taking place in the Soviet bloc and wished him success in his endeavors. Public opinion polls showed Gorbachev to be extremely popular among Americans and *TIME* magazine (January 1, 1990) named

Gorbachev as its "Man of the Decade." The reunification of Germany, divided since the end of World War II, occurred with the Soviet Union agreeing that a united Germany could be a member of NATO. But in early 1991, the Soviet crackdown in Latvia and Lithuania raised doubts about the optimism of 1990 and the future of Soviet–American relations.

In the United States, the political changes between 1988 and early 1991 were also dramatic. After finishing third in the Iowa precinct caucuses behind Sen. Bob Dole and evangelist Pat Robertson, George Bush's bid for the Republican presidential nomination seemed likely to expire quickly as polls from New Hampshire showed Bush losing there also. But a weekend television blitz before the primary, characterized by sharp attacks on Dole, gave Bush a New Hampshire win and an easy road to the GOP nomination.

Despite the hardball tone of his New Hampshire campaign, George Bush was seen as a "wimp," and Michael Dukakis enjoyed a big lead in the polls in late spring and early summer of 1988. By September, the political fortunes of the two candidates had switched, and Bush held on to score a solid popular vote victory and an electoral college landslide on Election Day. The tactical brilliance of the Bush campaign was, for many Americans, overshadowed by its cynical manipulation of symbols, both racial and patriotic, and its irrelevance to the major issues of public policy facing the United States. A mean-spirited campaign left many Americans wondering about their new president. And yet a year after his inauguration, Bush's presidential approval ratings hit historic highs as Americans responded to his style of leadership and his call for a "kinder and gentler" nation. The wimp of early 1988 had become a strong and popular president. As the economy remained strong, as democracy seemed to be emerging in many parts of the world, and as the president continued to enjoy record high levels of popularity through mid-1990, it appeared that no credible Democrat wanted to step forward to challenge Bush for reelection in 1992. In the 1988 campaign, aspiring Democratic nominees began their jockeying soon after Reagan's reelection in 1984, with the knowledge that no incumbent would be running in 1988. In contrast, the battle for the 1992 Democratic nomination was slower in starting, in part because of the perceived unattractiveness of the nomination in the face of a popular incumbent seeking reelection. Indeed, the first two likely entrants for the 1992 Democratic nomination contest were Virginia Gov. L. Douglas Wilder and former Massachusetts U.S. Sen. Paul Tsongas, two aspirants widely viewed as very long shots in the presidential sweepstakes.

But by the second half of 1990, the political tides appeared to be shifting once again. The savings and loan scandal was at last entering the public's consciousness, and while both political parties could share the blame for the scandal, the Republican party was in the more vulnerable position since the misdeeds occurred largely during Republican presidential administrations in an aura of unregulated entrepreneurship that reflected a GOP philosophy of government. The fact that the president's son Neil Bush was connected to a failed savings and loan after receiving what he himself called "an incredibly sweet deal" brought the scandal a bit closer to the White House and to the Republican party. The savings and loan crisis on top of the HUD scandals left many Americans with the impression that rampant greed was running amok in Washington.

Other developments in the second half of 1990 also seemed to looosen the Republican lock on the 1992 election. As the budget deficit worsened, President Bush moved away from his election statement of "read my lips, no new taxes" to a position that called for "tax revenue increases," thereby creating great consternation among Republican party officials. The abortion issue threatened to create divisiveness within the GOP as pro-choice Republicans objected to their party's national policy. Some of the policies that had unified the Republican party, such as anticommunism, hostility to the Soviet Union, and a strong national defense, were no longer as compelling with the dramatic changes in the Soviet Union and Eastern Europe. Indeed, both political parties called for scaled-back defense spending in response to international developments and as a way of reducing the budget deficit.

Nineteen ninety had begun as a year of great promise and popularity for George Bush. And although early 1991 witnessed even higher levels of popularity for the president, because of the Gulf war, the domestic and international situations had become much more precarious and fraught with peril. At home the country entered a recession, the duration of which could not be forecast. The president received poor marks from Americans on his handling of the economy, and more and more citizens worried about the direction the country was going. Was the United States becoming a second-rate economic power? Was America losing control of its economic destiny to the Japanese and to the emerging European community? Were Americans once again putting themselves at the mercy of unpredictable Middle Eastern politics by their growing dependence on imported oil? Could Americans make the tough choices and commit the appropriate resources so that the products of the American educational system would be competitive with their counterparts in Europe and Japan? Would America's traditional strengths and leadership in basic and applied research and technology transfer continue to erode? Were our leaders in Washington capable of addressing fundamental problems from a broad perspective, or were they so caught up with concern about the next election that real solutions to serious problems were continually postponed? A *Washington Post* /ABC News poll (Balz and Morin, July 26, 1990), conducted in July 1990, showed that only 37 percent of Americans thought "things in this country were generally going in the right direction," while 60 percent believed that "things had gotten pretty seriously off on the wrong track." Likewise, only 9 percent of Amerians thought the nation's economy was getting better, while 58 percent thought it was getting worse. By October 1990, the percentage of Americans believing that the country was moving in the right direction had plummeted to 19 percent, with fully 79 percent believing that things had gotten off track (Dionne and Morin, April 12, 1991).

The international scene also became more dangerous, with instability and renewed repression in the Soviet Union and the outbreak of war in the Mideast when Iraq failed to remove its troops from Kuwait by the January 15, 1991 deadline specified by the United Nations. Although a coalition of nations opposed Iraq, the actual conduct of the war was largely an American enterprise that at the outset had both risks and opportunities for George Bush. But fortunately the war effort was highly successful, with the duration and number of casualties far less than expected. The president received very high marks for his skill in establishing the international coalition that opposed Iraqi aggression and for his resoluteness in pursuing his objectives. The quick and decisive end to the war made Americans proud and encouraged perceptions that the country was moving in the right direction once again. A February 1991 *Washington Post* poll indicated that 58 percent of Americans saw the country as moving in the right direction compared to 39 percent who believed it had gone off track. Bush's effective leadership throughout the crisis led some observers to conclude that Bush was unbeatable in 1992, assuming the economy was in good shape, and that the postwar situation in the Persian Gulf area was favorable for the United States. The euphoria of the military victory diminished as the domestic economy remained weak and the plight of the Kurds became increasingly prominent in news reports. Thus, by April of 1991, a majority of Americans (51 percent) once again thought things had gone off track compared to 42 percent who thought things were moving in the right direction.

As the 1990s began, the Reagan legacy became a topic of much debate. Reagan supporters described his legacy as peace and prosperity. They argued that it was the massive defense buildup of the early Reagan years that was in large part responsible for the willingness of the Soviet Union to seek an accommodation with the West and to allow fundamental political change in the nations of Eastern Europe. Moreover, Reagan loyalists argued that his administration helped restore confidence in America and a renewed sense of patriotism and pride. On the economic front, they pointed to the solid and enduring record of economic growth following the recession of the early 1980s.

Critics of the Reagan administration disputed all of these accomplishments. Critics claimed that the defense buildup was excessive and wasteful, thereby contributing to the deficit and other economic problems. They pointed out that the prosperity of the Reagan years did not benefit all Americans but, instead, favored the rich. Conservative political analyst Kevin Phillips (1990) lambasted the Reagan administration, charging that its policies increased the maldistribution of wealth in America, making the rich even richer and the poor even poorer. Other observers claimed that the Reagan view of government as the enemy weakened the government and its ability and willingness to tackle major problems and undermined the citizenry's faith in the effectiveness of governmental initiatives. And, finally, the critics argued that the combination of Reagan's defense buildup and his tax policies served to convert the United States to the world's largest debtor nation, one that did not have the economic ability to play a major role as dramatic changes took place in Eastern Europe, the Soviet Union, and elsewhere. The Reagan years, to these critics, sold the American people a bill of goods that they could have it all and not have to pay for it.

There were other developments in the American polity that generated concern as the 1990s began. Foremost among these was a general sense of disengagement, even estrangement, from politics and political matters among many Americans. Many reasons were cited for this disengagement, including the Reagan administration's antigovernment philosophy as well as the presence of a truncated and weakened party system that provided voters only two alternatives unlike the multiparty systems of other democracies. The media and the politicians were also blamed for voter disinterest: the media because of their often negative and adversarial coverage of political affairs and the politicians because of their inability and unwillingness to address crucial issues.

This disengagement from political matters manifested itself in different ways, including low voter participation; in 1988, the turnout rate among adult Americans fell to about 50 percent, the lowest rate since 1948. Other indicators of estrangement were the low initial response rates to the 1990 census and widespread tax evasion (Taylor, May 14–20, 1990, pp. 6–7). A related phenomenon was the sudden popularity of proposals to limit the number of terms that legislative incumbents could seve. Citizen-sponsored propositions and initiatives to restrict incumbents' careers were successful in a number of states and were being considered in many others.

Probably the most disheartening signs of disengagement were the low levels of interest and information about public affairs uncovered in several studies conducted in the late 1980s and early 1990s. Richard Morin (December 18–24, 1989) wryly commented, "If ignorance is bliss, then the decade of the '80s was one howling good time." For example, a survey conducted shortly before George Bush took office, but after his cabinet had been announced, showed that only 19 percent of Americans could name even one member of the cabinet, with only 10 percent identifying the secretary of state correctly (Morin, January 23–29, 1989). A dismayed Morin (December 18–24, 1989) commented that what Americans do not know is often as upsetting as what they do know, citing a *Washington Post* poll that showed 54 percent of Americans could name the judge on the television show "The People's Court," but only 9 percent could identify the chief justice of the United States. Bennett (1988) constructed a measure of political knowledge that included such measures as awareness of political figures and knowledge of candidates' and political parties' issue positions. Using a very lenient grading system, Bennett concluded that 30 percent of Americans could be classified as know-nothings, largely concentrated among the least educated, the very young and the very old, women, and the politically apathetic. Bennett expressed concern that the existence of such a large block of ignorant citizens could pose a potential threat to the viability of American democracy, since such citizens least appreciate the values that are core to a democratic political system.

Surveys of young Americans conducted by the Times Mirror Center for the People and the Press found that young citizens between the ages of eighteen and thirty were woefully uninformed about politics. The Times Mirror study, *The Age of Indifference*, talked of a new generation gap characterized by a young cohort of Americans that "knows less . . . cares less . . . reads newspapers less . . . votes less and is less critical of its leaders and institutions than young people in the past" (p. 1). For example, the Times Mirror study found that young Americans were less interested in news about Eastern Europe in 1989 than the over-fifty cohort, despite having higher educational attainment than the older age group. Across a wide range of major news stories, young Americans were less attentive and interested than their older compatriots (who themselves often had levels of attentiveness that were low). Only on the issue of abortion, which affected young people directly, were there no differences in interest between younger and older citizens: 47 percent of Americans between eighteen and thirty followed stories about the Webster decision very closely compared to 48 percent for Americans over fifty. Moreover, the Times Mirror study documented that this generation gap first arose around the mid-1970s; before that time Americans of different ages had similar levels of attentiveness to political events.

One can speculate why today's youth are less interested in news and current affairs. One reason might be that few of the major issues (abortion being a key exception) affect them directly. Or blame could be placed on the lack of effective leadership, the irrelevance of political parties, and the performance of the media. Whatever the cause, the Times Mirror study concluded (p. 28):

> The 30-second commercial spot is a particularly appropriate medium for the MTV generation. At the conclusion of the 1988 presidential campaign, Times Mirror's research showed that young voters, who began the campaign knowing less than older voters, were every bit as likely to recall advertised political themes such as pollution in Boston Harbor, Willie Horton, and the flag.
>
> Sound-bites and symbolism, the principal fuel of modern political campaigns, are well-suited to young voters who know less and have limited interest in politics and public policy. Their limited appetites and aptitudes are shaping the practice of politics and the nature of our democracy.

Future campaign managers will certainly fit campaign tactics and strategy to the need of the audience being targeted. This surely does not bode well for avoiding vacuous and irrelevant campaigns such as that of 1988.

As 1990 drew to a close, there was concern among Republican strategists that their period of ascendancy was coming to a close, that voters were questioning the direction that America had moved under the Republicans and were considering other alternatives. Unfortunately for the Democratic party, it still had not been able to identify what it collectively stood for and how it would address the serious problems facing the country. Because the Democratic party had lost seven of the last ten presidential elections, many observers felt comfortable in offering the Democrats advice on how to improve their political fortunes. Some analysts (Cohen, June 28, 1990; Germond and Witcover, July 7, 1990) recommended that the Democrats get back to their roots as the party of the little guy; that the party be willing once again to emphasize social class differences in elections and even engage in some class warfare, pegging the GOP as the party of the rich and privileged as was done in the 1930s through the 1960s. There are many problems with this strategy, including the fact that when the strategy worked, the Democrats portrayed themselves as the party of the poor and the working class, while the Republicans were depicted as the party of the wealthy. In those days, however, the poor and the working class were numerically dominant. Today, it is the middle class that is politically and numerically dominant, and advocacy for the poor may result in electoral problems among the middle class. Indeed, one of the political successes of the Reagan administrations was convincing a large segment of the American middle class that its political and economic interests were better represented by the GOP.

The problem for the Democratic party is how to win back the middle class without merely mimicking the GOP. The HUD and savings and loan scandals might provide Democrats with the opportunity to run a populist campaign that emphasizes how the middle class is paying for the misdeeds of the wealthy elite. Polls in mid-1990 showed Americans increasingly angry about the savings and loan scandal and more likely to blame the Republicans, especially the Reagan administration. However, the Democratic track record was not pure on matters of ethics, with the resignation of House Speaker Jim Wright and House Whip Tony Coelho and the presence of four Democratic U.S. senators among the "Keating Five." Moreover, populism is associated with an antigovernemnt theme, a position on which the Democratic party might not be all that believable. Populism may also be linked to support for traditional values and culture, yet it is the Democratic party that is more closely associated with support for unpopular causes and nontraditional lifestyles and values. Finally, the Democrats might have difficulty producing a presidential nominee who could run comfortably under the populist banner. Late in the 1988 campaign, Dukakis seized upon populist themes to energize this campaign but many Americans were skeptical of how true a populist the liberal Democratic governor from Massachusetts really was. Should the economy be sour in 1992 and the savings and loan scandal still salient to the public, then a populist campaign that resembled more traditional New Deal themes might have reasonable prospects for success.

Another problem for the Democratic party is the heterogeneity of its coalition in contrast to the Republican support base. A party that includes (or at least once included) conservative southern whites, blacks, northern urban Catholic ethnics, Jews, and other disparate groups is a party that has greater difficulty nominating candidates who can appeal to its disparate coalition members. Indeed, many would argue that as black support for and involvement in the Democratic party increased, many whites deserted the party, especially in the South. As the Democratic party became increasingly associated with the agenda of poor people, especially blacks, many Democratic white citizens in the working and middle classes felt that their party had deserted them. The historic candidacies of Jesse Jackson in 1984 and 1988 may have energized many black citizens, but they also turned many white citizens toward the GOP.

Race clearly remains an important factor in American politics, and for the Democratic party this manifests itself in questions about how to handle Jesse Jackson. Some Democrats were pleased with the outcome of the Virginia gubernational and New York City mayoralty elections in 1989, since black Democrats—Douglas Wilder and David Dinkins—won both contests. It was argued that the emergence of more mainstream (both in terms of policies and campaign styles) black leaders would weaken Jackson's influence and thereby lessen the difficulty the Democrats faced in holding on to black support and regaining some of the lost white support. But race as a meaningful cleavage in American politics goes far beyond the Jackson presence, and the task for the Democrats will be to identify issues and candidates that cross racial lines. The Democratic party must convince former white supporters that its advocacy of affirmative action and civil rights does not come at the expense of the white middle class and does not constitute reverse discrimination.

Each time the Democratic party loses a presidential election, it reexamines the presidential nominating process to see whether it could be "reformed" to yield a more electable Democratic candidate. After their 1984 debacle, the Democrats encouraged the creation of an early southern regional primary, which became "Super Tuesday," a day in which fourteen southern and border states, as well as six other states, selected (or began the selection of) their delegates to the national nominating conventions. The rationale for this was to reduce the importance of the Iowa precinct caucuses and the New Hampshire primary, the most prominent early delegate selection events, and to increase the influence of the South in determining the Democratic nominee. The reason for enhancing southern influence was to promote the changes of a more moderate, more centrist Democrat winning the nomination who then would be more electable in November. But as is the case with many reforms, the results were not as intended. Super Tuesday promoted three candidates—Jesse Jackson, Michael Dukakis, and Al Gore—and effectively ended the candidacy of Richard Gephardt. As the primaries moved north after Super Tuesday, Gore was quckly eliminated and the Democratic contest became a struggle between the liberal Dukakis and the even more liberal Jackson, just the opposite of what was hoped for by many Democratic party leaders.

After their 1988 loss, Democratic leaders once again acted to modify the nomination process. The major proposal was to move the California primary up from June to the first Tuesday in March, very early in the delegate-selection season. The argument once again was to reduce the influence of New Hampshire and Iowa. In these small states, relatively unknown candidates with little national support and following could perform unexpectedly well and be vaulted to the head of the pack because of the orgy of media coverage that Iowa and New Hampshire receive. It was also argued that Iowa and New Hampshire were unrepresentative and that moving up the California primary would ensure that a more representative, diverse, and cosmopolitan state—indeed, the largest state in the union—would play a more significant role in determining the identity of the Democratic nominee. As of this writing, the effort to move the California primary appears to have failed. Instead, California Democrats are considering electing about one-third of their delegates in a caucus that would occur about three months before the primary election, thereby giving California an earlier voice in the presidential selection process.

If this proposed change occurs, it may not work as Democratic leaders hope. For one thing, it is still possible for a relatively unknown candidate to emerge from the Iowa and New Hampshire contests and, because of the tremendous publicity given to those results, be propelled to victory in the California caucuses shortly thereafter. More importantly, California is a state in which distinctive single-issue politics could play a major role in generating a victor who may be out of step with other areas of the nation on certain issues. For example, the environmental movement is stronger in California than in other major states. One can envisage a candidate doing well in California on environmental concerns, perhaps even antigrowth appeals, thereby becoming a leading contender for the nomination. But such a candidate, should he or she ultimately win the nomination, might turn out to be a weak general-election nominee. Or certain cultural or lifestyle issues, particularly distinctive to California, could dominate the caucuses, yielding a victor unpopular with rank-and-file Democrats in other regions of the country. The Democrats also approved several rule changes for 1992, which may have the effect of making it more difficult for a candidate to secure the nomination early on, thereby fostering divisiveness within the party; these are discussed in chapter 7.

Although the 1992 campaign did begin later than recent presidential contests, there was much speculation about 1992 even before the 1990 midterm elections. On the Republican side, the major speculation focused on the likely future of Vice-President Quayle: would the president keep him on the ticket or dump him? On the Democratic side, the major topic was, of course, the likely identity of the 1992 nominee. Much of the speculation focused on the intentions of New York Governor Mario Cuomo. Many "Mario scenarios" were floating around. Other names were also prominently mentioned: senators Lloyd Bentsen, Bill Bradley, Joe Biden, Al Gore, and Sam Nunn; House members Richard Gephardt and Patricia Schroeder; Reverend Jesse Jackson; and the dark-horse candidacies of former Sen. Paul Tsongas and Virginia Gov. Douglas Wilder mentioned earlier.

After the 1990 midterm elections, the campaign for the presidency in 1992 became more prominent, although the Persian Gulf war initially suppressed overt presidential campaign activities. Three themes dominated news coverage of the 1990 elections: (1) How would President Bush cope with a Congress in which Democrats still controlled both Houses and how would this affect his reelection chances? (2) What did the election outcome mean for the future of the Democratic and Republican parties? (3) What did the 1990 results signify for Democrats who might seek their party's presidential nomination in 1992?

Even before all the votes were tallied in the 1990 midterm elections, the spin doctors for both political parties were trying to shape media interpretations of the outcome. The Republican spin doctors pointed to the average historical losses that the president's party in Congress typically suffers in a midterm election. And when Republicans lost only nine House seats and one Senate seat, GOP spokespersons tried to put a very positive light on the election results. Before the election, the Democratic spin doctors instead focused on how difficult it would be for the Democratic party to make substantial gains since it already held so many seats. Hence the Democrats argued that their relatively small gains actually constituted a substantial victory. Certainly the mood of the Democrats after the election was more upbeat than the GOP. And given that six months before the election, Republicans were talking confidently about reducing the Democratic margin in the U.S. Senate as the first step in regaining control of the Senate in 1992, the Democratic gain of one seat in 1990 was a setback to the GOP's 1992 aspirations.

With respect to the 1992 presidential contest, numerous political commentators argued that a number of potential 1992 candidates had been hurt by the 1990 election results. First was George Bush, since much of the blame for the GOP's losses centered on the clumsy way the White House dealt with the budget deficit and tax negotiations. Moreover, the fact that the GOP had lost congressional seats in two consecutive elections was seen as a potential sign of weakness for 1992. On the Democratic side, two oft-mentioned potential 1992 nominees—New York Gov. Mario Cuomo and Sen. Bill Bradley of New Jersey—were viewed as having suffered setbacks since their reelection margins were smaller than expected. In contrast, the sweeping victory of Sen. Al Gore of Tennessee was seen as providing a boost to his 1992 prospects.

The contest for the presidency is an extremely drawn out affair in which incumbent presidents may *formally* declare their candidacy for reelection a year or fifteen months before the election, and nonincumbents may announce their candidacies up to two years in advance of the election. But the actual contest for the nomination usually begins even earlier. Aspirants, especially those from the out-of-power party, need to test the waters early and raise funds. They should build campaign organizations, especially in such early critical states as Iowa and New Hampshire that enjoy disproportionate influence in the presidential selection process. Indeed, lesser known presidential candidates typically start campaigning in Iowa more than a year before the actual precinct caucuses and spend weeks and weeks in Iowa hoping for a strong showing in this important state.

The presidential selection process has become very lengthy despite efforts by the political parties to compress the formal delegate selection into a three-and-a-half month period beginning in late February. Increasingly, more and more primaries are bunched together in the first month of the formal delegate-selection season. This phenomenon, known as *front-loading*, means that presidential hopefuls have to be ready to make a major and sustained effort from the outset, which in turn requires them to start their candidacies months and even years in advance.

When many potential nominees seek voter support and media coverage, candidates must demonstrate their viability and credibility in a variety of ways to distinguish themselves from the pack. One such way is to be successful in fund-raising and to be among the first to qualify for public matching funds in the primary season. Another method is to establish a political action committee (PAC), a tactic used widely in preparation for the 1988 contest but less so in 1992. Would-be presidential aspirants ostensibly set up a PAC to raise and spend money on behalf of other candidates and party committees. In this way the aspirants are able to win the favor and support of key party leaders. Presidential PACs do much more than just funnel contributions to other candidates. A typical PAC raises funds, produces newsletters, and builds a mailing list of potential donors who may become critically important during the nomination campaign. Moreover, PACs enable prospective candidates to travel around the country giving speeches, generating media coverage, and having their expenses paid by the PAC.

Polls are another way for a candidate to demonstrate his or her viability. For example, polls conducted in 1990 regularly showed Jesse Jackson and Mario Cuomo to be the two leading Democratic candidates for the 1992 nomination when Ted Kennedy was not included among the choices. Another poll-related measure of strength is how well a candidate runs against likely general-election opponents in trial heats, matching pairs of possible Democratic and Republican candidates. Because polls taken so far in advance of the primary season can fluctuate dramatically, they do not provide very precise estimates of a candidate's support. However, these early polls are analyzed very closely by the media and political strategists for signs of how the presidential horse race is unfolding and for indications of which candidates are gaining or losing momentum and support. The widespread publicity given these early polls is particularly important for party activists, potential campaign contributors and volunteers, and other attentive observers who monitor the presidential campaign closely from the start.

Media coverage is another measure of the early strength and credibility of the candidates. It is particularly important to be mentioned in columns by prominent, nationally syndicated journalists such as David Broder of the *Washington Post* and Tom Wicker of the *New York Times*, and in such reputable publications as the *National Journal* and the national news magazines. Clearly, the more often a well-known journalist covers a candidate, the more likely it is that other journalists will also cover that candidate. The more coverage a candidate receives, the more likely it is that his or her standing in the polls will rise. And the higher a candidate's poll standing, the more likely it is that he or she will receive media coverage, particularly when there is a crowded field of candidates.

Endorsements are another measure of the early strength of candidates. Picking up key political endorsements and the backing of major interest groups gives candidates a substantial boost, while the failure to receive certain endorsements may be viewed as a setback. The Mondale candidacy in 1984 illustrated the benefits and pitfalls of endorsements. Early on, organized labor endorsed Mondale, as did women's groups. Labor support was critical to Mondale's success in winning the nomination, particularly after he stumbled badly in New Hampshire. Gary Hart tried to convert Mondale's endorsements into a liability by portraying Mondale as the candidate of special interests. Although Hart was not able to defeat Mondale, the special interest tag was a burden for Mondale throughout the general election. Nevertheless, key endorsements accompanied by money and staff workers can be very critical to a candidate's performance in the primaries.

Finally, candidates can demonstrate early strength through their showing in straw polls held by various state parties, in conventions, and in similar contests. Typically, these events are inconclusive, since no convention delegates are selected. But they have great importance because of the media coverage. Indeed, they might quite accurately be called *media events*. Because of the horse race perspective the media bring to their coverage of the presidential campaign, these early events receive heavy coverage. Television and press reporters seek out early signs of who's ahead, who's behind, who's gaining, and who's trailing. Candidates participate in media events because the media are there (as are party leaders and activists from the various states); the media come because the candidates are there. Such events have become more frequent in recent presidential campaigns and are commonly referred to as meat markets and cattle shows dominated by puffery, narrow appeals to specific constituencies, and behind-the-scenes machinations. Nevertheless, these pseudo events become tests that candidates must pass in their pursuit of the nomination.

The media role in reporting pseudo events is simply one example of a more general phenomenon—the extensiveness and even intrusiveness of media involvement in the presidential selection process (chapter 9 will discuss this subject more fully). The presence of the media distorts the process in a variety of ways. Pseudo events receive more coverage than they merit. Even the formal aspects of the selection process—the caucuses and primaries that actually choose delegates—are distorted by patterns of media coverage. The early primaries and caucuses receive far more coverage than the later ones. Winning the Iowa caucus or the New Hampshire primary is worth much more television airtime and newspaper and newsmagazine coverage than winning the California and New Jersey primaries, which in recent years have been held very late in the primary season. The heavy importance given to the early states is recognized by the legislatures of these states. The New Hampshire legislature regularly threatens to move its primary to one week before any other state's primary because New Hampshire does not want to lose the political and economic benefits of its early primary. Likewise, the Iowa legislature is just as adamant in protecting Iowa's early status. Thus, when the Democratic party reformed its delegate selection procedures for the 1984, 1888, and 1992 campaigns, it granted exemptions to Iowa and New Hampshire so that they might continue to make early delegate selections. By way of contrast, all other states had to conduct their primaries and caucuses in a three-month period between early March and early June.

The 1992 primaries and caucuses will again take place within an approximate three-month period. But because of the front-loading occurring as more and more states move up their primaries and caucuses, candidates in 1992 will have to contest many states in rapid succession. As a result, candidates could be expected to begin campaigning even earlier than in the past, although this was not the case for 1992. Thus, paradoxically, shortening the formal delegate-selection process has actually lengthened the contest for the presidency. The presidential selection system is lengthy, exhausting, and overly dependent on the media.

Even more fundamental questions about the presidential nomination system should be raised. For example, does the system favor certain types of candidates over others? More important, does the system produce nominees qualified to be president? The tremendous campaign demands of the nomination process may work to the disadvantage of conscientious officials currently holding public office. For example, according to some observers, Sen. Howard Baker's poor showing in the 1980 Republican nomination contest was due to his late start. One reason for this late start was said to be Baker's fulfilling first his responsibilities as U.S. senator and GOP minority leader. Because Baker's presidential aspirations were still alive, he decided not to seek reelection to the Senate in 1986 so that he could contemplate a full-time bid for the Republican nomination in 1988. The Baker example suggests that being unemployed, in the sense of not holding public office, may be advantageous in running for president. Certainly recent political history provides some support for this proposition. Jimmy Carter ran successfully in 1976 as a *former* governor of Georgia. In 1980 neither of the two leading GOP contenders—Ronald Reagan and George Bush—held public office when they sought the Republican nomination. And in 1984 Walter Mondale did not hold public office as he successfully sought the nomination. It might be well to question a nomination system that appears to favor the unemployed candidate.

In addition, the physical strains and stresses of the nomination process may deter some would-be candidates from seeking the office. The process may be so dispiriting that distinguished citizens opt out. Walter Mondale was the first candidate for the 1976 Democratic nomination to drop out of the race, asserting, "Basically I found I did not have the overwhelming desire to be president which is essential for the kind of campaign that is required. I don't think anyone should be president who is not willing to go through fire" (*Congressional Quarterly Weekly Report*, November 30, 1974, p. 3214). Although Mondale evidently possessed the "overwhelming desire" in 1984, the question is whether surviving an endurance contest is really a central requirement for being president. The presidency may be a stressful position, but it is not characterized by the indignities of interminable evenings on the road, extensive separation from one's family, and the like. Perhaps the grueling pace of the primaries and caucuses is a proper test of presidential capabilities. Others, however, have argued just the opposite, asserting that the endurance-contest features of the primaries have little, if anything, to say about a person's presidential fitness. Michael Robinson has extended this argument to claim that primaries are dysfunctional for both the candidates and the country. He writes (1975):

> The primary system has made it so that the nice guys, including the competent ones, stay out of the whole ordeal. Right from the start, the primary system means that only those who possess near psychopathic ambition and temperament will get involved and stay involved.
>
> All told, the primary system is a disaster. It costs too much; it takes too long; it makes pseudo-enemies out of true political allies; and it makes pseudo-winners out of true losers. And, more importantly, the primary system has made the process of becoming President so dispiriting, so distasteful, that those who would become, shouldn't.

There is most likely an element of exaggeration in Robinson's comments, but nevertheless the question remains: Does the presidential selection system produce nominees with the qualities to be president? The answer, of course, is, "Not necessarily." What might some of these qualities be? Certainly presidents should be persons of integrity and character as well as good judges of the integrity and character of others. Presidents should be informed and knowledgeable and understanding of the ways and means of presidential influence and power. They should have a sense of priorities and the administrative and organizational skills to pursue those priorities effectively. And certainly presidents should be effective communicators. Many other qualities could be listed. The point is that only some of these qualities are truly tested in the quest for the presidency. Governing the country and running for president require different skills and talents, yet the presidential selection process provides voters with much more insight about candidates' campaign skills than about their governing abilities.

Finally, the presidential selection process often seems contrary to the needs of the political parties. Although the Democratic party adopted reforms for its 1984, 1988, and 1992 conventions to guarantee greater participation by party officials and elected officeholders, the process of obtaining the nomination may undermine the party. This is particularly so for the Democratic party, which is much more of an umbrella party than is the GOP. Indeed, some observers have argued that there is no Democratic party per se, but instead a collection of interests—labor, blacks, feminists, gays, environmentalists, and so on—that find the Democratic party a useful vehicle for pursuing their own particular ends. Since their 1984 debacle, the Democrats, under the leadership of their national chairmen Paul Kirk and Ron Brown, have attempted to limit the number and the influence of special interest caucuses.

The problem for both Democrats and Republicans is that often the strategy appropriate for winning the nomination may be counterproductive in the general election unless the candidate is extremely skillful in shifting from a narrowly defined support group to a more broadly based coalition. For example, many observers argued that the Mondale candidacy in the general election of 1984 was doomed to defeat because of widespread perceptions that the Democratic nominee was the captive of special interests. Such perceptions arose because of the manner in which Mondale won the Democratic nomination. The point to keep in mind is that the current nomination system encourages candidates to seek out specific bases of support. This is particularly the case when many candidates are running, in view of the diverse groups making up the Democratic party. In fact, the candidate with the broadest appeal to the electorate and with the best chance to win the general election may be less favored to win the nomination because he or she has a limited appeal to specific groups within the party. Thus the candidate of special interests in the primaries may have to perform a very delicate balancing act in order to become the candidate of Middle America in the general election.

This brief overview of the nomination system indicates that for some Americans—prospective candidates and their staff, public opinion pollsters, and political commentators and journalists—presidential politics is always in season. But for the average citizen, the presidential contest may become prominent only during the general-election campaign every four years, and then perhaps only in the latter weeks of the campaign. Citizen involvement in the presidential race is largely confined to the later, highly visible stages of the campaign; but for the candidate and the campaign team, the serious effort now extends into years. This difference in political attention and activity suggests that presidential elections can be viewed from two differing perspectives—that of the citizen who selects the nation's leader and that of the candidate who seeks support from the citizenry. Elections involve inter-action between citizens and candidates, and it is this interaction that provides the organizing themes of this book. Part I of the book deals with elections from the perspective of citizens; it focuses on such topics as the elements that determine the citizen's vote, and it examines such factors as party identifica-tion and the candidates and issues unique to an election. Part 2 concentrates on campaign strategy and the conduct of presidential campaigns, mainly from the vantage point of political elites such as candidates and party strategists.

Unfortunately, there are disparities in the information available for the analysis of the behavior of citizens as compared to the behavior of political elites. On the citizen side, numerous surveys and public opinion polls provide detailed information about the attitudes and preferences of voters. The series of national sample surveys conducted since 1948 by the Survey Research Center and the Center for Political Studies of the University of Michigan is of particular importance. These surveys (hereafter referred to as SRC/CPS) are designed to explain and not simply predict electoral outcomes and are an invaluable source of data for studying citizen behavior over time, since many of the same or similar questions were asked at each election. Other important sources of information about citizen behavior are the public opinion polls conducted regularly by, among others, the Gallup and Harris organizations, major newspapers and the national television networks, and the National Opinion Research Center and the election statistics and census information published periodically by the U.S. government.

Political elites such as candidates and party strategists are far less accessible than voters, and much of their behavior is less public than that of voters. While published statements and documents are available, it must be recognized that public utterances may have strategic purposes, such as winning support or covering up problems, and therefore may not accurately reflect elite preferences and motivations. Similarly, the various interpreta-tions of elite behavior published by respected observers of American politics should not necessarily be viewed as factual or correct since each author (including me) has certain values and preferences that influence his or her analysis of political events. This results in sharply different interpretations being given to the same event or set of events.

Hence, there is much speculation about the reasons and motivations underlying elite behavior, campaign tactics, and the like. Speculation is not necessarily bad, but it may leave many interesting questions unanswered. For example, did Senator Goldwater really believe in 1964 that there were millions of conservative citizens just waiting for the opportunity to vote for a genuinely conservative candidate? Did Lyndon Johnson know in 1964 that his promises to keep American soldiers out of a land war in Southeast Asia would soon be broken? Did Richard Nixon in 1968 really have a plan for peace in Vietnam in his coat pocket that he could not or would not reveal for fear of upsetting the Paris peace negotiations? Did Ronald Reagan truly believe in 1980 that taxes could be cut substantially, defense spending increased sizably, and the federal budget brought into balance? All of these questions are at the heart of politics, yet we are less able to answer them conclusively than we are to investigate the bases of vote choice by the average citizen.

The 1952–1988 Era

This book's aim is to understand the dynamics of presidential elections—not simply to describe a specific election in unique terms but to develop a more general approach that will enable readers to comprehend the similarities and dissimilarities in elections over time and perhaps even to project to future elections. The ten presidential elections from 1952 through 1988 are instructive for a variety of reasons. They span an unusually diverse period of American history, ranging from the relatively tranquil and issueless 1950s to the more turbulent and issues-oriented 1960s and 1970s to the more optimistic and even nostalgic Reagan years. The elections of this era are characterized by the decline in the early 1970s in the importance of traditional New Deal–economic prosperity issues and the rise of new issues centering on race, war, and lifestyles. Yet the raging inflation, high interest rates, and recession of the late 1970s produced a presidential election in 1980 in which economic concerns were once again paramount—this time favoring the Republican challenger.

The 1952–1988 era includes elections in which the candidate's personality was of paramount importance (1952 and 1956); an election in which religion played a major role (1960); contests in which race and civil rights were both above and beneath the surface (1964 and 1968); a race in which a third-party candidate almost forced the election into the House of Representatives (1968); an election in which one party scored a smashing victory (1972) only to have the significance of that victory called into question by subsequent revelations of serious misdeeds; two contests (1976 and 1980) in which economic concerns contributed to the defeat of incumbent presidents; and one election (1988) in which the conduct of the campaign itself became the focus of widespread dismay. The circumstances under which presidents left office in this period suggest the volatility and diversity of the era. Two presidents (Eisenhower and Reagan) left office to widespread acclaim and affection; another (Kennedy) was assassinated; another (Johnson) was practically prevented from seeking reelection; another (Nixon) was forced to resign from office in the face of inevitable impeachment in the House of Representatives and conviction in the Senate; and two (Ford and Carter) experienced the rare electoral defeat of an incumbent president.

Beyond their intrinsic interest, the presidential elections between 1952 and 1988 are important to analyze because they span a period of significant trends in American politics. In this era the conduct of presidential campaigns underwent substantial change, as did the composition of the electorate itself. Citizens became more critical of the political system. At the elite level, there was a fundamental shift in the meanings of the ideological labels that often occupy prominent positions in presidential election contests. Finally, the years 1952–1988 can be viewed as a transitional period during which the partisan alignments emerging from the Great Depression of the 1930s gradually weakened, to be replaced by a structure of partisan allegiances as yet unclear. Discussion will center around trends and topics and their implications for American presidential politics in the following sections.

CHANGES IN THE CONDUCT OF CAMPAIGNS

The advent of television in the 1950s drastically altered the conduct of presidential campaigns and the strategies candidates used to win the presidential nomination; television made it possible for candidates to go directly to the public on a massive scale, thereby reducing reliance on the party organization. Observers have bemoaned the impact of television on presidential politics, citing its tremendous cost, which has led to a decline in more traditional grass-roots campaign activities. Furthermore, the effective use of television requires skilled media personnel; hence, campaigns are increasingly managed by market research and advertising companies, to the detriment of the political party organizations. The prominence of media experts in campaigns has led to overblown descriptions of the influence of television, a topic addressed in chapter 9.

The late 1960s and 1970s also witnessed substantial reforms in the presidential selection process. Public funding was provided to the presidential candidates for the first time in 1976. More important, since 1968 the political parties, especially the Democrats, have adopted a series of reforms to make the presidential nomination process more open and democratic. Because of some unanticipated consequences of these reforms, the Democrats in the 1980s adopted some rule changes to return the political party to a more prominent position in presidential politics. The reforms in conjunction with media coverage of the presidential selection process have dramatically changed the way in which a presidential nomination is obtained and the role of the political party in that process—themes developed in chapters 8 and 9.

CHANGES IN THE CHARACTERISTICS OF THE ELECTORATE

The eligible electorate expanded dramatically between 1952 and 1988. In particular, the role of black citizens, especially in the South, changed markedly. From systematic disenfranchisement and low levels of participation, black citizens today are sometimes more politically active than their white compatriots. The extension of the vote to eighteen year olds has also increased the eligible electorate; it added 11 million citizens to the list of potential voters in 1972.

Certain characteristics of the electorate have changed noticeably since 1952. For example, in 1952 more than 40 percent of the electorate had an eighth-grade education or less, while by 1988 this proportion was about 10 percent. At the other end of the education continuum, less than 15 percent of the people had had some college education in 1952, while by 1988 more than 42 percent had had at least some college experience. Given the emphasis in classical democratic theory on the competence of the individual citizen to make informed, rational decisions (a topic developed in chapter 4), the trend toward higher educational levels in assessing the performance of the American electoral system cannot be ignored.

The age distribution of the American electorate is another changing characteristic, the effect of which is difficult to identify precisely. In the 1960s the electorate was becoming younger as the World War II baby boom reached voting age. As younger people generally have weaker attachments to political parties (a theme developed in chapter 3), the presence of a large segment of potentially mobilizable young voters could have a substantial impact on American politics under the proper conditions. But the long-range trend now appears to be one of an increasingly older electorate because of the end of the postwar baby boom and the gradual reduction in the U.S. birthrate.

CHANGES IN CITIZEN EVALUATIONS OF THE POLITICAL SYSTEM

In addition to changes in the characteristics of the electorate, there have been potentially significant trends in the public's attitudes toward the political system. People's loss of confidence in government, indicated by responses to a set of five questions asked periodically by SRC/CPS is particularly important. Presented in table 1.1, these responses indicate a dramatic increase in cynicism toward government, a trend that predates the Watergate affair. Substantial rises in cynicism occurred between 1964 and 1968; for example, in this period the percentage of citizens believing that government was run for the benefit of a few big interests rose by 13 percent, while the percentage saying that the government could be trusted to do what was right only some of the time jumped by 15 percent. Between 1972 and 1973, the period of the Watergate revelations, there were additional, sharp increases in levels of cynicism. The percentage of citizens who believed that quite a few government officials were a little crooked rose by 17 points, while the percentage of citizens who thought government was run for the benefit of big interests jumped by 19 points.

Note that even with the resignation of Richard Nixon in 1974 and the passing of the Watergate affair into history, citizen confidence in government

TABLE 1.1

Trends in Trust in Government, 1958–1988 (in percentages)

Attitudes of trust or distrust	Response categories	1958	1964	1968	1970	1972	1973	1974	1976	1980	1984	1988
1. How much of the time do you think you can trust the government in Washington to do what is right?	Always	16%	15%	8%	7%	7%	4%	3%	4%	2%	4%	4%
	Most of the time	59	63	55	48	47	30	35	31	25	42	38
	Some of the time	24	22	37	45	46	66	63	65	73	55	58
	Total	99	100	100	100	100	100	101	100	100	101	100
	Number of cases	1,711	1,423	1,310	1,539	1,286	1,383	2,413	2,727	1,512	1,861	1,704
2. Would you say the government is pretty much run by a few big interests looking out for themselves or that it is run for the benefit of all of the people?	For benefit of all	—	69	56	45	47	28	27	27	23	41	33
	Few big interests	—	31	44	55	53	72	73	73	77	59	67
	Total		100	100	100	100	100	100	100	100	100	100
	Number of cases		1,335	1,212	1,423	1,223	1,317	2,270	2,565	1,457	1,783	1,665
3. Do you think that people in the government waste a lot of money we pay in taxes, waste some of it, or don't waste very much of it?	Not much	11	7	4	4	3	3	1	3	2	4	2
	Some	44	45	35	27	28	22	23	21	18	30	34
	A lot	45	48	61	69	69	75	76	76	80	66	64
	Total	100	100	100	100	100	100	100	100	100	100	100
	Number of cases	1,704	1,413	1,309	1,555	1,303	1,394	2,458	2,772	1,572	1,879	1,738
4. Do you feel that almost all of the people running the government are smart people who usually know what they are doing, or do you think that quite a few of them don't seem to know what they are doing?	Know what they are doing	61	72	61	54	56	53	52	47	35		
	Don't know what they are doing	39	28	39	46	44	47	48	53	65		
	Total	100	100	100	100	100	100	100	100	100		
	Number of cases	1,681	1,386	1,280	1,508	1,262	1,348	2,378	2,660	1,532		
5. Do you think that quite a few of the people running the government are a little crooked, not very many are, or do you think hardly any of them are crooked at all?	Hardly any	28	19	20	17	17	12	10	14	9	15	12
	Not very many	46	51	54	50	48	35	43	42	43	52	47
	Quite a few	26	30	26	33	36	53	47	44	49	33	42
	Total	100	100	100	100	101	100	100	100	101	100	101
	Number of cases	1,670	1,383	1,283	1,517	1,284	1,373	2,412	2,684	1,543	1,831	1,694

SOURCES: SRC/CPS election studies of 1958, 1964, 1968, 1970, 1972, 1973, 1974, 1976, 1980, 1984, and 1988. Item 4 was not included in the 1984 and 1988 surveys.

had not by 1988 resumed the high levels characteristic of the early 1960s, although there was a sizable increase in trust in government between 1980 and 1984. This suggests that the sources of cynicism and dissatisfaction go beyond mere approval or disapproval of incumbent officeholders. Arthur Miller found that one reason for the decline in political trust between 1964 and 1970 was citizen dissatisfaction with federal government actions on various issues, particularly Vietnam and civil rights (1974). Miller identified two groups of cynics—cynics of the left and cynics of the right—who disagreed with federal governmental policies. The left-wing cynics were generally favorable to political and social change and thought that many social and political ills could be cured by changing the existing political system. For example, left-wing cynics thought that urban riots could best be prevented by solving the problems of poverty and unemployment. Right-wing cynics were more supportive of the existing political arrangements and favored authorities who would act to control disruptive elements by whatever means necessary. Thus, right-wing cynics tended to believe that urban unrest should be handled by the use of police force. The point is that both groups of cynics were dissatisfied with governmental policies, which they perceived as being middle-of-the-road, that is, some distance from their own preferred positions.

These findings have direct relevance for the discussion in chapter 11 of a possible political realignment in the United States. Miller's research suggests that dissatisfaction is more policy related than personality oriented. Therefore, simply changing the incumbent leadership, for example, the president, may not necessarily reduce the level of distrust. Of course, another source of distrust in government is dissatisfaction with the incumbent leadership, which eventually may be generalized to the political system at large. Hence, replacement of that leadership may produce some increase in popular confidence in government. But if dissatisfaction is largely rooted in policy concerns, then leaders must at some point confront these issues. And if the issues and problems are themselves intractable, this bodes poorly for governmental performance that would be likely to generate public confidence. Undoubtedly, the inability of the federal government in the late 1970s and the early 1980s to resolve the nation's economic woes contributed to a further decline in the public's confidence in political authorities and institutions. Similarly, the improved economic situation and the confident leadership style of Ronald Reagan contributed to a growth in public confidence by 1984. By 1988, the proportion of Americans believing that government was run by a few big interests and that quite a few government officials were crooked grew by about 9 percent, perhaps in response to the Iranian arms scandal and revelations about American dealings with Pananamian dictator Noriega. One can reasonably speculate that popular distrust of government will increase further if the savings and loan scandal expands.

There are also important trends in public support for the institutions of elections and the political party system. Jack Dennis found that the institution of elections received widespread support in the electorate, particularly with respect to the belief that it is the duty of citizens to vote (1970). Dennis also found more negative evaluations of the political party system in comparison to the electoral system. For example, in response to a question as to which part of the government had done the best job in recent years, only about 4 percent of a 1973 sample of citizens said the political parties, compared to 45 percent for Congress, 26 percent for the Supreme Court, and 25 percent for the president—this at a time when the president was under widespread attack (Dennis, 1974: 11a). These varying perceptions of elections versus parties are laid out clearly in figure 1.1, which shows the percentage of citizens believing that political parties and elections help make the government responsive to the people. Note that while elections are evaluated more positively, both trend lines slope downward, indicating decreased support for both elections and parties. For most Americans, political parties are largely seen as irrelevant in promoting governmental responsiveness.

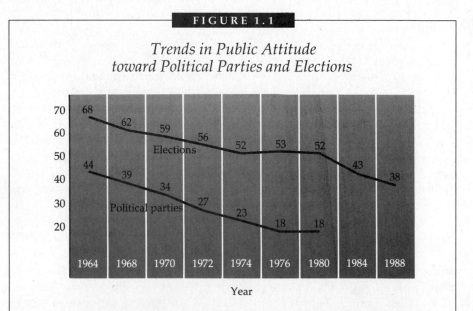

FIGURE 1.1

Trends in Public Attitude toward Political Parties and Elections

Year

Percentage of respondents saying that the institution helps a good deal in making government responsive to the people

SOURCES: SRC/CPS surveys of 1964, 1968, 1970, 1972, 1974, 1976, 1980, 1984, and 1988. The actual questions were: "How much do you feel that political parties help to make the government pay attention to what the people think: a good deal, some, or not much?" and "How much do you feel that having elections makes the government pay attention to what the people think: a good deal, some, or not much?" The item on political parties was not included in the 1984 and 1988 surveys.

It is clear that political parties are held in relatively low esteem by citizens. Popular attitudes toward the parties are reflected in the pridefully uttered statement "I vote for the man, not the party," in the common description of party workers as hacks, and in the widespread disdain expressed about party patronage positions. Political parties were never specifically mentioned in the Constitution and were often referred to pejoratively as *factions* by the Founding Fathers.

The negative evaluation of parties is paradoxical, given the central role that they play in the organization and processes of electoral politics. Indeed, a major goal of the newly transformed nations of Eastern Europe is the development of a well-functioning political party system. The decline in popular support for the political parties has been a source of major concern for numerous observers of American politics. A political scientist, Walter Dean Burnham, has written:

> The New Deal might come to be regarded one day as a temporary if massive deviation from a secular trend toward the gradual disappearance of the political party in the United States. It is clear that the significance of the party as an intermediary link between voters and rulers has again come into serious question. . . .
>
> It seems fairly evident that if this secular trend toward politics without parties continues to unfold, the policy consequences will be profound. To state the matter with utmost simplicity: Political parties, with all their well-known human and structural shortcomings, are the only devices thus far invented by the wit of Western man which with some effectiveness can generate countervailing collective power on behalf of the many individually powerless against the relatively few who are individually—or organizationally—powerful. Their disappearance could only entail the unchallenged ascendancy of the latter unless new structures of collective power were developed to replace them. . . . This contingency, despite recent publicity for the term "participatory democracy," seems precisely what is not likely to occur (1970: 132–33).

In a similar vein, David Broder, a respected political journalist, wrote a book entitled *The Party's Over* in which he expressed fear for the disintegration of the political parties. He cited as evidence for his concern the increase in the number of citizens who did not identify with either political party and the tremendous jump in the number of split-ticket votes cast in recent years—topics addressed more fully in chapter 3. Broder also discussed the weakening of the party organization, citing such causes as the reduction in the number of patronage positions brought about by civil service reforms; the advent of technology, particularly television, that makes the party organization less necessary to conduct campaigns; and the increase in political work done by volunteers with loyalties to candidates and not to parties. To Broder's list might be added the campaign-financing and delegate-selection reforms that to a substantial degree have taken the traditional political party organization out of the business of nominating and electing its own presidential candidates, and recent court decisions that have further weakened political patronage.

The implications of these trends will be considered further in the discussion of a potential partisan realignment in the United States in chapter 11. For now, note that the weakening of partisan attachments and the party organization is likely to lead to vote decisions based on factors other than party and to campaigns conducted by persons other than party elites. Furthermore, the decline in the two traditional parties may facilitate the emergence of new organizations built around different issues or principles, or both. While it is fashionable to criticize the Republican and Democratic parties as archaic and unresponsive despite the far-reaching party reforms instituted in recent years, several critical functions that the parties do perform must be kept in mind:

> The American parties . . . serve democracy by reaffirming and promoting its basic values. The very activities of the two gigantic and diversified American parties promote a commitment to the values of compromise, moderation, and the pursuit of limited goals. They also encourage the political activity and participation that a democracy depends on. . . .
>
> In addition, the parties offer an operating mechanism for the processes of democracy. By organizing aggregates of voters, the major American parties express the demands and wishes of countless Americans with meaningful political power. They are mobilizers of both democratic consent and dissent. By channeling choices into a few realistic alternatives, they organize the majorities by which the country is governed. . . . The party is, moreover, the instrument of compromise among competing claims on public policy. . . . To put the matter briefly, the political parties have helped fashion a workable system of representation for the mass democracies of the twentieth century (Sorauf, 1972: 54–55).

The possible demise of the traditional political parties without any clear indication as to what is likely to emerge as their replacement should be viewed with mixed feelings. This is not to say that the two-party system should be preserved as is, no matter what its shortcomings are, but rather replacing the present party system offers no necessary assurances of improvement.

CHANGES IN POLITICAL DISCOURSE

In addition to trends in popular evaluations of government, the years 1952–1988 witnessed startling changes in the meanings given to political labels, such as liberal and conservative—changes with important consequences for understanding American politics and assessing the presidency as a governmental institution. Despite the tendency of labels to distort and oversimplify, their use in political discourse often serves as a useful shorthand to describe where an individual stands on a broad range of issues. Throughout the 1950s and up through the mid-1960s, the meanings of such terms as *liberal* and *conservative* were fairly clear, particularly when applied to political elites rather than to the average citizen. For example, a conservative was commonly portrayed as a person opposed to federal governmental intervention in the economy and society. Knowing this general position, one could predict fairly accurately how a conservative would feel about a variety of domestic social welfare programs, such as federal aid to education and public housing. A liberal, on the other hand, was most often described as an advocate of federal intervention.

Because of their different policy preferences, conservatives and liberals had different opinions about the optimal relative strength of Congress versus the president. The liberals favored a strong, activist president and viewed Congress with its seniority system, conservative southern committee chairmen, and Rules Committee (particularly during the Kennedy administration) as a major roadblock to progressive legislation. The conservatives, on the other hand, looked to Congress to block the advances of an activist president. The liberal idealization of presidential power reached its peak in 1964 and 1965 during the Johnson administration, when presidential initiatives led to passage of two major civil rights bills and a host of domestic welfare programs, many of which had been bottled up in Congress for years.

Until the late 1960s and 1970s, it appeared that power was flowing to the president at the expense of Congress, the process reaching its culmination during the Johnson and Nixon administrations, when an unpopular, costly, and undeclared war continued to be prosecuted in the face of ever-rising congressional opposition. Given the apparently unlimited ends to which presidents employed their power, the attitudes of liberals and conservatives toward the relative power of Congress and the president and the role of the federal government began to change in the late 1960s. Johnson's conduct of the Vietnam War was a major catalyst in this change, as were the abuses of presidential power (enemies lists, illegal wiretaps, and burglaries) revealed during the Nixon administration. Beyond presidential misconduct there were growing fears about centralized government acting as Big Brother. These fears were exacerbated by the development of computer-related technology that made it possible for the government to maintain massive data banks on its citizens. Liberals no longer sanctified presidential and national power, recognizing that such power could be put to bad as well as good ends. Liberals praised Congress for its attempts to resist presidential incursions in such areas as impoundment of funds, control over the national budget, war powers, and executive privilege. Conservatives, however, tended to rally behind the president (especially Nixon), particularly in the areas of foreign policy and fiscal affairs. Conservatives warned of tying the hands of the president and at times berated Congress for its efforts to regain power. Liberals, who had once been firm supporters of foreign aid and international involvement, were now dubbed the *new isolationists* because of their reaction to the Vietnam War and to American military aid policies that resulted in

American allies fighting each other with American-supplied arms. Conservatives did not switch en masse to an endorsement of presidential initiatives in the realm of foreign affairs, although they did provide the bulk of the president's support in Congress on the war powers issue. Actions of the Nixon administration contributed further to the confusion in the meaning of liberal and conservative. A "conservative" administration instituted peacetime wage and price controls, formulated budgets with sizable deficits, established diplomatic contact with the People's Republic of China and détente with the Soviet Union, and used agencies of the federal government to invade the privacy and rights of citizens. Such actions are not normally associated with a conservative administration.

The meanings of the terms *liberal* and *conservative* were further muddied by the rise of new issues in the 1970s that did not coincide with the New Deal issues that had traditionally divided liberals and conservatives (and Democrats and Republicans). Whereas liberals had traditionally supported and conservatives opposed governmental intervention in the economy, the advent of such issues as drug regulation and testing, abortion, and sexual behavior often saw liberals opposing governmental involvement and conservatives favoring governmental regulation to protect traditional values. The rise of the feminist, environmental, and consumer movements placed issues on the political agenda that did not neatly fit into existing ideological and partisan labels.

Figure 1.2 presents a pictorial representation of the issues facing the United States today. Of course, this is an oversimplification of reality, as are the labels that anchor each dimension. Nevertheless, the figure suggests that when the issue domain is characterized by at least two dimensions, it becomes very difficult to classify a person under the overarching label of liberal or conservative. For example, how does one label the citizen who favors federal sponsorship of social welfare programs but strenuously objects to recent liberal trends in lifestyles? Given two dimensions, four ideal ideological types can be identified—the economic and lifestyle liberal, the economic and lifestyle conservative, the economic liberal and lifestyle conservative, and the economic conservative and lifestyle liberal. Despite the possibility of at least four clusters of issue positions, there are usually only two major candidates in presidential contests, which may result in many voters believing that their own policy preferences are not adequately represented by the available choices. There is currently a minor party (the Libertarian party) that explicitly takes the conservative position on the economic dimension and the liberal position on the lifestyle dimension, thereby providing the electorate with another choice—one with poor prospects of victory.

The complexity of the issue space depicted in figure 1.2 may help explain a number of seeming paradoxes of contemporary American politics. One such paradox is a citizenry that is more likely to call itself conservative even as it registers strong majorities in favor of traditional liberal social welfare programs in such areas as housing, health care, and education. There may be no inconsistency here if the sources of conservative identifications are stances on new issues and not positions on New Deal issues. This, however, is not the case. Polls have shown Americans to be more liberal than ever on such matters as the role of women, sexual mores, abortion, and some other lifestyle issues (Sussman, January 5, 1987). A *New York Times*/CBS News poll conducted in late 1985 found that the label *liberal* was relatively unpopular among a national sample of Americans but that the label *progressive* was viewed much more positively (Clymer, November 24, 1985). When asked whether they would think better or worse of a public figure if he or she were labeled a liberal or a conservative, 15 percent of Americans said they would think better of a public figure if he or she were liberal, while 17 percent would feel worse about that person. In contrast, 27 percent would feel better about conservative public figures and only 13 percent would feel worse. Yet 37 percent of Americans would think better of public figures labeled as progressives and only 7 percent would feel worse. All of this suggests that while the liberal label may be unpopular, liberal policy positions on a wide range of issues may enjoy broader support than expected in view of the outcomes of the 1980, 1984, and 1988 elections. Certainly the conservatism of Ronald Reagan in both economic and lifestyle matters poses problems for citizens who, while believing in limited governmental interference in the marketplace, still support the Equal Rights Amendment, abortion, and an activist role in environmental protection.

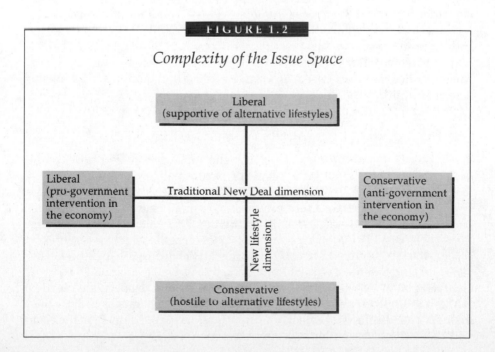

FIGURE 1.2

Complexity of the Issue Space

Liberal
(supportive of alternative lifestyles)

Liberal
(pro-government intervention in the economy)

Traditional New Deal dimension

Conservative
(anti-government intervention in the economy)

New lifestyle dimension

Conservative
(hostile to alternative lifestyles)

Additional complications in the interpretation of political labels arise when distinguishing between political discourse at the elite level versus the citizen level. The average citizen generally does not think about politics in such broad, overarching terms as *liberal* and *conservative.* Instead, citizens tend to view politics more from a self-interest perspective. Inappropriate interpretations must not be imposed on citizen attitudes and behavior. Philip Converse argues that the interpretation of the 1952 election outcome as a move to the right was correct only at the elite level where more conservative Republicans replaced Democrats in office (1974: 310–11). But survey data showed little evidence suggesting that the individual citizen had moved toward a more conservative position. Similar arguments could be made about the 1980 and 1984 elections. The question of how average citizens conceptualize politics will be discussed extensively in chapter 4.

Elites such as candidates for office are likely to have more coherent views of current political affairs than do average citizens. In addition, elites tend to rely more on general criteria for evaluating political events. That is, the assertion that a candidate is a conservative gives a lot of information about the candidate's stands on a wide variety of issues, while the same would probably not hold for the average citizen. In the 1950s an example of this situation occurred when positions on international and domestic issues were related at the elite level, but not so for citizens. Knowing whether a citizen preferred liberal or conservative policies in the realm of domestic affairs gave one no clue as to where the person stood on issues of internationalism versus isolationism. In contrast, positions on domestic and international issues were related at the elite level: domestic liberals tended to be internationalists and domestic conservatives isolationists (Converse, 1974: 324–29). The impact of foreign policy events since the 1950s, particularly the Vietnam War, has upset this neat pattern—a situation reflected in the parties' reactions to American military involvement in Central America.

1952–1988 AS A TRANSITIONAL ERA

When placed in a historical perspective, the 1952–1988 period raises some basic questions about the future shape of partisan alignments in the United States. The 1952–1988 presidential election outcomes varied markedly despite the fact that the Democratic party was commonly viewed as the majority party throughout the era. Dwight Eisenhower's 1952 victory marked the first Republican presidential success since the election of Herbert Hoover in 1928. The narrow 1968 and massive 1972 victories of Richard Nixon and the sizable 1980 and landslide 1984 wins of Ronald Reagan as well as the solid victory of George Bush in 1988 led many political commentators to speculate whether the Republican party was about to supplant the Democrats as the national majority party—that is, whether a substantial shift or realignment in the basic party loyalties of the nation was about to occur.

The politics of the 1952–1988 years was in part a legacy of the realignment of the 1930s in which the nation moved from majority Republican to majority Democratic, mainly because of the impact of the Great Depression and the efforts of the Roosevelt administration to alleviate the economic miseries. Prior to 1932, the first Roosevelt election, the GOP had been the dominant party nationwide, although the South was heavily Democratic. The 1928 candidacy of a Catholic New Yorker, Al Smith, attracted to the Democratic party many urban northern Catholic immigrant voters and repelled many traditional Protestant Democrats, especially in the South, because of the religious factor. This is graphically illustrated in the first column of table 1.2, which shows that five normally Democratic southern states went Republican in 1928. Since the 1930s, it has been common to refer to the majority Democratic support for FDR as the *New Deal coalition*, composed primarily of the South, labor, urban Catholics, and blacks.

The New Deal coalition reached its peak strength in the 1936 presidential and congressional elections and thereafter suffered erosion, so that the 1936 Roosevelt sweep of forty-six of forty-eight states and 60.8 percent of the total vote had by 1944 fallen to 53.4 percent of the vote, although Roosevelt carried thirty-seven states. Prior to the election of Eisenhower in 1952, the most serious threat to the dominance of the New Deal coalition occurred in 1948, when Harry Truman was challenged not only by the Republican candidate, Thomas Dewey, but also by third- and fourth-party candidates from the right and left wings of the Democratic party. Of the latter two challenges, the more notable was that raised by Strom Thurmond, then governor of South Carolina, whose States' Rights candidacy carried the four deep-southern states of South Carolina, Alabama, Mississippi, and Louisiana. The immediate cause of the Dixiecrat revolt was the adoption of a liberal civil rights platform at the Democratic National Convention, a major controversy that previewed North–South splits in the Democratic party during the 1960s on racial issues.

The apparent decline of the New Deal coalition has raised the question of the future of the Democratic and Republican parties. After the 1968 and 1972 Republican presidential victories, some observers thought the country was in the midst of a realignment from Democratic to Republican dominance. Then there came the debacle suffered by the Republicans in the 1974 midterm elections, the Democratic presidential victory in 1976, and the minimal gains of the GOP in 1978. All these events raised speculation that the GOP was permanently the minority party that could only occasionally win the presidency because of internal contradictions in the Democratic coalition. But the Republican presidential and senatorial victories of 1980 once again caused observers to speculate that the GOP might emerge as the majority party. In fact, poll results in the first years of the Reagan administration showed an increase of Republican loyalists. However, the decline in the economy, the drop in president Reagan's popularity, and the substantial Democratic gains in 1982 put to rest for a time such speculation. This speculation revived as a

TABLE 1.2

Presidential Voting in the South Since 1928

	1928	1932	1936	1940	1944	1948	1952	1956	1960	1964	1968	1972	1976	1980	1984	1988	Dem.	Rep.	Other
Alabama	D	D	D	D	D	SR	D	D	D	R	W	R	D	R	R	R	9	5	2
Arkansas	D	D	D	D	D	D	D	D	D	D	W	R	D	R	R	R	11	4	1
Florida	R	D	D	D	D	D	R	R	R	D	R	R	D	R	R	R	7	9	0
Georgia	D	D	D	D	D	D	D	R	D	D	W	R	D	R	R	R	11	4	1
Louisiana	D	D	D	D	D	SR	D	D	D	R	W	R	D	R	R	R	8	6	2
Mississippi	D	D	D	D	D	SR	D	D	D	R	W	R	D	R	R	R	9	5	2
North Carolina	R	D	D	D	D	D	D	D	D	D	R	R	D	R	R	R	10	6	0
South Carolina	D	D	D	D	D	SR	D	D	D	D	R	R	D	R	R	R	9	6	1
Tennessee	R	D	D	D	D	D	R	R	D	D	R	R	D	R	R	R	7	9	0
Texas	R	D	D	D	D	D	R	R	D	D	R	R	R	R	R	R	9	7	0
Virginia	R	D	D	D	D	D	R	R	R	D	R	R	R	R	R	R	6	10	0
Number of states won by Democrats	6	11	11	11	11	7	7	6	8	6	1	0	10	1	0	0			

Key to abbreviations: R–Republican, D–Democratic, SR–States' Rights, W–Wallace.
SOURCES: *Politics in America*, 4th ed. (Washington, D.C.: Congressional Quarterly, 1974), p. 87; *Guide to 1976 Elections* (Washington, D.C.: Congressional Quarterly, 1977), p. 25; and *Congressional Quarterly Weekly Report*, November 8, 1980, p. 3299.

result of the economic recovery of the mid-1980s, President Reagan's unprec edented popularity, and his massive reelection in 1984. Yet once again discussion of a Republican realignment was tempered temporarily by the Democratic recapture of the Senate in 1986 along with a decline in presidential popularity because of the Iranian arms scandal. Bush's victory in 1988 once again stimulated talk about a Republican lock on the White House with gains in state and local races likely to follow. But in 1989, Democrats held on to the Virginia governorship, brought the New Jersey governorship back into the Democratic column, and won many important local contests.

Angus Campbell of the Michigan Survey Research Center has developed a threefold typology of presidential elections (1966a). He labels the first kind of election *maintaining;* its chief characteristic is that the majority party (the party commanding the professed allegiances of a majority of voters) wins the election. The second type of election is termed *deviating;* this is an election in which the basic partisan loyalties of the electorate do not change much, but the influence of forces specific to the election leads to the defeat of the majority party. The Eisenhower victories of 1952 and 1956 are commonly viewed as deviating elections, resulting mainly from Eisenhower's immense popular appeal. Survey evidence about party loyalties as well as the congressional election results (the Republicans controlled Congress in only the first two of the eight Eisenhower years) are often cited to show that the Democrats were still the majority party in the Eisenhower years.

The third type of election discussed by Campbell—*realigning*— refers to a situation in which the basic partisan attachments of the electorate change. This results in a new partisan balance, one possible outcome being that the previous majority party becomes the minority, and vice versa. Other outcomes are possible. James Sundquist asserts that realignment can occur when one or both of the major parties are replaced, or when third parties are absorbed into the existing party system (1973). When supporters of George Wallace and the American Independent party in 1968 voted heavily for Richard Nixon in 1972, many observers thought that the Wallace candidacy had served as a way station for Democrats en route to becoming Republicans. However, survey evidence showed that the Wallace adherents maintained their Democratic partisan loyalties and supported Carter strongly in 1976.

Realignment occurs infrequently, but when it does, it is usually associated with severe crises and upheavals, such as wars or depressions. The best example of realignment thus far in this century has been the transformation in party loyalties brought on by the depression of the 1930s. Other elections generally referred to as realigning occurred in 1860, when the relatively new Republican party elected its presidential candidate (Abraham Lincoln) for the first time, and in 1896, when almost balanced partisan competition in the post–Civil War era gave way to a period of Republican dominance as the GOP made sizable gains in the Northeast. Rather than talk about a specific realigning election, some observers argue that discussion should center on a realigning era or period, thereby recognizing that realignment is an ongoing process, the end result of which depends on a variety of factors, including elite behavior, societal conditions, and chance (MacRae and Meldrum, 1960). The validity of this point is illustrated by the fact that the peak Democratic strength was reached in 1936, even though 1932 is commonly viewed as the critical or realigning election.

Gerald Pomper has offered a more elaborate classification of presidential elections. (Table 1.3 presents a schematic representation of this classification.) Its main contribution is the category of a *converting election*—an election in which the majority party wins, but the nature of its support coalition changes. Pomper's classification is useful since it explicitly incorporates two dimensions of electoral outcomes: the electoral fate of the majority party and the stability/instability in the existing electoral cleavages. The converting category suggests that one example of realignment in the United States would be to have the Democratic party remain as the majority party, but to have the sources of Democratic support shift substantially. Pomper labels the 1964 election *converting* since the Democrats were victorious and won increased support in the Northeast and Midwest. At the same time they lost tremendous support in the South, particularly in the five deep-southern states of South Carolina, Georgia, Alabama, Louisiana, and Mississippi (where Johnson received only 13 percent of the vote). Campbell, however, would classify the 1964 election as *maintaining*.

It cannot be said with certainty whether the United States is currently in a realignment era of Republican ascendancy or in an era of a permanent majority status for the Democrats; the ultimate outcome depends on a configuration of forces, some of which cannot yet be charted. Note, however, that, with the exception of the 1976 election, sectional realignment appeared to have taken place as the once Democratic Solid South seemed to have become the Republican Solid South, at least in presidential voting. Whereas Roosevelt carried all of the southern states in 1932 with vote tallies above 85

TABLE 1.3

Pomper's Classification
of Presidential Elections

	Fate of majority party	
Stability of electoral cleavage	*Victory*	*Defeat*
Continuity	Maintaining	Deviating
Change	Converting	Realigning

SOURCE: Gerald M. Pomper, *Elections in America* (New York: Dodd, Mead, 1968), fig. 2, p. 104.

percent in all the deep-southern states, in 1972 McGovern failed to carry a single southern state, and in 1968 Humphrey carried only Texas, eking out a tiny plurality over Nixon mainly because of the presence of Wallace in the race. In 1976 the South appeared solidly Democratic once again as native son Carter swept the entire region with the exception of Virginia. Table 1.2 presents the statewide presidential voting patterns of the South.

Even in 1976, Carter failed to carry the white vote in the South; his success depended heavily on the overwhelming support of black voters. In 1980 the South went strongly for Reagan, and Carter was able to carry only his home state of Georgia. In contrast, Reagan carried every southern state in 1984, as did Bush in 1988. Presidential Republicanism is flourishing in the South. But on the state and local levels, Republican dominance is far from established in the region. In fact, moderate Democrats with good ties to the national Democratic party have succeeded in recent years in winning southern governorships and replacing conservative patriarchs who have departed from Congress. Note, however, that in 1986 the GOP won a number of southern governorships, including those of Florida and Texas. This topic will be discussed further in chapter 11, which focuses on various aspects of realignment, including a discussion of the groups most likely to realign and the issues likely to bring about realignment. Explicit consideration will be given to an alternative scenario—*dealignment*—in which the shape of the present party system is maintained even as it becomes progressively weaker.

A Personal Assessment of Elections

Before turning to Part One and citizen voting behavior, I should make clear my evaluation of elections and their role in a democratic political system. Obviously, elections occupy a central role in democratic theory, especially as they provide a linkage between the preferences of citizens and the actions of government. Elections serve a legitimizing function in that they presumably enable leaders to act in the name of the people. Numerous consequences of elections are often suggested. For example, some observers argue that elections promote stability in the political system since they provide a regularized means for making potentially controversial decisions about political succession (even though two of the six most recent presidents took office by means other than elections). Furthermore, decisions made by popularly elected officials are more likely to receive the support of a citizenry responsible for choosing its leaders in the first place. At the individual level, the claim is often made that participation in elections (and other forms of political activity) contributes to the fullest growth of the individual.

While there is little dispute that elections serve as a mechanism whereby citizens choose their leaders, there is a major controversy over the significance of elections with respect to the policies subsequently adopted by the elected officials. What significance can elections have, some people ask, if the voter is forced to choose between two evils? What does it mean to talk of a choice when the competing candidates do not differ in important respects? How meaningful are elections if the victorious candidate subsequently reneges on campaign promises?

All of these questions have been raised about American presidential elections in recent years, and not only by people with a radical viewpoint. For example, the underlying thesis of the Goldwater campaign in 1964 was that there existed a vast number of conservative voters who refrained from voting because the Republican party offered candidates too similar to those of the Democrats. If the GOP were to nominate a genuine conservative, the argument went, millions of "stay-at-home" voters would flock to the polls to elect Goldwater. Richard Nixon and John Kennedy were often referred to as Tweedledee and Tweedledum in 1960; Barry Goldwater promised "a choice, not an echo" in 1964. In 1968, at the height of the "New Politics," the two major parties nominated familiar representatives of the old politics— Richard Nixon and Hubert Humphrey. George Wallace claimed that there was "not a dime's worth of difference between them," and evidently many voters agreed with him. A study of the Vietnam positions of Humphrey and Nixon by two political scientists showed that there was scarcely any difference between the candidates as determined from campaign speeches—this in a year when Vietnam was a major issue, with the Democrats attempting to defend their record and the Republicans promising to end the war in unspecified ways (Page and Brody, 1972). In 1976 the subtleties, nuances, and shadings of meaning expressed by the candidates, especially Carter, left many voters wondering just how the candidates differed. In 1988, neither candidate addressed the savings and loan situation when most experts knew the crisis already existed.

Do these examples indicate that presidential elections offer no choice to the voter? Not necessarily. By counterexample, note Reagan and Mondale in 1984, Carter and Reagan in 1980, and McGovern and Nixon in 1972 as candidates certainly representing sharply differing positions across a wide spectrum of issues. Likewise, there were substantial differences between Humphrey and Nixon on matters ranging from general philosophy of government to specific issues of social welfare and arms control. Who could deny that Adlai Stevenson was ahead of his time in raising the issue of disarmament in 1956? The point is that there are differences between the candidates, sometimes large, sometimes small. At some times these differences are on issues of immediate concern to the voter; at other times the voter seems to be left without a choice. In most cases there is no single candidate with whom one agrees on all issues; rather, the voter must decide which issues are most important to him or her and vote accordingly. Some observers call this selecting "the lesser of two evils." Perhaps so, but if presidential elections are to yield definitive results, the list of alternatives must be kept relatively narrow, although there is nothing sacred about the number two.

The charge is often raised that once elected, victorious candidates may break their campaign promises. An amusing article by political satirist Art Buchwald makes this point very effectively. Buchwald wrote about what would have happened had Barry Goldwater and not Lyndon Johnson been elected in 1964. He asserted that had Goldwater won, the United States would have become entangled in a major land war in Southeast Asia that would have involved hundreds of thousands of American troops and cost billions of dollars. Fortunately, Buchwald concluded, Lyndon Johnson, the peace candidate, won the election and thus this war never occurred.

But in prosecuting the Vietnam War, did Johnson really violate a mandate for peace? John Kessel reports that about 63 percent of the people who favored pulling out of Vietnam voted for Johnson in 1964 (1968: 290). Kessel also reports, however, that Johnson received almost 52 percent of the vote from those citizens who favored taking a stronger stand in Vietnam even if it meant invading North Vietnam. Or consider the case of conservative Republicans who supported Richard Nixon in 1968, in part because of his longtime opposition to Communist expansion abroad and to federal intervention at home. Did Nixon violate a trust by seeking détente with China and the Soviet Union and by instituting wage and price controls? Were not his China and Soviet policies bold ventures that held promise for building "a structure of peace"? And what about Bush in 1990 retreating from his pledge of "no new taxes"? In short, when does breaking campaign promises or changing from past behavior constitute a serious violation of trust? Campaign promises are made within a political, social, and economic context that can change dramatically during the four years of a president's term. Insisting that a president adhere faithfully to outmoded promises may lead to irrelevant and even disastrous policies. But where is the line between duplicity and flexibility? The individual citizen will have to make that judgment on his or her own grounds and behave accordingly.

If at some times elections do not offer meaningful choices and at other times campaign promises are broken, then where does this leave the average voter? Perhaps the central question of Part One of this book should be "Why does the citizen vote at all?" rather than "Why does the citizen vote as he or she does?" I think there are several good reasons to vote. One is to punish incumbents and parties that have performed less than admirably. In this situation, voting becomes a sanction to be employed after the fact. The vote signifies that one is unhappy with what has transpired, but it may have little policy directive for future governmental actions. This view of voting constitutes a procedural view of democracy in which the defining characteristic of a democratic political system is free and open competition among competing sets of elites. The role of citizens in such a system is minimal—the selection of leaders who are then free to make policy decisions unconstrained by popular directives. If the people are not content with the incumbents' performance, they can be voted out of office at the *next* election.

I would argue that the procedural view is a fairly accurate description of contemporary American politics; this in no way implies an endorsement of a limited role for the voters. While my assessment may be disturbing to the reader, it should be recognized that leaders often engage in anticipatory behaviors that result in indirect influence on policy decisions for the citizen. That is, the argument is made that since leaders want to remain in office, they try to anticipate what the people want and act accordingly, thereby resulting in indirect citizen inputs into decisions. The notion of anticipatory behavior by elites, if accepted too uncritically, can very quickly lead to overly optimistic evaluations of citizen influence. Some observers agree that leaders engage in anticipatory behavior, but what they try to anticipate is what they can get away with—not what the people want. Other observers have a markedly different view of the American political system, arguing that it provides maximum citizen initiative in decision making. The reader must make his or her own evaluations.

Before turning to chapter 2, 1 wish to explicitly lay out my own values and preferences here so that the reader can evaluate subsequent arguments more knowledgeably. I think that elections are consequential, that it is worthwhile to vote, and that reasonable choices are often available. In particular, I think that the types of public policies likely to be adopted differ, depending upon whether Democratic elites versus Republican elites versus some third set of elites control the national government. I am not content with a procedural or elitist view of democracy that assigns citizens to a minor role in influencing governmental policies, yet I recognize this as a fact of political life because of inequalities in the distribution of resources necessary to exercise influence, widespread lack of citizen interest on many issues, and the presence of uncontrollable external forces that impinge upon leaders. Besides voting, there are other kinds of participatory behaviors that may more directly affect elite behavior; protests, demonstrations, even riots may quickly obtain desired responses from leaders. Furthermore, there are elections other than presidential elections (for example, referenda) in which one's vote is more likely to have a direct bearing on the outcome and to have a clearer policy import. Yet all of these provisos suggest to me, not that voting in presidential elections is futile, but rather that greater efforts must be made to organize, to mobilize, to vote, and to carefully scrutinize the behavior of officials if government is to remain at least minimally controllable. Perhaps elected officials such as presidents cannot be controlled effectively. If so, it becomes even more important to place in office persons of good intentions and conscience who, in exercising relatively unlimited power, will not bring dishonor to the country and its people.

PART ONE

Citizens & Elections

CHAPTER 2

A Framework for Analyzing Voting Behavior

Many different forces have influenced presidential election outcomes since 1952. Analyzing voting behavior systematically requires a terminology that will facilitate comparisons over time. Two kinds of forces affect election outcomes— long-term and short-term forces. Long-term forces are those that exhibit continuity across a series of elections and include the generalized images that many people have of the political parties. For some people, the Democratic party is the party of prosperity and the Republican party the party of depression. For others, the Democrats are the party of war and the Republicans the party of peace. These generalized images reflect historical events: the Great Depression commenced during a Republican administration, while World Wars I and II and the Korean and Vietnam wars all broke out during Democratic administrations. These images do vary, depending on the specific election context. For example, Donald Stokes (1966) shows that the traditional Republican advantage in the area of foreign policy was eroded by the Goldwater candidacy in 1964; Goldwater was seen by many voters at that time as being too impulsive in the foreign policy arena. Likewise, the traditional Democratic advantage as the party of prosperity was undermined by the economic record of the Carter administration and by the sustained economic recovery during the Reagan administration.

The long-term force that has received the greatest attention from political scientists and political practitioners is the basic distribution of partisan loyalties in the electorate, commonly called *party identification*. Party identification is a psychological commitment or attachment to a political party that normally predisposes us to evaluate that party and its candidates in a favorable light. As table 2.1 indicates, the distribution of party attachments has remained fairly stable over the series of elections, studied herein, with the Democrats having an advantage over the Republicans in partisan loyalties since the 1930s. Note, however, that this Democratic advantage was smallest in 1988.

Further discussion about party identification will appear in chapter 3. The important point for now is that if the long-term force of party identification had been the only influence on presidential elections since 1952, then the Democrats should have won every election in that period, assuming a fairly even split in the independent vote and reasonably comparable turnout rates among each party's supporters. Yet not only did the Democrats lose seven of the ten elections, but in six of the seven they were solidly trounced by the Republicans, as shown in table 2.2.

Obviously, then, explanations of election outcomes since 1952 must be looked for beyond party identification. The unique features of each election that help account for departures from the prevailing patterns of party loyalties must be found. These unique features are the short-term forces, examples of which include Bush's vow of "no new taxes" and his exploitation of Willie Horton and the Pledge of Allegiance in 1988, Mondale's advocacy of a tax increase in 1984, the Americans held hostage by Iran in 1980, Carter's *Playboy* interview and Ford's misstatement about Soviet domination in Eastern Europe in 1976, the Eagleton affair and the short-lived McGovern $1,000 per person welfare program in 1972, the violence-torn Democratic National Convention in Chicago in 1968, perceptions of Barry Goldwater as "trigger-happy" in 1964, Kennedy's Catholicism in 1960, and Eisenhower's personal appeal in 1952 and 1956. Two types of short-term forces will be examined in this book—the candidates and the issues specific to each election.

The analysis of issues and candidates occupies a prominent place in the social psychological approach to the study of elections. This approach focuses on a set of attitudes that is viewed as the immediate determinant of the vote decision. An early work with a social psychological orientation was *The Voter Decides* by Angus Campbell and his associates, a study of the 1952 election. The authors were concerned with the psychology of the voting

The Distribution of Party Identification in the United States, 1952–1988 (in percentages)

	1952	1954	1956	1958	1960	1962	1964	1966	1968	1970	1972	1974	1976	1978	1980	1982	1984	1986	1988
Strong Democrat	22%	22%	21%	23%	21%	23%	26%	18%	20%	20%	15%	17%	15%	15%	18%	20%	17%	18%	17%
Weak Democrat	25	25	23	24	25	23	25	27	25	23	25	21	25	24	23	24	20	22	18
Independent leaning Democrat	10	9	7	7	8	8	9	9	10	10	11	13	12	14	11	11	11	10	12
Pure Independent	5	7	9	8	8	8	8	12	11	13	13	15	14	14	13	11	11	12	11
Independent leaning Republican	7	6	8	4	7	6	6	7	9	8	10	9	10	9	10	8	12	11	13
Weak Republican	14	14	14	16	13	16	13	15	14	15	13	14	14	13	14	14	15	15	14
Strong Republican	13	13	15	13	14	12	11	10	10	10	10	8	9	8	9	10	12	10	14
Apolitical, don't know	4	4	3	5	4	4	2	2	1	1	3	3	1	3	2	2	2	2	2
Total percent	100	100	100	100	100	100	100	100	100	100	100	100	100	100	100	100	100	100	101

SOURCES: SRC/CPS election surveys, Center for Political Studies, University of Michigan.

TABLE 2.2

Election Returns and Turnout Rate, 1952–1988

Candidates	Popular vote	Percentage of total vote	Presidential turnout rate
1952			
Dwight D. Eisenhower (Rep.)	33,939,137	55.1	61.6
Adlai E. Stevenson (Dem.)	27,314,649	44.4	
1956			
Dwight D. Eisenhower (Rep.)	35,585,245	57.4	59.3
Adlai E. Stevenson (Dem.)	26,030,172	42.0	
1960			
John F. Kennedy (Dem.)	34,221,344	49.7	62.8
Richard M. Nixon (Rep.)	34,106,671	49.5	
1964			
Lyndon B. Johnson (Dem.)	43,126,584	61.1	61.9
Barry M. Goldwater (Rep.)	27,177,838	38.5	
1968			
Richard M. Nixon (Rep.)	31,785,148	43.4	
Hubert H. Humphrey (Dem.)	31,274,503	42.7	60.9
George C. Wallace (AIP)	9,901,151	13.5	
1972			
Richard M. Nixon (Rep.)	47,170,179	60.7	55.5
George S. McGovern (Dem.)	27,171,791	37.5	
1976			
Jimmy Carter (Dem.)	40,829,046	50.1	54.4
Gerald R. Ford (Rep.)	39,146,006	48.0	
1980			
Ronald Reagan (Rep.)	43,901,812	50.8	
Jimmy Carter (Dem.)	35,483,820	41.0	53.9
John Anderson	5,719,437	6.6	
1984			
Ronald Reagan (Rep.)	54,455,075	58.8	53.3
Walter Mondale (Dem.)	37,577,185	40.6	
1988			
George Bush (Rep.)	48,886,097	53.4	50.2
Michael Dukakis (Dem.)	41,809,074	45.6	

SOURCES: *Guide to U.S. Elections* (Washington, D.C.: Congressional Quarterly, 1975); *Guide To 1976 Elections* (Washington, D.C.: Congressional Quarterly, 1977); *Statistical Abstract of the United States: 1971* (Washington, D.C.: U.S. Bureau of the Census, 1971); *Statistical Abstract of the United States: 1977* (Washington, D.C.: U.S. Bureau of the Census, 1977); *Congressional Quarterly Weekly Report,* April 25, 1981; *America Votes 16: A Handbook of American Election Statistics* (Washington, D.C.: Congressional Quarterly, 1985); and *American Votes 18: A Handbook of Contemporary American Election Statistics* (Washington, D.C.: Congressional Quarterly, 1989).

The presidential turnout rate is based on the number of citizens of voting age who cast votes in the presidential contest.

choice, arguing that the immediate determinants of human behavior are to be found in attitudes and perceptual organization of the environment rather than in social position or demographic characteristics, such as race and religion. Campbell and his colleagues were particularly interested in why voters chose one candidate over another. They identified three attitudinal variables that helped answer this question: party identification, issue orientation, and candidate orientation. Party identification will be considered extensively in the next chapter, while issue and candidate orientations are recurrent themes in chapters 4 through 6.

Probably the most influential work in the social psychological tradition is *The American Voter*, a study of the 1952 and 1956 Eisenhower–Stevenson elections by Angus Campbell and his associates. The authors examined six attitudes that were presumed to be strongly related to the partisan direction of one's vote. Each of the attitudes could easily be classified under the general headings of candidate-related and issue-related attitudes. The six partisan attitudes studied were:

1. Attitudes toward the personal attributes of Eisenhower.
2. Attitudes toward the personal attributes of Stevenson.
3. Attitudes toward the groups involved in politics and the questions of group interest affecting them.
4. Attitudes toward the issues of domestic policy.
5. Attitudes toward the issues of foreign policy.
6. Attitudes toward the comparative record of the two parties as managers of government.

Thus, in 1952 and 1956 samples of the mass electorate were asked a variety of questions about the parties, candidates, and issues. The flavor of this approach is captured by the following responses from an interview of an Ohio farm woman reported in *The American Voter* (p. 236).

> *Like about Democrats?* I think they have always helped the farmers. To tell you the truth, I don't see how any farmer could vote for Mr. Eisenhower.
> *Is there anything else you like about the Democratic party?* We have always had good times under their Administration. They are more for the working class of people. Any farmer would be a fool to vote for Eisenhower.
> *Dislike about Democrats?* No, I can't say there is.
> *Like about Republicans?* No.
> *Dislike about Republicans?* About everything.
> *What are you thinking of?* They promise so much but they don't do anything.
> *Anything else?* I think the Republicans favor the richer folks. I never did think much of the Republicans for putting into office a military man.

Now I'd like to ask you about the good and bad points of the two candidates for President. Is there anything in particular about Stevenson that might make you want to vote for him?   I think he is a *very smart* man.

Is there anything else?   I think he will do what he says, will help the farmer. We will have higher prices.

Anything else?   No.

Is there anything in particular about Stevenson that might make you want to vote against him?   No. But I have this against Stevenson, but I wouldn't vote against him. In the Illinois National Guards he had Negroes and whites together. They ate and slept together. I don't like that. I think Negroes should have their own place. I don't see why they would want to mix.

Is there anything in particular about Eisenhower that might make you want to vote for him?   No.

Is there anything in particular about Eisenhower that might make you want to vote against him?   Yes. He favors Wall Street. I don't think he is physically able, and he will step aside and that Richard Nixon will be President.

Anything else?   To tell the truth, I never thought he knew enough about politics to be a President. He is a military man. He takes too many vacations and I don't see how he can do the job.

In general, *The American Voter* demonstrated that the behavior of the electorate was better understood by examining all six attitudes rather than focusing on only one. For example, one could predict correctly how three fourths of the electorate would vote by simply relying on their attitudes toward Eisenhower. When all six partisan attitudes were examined, the correct prediction rate rose to 86 percent (Campbell, Converse, Miller, and Stokes, 1960, p. 74). More impressive, at the same time that information about the six partisan attitudes was collected, the respondents were asked to indicate how they intended to vote, which, in effect, were the voters' own predictions about their November vote. It turned out that one could predict slightly better how a person would actually vote by relying on partisan attitudes rather than on his or her own statement of vote intention. This clearly suggests the importance of partisan attitudes to vote choice.

The six partisan attitudes are obviously not independent of the voter's party identification. That is, attitudes toward the candidates, issues, performance of the parties, and the like are very likely to be influenced by party identification. It is argued in *The American Voter* that party identification serves as a perceptual screen through which the elements of politics are evaluated. This implies that party identification may lead to selective processes in the collection, retention, and interpretation of political communications. For example, longtime Democrats may be more receptive to information favorable to their own party and detrimental to the Republicans and may be more likely to retain or remember supportive information.

Thus, recognizing that party identification influences partisan attitudes, the long- and short-term forces affecting the vote decision can be arrayed as illustrated in the accompanying diagram. The terms in this diagram should be viewed in relation to their temporal proximity to the vote decision. Partisan attitudes that include attitudes about the short-term forces in an election are the most immediate determinants of the vote. Party

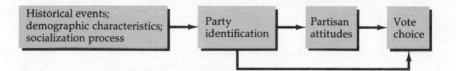

identification is viewed as more remote from the vote decision, generally influencing votes through its impact on partisan attitudes. Note, however, that an arrow is drawn directly from party identification to vote choice; that is done to reflect those citizens who make their vote choice solely on the basis of party without reference to specific issue and candidate attitudes. This type of voter is typified by the following interview responses from a California woman in *The American Voter* (p. 247):

> *Like about Democrats?* I'm a Democrat.
> *Is there anything you like about the Democratic party?* I don't know.
> *Dislike about Democrats?* I'm a Democrat, that's all I know. My
>   husband's dead now—he was a Democrat.
> *Is there anything you don't like about the party?* I don't know.
> *Like about Republicans?* I don't know.
> *Dislike about Republicans?* I don't know.
> *Like about Stevenson?* Stevenson is a good Democrat.
> *Is there anything else about him that might make you want to vote for
> him?* No. Nothing.
> *Dislike about Stevenson?* I don't know.
> *Is there anything about him that might make you want to vote against
> him?* No.
> *Like about Eisenhower?* I don't know.
> *Is there anything about Eisenhower that might make you want to vote for
> him?* I don't know.
> *Dislike about Eisenhower?* I don't know.
> *Is there anything about him that might make you want to vote against
> him?* No.

Clearly, this is a citizen for whom partisan loyalty is the paramount concern.

Finally, as shown in the diagram, the basic distribution of party identification in the electorate is seen as produced by major historical events (for example, the Great Depression) and processes (for example, the receptivity of urban Democratic machines to immigrant populations) that differentially affected various groups in society. The distribution of party identification tends to be maintained by a family-dominated political socialization process (discussed in chapter 3) even when memory of the crucial historical era has faded into the dim past. Hence, demographic characteristics such as race and religion are included in the diagram as farthest away from the vote decision, although these characteristics may become extremely important under appropriate circumstances. For example, the impact of religion on the 1960 Kennedy–Nixon election was far more immediate than the diagram indicates. Because of the salience of Kennedy's Catholicism to many voters in 1960, religion was transformed to the status of an immediate attitudinal determinant with major consequences for voting behavior.

The diagram oversimplifies reality, particularly as it treats the relationship between party identification and partisan attitudes, especially issue-related attitudes. A person may change loyalty to a party or forge a new loyalty on the basis of some issue or set of issues very crucial to him or her. The discussion of the possibility of major political realignment in the last section of this book reflects the potential power of "new" issues to upset the traditional alignments forged during the New Deal, which focused on issues of economic prosperity. Perhaps one reason the Democratic party no longer routinely carries the South in presidential elections is because many white southern Democrats see their national party and its candidates as taking too liberal and interventionist a position on matters of civil rights and social welfare and too tolerant a position on a variety of "social" issues dealing with lifestyles, law and order, and the like. Whether this means that white southern Democrats are inexorably converting to Republicanism is discussed later. The point is that issues can and do influence partisan attachments.

The framework to be employed in Part One treats the presidential vote in any election as being composed of two components—the normal or baseline vote and deviations from the normal vote. The term *normal vote* usually refers to the partisan division of the vote that would occur if the long-term force of party identification were the only force influencing the election outcome, or if party identification were operating and the short-term forces canceled themselves out; that is, if the pro–Republican forces balanced the pro–Democratic forces. The normal vote has actually been calculated by Philip Converse (1966a); the expected vote outcome when there are no short-term forces, or when the short-term forces cancel, is about 54 percent to 46 percent in favor of the Democratic party.[1]

The other component of the presidential vote is the *deviations* from the normal vote, and these deviations are a result of the short-term forces operating in a specific election. An example may help to clarify this notion. Converse decomposed the nonsouthern presidential vote in 1952 into its two components for both Protestants and Catholics, as shown in the accompanying table (1966a: 31). These numbers mean that the normal Democratic vote is 44 percent for Protestants and 64 percent for Catholics. The actual Democratic vote in 1952 for Protestants and Catholics was 31 percent and 51 percent. These 13 percent deviations for each religious group were due to the short-term forces acting on the 1952 election. Since the short-term component produced identical deviations for Protestants and Catholics, this implies that it was not related to any religious issue. Undoubtedly, the major part of the 13 percent deviation in each group is to be explained by the attractiveness of Eisenhower's personality. In contrast, in 1960 the actual Protestant vote was less Democratic than expected and the actual Catholic vote more Democratic. These opposite deviations for Catholics and Protestants in 1960 suggest that religion-related short-term forces were influencing the election outcome. Certainly one such force was Kennedy's Catholicism, which attracted some Catholic voters and repelled some Protestant voters.

The normal vote is an important concept because it helps disentangle the effects of short- and long-term forces, and it implies that any election outcome is the result of short-term forces acting upon a certain distribution of partisan loyalties in the electorate. It should be noted that the use of the normal vote concept and the classification of presidential elections discussed in chapter 1 make sense only if there is some stability in partisan affiliations from which a baseline or normal vote can be calculated. That is, if there is little continuity in party loyalties across a series of elections, then it is difficult to determine a normal vote as well as identify which is the majority party, thereby calling into question the applicability of classifying elections. Fortunately, there was substantial continuity in partisan allegiances in the first half of the period under investigation. This provides a baseline from which to analyze current developments in electoral commitments.

Converse distinguishes between two general kinds of short-term forces that can produce deviations from the normal vote: forces of stimulation, which act to increase turnout, and partisan forces, which tend to favor one party over the other and thus influence the election outcome directly (1966a: 15). These partisan forces receive substantial attention in the chapters on issues and candidates, so this chapter will discuss patterns and determinants of turnout in presidential elections since 1952.

Non–South	Long-term expected proportion Democratic, normal vote	Short-term deviation of 1952 vote from expected vote
Protestants	44%	−13%*
Catholics	64	−13

*A negative deviation means a vote more Republican than normal.

Turnout in Presidential Elections Since 1952

As shown in the last column of table 2.2, turnout in presidential elections has dropped steadily after reaching a peak in 1960. The reasons for this decline have sparked a major controversy, with some analysts citing institutional factors, such as registration requirements, and others emphasizing psychological determinants, such as citizen dissatisfaction with the political system. The various explanations will be discussed shortly; for now note that turnout has declined even as the act of voting has been made easier. For example, there has been a major relaxation of residency requirements and an easing of registration procedures. In 1960 about half the population lived in states where the state residency requirement for voting was one year; counties and municipalities also had their own residency requirements. Obviously, in a highly mobile society many people were disenfranchised by such conditions. Today a series of court decisions has led to a shortening of residency requirements in state and local elections, while the Voting Rights Act Amendments of 1970 forbade residency requirements of more than thirty days for presidential elections. Since young people and upper-status individuals tend to be the most mobile, the relaxation of residency requirements should contribute to higher voting rates among those groups. Likewise, many states have eased their registration procedures by, for example, conducting registration at multiple sites throughout the community, by publicizing more widely the opportunities and procedures for registration, and by making it more difficult to strike a person from the election rolls. Hence, the decline in turnout since 1960 might have been larger had not residency and registration requirements been weakened.

Contemporary turnout rates are not as high as those in the last half of the nineteenth century, when presidential turnout averaged more than 75 percent and approached 82 percent in 1876. Turnout fell sharply in the early years of the twentieth century, to an average of just over 50 percent by the 1920s, then gradually increased, reaching a contemporary peak in 1960 and declining once again afterward. If turnout figures are based on the total adult population, then American turnout rates seem low in comparison to the 80 percent to 90 percent figures commonly observed in Western European parliamentary elections. These comparisons are misleading since European turnout rates are often constructed on the basis of registered voters and not the total adult population. More important, most Western European nations make registration a much easier task than it is in the United States, where registration procedures often deter people from voting. Also, many nations have compulsory voting or at least impose sanctions on citizens who do not vote. For example, in Italy citizens who do not vote have their official documents marked as "failed to vote," which can create problems in obtaining other papers from the government. This threat may be one reason for the very high Italian turnout, which regularly exceeds 90 percent. American turnout would undoubtedly be much higher if the United States adopted registration and voting procedures similar to those used in many Western European nations; more on this point later.

One institutional development that has served to lower the turnout rate was the extension of the suffrage to eighteen year olds. The Voting Rights Act extension of 1970 gave young people the franchise for federal elections, and the ratification of the Twenty-sixth Amendment to the Constitution extended the franchise of eighteen year olds to all elections. These actions increased the potential universe of voters by more than 11 million in 1972. Because young citizens vote at a lower rate than their elders, their recent enfranchisement has served to lower the turnout rate.

Probably the most important development in increasing the opportunities for registration and voting has been the breakdown of the legal barriers, particularly in the South, that had prevented blacks and other minorities from voting. The Twenty-fourth Amendment to the Constitution abolished the poll tax, while congressional passage in 1965 of the Voting Rights Act enabled federal examiners to register citizens in counties (mostly southern) where literacy tests were used and fewer than 50 percent of the people were registered. Low registration rates in conjunction with literacy tests were viewed as evidence of discriminatory administration of the tests and hence justified federal intervention. Moreover, a number of organizations sponsored massive mobilization and registration drives among blacks. Table 2.3 shows how highly successful these activities of the federal government and private organizations were in registering blacks. For example, less than 7 percent of Mississippi blacks were registered prior to passage of the Voting Rights Act, while three years after passage the percentage had jumped to about 60 percent. Note that white registration levels also increased sharply; for example, over 90 percent of the white population of Mississippi has been registered in recent years. This may represent a countermobilization by whites in response to increased black participation.

Table 2.4 illustrates the turnout trends in the fifty states and the District of Columbia since 1960—the recent high point in presidential turnout nationally. A comparison of the 1960 and 1988 turnout rates shows that voting participation increased in only nine states over this period and that eight of the nine states were in the South. Hence, if turnout trends were analyzed for nonsouthern states only, the decline would be even more pronounced, which would further heighten concerns about the viability of voting and elections as instruments of popular control.

THE DETERMINANTS OF TURNOUT

Turnout is sensitive to the characteristics of the individual citizen as well as to the properties of the political system in which elections are conducted. With respect to the attributes of the political system, the fifty states have the major responsibility for election administration, which includes such matters

TABLE 2.3

Voter Registration Rates in the South Before and After the Voting Rights Act of 1965 (by race)

State	Percentage Registered						
	1960	1964	1968	1976	1980	1984	1986
Alabama							
Nonwhite	13.7%	19.3%	51.6%	58.4%	57.5%	69.2%	68.9%
White	63.6	69.2	89.6	79.3	81.8	74.3	77.5
Arkansas							
Nonwhite	38.0	40.4	62.8	54.0	59.9	60.9	57.9
White	60.9	65.5	72.4	62.6	81.0	65.4	67.2
Florida							
Nonwhite	39.4	51.2	63.4	61.1	61.4	55.5	58.2
White	69.3	74.8	81.4	61.3	72.0	64.0	66.9
Georgia							
Nonwhite	29.3	27.4	52.6	74.8	51.9	49.8	52.8
White	56.8	62.2	80.3	65.9	65.6	58.3	62.3
Louisiana							
Nonwhite	31.1	31.6	58.9	63.0	61.3	62.5	60.6
White	76.9	80.5	93.1	78.4	77.2	71.8	67.8
Mississippi							
Nonwhite	5.2	6.7	59.8	60.7	64.1	68.2	70.8
White	63.9	69.9	91.5	80.0	95.0	91.4	91.6
North Carolina							
Nonwhite	39.1	46.8	51.3	54.8	55.3	59.7	58.4
White	92.1	96.8	83.0	69.2	72.0	67.2	67.4
South Carolina							
Nonwhite	13.7	37.3	51.2	56.5	55.8	49.8	52.5
White	57.1	75.7	81.7	58.4	61.8	50.5	53.4
Tennessee							
Nonwhite	59.1	69.5	71.7	66.4	66.7	67.1	65.3
White	73.0	72.9	80.6	73.7	80.2	69.3	70.0
Texas							
Nonwhite	35.5	53.1*	61.6	65.0	54.8	59.1	68.0
White	42.5		53.3	69.1	71.2	70.2	79.0
Virginia							
Nonwhite	23.1	38.3	55.6	54.7	54.1	50.7	56.2
White	46.1	61.6	63.4	61.6	62.5	57.0	60.3

*A breakdown by race is not available.
SOURCES: *Political Participation: A Report of the United States Commission on Civil Rights* (Washington, D.C.: U.S. Government Printing Office, 1968), pp. 12–13; *Statistical Abstract of the United States: 1977* (Washington, D.C.: U.S. Bureau of the Census, 1977), p. 507; *Statistical Abstract of the United States: 1981* (Washington, D.C.: U.S. Bureau of the Census, 1981), p. 495; *Statistical Abstract of the United States: 1985* (Washington, D.C.: U.S. Bureau of the Census, 1985), p.253; and *Statistical Abstract of the United States: 1990* (Washington, D.C: U.S. Bureau of the Census, 1990), p. 264.

as registration and absentee ballot procedures, the hours in which the polls are open, and many more. One might hypothesize that states that make registration and absentee voting easy and keep the polls open longer will (all things being equal) have higher turnout. The nature of a state's political party system can also affect turnout. One might expect turnout to be higher where the competition between the two parties is more evenly balanced and citizens therefore see their votes as being more consequential for the election outcome. The effects of election administration and party competition on turnout are demonstrated in a study done by three political scientists on presidential voting in 1960 (Kim, Petrocik, and Enokson, 1975). Their research shows that one reason for the low southern turnout in 1960 (and earlier) was the presence of election laws designed to hinder participation and the absence of meaningful party competition in the general election. By implication, as legal barriers have been struck down in the South and as the region has become more politically competitive, one would expect that southern turnout would increase and begin to approach levels outside the South. That, of course, is the pattern observed for the 1960–1968 period. Moreover, Wolfinger and Rosenstone argue that, as the older generations of Southerners who were socialized in an era of nonparticipation depart from

TABLE 2.4

Turnout in Presidential Elections by States, 1960–1988*

State	1960	1964	1968	1972	1976	1980	1984	1988
Alabama	30.8%	35.9%	52.7%	43.4%	47.3%	49.2%	50.2%	45.8%
Alaska	43.7	44.0	50.0	48.3	53.5	58.5	60.2	51.9
Arizona	52.4	54.8	49.9	48.1	47.8	45.4	46.6	45.0
Arkansas	40.9	50.6	54.2	48.1	51.1	51.9	52.2	47.0
California	65.8	63.9	61.0	59.9	51.4	49.7	49.9	47.4
Colorado	69.2	68.0	64.8	60.1	61.0	56.9	54.8	41.7
Connecticut	76.1	70.7	68.8	66.3	62.5	61.5	61.0	57.9
Delaware	72.3	68.9	68.3	62.3	58.5	55.1	55.7	51.0
District of Columbia	(X)	38.7	34.5	43.2	32.8	35.4	43.8	39.5
Florida	48.6	51.2	53.1	49.3	49.8	50.0	49.0	44.7
Georgia	29.3	43.3	43.9	37.9	43.5	41.8	42.2	38.8
Hawaii	49.8	51.3	53.8	50.4	48.6	44.0	44.5	43.0
Idaho	79.7	77.2	73.4	63.2	60.7	68.6	60.4	58.3
Illinois	75.5	73.2	69.3	62.7	61.1	58.1	57.3	53.3
Indiana	76.3	73.5	70.7	60.8	61.0	57.9	56.3	53.3

(continued)

TABLE 2.4

Turnout in Presidential Elections
by States, 1960–1988* (continued)

State	1960	1964	1968	1972	1976	1980	1984	1988
Iowa	76.5%	72.9%	69.8%	63.3%	63.6%	63.1%	62.3%	59.3%
Kansas	69.6	65.1	64.8	59.0	59.5	57.2	57.0	54.3
Kentucky	57.7	53.3	51.2	48.4	49.2	50.2	50.7	48.2
Louisiana	44.6	47.3	54.8	44.3	50.5	53.9	54.2	51.3
Maine	71.7	65.1	66.4	61.1	65.2	65.1	65.2	62.2
Maryland	56.5	54.1	54.4	50.3	50.3	50.5	51.4	49.1
Massachusetts	75.0	70.0	67.4	62.0	61.0	59.4	57.9	58.1
Michigan	72.2	67.9	65.7	59.5	58.3	60.1	58.2	54.0
Minnesota	76.4	75.8	73.8	68.4	71.7	70.6	68.5	66.3
Mississippi	25.3	33.9	53.3	45.0	49.8	52.3	52.0	49.9
Missouri	71.5	67.1	64.3	57.5	58.4	59.1	57.7	54.8
Montana	70.2	69.3	68.1	67.7	63.5	65.6	65.0	62.5
Nebraska	70.6	66.5	60.9	56.0	56.2	57.1	56.1	56.6
Nevada	58.3	52.1	54.3	50.9	47.6	42.5	41.6	44.9
New Hampshire	78.7	72.4	69.9	64.2	59.2	57.9	53.9	54.8
New Jersey	70.8	68.8	66.0	60.0	58.5	55.4	56.9	49.6
New Mexico	61.7	62.0	60.7	57.6	54.3	51.7	51.6	47.3
New York	66.5	64.8	59.9	56.6	50.6	48.2	51.1	48.1
North Carolina	52.9	52.3	54.4	43.4	43.6	44.0	47.7	43.4
North Dakota	78.0	71.4	70.0	67.9	68.8	65.4	62.9	61.5
Ohio	70.7	66.6	63.3	57.5	55.1	55.6	58.2	55.1
Oklahoma	63.1	63.4	61.2	56.9	56.4	53.0	51.2	48.7
Oregon	72.0	68.9	66.6	61.7	62.3	61.9	62.6	58.6
Pennsylvania	70.3	67.9	65.3	56.1	54.7	52.2	53.9	50.1
Rhode Island	75.1	71.6	67.2	62.0	63.5	59.1	56.0	53.0
South Carolina	30.4	39.4	46.7	38.6	41.5	41.0	40.6	38.9
South Dakota	77.6	74.2	73.3	68.8	64.1	67.6	63.8	61.5
Tennessee	49.8	51.7	53.7	43.6	49.9	49.1	49.3	44.7
Texas	41.2	44.6	48.7	45.4	47.9	45.8	47.0	44.2
Utah	78.2	78.4	76.7	68.5	69.1	65.6	60.5	60.0
Vermont	72.4	70.3	64.1	61.1	56.2	58.2	60.8	59.0
Virginia	32.8	41.1	50.1	45.5	48.1	48.2	51.1	48.2
Washington	71.9	71.8	66.0	63.8	61.3	58.2	58.5	54.6
West Virginia	77.9	75.5	71.7	62.4	58.6	53.1	51.3	46.7
Wisconsin	72.9	69.5	66.5	62.0	65.5	67.9	63.4	62.0
Wyoming	73.3	74.3	67.0	63.6	58.8	54.5	51.8	50.4

*Turnout rates are based on the voting age population.
SOURCES: *Statistical Abstract of the United States: 1977* (Washington, D.C.: U.S. Bureau of the Census, 1977), p. 511; *Statistical Abstract of the United States: 1981* (Washington, D.C.: U.S. Bureau of the Census, 1981), p. 499; *Statistical Abstract of the United States: 1985* (Washington, D.C.: U.S. Bureau of the Census, 1985), p. 255; and *Statistical Abstract of the United States: 1990* (Washington, D.C.: U.S. Bureau of the Census, 1990), p. 265.

the political scene, southern and nonsouthern turnout rates will further converge (1977: 57-58).

Individual characteristics can also affect turnout, and here one might distinguish between such demographic or background variables as race, education, and place of residence and such attitudinal variables as interest in politics, feelings about the obligation to vote, and concerns about the election outcome. It should be recognized that systemic factors do not affect all citizens uniformly; rather, their impact will depend on the individual characteristics of citizens. For example, election laws designed to deter participation are most likely to be effective among citizens with little interest in politics in the first place; citizens highly interested in politics will more readily overcome legal obstacles to participation.

Table 2.5 presents the turnout rate in 1988 by selected background characteristics of Americans. A fair summary statement is that the electorate is disproportionately white, middle-aged, and of higher socioeconomic status.[2] More specifically, the table indicates that turnout is positively related to education and age; that is, the more educated and older groups have higher

TABLE 2.5

Turnout in the 1988 Election
by Population Characteristics

Characteristic	Percent turnout	Characteristic	Percent turnout
Sex		Employment status	
Male	56.4%	Employed	58.4%
Female	58.3	Unemployed	38.6
Race/ethnicity		Not in labor force	57.3
White	59.1	Age	
Black	51.5	18–20 years	33.2
Spanish origin	28.8	21–24	38.3
Region		25–34	48.0
Northeast	57.4	35–44	61.3
Midwest	62.9	45–64	67.9
South	54.5	65 and over	68.8
West	55.6		
Education			
8th grade or less	36.7		
9–11	41.3		
High school	54.7		
1–3 yrs. college	64.5		
4 or more yrs. college	77.6		

SOURCE: *Statistical Abstract of the United States: 1990* (Washington, D.C.: U.S. Bureau of the Census, 1990), p. 262.

turnout rates. The more highly educated vote with greater regularity because they tend to have more information about politics, to be more aware of the impact of government on citizens, and to feel that they are competent to influence government (Milbrath, 1965: 122–123). Younger citizens have lower turnout rates in part because they have other important matters, such as career and family decisions, vying for their attention along with political affairs, while the oldest age groups have lower voting rates because of the physical and financial burdens of age (Converse, 1963) and because of their lower average level of education (Wolfinger and Rosenstone, 1977). Turnout also tends to be higher among high-income and higher status occupation groups. Milbrath cites three reasons for this situation: such groups tend to be better educated; they are more likely to perceive that they have a stake in politics; and they are more likely to interact with persons active in politics (1965: 116–121). Robert Lane cites some additional factors that help explain why lower-status citizens do not participate as much, including the basic fact that such individuals have less of the resources (for example, time and money) that are conducive to participation and voting (1959: 233–234). He also argues that the social roles and norms of lower-status citizens tend to encourage more passive political behavior in comparison to the social roles and norms of middle- and upper-class citizens.

Among religious groups, Jews and Catholics tend to have higher turnout rates, while white citizens generally still vote more regularly than black citizens. One reason black citizens vote less than white citizens is that they are disproportionately in the lower levels of income, occupation, and education, characteristics associated with lower levels of political activity in general. The difference in black and white turnout rates has narrowed substantially since the 1950s throughout the nation, reaching a minimum outside the South in 1964, when the gap between black and white turnout rates was less than 3 percent (72 percent and 74.4 percent, respectively). This occurrence probably reflected the fact that in 1964 blacks had the strongest positive incentives to support Lyndon Johnson, who pushed the Civil Rights Act through Congress, and to vote against Barry Goldwater who opposed the act.[3] The gap between black and white turnout rates actually widened to more than 10 percent in the 1970s, although this was much less than that observed in the 1950s. In 1988 the difference in white and black turnout rates was less than 8 percent. Note that the ethnic category with the lowest turnout in table 2.5 is people of Spanish origin. Although this is a very broad classification—which does not distinguish between citizens of Puerto Rican origin, who reside mainly in cities of the northeastern United States, and Mexican-Americans, who live mainly in the Southwest and California—the very low turnout of Hispanics suggests that they are a potentially rich target for political mobilization. In many areas, particularly in the Southwest where geographic concentration may be readily convertible into political power, there is a rising political consciousness and an increasingly effective political organization among Hispanics. Moreover, when Congress extended the

Voting Rights Act for seven years in 1975, it also added guarantees to protect the voting rights of Spanish-speaking Americans, thereby providing that institutional and legal basis upon which a major mobilization effort might be built.

A number of attitudinal factors that affect turnout were identified in *The American Voter* (pp. 89–115). Party identification has an impact on turnout; people with stronger attachments to a party vote at higher rates than do people with weaker or nonexistent attachments. *The American Voter* also found that the more involved in politics a person was, the more likely that person was to vote. Citizens with higher levels of interest in politics, greater concern about the election outcome, and greater feelings of effectiveness in influencing political affairs were more apt to vote. And, as previously suggested, citizens in the higher-status categories tend to have higher levels of political interest, concern, and effectiveness. A respectable proportion of people with low interest, little concern about the election, and low efficacy with respect to politics actually voted, and *The American Voter* attributed this to a sense of citizen duty that was socialized in the person by civics courses, media appeals, and the like. The good citizen is commonly described as someone who performs his or her civic duty of voting.

THE TURNOUT CONTROVERSY

The reasons for the decline in turnout, the effectiveness of possible remedies, and the consequences of low voter turnout for the political system have been controversial topics in recent political debate. With respect to the decline in turnout, one line of argument (for example, Piven and Cloward, 1988) emphasizes the depressing effects on turnout of institutional barriers, particularly restrictive registration systems. It is observed that turnout among registered voters is very high (averaging about 84 percent in the five national elections between 1968 and 1976, according to Census Bureau reports) and that therefore the turnout problem can be reduced to registering more citizens by creating a more facilitative registration system. The obvious flaw in this argument is that institutional barriers have been weakened substantially since 1960, yet throughout this period turnout has fallen. Hence, although registration requirements may deter some people from voting, they cannot account for the decline in turnout in the past two decades.

In a very comprehensive study of the effects of registration laws on turnout, Rosenstone and Wolfinger argued that if the most permissive laws were on the books in all fifty states, national turnout would increase by about 9 percent (1978). The most important reforms they identified were expanding the hours during which one could register and establishing a deadline for registration much closer to election day. The liberalized registration laws they analyzed would still leave a registration system in which the primary responsibility for registering falls upon the citizen, in contrast to the registration system in most European democracies, where the government takes the initiative in enrolling citizens by such means as door-to-door registrars and postcard registration. Hence, Rosenstone and Wolfinger argued that if relatively minor changes in registration laws could increase turnout by 9 percent, then a revamped system in which the government played a more active role could increase turnout substantially more. In fact, in a comparative analysis of democratic nations, Powell (1986) showed that turnout levels in the United States were depressed by about 14 percent because of characteristics of American registration systems.[4]

The analyses of Rosenstone and Wolfinger, and Powell are very convincing, but they do not explain the *drop* in turnout in the United States. In fact, if liberalized registration laws increased voting by 9 percent, voting participation would be back only to its 1960 level. Moreover, demographic changes in the electorate, such as rising educational levels and the passing of the oldest generation (characterized by lower female participation), suggest that turnout should be increasing rather than the reverse. The one demographic change that does help account for lower turnout is the age distribution of Americans, which has become more skewed to the youngest and oldest adults since 1960. Because a greater proportion of Americans are in the youngest and oldest age cohorts and because these cohorts tend to have the lowest turnout rates (see table 2.5), turnout has declined. Boyd cites a Census Bureau estimate that 30 percent of the decline in turnout since 1964 can be traced to the changing age distribution of the electorate (1979: 5). Overall, institutional and demographic explanations of turnout trends are neither definitive nor complete, and thus individual attitudes and motivations as possible sources of the decline in turnout must be examined.[5]

Chapter 1 detailed the decline in trust in government (table 1.1) and the loss of confidence in elections and political parties (figure 1.1) as being institutions that promote governmental responsiveness. And table 2.1 indicates a weakening of party loyalties in the past decade. It is certainly plausible to expect that as support for various political institutions goes down, the rate of nonvoting will increase. Many citizens believe that voting is not worth the effort, that government is distant and unresponsive, that the bureaucracy is an incomprehensible, uncontrollable maze, and that the link between one's vote and policy outcomes is minimal at best.[6] Various polls have shown that attitudes toward presidential candidates have become more negative, with fewer voters able to see meaningful differences in the choices offered them. Reiter found that the decline in turnout has occurred mainly among white citizens of low education and low income (1977). He speculates that the reason this group is dropping out of the electorate at a faster rate is that the available party choices, which do not include a workers' party or a socialist party, are least relevant to lower-status citizens.

All of the above attitudinal explanations emphasize voter discontent and antipathy toward the political system. Yet voters may refrain from voting because of a basic sense of satisfaction with the course of politics. A study of nonvoting established six categories of nonvoters, the first of which was labeled the *positive apathetics*—satisfied citizens who thought voting was unnecessary and who comprised 35 percent of all nonvoters (Hadley, 1978). In Hadley's scheme, only 18 percent of the nonvoters were classified as physically or legally disenfranchised, which means that institutional reforms could at best have only a marginal effect in increasing turnout. In a polemical conclusion Hadley asserts that politicians emphasize institutional reforms that would increase turnout to avoid the unpleasant fact that many Americans despise politicians or at least see them as irrelevant.

Hence, many factors are possible sources of the downward trend in turnout, but the various pieces of the puzzle have not yet been fitted together. For those who interpret low turnout as a sign of voter satisfaction, the decline in voting rates poses no problems. In fact, some analysts (for example, Berelson, Lazarsfeld, and McPhee, chapter 14) would argue that low turnout can provide political leadership flexibility in decision making and contribute to the maintenance and stability of the political system. But for other observers, nonvoting has more worrisome ramifications. Substantial nonvoting may indicate a low degree of legitimacy accorded by the citizenry to the political system. Moreover, the presence of numerous citizens not actively involved in politics suggests the existence of a large pool of potentially mobilizable voters who might succumb to the antidemocratic blandishments of a charismatic demagogue in a time of crisis. And if elections do have policy consequences, then the question is whether the policy preferences of voters differ from those of nonvoters; it may be that nonvoting results in certain policy alternatives being ignored.

Nothing more will be said about turnout, although turnout can be as influential in affecting the election outcome as the partisan forces to be discussed in the next chapters. If parties appeal differentially to a variety of societal groups, then the party with supporters characterized by higher turnout rates is obviously in a more advantageous position. It is commonly noted that the groups associated with the Democratic party exhibit lower turnout levels.[7] Thus, turnout becomes an important strategic consideration for the candidate attempting to build a majority coalition. For example, the McGovern hope to win an overwhelming proportion of the youth vote in 1972, even if achieved (and it was not), was still a fragile strategy since young people have traditionally had very low turnout rates. As another example, if black voters had turned out in 1968 for Hubert Humphrey at the same rate they did for Lyndon Johnson in 1964, Humphrey might have carried a few additional states, which at the least might have thrown the election into the House of Representatives. Finally, in all the presidential elections since 1952, the difference in vote totals between the two major party candidates was far less than the number of eligible citizens who did not vote. If these nonvoters could be mobilized to vote, they would directly influence the kinds of electoral strategies that major and minor party candidates would adopt.

Notes

1. Converse computed the normal vote on data from 1952 to 1960. A recalculation of the normal vote with more recent data yields essentially the same result. (Miller, 1979). Petrocik (1989) has proposed a reformulation of the normal vote construct that addresses criticisms of the concept, yet preserves its utility as an analytical tool.

2. Until recently, there had been a small but statistically significant difference in the turnout rates of men and women, with men voting at a higher rate. This difference has almost vanished for a number of reasons: the dying out of the older female age cohort, socialized at a time when women's political role was more passive; the higher proportion of women going on to a higher education today; and the greater number of women in the work force.

3. When one looks at types of political participation other than voting, such as campaign activity and contacting public officials, the differences in white and black participation rates vary markedly. In a nationwide study, Verba and Nie found that whites were about twice as likely to contact public officials about a problem, in part because most public officials are white. For other types of political activity, however, blacks were just as likely, if not more so, to participate as whites. And when the effects of the lower-class characteristics of blacks were eliminated, blacks performed many political activities at rates substantially higher than those of whites. One reason for this was the presence among blacks of a group consciousness. Verba and Nie wrote: "Consciousness of race as a problem or a basis of conflict appears to bring those blacks who are conscious up to a level of participation equivalent to that of whites. Or, to put it another way, this awareness overcomes the socioeconomic disadvantages of blacks and makes them as active as whites." See Verba and Nie (1972: 149–173).

4. Squire, Wolfinger, and Glass (1987) studied the impact of registration on turnout from the perspective of residential mobility. When citizens move, they must reregister in order to be eligible to vote. This requirement keeps many Americans who have recently moved from voting. Squire, Wolfinger, and Glass estimated that national turnout rates would be 9 percent higher if there were no residential mobility.

5. One institutional explanation of turnout decline concerns the American election calendar. Boyd observes that Americans have many opportunities to vote beyond the presidential contest; in addition to the multitude of offices on the November ballot, there are primary elections, referenda, special tax levies, and so forth (1979). It may be that citizens are voting, but not always in the presidential contest. Boyd further notes that between 1932 and 1976 the number of states holding their gubernatorial election simultaneously with the presidential contest fell from 34 to 14. If the gubernatorial contest and the concomitant political party activity helped stimulate overall turnout, then the current separation of the two races may help explain the

decline in presidential turnout. Of course, the downward trend in turnout has been evident in most election contests. In a subsequent analysis, Boyd (1989) showed that the turnout rate in presidential elections would be about 6 percent higher if all states held their gubernatorial elections in the same year as the presidential contest.

6. Abramson and Aldrich (1982) attributed most of the decline in turnout to weakened political party loyalties and to lessened feelings of political efficacy and effectiveness among Americans. To these two explanations, Shaffer (1981) also cited the importance of the changing age distribution of the American population as well as the lower reliance on newspapers as a source of campaign information. It is likely that all these factors have played some role in the decline in turnout, although Cassel and Luskin (1988) argue that these analyses are flawed and that most of the decline in turnout remains unexplained.

7. There is an ongoing debate whether high turnout helps the Democrats in presidential elections. See De Nardo (1980), Tucker and Vedlitz (1986), and De Nardo (1986).

CHAPTER 3

Party Identification

As discussed earlier, the long-term force of party identification plays a central role in any analysis of American presidential elections. According to most observers, party identification in the United States is a psychological attachment or feeling of loyalty to a political party. It develops during childhood and becomes more intense the longer one remains identified with that party. While party identification predisposes voters to vote for the party of their choice, this is not the same thing as voting for the party candidate. This point was made clear by the substantial defection of Republican loyalists from Goldwater in 1964 and of Democratic partisans from McGovern in 1972, from Carter in 1980, and from Mondale in 1984.

Functions of Party Identification

Party identification often serves useful functions for the individual citizen and for the political system of which he or she is a part. At the individual level, party identification provides a vantage point from which the citizen can more economically collect and evaluate information about political affairs and behave accordingly. The citizen requires some screening device to make the burdens of collecting and evaluating information manageable; party identification provides that device and thereby eases the difficulties involved in making decisions about a broad range of political matters. Of course, as discussed in chapter 2, reliance on party identification as an orienting framework toward politics may cause one to acquire and interpret political information in a highly selective way, upsetting results for those who (somewhat naively) believe that one can and should make political decisions without any regard for a partisan context.

This argument does not imply that attachment to a party causes voters to screen out all information unfavorable to their party and its candidates; if such were the case, then there would be very few instances of partisans defecting from their party to support the candidate of the opposition. Yet in 1964, 1972, 1980, and 1984 there were substantial defections. Furthermore, when citizens have changed their partisan affiliation (as might occur in a realigning era), information unfavorable to the initial partisan loyalties must have filtered through the voters' perceptual screens. Finally, the screening effect of party identification should be weaker among younger voters, whose attachments to the parties tend to be less intense a point that will be discussed more fully.

At the system level, the presence of widespread partisan attachment helps maintain the stability of the political system. Jack Dennis and Donald McCrone have given the following analysis of this function of party identification (1970: 247).

> Party system stability, in the sense of a persisting configuration of organized partisan competition, is a function of how widely rooted in mass public consciousness is the sense of identification with the parties. Two aspects of mass identification are important: *(a)* the extent of partisan identification as measured by the proportion of the general public who identify themselves psychologically with one or another of the parties, however intensely; *(b)* the intensity of party affiliation, seen as the percent of identifiers who have a strong (and thus, more enduring) sense of commitment to one of the parties.

According to this argument, political systems characterized by widespread and enduring partisan attachments are more likely to remain immune to profound upheavals brought on by severe societal stresses, such as depression and war. Thus, the existence of widespread partisan loyalties becomes highly desirable for some observers whose major concern is maintaining the stability of the political system. Hence, the fact that in recent years there has been a marked decrease in the proportion of Americans identifying with one of the two major parties (as was shown in table 2.1) is a source of genuine worry to these observers, who fear that an uncommitted electorate will be more susceptible to the appeals of a demagogue under the appropriate circumstances. While there is certainly a conservative or status quo bias in this argument, it is instructive to note that in the 1968 presidential election the nonsouthern vote of George Wallace came disproportionately from young voters and not from the older age cohorts, a finding that surprises many students. As Converse and his colleagues (1969: 1103) note, "Wallace captured less than 3 percent of the vote among people over seventy outside the South, but 13 percent of those under thirty, with a regular gradient connecting these two extremes." The explanation for this finding is that young people generally have weaker attachments to the two major parties and therefore are more susceptible to the appeals of a third-party candidacy. Table 3.1, which breaks down the various classes of partisan identities by age groups, offers evidence to support this explanation. Keep two key points in mind in studying this table. First, the proportion of Independents is much higher among younger age cohorts than among older ones. For example, in the eighteen to twenty age cohort, 46 percent were Independents of one type or another, while in the oldest age group only 22 percent were Independents.

TABLE 3.1

Party Identification
by Age Cohorts, 1988 (in percentages)

Party identification	Age				
	18–20	21–30	31–54	55–70	71 and over
Democrat					
Strong	9%	14%	16%	22%	27%
Weak	20	15	19	17	19
Independent					
Democrat	10	16	12	10	6
Independent	19	13	11	7	7
Republican	17	15	15	10	9
Republican					
Weak	14	15	12	15	17
Strong	11	11	14	18	15
Total	100	99	99	99	100
Number of cases	70	408	906	393	218

SOURCE: 1988 CPS election study.

Second, the relative frequency of strong versus weak partisan identifiers differs sharply across age cohorts. For example, only 20 percent of the youngest age cohort are strong (more intense) Democrats or strong Republicans, compared to 42 percent of the oldest age group, with fairly regular gradients in the intermediate age categories. Thus, party identification serves as a conservatizing force; and the decline in partisan attachments has major implications for the future of American politics. (This theme is developed further in the last chapter of the book.)

The Measurement and Conceptualization of Party Identification

This chapter has discussed citizens' attachments to the Democratic and Republican parties and whether these attachments are strong or weak. Discussion will now center on how the partisan affiliations of American citizens are determined. The most common way of measuring party identification is simply to ask people whether they consider themselves to be Democrats, Republicans, or Independents. This question is evidently a very meaningful one for a substantial proportion of the American adult population—as witnessed by the fact that from 1952 to 1988 between 60 and 74 percent of the electorate could cite an allegiance to one of the two parties when questioned about their partisan loyalties (see table 2.1).

The SRC of the University of Michigan has measured party identification by a two-part question that results in a more refined way of classifying party affiliation beyond the three basic choices of Democrat, Republican, and Independent. People were first asked: "Generally speaking, do you think of yourself as a Republican, a Democrat, an Independent, or what?" Those who classified themselves as Republicans or Democrats were then asked: "Would you call yourself a strong (Republican, Democrat) or a not very strong (Republican, Democrat)?" Those who termed themselves Independents were then asked: "Do you think of yourself as closer to the Republican or the Democratic party?"

Table 2-1 shows the seven categories of party identification obtained as a result of this two-part question—strong Republican, weak Republican, Independent Republican, Independent, Independent Democrat, weak Democrat, and strong Democrat.

Note that to be classified a "pure" Independent, a person would have had to have answered the first question "Independent" and said that he or she was closer to neither the Democratic nor the Republican party in reply to the second question. Similarly, to be classified a weak Democrat requires a response of "Democrat" to the first question and a reply of "not very strong" to the second. For certain purposes this discussion will rely on the simple threefold categories of party identification, while for others this discussion will employ the more elaborate sevenfold classification.

According to the concept of partisanship reflected by the two-part question, Independent represents the midpoint of a single continuum ranging from strong Democrat to strong Republican. Thus, Democratic and Republican identifications are opposite points along this continuum. This unidimensional concept of party identification seems intuitively plausible, and it yields excellent results in understanding election outcomes. All the same, a number of irregular results of this two-part question raise doubts about how unidimensional party identification really is. For example, research by John Petrocik (1974) found inconsistencies in the measure of party identification with respect to other variables. For example, those persons leaning toward Independent were more likely than weak identifiers to be involved and interested in politics. Such a result is surprising if one thinks of weak identifiers as having stronger partisan feelings than those leaning to Independent. Thus, one might logically expect weak identifiers to have a greater political involvement. But Petrocik shows that Independent leaners have more characteristics generally associated with higher levels of political involvement than do weak partisans. Such characteristics include higher education and higher income.

Petrocik's inconsistencies dealt mainly with measures of political involvement. In addition, other inconsistencies have arisen with respect to partisanship-related measures, such as the evaluation of the parties and candidates as well as voting loyally for one's party. Table 3.2 presents the average evaluation of four partisan objects—the Democratic and Republican parties and the Democratic and Republican nominees in 1988—for each

TABLE 3.2

Mean Evaluations of Four Partisan Objects in 1988, by Party Identification*

Object	Strong Demo-crats	Weak Demo-crats	Indepen-dent Democrats	Indepen-dents	Indepen-dent Republicans	Weak Repub-licans	Strong Repub-licans
Democratic party	85	72	71	54	49	49	38
Republican party	39	50	50	55	71	72	84
Dukakis	77	66	69	54	46	46	34
Bush	38	51	48	60	75	73	86

*Table entries are mean thermometer ratings. The higher the rating, the more positive or favorable is the evaluation of the object.
SOURCE: CPS 1988 election study.

category of party identification. These evaluations are obtained by a ther mometer scale that asks respondents to indicate how warm or cold they feel toward an object along a 0 to 100 continuum, where 100 represents the warmest (most positive) evaluation and 0 the coldest. The analogy to a thermometer is helpful to the person making the evaluation. Thus, the first entry of 85 in table 3.2 means that the average rating of the Democratic party by strong Democrats was 85, a very warm or positive rating, as expected. Likewise, the mean evaluation of the Democratic party by strong Republicans was only 38.

Note that the differences in the mean ratings of the various objects for weak identifiers versus leaners of the same party are often very small and sometimes in the opposite direction than expected. For example, there is no difference in ratings of Dukakis by independent and weak Republicans. Yet if weak Republicans are really more partisan than Independent Republicans, we would expect their assessments of Dukakis to be more negative. Similarly, observe that there are scant differences in the evaluations made of Bush by weak versus Independent Republicans, while weak Democrats are more favorable toward Bush than are independent Democrats, clearly an inconsistent pattern. In general, table 3.2 indicates numerous instances where the discriminatory power of the sevenfold classification of party identification is at best minimal and where obvious inconsistencies arise.

A final inconsistent result of the traditional measurement of party identification concerns the actual votes cast by citizens. If party identification is unidimensional, strong identifiers should be more loyal to their party than weak identifiers. Weak identifiers should be more faithful than leaning Independents. Yet a quick glance at figures 3.4 and 3.5 (see pages 69 and 71) reveals that more often than not Independent leaners were more loyal than weak identifiers in supporting their party's presidential nominee. Indeed, because of such patterns some researchers question whether leaners should be classified as Independents or as partisans. See Asher (1983: n. 7) for a discussion of this controversy.

As a result of these inconsistencies, investigators have proposed multidimensional ways of conceptualizing party identification. Niemi, Wright, and Powell (1987) attributed some of the inconsistencies to the fact that some Americans identify with different political parties at different levels of government. These multiple identifications (for example, Republican at the national level, but Democrat at the state level) suggest that party identification is a multidimensional phenomenon. Weisberg (1980) also posited a multidimensional approach to partisanship. He argued that independence may be a separate entity with which people can identify, regardless of whether they are neutral between the two parties. Moreover, Republican versus Democratic loyalty may not be polar opposites; certainly citizens can simultaneously like or dislike both parties. Hence, Weisberg advocates a three-dimensional approach, consisting of attitudes toward the Republican party, the Democratic party, and independence. One immediate payoff of this multidimensional perspective is the ability to distinguish between party loyalists openly hostile toward the opposition party and party loyalists indifferent to it. Clearly, one would expect greater loyalty toward one's own party in the former case; two researchers (Maggiotto and Piereson, 1977) found that evaluations of the other party exerted an independent effect on vote above and beyond the influence of party loyalty.

Other researchers have argued for two dimensions of partisanship. Katz (1979) found that strong party identifiers who switched their party loyalty were more likely to move all the way to strong identification with a new party than to move to some intermediate position. This suggested to Katz that strong Democrat and strong Republican were actually close points and not opposite ends of a unidimensional continuum. Valentine and Van Wingen (1980) and Howell (1980) also argue for two dimensions of party identification—partisanship and independence. Van Wingen and Valentine argue that the problems inherent in interpreting the standard party identification measure arise from the fact that the measure is inadequately tapping two dimensions simultaneouosly. They therefore call for the development of direct unidimensional measures of partisanship and independence.

These new ways of formulating party identification raise very directly a fundamental question: Can we continue to use the traditional measure of partisanship? This standard measure has the advantages of familiarity, availability, and comparability over time. Thus, giving it up would impose hardships on many analyses. Nevertheless, standard measures of party identification do not reflect well the underlying unidimensional concept of partisanship. Weisberg (1980: 49) takes the reasonable position that it would be silly to give up the traditional measure, even with its known flaws, unless alternative measures provide "real theoretical and substantive gains." Certainly the traditional measure needs to be supplemented, if not replaced, in understanding political independence. But the traditional measure still powerfully represents the partisan predispositions and locations of citizens. Scholars (for example, Dennis, 1981) are currently studying other possible measures of partisanship. Initial results suggest that the traditional measure of party identification does a slightly better job of tapping long-term retrospective aspects of voting behavior, such as regularity of party voting. But the traditional method does no better than alternative measures in other areas.

In summary, the most frequently used measure of party identification is a self-report technique in which citizens respond verbally to a survey question about their partisanship. Despite some systematic distortion in their verbal response as compared to their actual behavior, people can be readily assigned to the three broad categories of Democrat, Republican, and Independent. While researchers may want to use a more elaborate classification of party identification for certain purposes, they should be careful not to get unnecessarily complicated. The method used to measure a concept often influences the results.

The Development and
Transmission of Party Identification

As stated earlier, citizens tend to acquire a party identification fairly early in their lives. In a study of school children in eight cities, Hess and Torney (1967: 90) found that only about 20 percent of a sample of fourth graders could not recognize what the terms *Democrat* and *Republican* meant, while almost half the children could express a clear partisan preference. Similarly, in a study of New Haven youngsters, Fred Greenstein (1965: 71) found that by the fourth grade more than 60 percent of the students could cite a partisan preference. Hence, it is meaningful to talk of the partisan attachments of young children; however, the policy content and informational support of this partisanship is weak to nonexistent. Greenstein discovered, for example, that only a third of the fourth graders could name one public official from either of the two parties and that fewer than one in five students could name a leader from each party. He also found that perceptions of issue differences between the parties were uncommon. These early partisan loyalties, despite being devoid of policy and informational content, may be consequential for what the child subsequently learns about the parties. That is, these early attachments may so facilitate the selective acquisition of information about parties that they tend to reinforce initial loyalties.

It is widely agreed that the family plays the greatest role in the child's acquisition of partisanship. In a nationwide study of high school seniors conducted in 1965, Jennings and Niemi (1974: 41) found substantial agreement in parental and child partisan affiliations, as shown in table 3.3. The Jennings and Niemi evidence is particularly interesting since it is based on responses from both the child and his or her parents and does not rely on the child's report of the parents' partisanship, which can be subject to serious distortion.

One factor that affected the degree of correspondence between the parents' and the child's identification was the politicization of the family. Correspondence was higher in situations where the parents engaged in political conversations frequently and where the child had a high level of interest in public affairs. Jennings and Niemi argued that in such situations there are more cues about the parents' political leanings and a greater likelihood that the child will accurately pick up such cues. Thus, the greater correspondence in party loyalties in politicized families is due to greater perceptual accuracy on the part of children in recognizing their parents' partisanship (Jennings and Niemi, 1974: 47–49).

The family plays the dominant role in the transmission of partisan attitudes, although it is less important with respect to other political attitudes.[1] Within the family, it had been traditional to describe the father's political role as dominant. This image of male political dominance arose in part because in some of the earlier studies of voting it was not uncommon for the wife to say that she was going to vote the way her husband voted. The work of Jennings and Langton (1969) calls into question the simplistic notion of male political dominance, particularly in the child's acquisition of partisan attachment. Jennings and Langton showed that in cases where the mother and father had different identifications, the child was more likely to take on the partisan affiliation of the mother, as shown in table 3.4. While the advantage for the mother is not overwhelming, it does suggest that any unqualified notion of male political dominance should be rejected.

One explanation for the mother's relatively advantageous position is simply that the child spends much more time with the mother in his or her formative years and therefore develops closer affective ties with the mother. While Jennings and Langton examine additional factors that affect the relative influence of the father versus the mother on the child, the basic result of the mother having greater influence still holds. For example, where the mother is more politically active in campaigns than the father, the child's identification agrees with the mother's over the father's by a margin of 59 percent to 28 percent, or a 31 percent advantage for the mother. But where the father is more politically active, his advantage over the mother in the child's loyalties is only 6 percent (36 percent versus 30 percent). The actual learning of partisanship by children occurs via a process of identification, described by Hess and Torney (1967: 21) as consisting of "the child's imitation of the behavior of some significant other person—usually a parent, or a teacher—when the adult has not attempted to persuade the child of his viewpoint." Thus, learning party identification is not a conscious activity;

TABLE 3.3

Student Party Identification by Parental Party Identification* (in percentages)

Student party identification	Parental party identification		
	Democrat	Independent	Republican
Democrat	66%	29%	13%
Independent	27	53	36
Republican	7	17	51
Total	100	100	100
Number of cases	914	442	495

*Party identification was measured by the standard SRC/CPS question. The categories of Democrat and Republican include strong and weak identifiers, while the Independent category includes leaners and pure Independents.
SOURCE: Jennings, M. Kent, and Richard G. Niemi, *The Political Character of Adolescence: The Influence of Families and Schools.* Copyright © 1974 by Princeton University Press. Table 2.2, p. 41 reprinted by permission.

rather, it is an informal process centered mainly in the family. One reason why the family is so crucial in this area is that other potential agents of political learning, such as teachers and school curricula, studiously avoid getting enmeshed in partisan questions.[2]

Although people acquire their party identification early in life, it need not remain stable throughout the life cycle. One reason for this is that the childhood learning of partisanship is often devoid of much issue and policy content. As people age, they may find themselves identifying with a political party that is not in harmony with their developing issue positions. In such a situation, it is not uncommon for adults to bring their partisanship into line with their issue preferences. Once they do so, the newly acquired partisanship is likely to remain stable so long as the issue–party linkage remains congruent. Franklin (1984) provides evidence that the partisanship of young adults is indeed responsive to their issue preferences. And Luskin, McIver, and Carmines (1989) demonstrate that issues, especially more complex economic matters, are important influences when children take on a partisan affiliation opposite that of their parents.

The Stability of Party Identification at the Individual Level

Although citizens' partisan orientations can and do change in response to new information and changed political environments, overall there is substantial stability in the party loyalties of Americans. Panel data collected as a result of repeated interviews with the *same* people offer the best evidence of this stability. Such data enable researchers to observe directly changes occurring in partisanship. Two major panel studies of the American electorate are

---

TABLE 3.4

Student's Party Identification in Cases in which the Parents' Party Identification Differs (in percentages)

Parents' partisanship		Student's partisanship				No. of
Mother	Father	Democrat	Independent	Republican	Total	Cases
Democrat	Republican	44%	21%	35%	100%	37
Republican	Democrat	29%	38%	35%	100%	23

SOURCE: M. Kent Jennings and Kenneth P. Langton, "Mothers versus Fathers: The Formation of Political Orientations among Young Americans," *Journal of Politics* 31 (May 1969), table 3, p. 341. By permission of the authors and the University of Texas Press.

available, one spanning the 1956–1958–1960 period, and the other encompassing 1972–1974–1976. Table 3.5 presents the relationship between the partisanship professed by a sample of Americans in 1972 and the partisanship of these same respondents in 1976.

Although the assessment of partisan stability shown in table 3.5 appears straightforward, problems inherent in the way partisanship is conceptualized and measured complicate this task. If the two-part party identification question assigns respondents to one of seven possible categories, does stability refer to both the direction and the strength of partisanship? That is, should a person who was at one time a strong Democrat and at another time was a weak Democrat be considered stable or unstable in partisanship? If stability is defined as *constancy in both direction and intensity*, then the more numerous the categories of partisanship, the less likely is it that the person will give identical responses over time. Hence, as shown in table 3.5, the level of stability with the sevenfold classification is about 50 percent compared to over 74 percent (the sum of the percentages within the broken lines) when party identification is divided into three categories: Democrat (strong and weak), Independent (leaners and pure Independents), and Republican (strong and weak). If the Independent leaners are included with the partisans rather than with the pure Independents, a third estimate of stability of just under 80 percent (the sum of the percentages within the solid lines) is obtained. Which of the three estimates gives the most accurate assessment of stability depends on what is required of party identification to call it stable.

Analyses of the 1956–1958–1960 panel have yielded varying judgments of stability. Dreyer (1973) concluded that party identification was very stable, with only random changes occurring over time. Subsequent analyses by Dobson and St. Angelo (1975), Brody (1977), and Howell (1981) have challenged this conclusion, arguing that changes in partisanship were indeed responsive to real-world events. For example, Dobson and St. Angelo found that Republicans were less stable in their partisanship than Democrats between 1956 and 1958, while both groups behaved similarly between 1958 and 1960. They attributed this pattern to the "Republican" recession of 1958. A similar pattern held in the 1972–1974–1976 era, with Republicans between 1972 and 1974 (the Nixon resignation year) much more likely than Democrats to move away from their partisanship, a party difference that practically vanished between 1974 and 1976. Brody argued that the economic climate and the low evaluation of the Republican president's performance made Republican identifiers more prone to changing their partisanship. Howell's analysis confirmed the responsiveness of party identification to short-term forces, although for Howell the major short-term force was past voting behavior.

In the first year of the Reagan presidency, public opinion polls showed that the traditional Democratic advantage in partisan allegiances had nearly vanished. The Republican resurgence was attributed to the popularity of the

TABLE 3.5

The Stability of Partisanship Between 1972 and 1976

1972 Partisanship	1976 Partisanship						
	Strong Democrat	Weak Democrat	Independent Democrat	Independent	Independent Republican	Weak Republican	Strong Republican
Strong Democrat	8.9	3.7	0.8	0.3	0.1	0.1	0.1
Weak Democrat	5.0	13.0	3.2	1.7	0.6	0.9	0.2
Independent Democrat	1.5	3.5	4.3	0.8	1.0	0.2	0.1
Independent	0.6	1.0	1.7	4.9	2.2	0.9	0.1
Independent Republican	0.5	0.4	1.0	2.6	4.8	1.8	0.5
Weak Republican	0.1	0.7	0.2	0.8	2.7	7.4	2.4
Strong Republican	0.3	0.4	0.2	0.2	0.9	4.1	6.5

Total percentage = 100.
SOURCE: CPS 1972–1976 election panel. Table entries are corner or total percentages based on a total of 1,276 panel respondents who expressed a partisanship in both 1972 and 1976. The stable proportion is simply the percentage of respondents who gave identical responses over time.

president, his grace and good humor in recovering from the assassination attempt, and optimism (in 1981) about the likely success of his economic program. By 1982, when the economy had sunk into a deep recession and the president's popularity had declined, public opinion polls once again showed the Democrats with a sizable advantage in partisan allegiances. Although these public opinion polls in 1981 and 1982 were not panel surveys, they did suggest that the distribution of partisanship responds to the short-term political climate. The work of Alsop and Weisberg (1988); Weisberg and Alsop (1990); and MacKuen, Erikson, and Stinson (1989) further demonstrated that party identification is responsive to short-term forces. Alsop and Weisberg showed that the distribution of partisanship changed in politically meaningful ways over the course of the 1984 campaign. And MacKuen, Erikson, and Stinson, examining partisanship over a forty-two-year period, showed that party loyalties were sensitive to economic conditions and presidential popularity.

Hence, there is much evidence that the conceptualization of party identification as primarily a long-term force unresponsive to current political stimuli should be revised. For party identification *does* respond to short-term influences. However, saying that it is sensitive to short-term forces is *not* the same as saying that it is unstable. On the contrary, party identification remains one of the most stable political attitudes. Party loyalties are far more stable than attitudes on a wide range of prominent political issues. Likewise, few attachments (with the exception of such loyalties as religious affiliation) are more durable than partisan stability. For example, Markus and Converse (1979) found that partisan stability in the 1972–1974–1976 CPS panel far exceeded the stability of respondents' stances on issues (with the exception of moral issues). Moreover, the direction of partisanship is more stable than its strength; the bulk of observed changes in the panel data are intraparty (for example, from strong Republican to weak Republican) rather than interparty. Various research findings suggest that the direction and strength of party identification are conceptually distinct. The former is more stable and long-term, while the latter is more responsive to the immediate political setting.

Finally, the work of Jennings and Niemi (1975) and Jennings and Markus (1984) provides an even stronger test of the stability of partisanship. The authors analyzed a sample of high school seniors and some of their parents in 1965; they then reinterviewed many of the same people in 1973 and again in 1982. Among the parental sample, partisan stability was very high at all three interviews with very little polar change in partisanship. Among the youth sample, partisan change was much more common between 1965 and 1973. But between 1973 and 1982 the youth sample (whose members were approximately thirty-five years old in 1982) registered a marked increase in partisan stability, although the proportion identifying with a political party was still less than in the parental generation. Hence, the stability of party identification over a seventeen-year period has been demonstrated very convincingly, as has the tendency of young adults to move toward more stable partisan loyalties.

Although panel data yield valuable evidence about partisan stability, their limited time span makes them less helpful in studying two related questions; namely, whether citizens become more conservative politically as they age and whether partisan loyalties become more intense over time.[3] With respect to the former question, it is commonplace in popular discussions of politics to assert that as adults get older, they get more conservative. Conservative in this context can mean different things, including an unwillingness to accept new ideas and a rigidity in thought. Or it might refer to more overtly political matters, for example, the assertion that older people become more conservative politically and hence more Republican because the Republican party is likely to take the more conservative, status quo position (that is, the position opposed to federal intervention) on a wide range of public policy issues.

If, in fact, older citizens are more conservative and Republican, two distinct processes might produce this effect. The first process— the so-called *life-cycle effect*—suggests that growing conservativism is an integral part of aging. But according to a different explanation, older citizens are more Republican because they learned their partisanship in a more Republican era. Hence, their greater Republicanism is not due to aging but to a generational effect reflecting the fact that this age cohort of citizens grew up in a more Republican era. Therefore, they are more Republican today because of the relative stability of partisan orientation over time.

The relative importance of life-cycle versus generational effects has sparked a major controversy among academic investigators. *The American Voter* (pp. 149–67) found substantial generational effect associated with the Great Depression and the New Deal and also observed that older citizens were somewhat more likely to switch from Democrat to Republican than the reverse. But overall *The American Voter* found little evidence to sustain the notion that aging leads to Republicanism. John Crittenden (1962, 1969–1970) found that the aging process does produce sizable conversions to Republicanism, although Neal Cutler (1969–70) has criticized this research as based on faulty methodology. A study by Glenn and Hefner (1972) concludes that there is no evidence for the proposition linking aging to Republicanism.

With respect to the intensification of partisanship, political analysts have long observed that older citizens exhibit stronger party loyalties than do their younger counterparts; see table 3.1 for an example of the positive relationship between age and strength of party identification. The question is what processes might account for the more intense loyalties of older citizens, and the life-cycle versus generational controversy again becomes relevant. Converse (1969, 1976, 1979) has espoused an intuitively appealing life-cycle explanation, which asserts that the longer a person supports a political party, the stronger the loyalties to that party will become; repeated and enduring commitment results in more intense commitment. The life-cycle explanation implies that as older citizens with firmer loyalties pass from the electorate, they are replaced by younger cohorts with intensifying party loyalties, thereby leaving the overall level of party support relatively unchanged.

Employing a cohort analysis, Abramson (1976, 1979) did not observe an increase in partisan intensity among age cohorts over time, as the life-cycle explanation would predict. Hence, he argued that the stronger party attachments of older citizens represent generational and not life-cycle effects because the older generation was socialized into partisanship at a time when party labels and loyalties were more meaningful. Thus, the older generation was imprinted with a stronger sense of partisanship at a young age and has carried this imprinting over time. Abramson asserts that the young cohorts of today receive weak partisan cues and that the resulting weak attachments will be characteristic of them even as they identify with a political party over a lengthy period.[4]

A two-wave panel study (Jennings and Niemi, 1975) of a sample of high school seniors and their parents provides additional evidence challenging the life-cycle explanation. Between 1965 and 1973 the proportion of Independents among the youth rose by 12 percent and the proportion of strong identifiers fell by half—movements opposite to those predicted by the life-cycle notion. For the parents, there was greater partisan stability over the eight-year period, with only a slight decline in the proportion of intense partisans. It is possible that life-cycle effects operative in this era were outweighed by even stronger period effects centered on such political crises as Vietnam, race relations, and Watergate.

How do these findings relate to the potential for political realignment? The generational explanation implies that the weaker partisan attachments of the contemporary youth generation will remain weak; this will result in a citizenry more susceptible to political realignment. In contrast, the life-cycle process predicts that younger cohorts will acquire a greater political colortion as they mature; hence, they will be more resistant to realignment.

Alternative Conceptualizations and Measurements of Party Identification

If party identification does respond to short-term stimuli, as suggested in the discussion of partisan stability, then a partial reconceptualization of partisanship may be required. Fiorina (1977, 1981) provides such a reformulation. He defines a person's identification with a party as the person's past experiences with that party minus the person's past experiences with the other party plus some adjustment representing the initial partisan bias that the person brings into the political arena. This formulation is useful because it incorporates past experiences yet weights them less than current experiences, thereby allowing recent events to alter partisan predispositions. In effect, party identification becomes "a running tally of retrospective evaluations" (1981: 89). The formulation grounds party identification in reality and allows past experiences to anchor party identification somewhat, thereby giving to party identification some element of a standing decision even as it responds to current political stimuli. In fact, Fiorina explicitly states (1981: 152) that "there is an inertial element [party identification] in voting behavior that cannot be ignored, but that inertial element has an experiential basis; it is *not* something learned at mommy's knee and never questioned thereafter." But overall, Fiorina rests party identification in evaluations of prior experiences and, as such, gives the acquisition of partisanship a more rational basis.

Shively (1979) also suggests a rational basis for the way in which people acquire and keep their party identification. His functional model argues very straightforwardly that people acquire party identifications in order to simplify the decisional burden facing them as voters. He sees party identification as an economizing device that reduces the costs of decision making. A person will be more likely to develop a partisanship if other economizing devices (for example, class and group loyalties) are not available. Shively presents some evidence for his model and develops some interesting implications.

The work of Fiorina and Shively is important because it moves the discussion of party identification away from a long-term attitude acquired in childhood, which is probably devoid of issue and policy content. Instead, it anchors party identification in the political reality experienced by the adult citizen. This does not deny child–adult party identification linkages, but it does suggest that people acquire partisanship through a more complex and dynamic process with a rational foundation.

There is still much evidence that people tend to learn party identification in childhood even before the party label has much issue content. However, this identification changes in response to individual experiences and to the dominant political forces of the era. Howell's (1980) analysis of the effects of voting behavior on changes in partisanship reaches a similar conclusion; the development of adult partisanship "involves an interplay between the stable component of that attitude [party identification] and adult behavior [in Howell's case, voting behavior] which can be either reinforcing or non-reinforcing. Past behavior does influence future identification, but that influence is specified by both the stability and direction of the initial identification" (p. 298).

All of the studies reviewed thus far have conceptualized party identification as a psychological phenomenon and measured it by means of attitudinal questions. Some observers, such as Walter DeVries and V. Lance Tarrance, the authors of *The Ticket-Splitter*, have argued that political scientists rely too much on attitudinal measures of partisanship rather than on measures based on actual behavior. For example, DeVries and Tarrance classify people as Independents, not according to their responses to a survey question but according to their actual voting behavior. Thus, an Independent for them is a person who cast a split-ticket vote, that is, supported candidates of both parties at the same election. Given their different definition of an Independent, it is not surprising that DeVries and Tarrance's description of Independents differs from other analyses.

In general, different measures of what is thought to be the same basic concept are likely to lead to disparities in research findings. This phenomenon is illustrated in the work of Everett Ladd and Charles Hadley (1973–1974), who employed an attitudinal and a behavioral measure of party identification to measure the similarity in policy preferences of Democrats and Republicans. Their attitudinal measure of partisanship was a standard survey item, while they defined behavioral Republicans and behavioral Democrats as voters who supported the same party's presidential nominees in two consecutive elections. Thus, the self-identified (attitudinal) Democrat who voted for Eisenhower in 1952 and 1956 would be classified as a behavioral Republican. Ladd and Hadley found that with the attitudinal measure, Republican and Democratic adherents took fairly similar positions on a wide variety of issues, while they were much further apart when measured behaviorally. In general, Ladd and Hadley found that behavioral Democrats were more liberal than their self-identified Democratic counterparts, while behavioral Republicans were more conservative.

Thus, the reader might ask which definition or measurement strategy is the correct one. The answer is that neither one is right or wrong; the choice between the two must be made on conceptual grounds. A self-identification measure of party identification is, to me, more useful when people do not vote according to their proclaimed identification because that leads to the crucial question "Why?" Hence, once again, party identification is a baseline from which to assess the impact of other factors impinging on the vote decision. Ladd and Hadley (p. 32) note that in times of rapid social change and partisan realignment, self-identification may lag behind actual behavior. That is, people may continue to identify with a party even though they no longer support its presidential candidates. But even in this situation, the self-identification measure seems superior. If realignment is conceptualized as a process occurring over time, then its ultimate outcome is in doubt. The fact that identification may lag behind behavior helps contribute to the uncertainty of the realignment outcome. Should events change suddenly, the lagged identification may facilitate the movement of people back to their original party. For example, one might speculate that the Watergate scandals and economic problems of the 1970s, coupled with the lagged Democratic identification in the South, made it easier for Southerners who supported Republican candidates in recent presidential elections to return to the Democratic party and Jimmy Carter in 1976. For the kinds of questions that concern us in this book, the attitudinal measure of party identification is preferable.

The Stability of Party Identification in the Aggregate

Although the partisanship of individual citizens has remained fairly stable, there have been significant trends in the overall distribution of partisanship in the electorate. The most noteworthy trend is the huge rise in the number of citizens claiming to be Independents, so that in 1988, there were more Independents than there were Democrats or Republicans (see table 2.1). Of course, if one treats leaning Independents as partisans rather than as pure Independents, the growth of independence is not nearly so impressive. The other major development has been the erosion in the Democratic numerical advantage over the GOP so that by 1988 the percentage of Democrats was only 7 percent greater than the proportion of Republicans in the electorate, a sizable decline in the Democratic lead of 18 percent in 1980 and 27 percent in 1964.

As depicted in figure 3.1, the major increase in Independents occurred between 1964 and 1972, with little additional growth since 1972. Overall, the gain in Independents about equals the decline in Democratic identifiers,

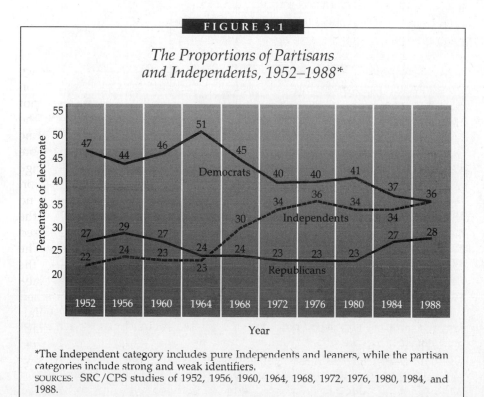

FIGURE 3.1

The Proportions of Partisans and Independents, 1952–1988*

*The Independent category includes pure Independents and leaners, while the partisan categories include strong and weak identifiers.
SOURCES: SRC/CPS studies of 1952, 1956, 1960, 1964, 1968, 1972, 1976, 1980, 1984, and 1988.

although this does not mean that Democrats have been switching to a position of independence. In fact, the major source of the increase is to be found in the party affiliations of the young generation. In 1964, 33 percent of the twenty-one to twenty-four age cohort were Independents, compared to over 50 percent in 1972. Likewise, 28 percent of the twenty-five to thirty-four year olds were Independents in 1964, a figure that jumped to 47 percent by 1972. In contrast, the older generation has not witnessed as substantial an increase in independence. For example, between 1964 and 1972 the proportion of Independents among citizens over sixty-five years old increased only 10 percent (from 14 to 24 percent Independent).

Thus, the young generation without solid attachments to a political party becomes a prime source of any potential realignment. It is reasonable to expect that as these young citizens age, a sizable proportion will find a home in one of the two political parties even if they never become as partisan as the older generation. But on what basis will they make this choice? One possibility is that the preponderance of these young citizens will end up as adherents of the party preferred by their parents. It appears, however, that the influence of the family has declined somewhat, perhaps to be replaced by the impact of political events, issues, and candidates. If so, the future shape of the party system is unpredictable.

The Social Characteristics of Partisans

It is a fact of American political life that support for the Democratic and Republican parties varies among different racial, religious, nationality, and economic groups. American politics is often discussed in terms of the black vote or the union vote or the Catholic vote, indicating that blocs of citizens may have distinctive partisan allegiances. Yet despite the relative homogeneity of these various groups, it should be noted that, with the exception of blacks and Jews, it is uncommon for any group to give more than 60 percent of its vote to a party. Thus, the Democratic party usually wins many more votes from union members and Catholics than does the Republican party; it is also correct, however, to say that the Republican party receives a substantial minority of the votes cast by Catholics and union members. Thus, the parties attract rather heterogeneous support even though they appeal much more to certain groups than to others.

Parties have a differential appeal to citizens with varying social characteristics because citizens do not act politically in a vacuum divorced from the influence of relevant others. Rather, Americans belong to a large number of groups, many of which are relevant for partisan preferences. The most important group is the primary group of the family, where many citizens acquire their initial partisanship. But many secondary groups to which an individual belongs, while entailing less group interaction than the family, still have notable consequences for political behavior. Such groups as religious and occupational organizations, while usually not overtly political, influence or appear to influence partisan choice because members of the group have shared politically relevant experiences or because the group reflects consequential political events of a previous era or because the group has the resources to educate and mobilize its members toward political goals. This is the case, for example, when labor unions rally their membership behind candidates endorsed by union governing bodies. As another example, Catholics are on the whole more Democratic than non-Catholics, not because the Democratic party currently espouses specifically pro-Catholic policies, but because of historical circumstance and the economic location of Catholic citizens in an earlier generation. That is, the Democratic party welcomed the massive waves of Catholic immigrants in the early part of this century and facilitated the movement of Catholics into the political system. Furthermore, Catholics were disproportionately of the lower and working class when the Great Depression struck. It was the Democratic party that proposed policies viewed as more beneficial to disadvantaged groups of that period. These Catholic Democratic loyalties, while less relevant to contemporary America, are maintained in part by a socialization process and by particular events, such as recessions and the Democratic nomination of Catholic candidates. Such events tend to resurrect the older images of the Democratic party as the party more beneficial to Catholic citizens.

The most interesting aspect of group loyalties is that frequently the members of the group do not see the political relevance of the group or perceive the group as having any significant impact on their behavior. Yet situations can arise in which the original basis of the group attachment assumes new life. For example, probably the most basic and most investigated social characteristic is social class, which is defined in a multitude of ways. While class cleavages are not as prominent in the United States as in other societies, the Democratic and Republican parties are perceived somewhat differently in terms of which class they favor, with the Democrats seen as the working-class party and the GOP as the middle-class party. Although these class-related perceptions of the two parties have weakened in recent decades, the presence of economic crises is likely to make class a more potent factor in partisan choice. The point is that the differential loyalties of various groups to the two parties most often have a "rational" basis in some set of events in the past. These loyalties may gradually decay as the original rationale for them fades into the past. But if the original basis for the loyalties become prominent once again, then these loyalties may be reinforced. This is why the Democratic party tries to contest elections on New Deal economic issues. If voters make their choices on the basis of such concerns, the Democratic party is likely to fare very well at election time.

Research has indicated that blacks are more Democratic than whites, that Catholics and Jews are more Democratic than Protestants (outside the South), and that lower- and working-class citizens are more Democratic than

middle- and upper-class citizens. These general patterns have held throughout the 1952–1988 period, although there have been some noteworthy deviations, which will be discussed further.

Figure 3.2 presents trends in Democratic identification among religious
groups. The proportion of Catholics who are strong and weak identifiers with
the Democratic party has declined by 23 percent from a peak in 1960, the year
in which the Democrats nominated a Catholic candidate for president.
Southern Protestant loyalties to the Democratic party have eroded even more
markedly, a decline that would be sharper if black citizens were excluded
from the analysis. Yet the Democrats still claim greater allegiance from
Catholics and southern Protestants than do the Republicans. Nonsouthern

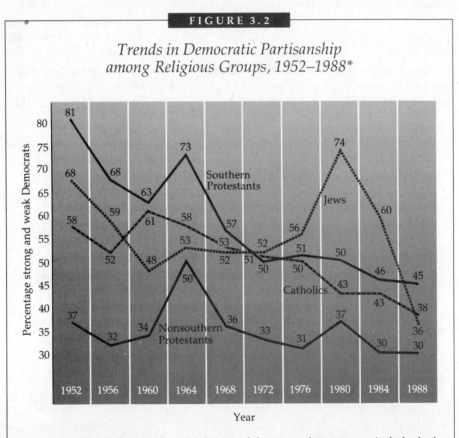

FIGURE 3.2

*Trends in Democratic Partisanship
among Religious Groups, 1952–1988**

*In this figure and the next, the complement of the reported percentages includes both
Independents and Republicans. That is, the fact that 58 percent of the Catholics in 1952
were Democrats means that the other 42 percent were either Independents or Republicans.
SOURCES: SRC/CPS studies of 1952, 1956, 1960, 1964, 1968, 1972, 1976, 1980, 1984, and
1988.

Protestants have traditionally been less Democratic, and there has been no consistent trend in their loyalties; while among Jews, Democratic strength was solid until 1988 (sampling error may be a problem here).

Within racial categories (see figure 3.3), the greatest volatility has occurred among black citizens, especially in the South. This is not surprising since southern blacks have only recently become electorally active and have not had the opportunity to develop as firm loyalties to a political party as have citizens who have been voting for a long time. Voting for a party regularly increases one's commitment to that party, an effect not very important among southern blacks in view of the fact that they have only recently achieved the franchise. In 1960 only half of all blacks claimed to be Democrats, while in 1968 this proportion jumped to 88 percent, an almost unheard-of degree of partisan loyalty by a group. But between 1968 and 1972 black identification with the Democratic party plummeted by almost 20 percent as the number of black Independents rose tremendously. Between 1972 and

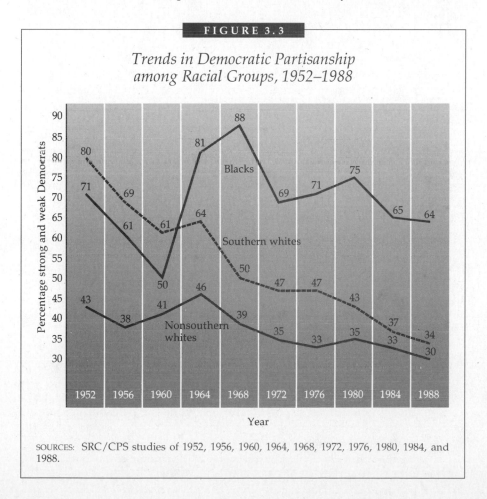

FIGURE 3.3

Trends in Democratic Partisanship among Racial Groups, 1952–1988

SOURCES: SRC/CPS studies of 1952, 1956, 1960, 1964, 1968, 1972, 1976, 1980, 1984, and 1988.

1988 black identification with the Democratic party ranged between 64 and 75 percent.

Among nonsouthern whites (see figure 3.3), partisan allegiances have not varied so much, even though there has been a long-term decline in white support for the Democrats. Among southern whites, the decline in Democratic loyalties has been much sharper; in 1952, 81 percent of white southerners were Democrats compared to only 34 percent in 1988. Fortunately for the Democrats, the GOP has not been the sole beneficiary of this decline; there has also been a sizable increase in the proportion of Independents among white southerners. Nevertheless, the GOP has made strong gains in national and state elections throughout the South. Overall, the 1952–1988 period has witnessed a marked convergence in the partisanship of southern and non-southern whites.

Among status groups, as measured by income, union membership, and citizens' perceptions of their social class, the trends in Democratic identification have not been as consistent or clear-cut. In general, Democratic identification dropped noticeably in 1972; this was particularly evident among union members, blue-collar workers, and people who call themselves working class. Fewer than half of these groups were classified as strong and weak Democrats in 1972 and in 1980. By 1988, only 44 percent of union members called themselves Democrats. While the Democrats still have a clear advantage over Republicans in the loyalties of these groups, erosion has occurred in these traditional pillars of Democratic support.

The previous analysis has investigated trends in the partisanship of various groups defined according to one or two characteristics. For example, Democrats tend to be strongest among southern and nonsouthern blacks, among nonsouthern and retired blue-collar Catholics, and among Jews. In contrast, Republicans claim the greatest loyalty among non-Southerners, Protestants, white-collar workers, housewives, and retired citizens in general.

Thus far, this analysis has focused on the partisan makeup of various social groups. (Chapter 10, which takes up the strategies employed by political elites to put together majority electoral coalitions, will also examine the social composition of various partisan groups.) This chapter will conclude with an examination of the actual voting behavior of citizens as opposed to the partisanship of various politically relevant social groups.

Robert Axelrod (1972) has described broad electoral coalitions for each party and determined the contribution made by each coalitional component to each party's vote at each election since 1952. The Democratic coalition, according to Axelrod, consists of the poor, blacks, Southerners, union members, Catholics, and residents of central cities, while the Republican coalition is practically the mirror image of the Democratic. Table 3.6 presents the voting loyalty rates of each element of both party coalitions.

Note that in 1988 Dukakis ran very well among three overlapping components of the traditional Democratic coalition—the poor, blacks, and

TABLE 3.6

Loyalty Rates Among Components of the Democratic
and Republican Electoral Coalitions, 1952–1988*

	Year									
Party and groups	1952	1956	1960	1964	1968	1972	1976	1980	1984	1988
Democrats										
Poor (income under $3,000, under $5,000 in 1980 and 1984, under $7,000 in 1988)	47%	47%	48%	69%	44%	45%	67%	71%	66%	68%
Black (and other nonwhite)	83	68	72	99	92	86	88	88	81	89
Union member (or union member in family)	59	55	66	80	51	45	63	50	55	59
Catholic (and other non-Protestant)	57	53	82	75	61	43	57	44	47	54
South (including border states)	55	52	52	58	39	36	53	47	44	49
Central cities (of 12 largest metropolitan areas)	51	55	65	74	58	61	61	69	70	74
Republicans										
Nonpoor	56	59	50	40	44	61	49	52	61	55
White	57	59	51	42	47	66	52	56	65	59
Nonunion	61	63	55	45	46	63	52	55	63	56
Protestant	61	62	63	44	49	64	53	54	62	58
Northern	57	60	50	38	47	60	49	51	60	54
Not in central cities	57	60	52	40	45	63	49	53	61	56

*The table entries are the percentages of each party's coalition components remaining loyal to the party in the presidential election.
SOURCE: Extracted from figures presented by Robert Axelrod, "Presidential Election Coalitions in 1984," American Political Science Review 80 (March 1986), pp. 281–284, and SRC/CPS 1988 election study.

central city residents—and reasonably well among labor union members. But his performance among Catholics and Southerners, while better than Mondale's performance four years earlier, still left Dukakis with relatively low support among groups that had been strongly Democratic in earlier decades.[5] Bush, in contrast, ran well among the components of the Republican coalition, though not as strongly as Reagan in 1984.

In the last six elections, Democratic candidates have received a majority of the southern vote only once—in 1976. Moreover, Catholic support for Democratic candidates in the five most recent elections of this period has on average been less than in the first five elections. Indeed, many observers have questioned whether Catholics and Southerners are undergoing a realignment of their partisan loyalties, a topic addressed in the last chapter of this book. Finally, note that the Republican coalition has held together fairly well over time, the major exception being the 1964 election, when the Goldwater candidacy resulted in many GOP defections.[6]

Turnout and Defection
Among Partisans and Independents

This chapter concludes with an examination of the relationship of party identification to turnout and vote defection over time. Comments will cen-

---

TABLE 3.7

Turnout Rates of Partisans
*and Independents, 1952–1988**

	Year									
	1952	1956	1960	1964	1968	1972	1976	1980	1984	1988
Strong Democrats	75%	79%	78%	82%	83%	75%	81%	84%	85%	80%
Strong Republicans	93	81	85	92	86	87	92	88	87	89
Weak Democrats	70	68	72	73	72	71	68	65	71	63
Weak Republicans	76	79	81	86	81	79	74	77	75	76
Independent Democrats	74	73	69	71	71	72	72	69	61	64
Independent Republicans	78	74	84	84	81	76	74	75	78	64
Independents	76	77	65	62	65	53	57	54	60	50

*The table entries are turnout rates expressed in percentages.
SOURCES: SRC/CPS studies of 1952, 1956, 1960, 1964, 1968, 1972, 1976, 1980, 1984, and 1988.

tcr on the implications of trends identified by analyzing presidential elections. Table 3.7 presents the turnout rate of partisans and Independents since 1952. There are three important points to be made about the table. First, as expected, turnout is highest among the strong identifiers, while the difference in turnout rates of weak versus Independent partisans is often small and inconsistent. Second, Republicans have higher turnout rates than Democrats, no matter what the year or type of partisan identifier. Thus, the numerical advantage the Democratic party enjoys in terms of allegiances is partially offset by the higher GOP turnout rate. In certain cases the difference in turnout rate is small, but it does exceed 10 percent in some instances. The differential turnout rate of Democratic and Republican partisans and the numerical advantage the Democrats enjoy help explain the oft-cited political strategy: the Democrats must get their supporters to the polls, while the Republicans must do the same and also attract a heavy share of the Independent vote and some Democratic defectors.

The third significant point to note in table 3.7 is the lower turnout rate of pure Independents in the five most recent elections. A major reason for this decline is the extension of the franchise to eighteen year olds, a group that is disproportionately Independent and has traditionally had the lowest turnout rates. Although the Independent turnout has been lower in recent elections, this does not mean that the contribution of Independents to the vote cast has declined. To the contrary, the lower turnout of Independents is more than compensated for by their larger numbers in recent years, so that the Independent proportion of the presidential vote (including pure and leaning Independents) has been highest in the five most recent elections. This is illustrated in table 3.8, which shows the proportion of the vote cast by different classes of party identifiers.

Note that between 1964 and 1988, the proportion of the vote cast by strong identifiers declined about 4 percent, while the share of the vote due to Independents (both pure and leaners) increased by 11 percent. These significant changes reflect millions of votes and have major implications for the conduct of politics. If citizens without strong partisan ties cast a greater proportion of the vote, then election outcomes can be expected to fluctuate more widely in the future. Landslide elections may become a common occurrence. Furthermore, as Independents cast more votes, candidates are more likely to appeal to citizens on grounds other than traditional party loyalties and party issues. It would be an electorally profitable strategy to seize upon issues that would mobilize the Independent vote, providing such a strategy would not frighten off the candidates' partisan adherents. If Independents had a comparable turnout rate to that of partisans, the influence of the Independent vote on election outcomes would be even more striking.

An examination of the relationship between party identification and loyalty to one's party in presidential elections provides another piece of evidence about the weakening of party ties. Figures 3.4 through 3.6 give the defection rates of Democrats and Republicans and the voting behavior of Independents. Note that the only party identifiers who consistently exhibited great loyalty to their party's nominees were strong Republicans who, even in the Democratic landslide of 1964, gave Barry Goldwater more than 90 percent of their vote. Among strong Democrats, the pattern of support for Democratic presidential candidates fluctuated more widely, reaching a peak in 1964 and a low point in 1972, when fewer than 75 percent of the strong Democrats supported McGovern. In 1988 strong Democrats and strong Republicans strongly supported their parties' nominees, the former giving Dukakis 94 percent of their vote and the latter giving Bush 98 percent.

The voting behaviors of weak and independent Democrats and Republicans exhibit greater defection from their parties to the extent that less than *half* of the weak Democrats in 1972 supported the McGovern candidacy and less than 60 percent of the weak Republicans voted for Goldwater in 1964. Likewise, the support given to the Democratic nominees in 1968, 1972, and 1980 by Independent Democrats was low. Finally, the voting behavior of Independents from 1952 to 1988 reveals the greatest variability, as might be expected in view of the absence of the anchoring effect of partisanship. Independent support for Democratic presidential candidates varied over 60 percent between 1952 and 1988.

TABLE 3.8

The Proportion of the Vote Cast by Partisans and Independents, 1952–1988*

	Year									
	1952	1956	1960	1964	1968	1972	1976	1980	1984	1988
Strong Democrats	23%	23%	21%	29%	22%	16%	16%	20%	19%	20%
Strong Republicans	17	17	18	13	11	13	12	11	15	18
Weak Democrats	23	21	24	24	24	25	23	21	19	17
Weak Republicans	14	15	15	15	16	15	15	16	15	15
Independent Democrats	10	6	6	8	9	10	12	11	9	11
Independent Republicans	8	9	8	6	10	11	11	11	13	12
Independents	5	9	9	6	9	9	11	10	9	7

*The table entries represent the percentage of the vote for president in a certain year cast by a specific partisan category.
SOURCES: SRC/CPS studies of 1952, 1956, 1960, 1964, 1968, 1972, 1976, 1980, 1984, and 1988.

Figures 3.4 through 3.6 indicate that while persons with partisan attachments are generally more likely to support their parties' nominees, there are numerous instances in which defections occur. Tables 2.1 and 3.8 document the growth in the number of Independents and the increase in the proportion of the vote cast by Independents. Furthermore, an examination of vote choice for other offices on the ballot in addition to the presidency would identify an increase in the frequency of split-ticket voting. All of these trends and patterns are signs that party identification has become less useful in accounting for why people vote for president as they do. If party identification now has a weaker effect on vote decisions, are there other factors that might have a stronger effect on vote choice? Chapters 4 through 6 will examine the role of issues and candidates in presidential voting since 1952.

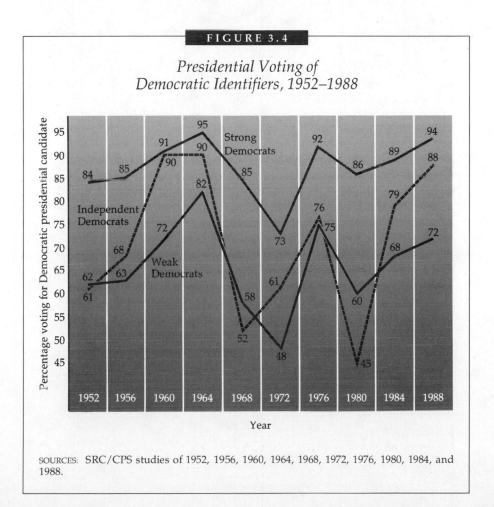

FIGURE 3.4

Presidential Voting of Democratic Identifiers, 1952–1988

SOURCES: SRC/CPS studies of 1952, 1956, 1960, 1964, 1968, 1972, 1976, 1980, 1984, and 1988.

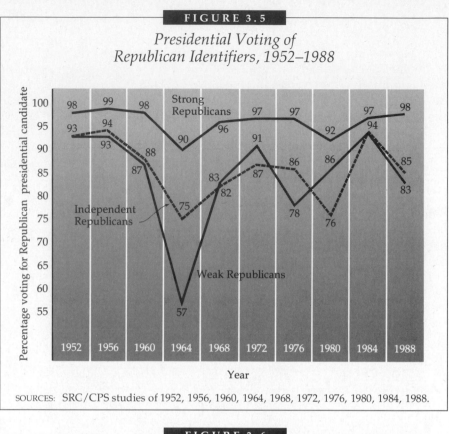

FIGURE 3.5

Presidential Voting of Republican Identifiers, 1952–1988

SOURCES: SRC/CPS studies of 1952, 1956, 1960, 1964, 1968, 1972, 1976, 1980, 1984, 1988.

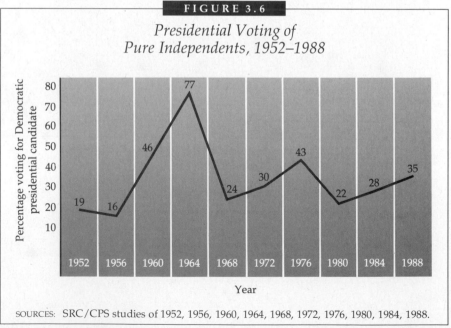

FIGURE 3.6

Presidential Voting of Pure Independents, 1952–1988

SOURCES: SRC/CPS studies of 1952, 1956, 1960, 1964, 1968, 1972, 1976, 1980, 1984, 1988.

Notes

1. For evidence that the family's role is less with respect to the transmission of political attitudes that are not overtly partisan, see Jennings and Niemi (1968).

2. For a discussion of the effects of the school and school curriculum, see Hess and Torney (1967: 93–115) and Langton and Jennings (1968). Rather than saying that the school has no impact on partisanship, it might be more accurate to say that the school moves children away from partisanship and toward independence. Jennings and Niemi observe that in comparison to the younger children studied by Hess and Torney and by Greenstein, the high school seniors they analyzed had a higher proportion of Independents. They attribute this to the impact of the school and teachers, arguing that "attempts to keep 'partisan bickering' out of the classroom as well as direct inculcation of the norm that one should vote for the man and not the party probably counteract the partisan cues which many children receive at home." See Jennings and Niemi (1974: 263).

3. Because such questions entail studying people over much longer time periods than four years and because panel data are very difficult and costly to collect over a lengthy time span, social scientists often rely on cohort analysis to make longitudinal inferences. Cohort analysis requires multiple surveys with different respondents conducted at different points in time. Respondents are then assigned to age-defined cohorts, and the behavior of these cohorts is traced over time. The CPS presidential election surveys, which have been conducted quadrennially since 1952, are a prime data source for cohort analysis. Imagine that the respondents in the 1952 CPS survey are divided into age groups, such as 21–24, 25–28, 29–32, and 33–36. Then the 21–24 cohort in 1952 will be the 25–28 cohort in the 1956 survey, the 29–32 cohort in the 1960 survey, and so on, and hence the behavior of the cohort (and not the individual) can be examined over time.

4. There are a number of substantive and methodological issues in the Converse–Abramson debate, dealing with such matters as appropriate cohort analysis techniques, the difficulty in sampling the youngest cohorts, and the possibility of period effects in addition to life-cycle and generational influences. See Converse (1976, 1979) and Abramson (1976, 1979). A period effect results from particular political circumstances and events that may differentially affect various segments of the population. The Vietnam War, issues relevant to race relations, and Watergate have produced period effects in the post-1964 era.

5. The 49 percent of the vote received by Dukakis in the South is based on a survey in which a sample of Americans was queried about its vote choice. When actual election returns are examined, the Democratic

share of the southern and border-state vote drops to approximately 42 percent.

6. For a different analytical approach to partisanship and group support, see Stanley, Bianco, and Niemi (1986) and Stanley and Niemi (1989).

CHAPTER 4

The Issue-Voting Controversy

According to classical democratic theory, issues should play the decisive role in electoral choice. This theory emphasized the importance of the rational citizen capable of choosing between alternatives on the basis of accurate information and sound reasoning. Classical democratic theory also stressed the need for a citizenry that was both highly motivated in public affairs and greatly concerned about such matters. The ideal citizen was the independent voter who based his or her decisions on the issues at hand and did not make electoral choices on the basis of mere group attachments or partisan affiliations or candidate attractiveness.

In an early empirical study of voting behavior, Berelson, Lazarsfeld, and McPhee (1954) discovered that classical democratic theory did not apply to the electorate. Instead of being informed and interested, voters were ignorant and apathetic. For example, on two hotly contested issues (the Taft-Hartley Act and price controls), which received extensive media coverage and on which Truman and Dewey took diametrically opposed positions in 1948, only 16 percent of a sample of citizens in Elmira, New York, knew correctly the stances of both candidates on both issues, while over 33 percent of the respondents knew only one position of one candidate correctly or none at all (Berelson, Lazarsfeld, and McPhee, 1954: 227–228). These early findings were upsetting to scholars who worried whether a democratic political system could survive if the basic requirements of democratic theory could not be met. Bernard Berelson gave one response to the tension between classical democratic theory and the findings of empirical research. In doing so, he essentially redefined the conditions necessary for a democratic political system to endure.

Berelson (pp. 305–323) argued that classical theory focused too much on the individual citizen; greater attention should be paid to the collective properties of the citizenry as well as to the consequences of these properties for the political system at large. Thus, Berelson claimed that the presence of substantial apathy and ignorance in the electorate was actually beneficial since apathetic and uninformed citizens were unlikely to concern themselves much about politics and policies. As a result, political leaders had greater independence and flexibility from popular pressures in making decisions. And, Berelson argued, elite decision making in the absence of mass pressures was likely to lead to wise choices that stabilized and maintained the political system. Thus, for Berelson, the stability of the political system and the ability of elites to govern became the overriding concerns, while the opinions of the citizenry became secondary. Berelson's reformulation of the conditions required for a democratic political system is often referred to as an *elitist theory of democracy*. Obviously, there are conservative, status quo values in Berelson's reformulation, but his argument represented an attempt to reconcile empirical research and democratic theory by fundamentally altering the meaning of and conditions for democracy.

The work of Berelson and his associates was the first major study to call into question the average citizen's competence to comprehend politics and make informed decisions at election time. Some years later *The American Voter* presented further evidence about the shortcomings of the electorate. For example, Angus Campbell and his colleagues established three conditions that were necessary for issues to influence vote choice. They found that these conditions, which will be discussed in the next section of this chapter, were hardly met by the electorate. *The American Voter* also examined the manner in which citizens thought about politics and found that few citizens could be classified as ideologues with coherent sets of beliefs who employed broad principles to evaluate the elements of politics.

The American Voter focused on the electorate of the 1950s, and since that time research based on more recent elections has challenged its findings. Thus, there is currently a controversy about the competence of the electorate to make informed voting decisions on the basis of issue-related considerations. The points of contention in this debate are both substantive and methodological, and they must be understood in order to evaluate accurately the issue awareness of the contemporary electorate. Hence, this chapter will discuss in detail the issue-voting controversy, beginning with the earlier findings presented in *The American Voter* and other works from the SRC. This chapter will also examine some more recent research and concludes with a summary evaluation of the competence of the American electorate.

The Traditional Image of the Voter

ISSUES

In *The American Voter,* Campbell and his associates (pp. 169–171) presented a number of analyses of issue voting. In the most direct analysis the authors posited three conditions necessary for issue-oriented electoral choices and then determined how well the electorate satisfied these conditions. The authors cogently argued that for an issue to influence a citizen's vote decision, the citizen must be aware of the issue in some form. Furthermore, the citizen must care at least minimally about the issue. And, finally, if the issue is to influence the citizen's partisan choice, the citizen must perceive that one party represents his or her position on the issue better than the other party; otherwise, the issue provides no reason to opt for one party over the other.

Thus, a national sample of citizens was presented with a series of sixteen significant issues in order to see how aware the citizens were of these issues. Overall, only between 18 and 36 percent of the citizens met the three conditions of issue voting on any specific issue. And this is no proof that issues actually influenced vote choice; they simply set an upper boundary on the number of citizens whose electoral choices could have been affected by the issues in question.

The authors of *The American Voter* explicitly recognized that the political nature of the times could have affected the degree to which citizens perceived party differences. That is, if the policy differences between the parties or the candidates, or both, were small in 1956, then there is little reason to expect that citizens could have perceived party differences. By way of contrast, perception of party differences by the citizenry should be greater when the parties and candidates take clear-cut, opposing positions on issues. This assertion is reflected in the findings of some recent research on voting behavior, which will be discussed shortly.

IDEOLOGY

A second analysis in *The American Voter* (pp. 216–265) of issue voting concerns the way in which citizens conceptualize politics. Do citizens employ broad, overarching concepts such as *liberal* and *conservative*, or do they rely on more specific and immediate frames of reference to interpret political affairs? This is an important question since political elites, such as party activists and media commentators, often employ ideological terminology in discussing and analyzing politics. But if citizens are not aware of or comfortable with such terms as *liberal* and *conservative*, then there may be substantial slippage in communications from elites to citizens. Such slippage may affect the way citizens interpret political events.

Citizen responses to a series of open-ended questions about their likes and dislikes of the candidates and parties were analyzed. This analysis resulted in a four-category classification of the way in which people conceptualize politics, ranging from ideology at the most sophisticated end to no issue content at the least sophisticated. By an *ideology* was meant an elaborate set of interrelated attitudes organized according to some underlying continuum. Issue voting should be more common among ideological citizens since such citizens employ a more general frame of reference in evaluating politics, including opinions on specific issues. This notion is supported by the fact that the only empirically common ideological perspective used by citizens was the liberal–conservative continuum, which is undoubtedly the one general dimension used most often in discussing American politics. While the specific meaning of a liberal or conservative position may vary at different times, depending on the immediate political circumstances, reliance on such an abstraction in evaluating politics will help citizens understand issues and their relationship to partisan and candidate choices. The absence of an ideological perspective does not mean that issues will be irrelevant to vote choice, but it does mean that citizens will need additional information about the issue to place it in a meaningful political context so that it might influence vote decisions.

Table 4.1 shows this distribution of the 1956 electorate into four levels of conceptualization: ideology, group benefits, nature of times, and no issue content. Note that more citizens are placed in the no issue content category than in the ideology category. To be considered an ideologue, a citizen need not have given highly sophisticated responses to questions about his or her likes and dislikes of the parties and candidates. For example, the following replies given by a woman from a Chicago suburb were enough to assign her to the category of ideology (*The American Voter*: pp. 228–229).

> *Like about Democrats?* No.
> *Is there anything at all you like about the Democratic party?* No, nothing at all.
> *Dislike about Democrats?* From being raised in a notoriously Republican section—a small town downstate—there were things I didn't like. There was family influence that way.
> *What in particular was there you didn't like about the Democratic party?* Well, the Democratic party tends to favor socialized medicine—

and I'm being influenced in that because I came from a
doctor's family.

Like about Republicans? Well, I think they're more middle-of-the
road—more conservative.

How do you mean, "conservative"? They are not so subject to radical
change.

*Is there anything else in particular that you like about the Republican
party?* Oh, I like their foreign policy—and the segregation business, that's a middle-of-the-road policy. You can't push it too
fast. You can instigate things, but you have to let them take
their course slowly.

According to the authors of *The American Voter*, these replies indicated that the
"respondent operates with a fairly clear sense of the liberal–conservative
distinction and uses it to locate both the major parties and the more specific
policy positions espoused" (p. 229). Thus, relatively few citizens used the
liberal–conservative continuum or any other overarching dimension to frame
their responses about their likes and dislikes of the parties and candidates.

TABLE 4.1

The Levels of Conceptualization in 1956
for the Total Sample and Voters (in percentages)

	Proportion of total sample	Proportion of voters
A. Ideology		
I. Ideology	2.5%	3.5%
II. Near-ideology	9	12
B. Group benefits		
I. Perception of conflict	14	16
Single-group interest	17	18
II. Shallow group benefit responses	11	11
C. Nature of times	24	23
D. No issue content		
I. Party orientation	4	3.5
II. Candidate orientation	9	7
III. No content	5	3
IV. Unclassified	4.5	4
	100	100

SOURCE: Angus Campbell et al., *The American Voter* (New York: John Wiley & Sons, 1960),
table 10-1, p. 249. Copyright © 1960. John Wiley & Sons, Inc. Reprinted by permission of
John Wiley & Sons, Inc.

The low frequency of ideological conceptualization does not mean that citizens not assigned to the ideology category are somehow deficient or irrational; many citizens classified in other categories would be recognized as acting in their own rational self-interest, that is, voting for the candidate or party that espouses policies of immediate benefit to the individual. For example, the quotation from the Ohio farm woman on page 43 indicates a preference for the Democratic party since she perceives that party as being good for farmers while the Republicans favor "the richer folks." Citizens who simply cite the nature of the times in response to questions about party and candidate likes and dislikes can be viewed as behaving according to rational self-interest. If times are good, vote for the incumbents; if times are bad, reject the incumbents. Citizens in the nature-of-the-times category may not have much specific information about politics organized in a coherent fashion, but they are aware in a vague, more general sense of their own and the country's condition.

What about people assigned to the category of no issue content? Among them—quite literally—no issues are cited for their support of a party or candidate. Yet it might be argued that even people in this category are concerned about issues; the questions asked by the interviewer simply did not raise such issues with them. Some of these respondents may base their support of a party on generalized, long-standing images of the party. For example, they may say that a party is the "party of the average citizen" or the "party of prosperity" or the "party of peace." When such citizens claim to vote on the basis of the party, they may really have an underlying issue rationale for their electoral choice. Nevertheless, the responses of people in this category clearly indicate that they are not much aware of the issue stances taken by the parties and candidates at a specific election. Most responses of people in the no-issue-content category are rather simple references to parties and candidates. A North Carolina man gives the following example of a party-oriented reply (p. 246):

> *Like about Democrats?*   No, Ma'am, not that I know of.
> *Dislike about Democrats?*   No, Ma'am, but I've always been a Democrat just like my daddy.
> *Like about Republicans?*   No.
> *Dislike about Republicans?*   No.
> *Like about Stevenson?*   No'm.
> *Dislike about Stevenson?*   No, Ma'am.
> *Like about Eisenhower?*   Not as I know of.
> *Dislike about Eisenhower?*   No, Ma'am.

A Texas woman provides an illustration of a candidate-oriented response (pp. 247–248):

> *Like about Democrats?*   No, I don't know anything about political parties. I'm not interested in them at all.
> *Dislike about Democrats?*   No, nothing.

Like about Republicans? No, I don't know about the *party.* I like Ike.
Dislike about Republicans? No, nothing I can put my finger on.
Like about Stevenson? Right now I can't think of anything I like well
    enough to vote for him.
Dislike about Stevenson? No, I just have my choice and it is not
    Stevenson. It is Ike.
Like about Eisenhower? I just like him, the way things have gone.
How do you mean? That's really all I know.
Dislike about Eisenhower? No.

Issue voting might occur at all levels of conceptualization except for
people in the no-issue-content category, a group that includes 22.5 percent of
people in the sample and 17.5 percent of the voters. This does not mean that
issue voting does occur, in fact, among people in the first three levels of
conceptualization. To be certain of this, there must be other assurances, including citizen concern about the issues and the perception that the election does
offer a choice.

To be classified as ideologues, the question used in the survey required
citizens to mention spontaneously an ideological perspective. Hence, Philip E.
Converse (1974) argued that a higher recognition of the terms *liberal* and
conservative might be expected if citizens were asked directly about them.
Therefore, in 1960 a sample of citizens was asked whether they thought one
candidate was more conservative than the other. In addition, they were asked
what they meant by the terms *liberal* and *conservative.*

Converse found (pp. 318–319) that at best about half of the sample had
a reasonable recognition of the terms *liberal* and *conservative.* He further
subdivided this recognition into broad versus narrow comprehension of the
terms. Many of the narrow understandings focused on questions of spending
and saving, which, according to Converse, do not begin to tap the richness of
the liberal–conservative dimension. Overall, only about 17 percent of the
respondents had a broad understanding of liberal–conservative differences,
while an additional 33 percent had a more narrow comprehension that was
accurately linked to the positions of the political parties.

Next, Converse investigated the coherence of positions taken on issues
by a sample of citizens and by a sample of political elites, that is, candidates
for Congress. The purpose of his analysis was to see if citizens might have
organized beliefs on specific issues that reflected a basic liberal–conservative
continuum even though they were unable to give ideological responses to
open-ended questions during an interview. Thus, Converse turns his attention
to mass belief systems, which he defined as patterns of "ideas and attitudes in
which the elements are bound together by some form of constraint" (p. 302).
In simpler terms, a *belief system* is a set of interrelated attitudes showing
constraint.

Converse discusses constraint in the static and dynamic cases. In the
static case, constraint refers to how well a person's position on an issue can be

predicted if his or her stance on another issue is known. For example, if a person favors using all available force to solve the problem of urban riots, one might also expect the person to support capital punishment. Constraint in the dynamic case refers to the extent to which a change in one element of a belief system leads to changes in other elements (p. 302).

Table 4.2 presents the results of Converse's analysis of the static constraints shown by citizens and congressional candidates on a series of specific issues. The entries in the table are correlation coefficients (tau-gammas), which give an indication of how related issue positions are on pairs of issues. The closer the value of the coefficient is to 1.0, the more closely related are the two issue positions. Another way of interpreting the coefficients is to say that the higher their value, the easier it is to predict an individual's position on one issue if his or her stance on the other issue is known.

The figures of table 4.2 indicate that constraint is higher among congressional candidates than average citizens. The average correlation between pairs of domestic issues is .53 for congressional candidates and only .23 for citizens, while the comparable correlations on foreign affairs issues are .25 and .11. Finally, the average relationship between issue position and party preference is a moderate .38 for candidates and a rather weak .11 for citizens.

These findings have three implications. First, yet another analysis has failed to uncover any substantial coherence in the issue beliefs held by citizens. With respect to the issues investigated, there was no underlying organization to the responses, such as the liberal–conservative dimension. Second, the fact that citizens' issue beliefs were only weakly related to their partisan affiliation indicates that issue positions cannot be accounted for by adherence to well-defined party programs and that citizen perceptions of distinct party differences were minimal. Finally, the findings suggest how important it is to distinguish between political discourse at the elite versus the mass level. Interpretations of politics based on such terminology as liberal and conservative may be more appropriate for political elites than for average citizens.

NONATTITUDES

An analysis by Converse (1970a) of the phenomenon of nonattitudes is the final piece of research from the SRC about the traditional view of the electorate. Converse argues that the survey approach to citizen opinions introduces the danger of measuring attitudes that do not really exist. That is, the very act of asking people about issues may create responses that do not represent any real attitudes about the topic at hand but simply reflect a desire on the part of the respondents to appear cooperative and informed about current issues. No matter how socially acceptable it is for the citizen to respond "I don't know" to a question, or no matter how carefully citizens who have no opinion on an issue are screened out, respondents still give replies to queries about which they know and care very little. These replies are labeled *nonattitudes*.

TABLE 4.2

The Constraint on Issue Opinions for a Sample of 1958 Congressional Candidates and for a Sample of Citizens*

	Employment	Education	Housing	FEPC**	Economic	Military	Isolationism	Party preference
Congressional candidates								
Employment	—	.62	.59	.35	.26	.06	.17	.68
Aid to education		—	.61	.53	.50	.06	.35	.55
Federal housing			—	.47	.41	-.03	.30	.68
FEPC**				—	.47	.11	.23	.34
Economic aid					—	.19	.59	.25
Military aid						—	.32	-.18
Isolationism							—	.05
Party preference								—
Cross-section sample								
Employment	—	.45	.03	.34	-.04	.10	-.22	.20
Aid to education		—	.12	.29	.06	.14	-.17	.16
Federal housing			—	.08	-.06	.02	.07	.18
FEPC**				—	.24	.13	.01	-.04
Economic aid					—	.16	.33	-.07
Soldiers abroad						—	.21	.12
Isolationism							—	-.03
Party preference								—

*The table entries are tau-gamma coefficients. The greater the value of the coefficient, the greater is the constraint between pairs of issues.

**Fair Employment Practices Commission

SOURCE: Adapted from "The Nature of Belief Systems in Mass Politics," by Philip E. Converse, in *Ideology and Discontent*, by David E. Apter. Copyright © 1964 by The Free Press of Glencoe, a Division of Macmillan Company. Used with the permission of David E. Apter.

To study nonattitudes, Converse examined the stability of responses to a series of issue questions asked of the same individuals over time. The results indicated that for many issues there was little stability in responses; persons who at one time claimed to favor a certain program expressed opposition to it at another time and support for it at an even later time. This instability of responses is, for Converse, evidence that nonattitudes have been measured.

This simple finding of response instability is potentially most damaging to any claim that issue-related voting is widespread, for it suggests that on many issues the citizen's position does not reflect any firm preferences but is instead a product of the interview situation. It also suggests the ease with which citizens might change their issue opinions, perhaps to bring them in line with positions of their preferred party or candidate, or both. Of course, all a citizen needs is one issue about which he or she cares enough to have it influence the citizen's vote. If such an issue exists, then there is no need to be so concerned about response instability or nonattitudes on other issues.

SUMMARY OF THE TRADITIONAL IMAGE

In summary, according to the traditional view of the voter's competence, citizens on many issues have no genuine, consistent opinions, and on other issues their concern is minimal and their perceptions of party differences are weak to nonexistent. Furthermore, citizens do not organize the elements of politics in broad frameworks; their beliefs are not integrated into a coherent whole; and they have a limited awareness of the terms *liberal* and *conservative*—terms that figure prominently in contemporary debates about politics. Thus, the image of the average citizen in the traditional literature is rather negative. It suggests that issue concerns are not likely to play a prominent role in electoral choice and that classical democratic theory may impose too severe demands on the contemporary electorate. Note that the conclusions of the traditional research were carefully qualified; there was no suggestion that the results presented held for all time and under all conditions. In fact, the conclusions were often phrased in a conditional sense, and the consideration of these conditions may partially reconcile the traditional and revisionist literature on voters' competence.

The Revisionist Image of the Voter

INTRODUCTION

Revisionist literature criticizes the traditional description of citizens' issue and ideological awareness on methodological and substantive grounds. This section will discuss a sample of this literature that illustrates the concerns guiding current research; no attempt will be made to provide an exhaustive account of the more recent research. Much of the revisionist literature itself has come under attack, mainly on methodological grounds; some of the more important criticisms will be highlighted.

The most prominent early revisionist work was *The Responsible Electorate* by V. O. Key, Jr., who argued that "voters are not fools" (1966: 7). Key examined voters who voted for the same party (stand-patters) and different parties (switchers) in successive presidential elections and found that switchers tended to move to the party closest to the voter's own position on some important issue. His work, which spans the 1936–1960 era, suggests that issues were more important to voters than the study of the 1952 and 1956 elections by *The American Voter* reported them to be. Although Key's analysis was quite insightful, it unfortunately suffered from data problems. Key's work relied on limited data sets that restricted the types of analyses; it also made use of recall data for past voting behavior; that is, the voters' recollections of how they had voted in the past. Key had no way to determine whether the voters had changed their issue positions to bring them in line with the views of the candidates they had chosen. Hence, this examination of the revisionist literature will concentrate more on recent research based on more extensive data resources.

ISSUES

Some methodological innovations.   *The American Voter* has been criticized for the way in which it chose the sixteen issues investigated. The issues were selected by the authors, who deemed them important on a priori grounds. David RePass (1971), among others, has argued that a list of predetermined issues may not include those issues that are of greatest importance to the voter, no matter how carefully major issues are identified. A better strategy, RePass argued, is to allow the respondents themselves to define the issues that are important to them and that are most likely to influence vote choice.

Thus, a prominent strategy in recent research has been to identify groups of citizens who express concern about specific issues and to focus on their voting behavior. In fact, since 1960 the SRC/CPS election studies have included questions that ask voters to name the most important problems that, in their opinion, the government should address. Such questions have helped this type of analysis. This approach generally results in more positive assessments of citizen competence. Partly this is because it focuses on subsets of citizens who are more likely to be issue oriented while, by way of contrast, *The American Voter* analyzes the electorate as a whole. Although the analysis of subsets of issue-oriented citizens may help describe the conditions under which issue voting is likely to occur, the results may be applicable to only a very small segment of the entire electorate. Some examples should suffice to give the reader the gist of this type of research.

After examining the responses to questions about the "most important problems" asked by SRC/CPS in the 1960 and 1964 presidential elections,

RePass found that more than twenty-five issues were cited with some frequency each year. Yet none of these issues could be named as the "dominant" issue. Moreover, the kinds of issues mentioned at each election differed dramatically. In 1960 foreign affairs were most important, while in 1964 domestic affairs, particularly those associated with civil rights, were paramount (pp. 391–392). Because of these findings, RePass believed that it would be difficult to construct a comprehensive list of issues, as *The American Voter* had done. He concluded that one reason for the low level of issue awareness described by *The American Voter* was the type of questions asked.

Discovering that more than 60 percent of the people were able to perceive party differences on nineteen of the twenty-five issues mentioned in 1964, RePass concluded that "the public does perceive party differences on these issues that are salient to them" (p. 394). This finding appears to contradict *The American Voter*'s assertion about the voters' minimal perception of party differences. In fact, RePass's finding is not directly comparable, since he examined only those citizens for whom an issue was salient or important. For example, according to RePass, over 80 percent of the citizens for whom medical care for the aged was a major concern could perceive party differences on this issue. But recall that less than 5 percent of the sample considered medical care an important problem (p. 396).

Isolating individuals whose partisanship and issue preferences are in conflict is a very straightforward way to demonstrate the impact issues can have on voters. That is, when voters' party identification and their perception of which party will better handle a particular issue are not in agreement, whether they voted according to the party or the issue can be determined. When the voters' partisanship and positions on issues are in harmony, however, it is difficult to judge the impact of each of these two factors on the votes. Hence, table 4.3 shows the relationship between party identification and voting record in the seven presidential elections between 1964 and 1988 for three groups of citizens—those who named the Republicans as the preferred party on their most important problem, those who named the Democrats, and those who preferred neither party on the issue.

For this discussion, the most interesting cells in the table are those in which partisanship and issue position conflict, for they enable us to see directly how citizens reacted to the conflict. Note that among Democratic identifiers in 1988 who preferred the Republicans on their most important issue, fully 79 percent defected from Dukakis. Among Republicans in 1988 who thought the Democratic party better on their key issue, only 40 percent remained loyal to Bush. Thus, there is substantial vote defection when the voters' issue stance and partisanship are out of agreement on an important issue—a development that provides some evidence of the impact of issues on voting. But since very few respondents display these incongruent preferences, issue-based defections do not appear to be very common, at least not on issues cited by the respondents as the most important. A relative infrequency of incongruence might be expected because of voters' tendency to bring their stance on issues

TABLE 4.3

The Relationship between Party Identification and Vote for Three Categories of Issue Partisanship in 1964, 1968, 1972, 1976, 1980, 1984, and 1988 (in percentages)

Year and vote	Republicans*			Neither*			Democrats*		
	Dem.†	Ind.†	Rep.†	Dem.†	Ind.†	Rep.†	Dem.†	Ind.†	Rep.†
1988									
Bush	79%	93%	98%	20%	53%	90%	4%	11%	40%
Dukakis	21	7	2	80	47	10	96	89	60
Total	100	100	100	100	100	100	100	100	100
Number of cases	29	68	197	179	208	175	198	66	20
1984									
Reagan	80	93	99	27	65	93	6	14	43
Mondale	20	7	1	73	35	7	94	86	57
Total	100	100	100	100	100	100	100	100	100
Number of cases	55	148	260	180	182	129	250	65	14
1980									
Reagan	58	80	92	17	40	78	2	14	33
Carter	37	9	1	77	42	16	92	57	67
Anderson	5	11	7	6	18	6	6	29	0
Total	100	100	100	100	100	100	100	100	100
Number of cases	84	141	197	184	122	50	84	14	3
1976									
Ford	86	94	99	33	70	88	4	14	48
Carter	14	6	1	67	30	12	96	86	52
Total	100	100	100	100	100	100	100	100	100
Number of cases	29	65	140	191	272	212	367	147	48
1972									
Nixon	81	94	99	51	71	92	21	21	67
McGovern	19	6	1	49	29	8	79	79	33
Total	100	100	100	100	100	100	100	100	100
Number of cases	37	64	105	111	92	72	118	47	15
1968									
Nixon	49	77	94	18	52	84	4	20	50
Humphrey	34	6	4	66	32	9	92	80	50
Wallace	17	17	2	16	16	7	4	0	0
Total	100	100	100	100	100	100	100	100	100
Number of cases	67	108	163	156	106	70	180	30	8
1964									
Goldwater	61	89	94	14	27	66	3	7	20
Johnson	39	11	6	86	73	34	97	93	80
Total	100	100	100	100	100	100	100	100	100
Number of cases	33	47	145	105	59	67	295	68	45

*Party preferred on most important issue.

†Party identification: Democratic and Republican identifiers include strong and weak partisans, while Independents include pure Independents and leaners.

SOURCES: SRC/CPS studies of 1964, 1968, 1972, 1976, 1980, 1984, and 1988.

into line with their partisanship. Note also the likelihood that partisanship itself is based on an issue or issues. Of course, people are much less likely to rationalize their positions on issues to bring them into harmony with their party identification when the issues are of great importance to the citizens.

When issue stance and party identification coincided in table 4.3, loyalty to the candidate of one's party was extremely high; for example, 99 percent of the consistent Republicans voted for Ford in 1976, 92 percent for Reagan in 1980, 99 percent for Reagan in 1984, and 98 percent for Bush in 1988. Likewise, 96 percent of the congruent Democrats supported Carter in 1976, 92 percent backed him in 1980, 94 percent of the congruent Democrats voted for Mondale in 1984, and 96 percent for Dukakis in 1988. Citizens who expressed no party preference on the issue most important to them in 1976, 1980, 1984, and 1988 tended to support their own party's nominee, with the Independents going heavily for Ford in 1976, Reagan in 1984, and splitting almost evenly in 1980 and 1988. The 1964, 1968, and 1972 results closely resemble the 1976, 1980, 1984, and 1988 findings.

In summary, methodological innovations (including one to be discussed in the next section) have led to findings of a greater issue awareness, a clearer perception of party differences, and a greater impact of issues on voting. By allowing the respondents themselves to determine the important issues and by analyzing the segments of the citizenry interested in particular issues it is certain that the issues investigated are those of greatest concern to the citizens and those about which the citizens are best informed. Yet the increased significance of issues and the greater frequency of issue voting are not simply due to the new ways of measuring the issues. Other factors, which may be termed the *nature of the times,* have played an important role in the increase of issue voting.

The nature of the times.   Much of the revisionist literature claims that the findings of *The American Voter* are time bound: that they refer to the relatively tranquil era of the 1950s when conflict between the parties and candidates was at a minimum and when many of the divisive issues of the 1960s and 1970s had not yet emerged. In more turbulent times, when the parties take more distinctive positions, it is argued, both perceptions of partisan differences on issues and issue voting itself will be higher. For example, RePass (1971: 393–393) claimed that a source of the higher levels of perceived party differences and issue awareness was the presidential campaign of 1964, particularly the ideological candidacy of Barry Goldwater, which sharpened party differences. Thus, the specific candidates and the kinds of campaigns they wage can have a direct effect on the extent of issue awareness and perceptions of party differences. The revisionist literature cites these contextual considerations in a number of places.

Gerald Pomper (1972) analyzed six issues for which comparable information was available in the four presidential elections between 1956 and 1968. He found that the relationship between party identification and issue position was strongest in 1964, particularly in the areas of social welfare and civil rights, issues on which Johnson and Goldwater expressed clear differences. The highest levels of perceived party differences also occurred in 1964, levels that substantially exceeded the figures cited in *The American Voter*. Since Pomper used questions identical to those employed in *The American Voter*, methodological differences could not account for the differences between his work and that of the SRC. Instead, Pomper claims that the presidential candidacy of Barry Goldwater was responsible for increasing the issue awareness and perception of party differences. Thus, Pomper supports RePass with respect to the potential impact of the political context on issue voting.

Michael Margolis (1977) criticized Pomper's findings on methodological grounds, arguing that much of the evidence of increased issue awareness was based on small subsets of the total sample. In reanalyzing Pomper's data, Margolis calculated percentages on the basis of the entire sample. He found much less impressive increases in issue awareness over time. Moreover, by extending Pomper's work to the 1972 election he found that the 1964–1968 patterns did not hold in 1972. In fact, the 1972 figures more closely resembled those of the 1950s than the 1968 results. Margolis's work implied that researchers need to sensitize themselves to the proportion of the American electorate to which a particular finding is applicable. It may not be possible to generalize high levels of issue awareness and issue voting among a small segment of the population to the broader electorate. Moreover, his work indirectly suggests another possibility: the supposedly quiescent 1950s may have been, in fact, no more atypical than the turbulent 1970s.

Benjamin I. Page and Richard Brody (1972) also depicted the important way in which a specific political context affected issue awareness by examining the impact of the Vietnam War on vote choice in 1968. Although Vietnam was mentioned by more than 50 percent of Americans as the most important problem facing the United States in 1968, Page and Brody found "that Vietnam policy preferences did not have a great effect on voting for the major party candidates in 1968" (p. 982). Support for Nixon varied little among citizens who favored escalating the war, maintaining the same policy, and pulling out of Vietnam entirely. The minimal effect of Vietnam on vote choice might seem surprising, given how often it was mentioned as a major problem. The authors explain this apparent paradox by asserting that the public saw very little difference between Humphrey and Nixon on the war. If the candidates offered little choice on the issue, then the issue could not have a great impact on vote decisions.

The interesting question becomes, "Why did people fail to perceive any substantial differences between Humphrey and Nixon on Vietnam?" Was it because of some deficiency or lack of information on the part of the electorate, or might there be another explanation? Page and Brody (1972) suggest an alternative explanation—namely, that Nixon and Humphrey did not take distinct stands on Vietnam and that citizens were simply responding to what the candidates offered. The authors based their conclusion on a systematic analysis of the speeches and statements of the candidates, which yielded few differences between Humphrey and Nixon (pp. 987–990). Thus, a political campaign variable—the respective positions of the candidates—must be taken into account in evaluating citizen awareness. Where the candidates or parties emit ambiguous signals by taking indistinct positions on issues, it is unreasonable to blame the electorate for its inability to recognize party or candidate differences. Page and Brody's conclusions are supported by the work of Aldrich, Sullivan, and Borgida (1989) who argue, contrary to the conventional wisdom, that foreign affairs issues can affect presidential vote choice when two conditions are met: candidates must emphasize foreign policy issues; *and* they must take distinct stances on the issues. They conclude that these conditions were met in the elections of 1972 and 1984 but not in 1968 when the candidates failed to provide distinct alternatives about the Vietnam War.

The methodological implication of the Page and Brody work is that it is not enough to relate the voter's own position on an issue to his or her vote choice. Where the voter perceives the candidate to stand on the issue must also be determined. For example, if one citizen claimed to be a hawk on Vietnam and another claimed to be a dove, yet both voted for Nixon, it might be concluded that issue position did not influence vote choice. This could be a faulty inference if the hawkish citizen thought Nixon was a hawk and thus voted for him, while the dovish voter saw Nixon as a dove and voted for him on that basis. In this hypothetical situation, the Vietnam issue directly influenced both citizens' votes for Nixon despite their own differing policy positions. Thus, a methodological innovation in the study of issue voting has been the development of proximity variables, which measure the distance between the citizen's own issue position and his or her perception of the candidate's or party's stance.[1]

However, even if citizens voted for the candidate closest to their own issue position on an issue or issues, this may not be definitive evidence that issues actually affected vote choice. Brody and Page (1972) discuss three processes that can result in voters selecting candidates nearest them on issues, but only the first process, in which the citizen evaluates the candidates' positions and votes accordingly, could be called *issue voting*. The second process, labeled *projection*, involves the voter seeing "a candidate as close to himself on an issue because he otherwise felt positive about the candidate" (p. 457). That is, a person who likes a candidate, for whatever reason (personality, party identification), may distort the candidate's policy position on an issue so that it corresponds with the voter's own position. *Persuasion* is the third process that can lead to proximity between citizen and candidate; here a preferred candidate moves the voter's own issue position toward that of the candidate. These processes are documented by Page and Brody, who write with respect to Humphrey and Nixon's Vietnam positions in 1968 (1972: 987):

> Those who saw a big difference between Humphrey and Nixon—a difference in either direction—were generally perceiving each candidate as standing wherever they wanted him to stand. They projected their own

opinions onto their favored candidate. Among Republicans, who mostly favored Nixon, extreme hawks thought that Nixon was an extreme hawk; extreme doves thought that he was an extreme dove; and those in the middle thought that Nixon stood in the middle.... Similarly, among Democrats, extreme hawks tended to think Humphrey was an extreme hawk; extreme doves thought Humphrey was an extreme dove; and those in the middle thought he stood in the middle....

Many of those who saw a big difference between Nixon and Humphrey, in other words, were responding to their own wishes. Their perceptions were the result of intended vote, not the cause. These people were not engaged in policy voting.

It becomes even more difficult to assess the impact of issues on votes if the notion of *rationality* is introduced, a term heretofore shunned because of its many meanings. RePass (1974) presents one definition of a rational vote, which asserts that voter concern about an issue is not sufficient to guarantee a rational vote. Rationality also requires citizens to be able to "correctly name the party which supports their position on that issue" (p. 3). While this is only one possible meaning of rationality, it is an interesting one since it raises the possibility that an issue vote may not be a rational vote if it is based on faulty information. For example, citizens who voted for Nixon over McGovern because they believed that Nixon was more likely to grant amnesty to draft evaders could be classified as issue voters but not as rational voters since their perception of Nixon's position seems to be incorrect.

While RePass finds that almost 40 percent of the voters were solidly rational in 1964 and only 25 percent irrational or nonrational, it nevertheless remains that assessing the amount of issue voting (let alone rational issue voting) is a very difficult task that, ideally, requires information about the temporal sequence linking citizens' own issue positions, their perceptions of the candidates' stances, and their evaluations of the candidates. If the citizens' positions and perceptions of the candidates are temporally prior to their candidate evaluation and vote intention, then concluding that issue voting occurred is substantiated. But information about such temporal ordering is costly to come by. It requires a panel design with repeated interviews with the same respondents periodically throughout the campaign. And deciding whether a vote is rational requires the ability to determine whether citizen perceptions of candidates are correct or not, a problematic task on issues in which candidate positions are vague. Thus, instead of attempting to measure the precise amount of issue voting that occurs at any specific election, the conclusion of this chapter will specify some general conditions that facilitate and depress the levels of issue voting and ideological awareness.

Edward Carmines and James Stimson (1980) have distinguished between two kinds of issue voting, one based on *hard issues* and the other on *easy issues*. Hard-issue voting results from a rational weighing of the alternatives and should be most prevalent in citizens with the cognitive and conceptual skills to make such comparative assessments. Easy-issue voting occurs for issues that are largely symbolic rather than technical, that deal with policy ends rather than means, and that have been on the political agenda for some time. Voters can respond to such issues on a gut level and hence need not possess any particular conceptual skills to cast an issue vote. Carmines and Stimson find that with respect to Vietnam, a hard issue, the level of information (a measure of cognitive and conceptual abilities) affected the relationship between policy position and vote. Issue voting was most pronounced among high-information respondents. For desegregation, an easy issue, information level had much weaker effects. One conclusion the authors draw is that issue voting is not necessarily a sign of political sophistication since easy-issue voting does not require any special intellectual skills. The Carmines and Stimson work will force future discussions of issue voting to be more careful about equating issue voting and citizen competence. High levels of issue voting do not necessarily indicate a highly competent electorate of rational decision makers.

In a related vein, Rabinowitz, Prothro, and Jacoby (1982) also provide insights about the properties and behavior of the electorate. Their study examined the effects of issue salience; that is, the importance of issues in vote decision. Unlike some earlier studies, their study found that the salience of an issue to the voter did shape his or her political behavior. However, the one most salient issue for each voter did not dominate the vote decision; the electorate was not a collection of single-issue voters. Carmines and Stimson (1980) and Rabinowitz, Prothro, and Jacoby (1982) jointly suggest that when salient issues are also easy issues, the amount of issue voting in an election is likely to be high. However, these works also suggest that issues are only one of a number of influences on the vote decision and that the extent of issue voting will depend on the characteristics of the voters, the campaign emphases of the candidates, and the nature of the issues themselves.

IDEOLOGY

Conceptualization. Revisionist literature on ideological awareness reaches conclusions similar to those of the issue-voting literature—namely, the level of ideological sophistication is higher than that found in *The American Voter*. This higher level is attributed both to measurement differences, including alternative definitions of an ideologue, and to changes in the political environment that have led to genuine increases in ideological awareness. For example, John Field and Ronald Anderson (1970) questioned whether in the elections characterized by ideological conflict at the elite level the amount of ideological conceptualization of politics might not be higher than the amount reported in *The American Voter*. Thus, they investigated the 1964 election, in which Barry Goldwater flaunted the fact that he was offering an ideological choice. Using a somewhat more lenient scheme for classifying citizens as ideologues, Field and Anderson found that the proportion of ideologues in the 1956, 1960, and 1964 electorates was 21 (*The American Voter* said 15), 27, and 35 percent. Since their more lenient coding system was used across all three elections, they concluded that the specific election context does indeed influence the extent of ideological awareness. They argued that *The American Voter* may have emphasized too strongly the importance of individual characteristics, such as education, information, and political involvement, to ideological sophistication. Of course, as Field and Anderson note, even in the ideological election of 1964, only 35 percent of the electorate could be classified as ideologues, which suggests that there are some upper limits to the proportion of ideologues in any election, perhaps because of the cognitive limitations of the electorate cited in *The American Voter* (p. 345).

The work of John C. Pierce and Paul R. Hagner (1982) and of Kathleen Knight and Carolyn Lewis (1986) provides a longitudinal portrait of the levels of conceptualization of politics by Americans between 1956 and 1984. As table 4.4 points out, the proportion of ideologues was highest in 1964 and 1968, two elections in which the voters were offered distinctive choices. In the elections since 1968, the percentage of ideologues has remained at about 20 percent of the electorate, regardless of the choices offered the electorate.

The fact that ideological conceptualization did not increase in 1980 and 1984, even with the election and reelection of an avowedly conservative president, indicates that factors (for example, education and political involvement) other than the stimulus of the campaign may affect the level of ideological conceptualization and suggests that the conclusions of Field and Anderson need to be tempered. Indeed, Fleishman (1986) examined ideological self-identification (whether people thought of themselves as liberals or conservatives) among Americans from 1972 to 1982 and, like the results in table 4.4 about conceptualization, found no increase in 1980 in the percentage of Americans

TABLE 4.4

Levels of Conceptualization, 1956–1984

Levels of conceptualization	1956	1960	1964	1968	1972	1976	1980	1984
Ideologues	12%	19%	27%	26%	22%	21%	22%	22%
Group benefit	42	31	27	24	27	26	30	27
Nature of times	24	26	20	29	34	30	31	34
No issue content	22	23	26	21	17	24	17	17
Total	100%	99%	100%	100%	100%	101%	100%	100%

SOURCES: John C. Pierce and Paul R. Hagner, "Conceptualization and Party Identification: 1956–76," *American Journal of Political Science* (May 1982), pp. 377–387 and Kathleen Knight and Carolyn Lewis, "the Growth of Conservatism in the American Mass Public: Measurement and Meaning" (Paper presented at the annual convention of the Southwest Social Science Association, San Antonio, Texas, March 19–22, 1986).

calling themselves conservatives. For him, this result challenged the notion that campaign context affects ideological awareness, although he recognized that campaign context may be a poorly formulated and measured concept. Krosnick and Weisberg (1988) found a decrease in ideological structuring in 1980 and a further decrease in 1984, with ideological organization more likely to occur among the better educated and more politically involved citizens. Finally, Jacoby (1986, 1989) studied the effect of ideological self-identification on citizens' attitudes. In a study of the 1980 election, he found that citizens at the ideology and near-ideology end of the conceptualization continuum relied more on the liberal–conservative dimension to evaluate candidates and hence exhibited greater structure and coherence in their candidate evaluations. In a study of the 1984 election, Jacoby found that citizens with higher levels of education and a more ideological conceptualization of politics were more likely to have their issue attitudes influenced by liberal–conservative identifications. He described the American public as being composed of two groups: one for whom liberal–conservative identifications are an important determinant of issue attitudes; and a second group for whom other orientations, such as party identification, are more important than ideology.

Thus, these results indicate that relatively few Americans organize their views about politics in an ideological fashion, and those that do are more likely to be characterized by higher levels of education and political involvement. But this does not mean that citizens' beliefs are without any organization. Feldman (1988) argued that citizens' specific attitudes and beliefs may reflect their underlying values and beliefs. He examined three core beliefs—support for equality of opportunity, economic individualism, and the free enterprise system—and found that the first two are related to positions on specific issues, evaluations of presidential performance, and support for particular candidates. Iyengar (1989) argued that citizens employ an "attribution of responsibility mechanism" to impose order on the complex political world in which they behave. Two aspects of responsibility are relevant: the cause of the issue or problem, and the locus of responsibility for its solution. Thus, the work of Feldman and Iyengar and others argue that there can be an underlying structure or organization to citizens' political views. But their proposed orientations are not the liberal–conservative dimension that receives so much attention in the media; therefore, one should be cautious in assigning ideological interpreations to citizens' political attitudes and behavior.

Constraint.   With respect to constraint in belief systems, the most far-reaching revisionist research is that of Norman Nie and Kristi Andersen (1974) and Norman Nie, Sidney Verba, and John Petrocik (1976), who examined the linkages among citizen issue opinions over time for an identical set of issues. Nie and Andersen determined the correlation between pairs of issue positions and used as their measure of constraint the average correlation for sets of issues. Figure 4.1 shows the average level of constraint on domestic and foreign issues over time; quite clearly, the consistency of responses in the post 1964 era far exceeds that of the 1956–1960 period. The authors summarize (p. 559):

> From 1964 onward, attitudes in the mass public on the issues of social welfare, welfare measures specific for blacks, racial integration in the schools, and positions on the cold war are substantially intercorrelated. That is, those who are liberal in one of these issue-areas tend to take liberal positions on the others, and the same is true for those at the conservative end of the attitude continuum.

Moreover, Nie and Andersen find that new issues, such as amnesty and the rights of radicals, are somewhat correlated with the more traditional issues.

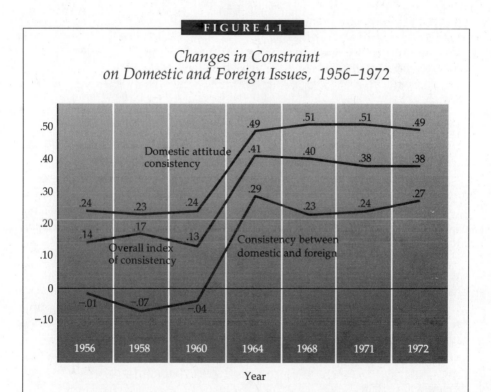

FIGURE 4.1

Changes in Constraint on Domestic and Foreign Issues, 1956–1972

SOURCE: Norman H. Nie and Kristi Andersen, "Mass Belief Systems Revisited: Political Change and Attitude Structure," *Journal of Politics* 36 (August 1974), Figure 4, p. 558 and text on p. 580. By permission of the authors and the University of Texas Press. Nie and Andersen examine citizen responses on five issues over time. Four of the issues are domestic in nature, dealing with questions of welfare, black welfare, integration, and size of government, while the fifth issue concerns the cold war. With five issues, ten correlations between pairs of issues can be calculated. The average of these ten correlations is represented by the overall index consistency, while the domestic attitude consistency is the average of the pairwise correlations among the four domestic issues. The domestic foreign consistency is simply the average of the correlations between the four domestic issues and the cold war item.

This suggests the presence of a general liberal–conservative ideology or, more accurately, constraint across a number of issues that fit a liberal–conservative pattern (pp. 562–563).

As did Converse, Nie and Andersen compared the level of constraint at the mass and elite levels. They found that the mass public of 1972 exhibited more constraint than did the sample of 1958 congressional candidates examined by Converse; unfortunately, more recent elite samples were not available.

The question arises as to the causes of the observed higher levels of constraint in mass belief systems. Nie and Andersen rule out rising educational levels as the explanation since there is increased constraint for citizens at all levels of education. The authors finally conclude that the explanation rests in the changed salience of politics itself, that the 1960s and 1970s were more exciting, dramatic, issue-oriented times than the 1950s. They write (p. 580):

> The pattern of attitudes found among Americans in the 1950s was a transient phenomenon and not an inevitable characteristic of mass politics. Of course, the pattern that emerged in the 1960s may be transient as well, but that does not change our argument about the lack of inevitability of the earlier pattern. Indeed, our data suggests that not only specific political attitudes but the *structure* of mass attitudes may be affected by politics in the real world. The average citizen may not be as apolitical as has been thought.

Plausible as the Nie and Andersen finding about increased issue constraint in the 1960s seems to be, it has come under serious challenge on methodological grounds. Numerous investigators (Sullivan, Piereson, and Marcus, 1978; George Bishop et al., 1978a, 1978b, 1978c) have argued that the increase in issue constraint attributed by Nie and his associates to the more politicized nature of the 1960s is in reality due to changes in the wording of the issue questions asked by the CPS in 1964. It has been shown that these changes have resulted in higher constraint.[2]

If the wording of the questions accounts for the rise in issue constraint, then where does this leave the revisionist literature about the competence of the average citizen? One answer is to downplay the constraint evidence and focus more directly on research that links ideology and issues to actual vote choice. In the CPS report on the 1972 election, Arthur Miller and his associates declare (1976: 754): "Ideology and issue voting . . . provide a means for better explaining the unique elements of the contest than do the voters' social characteristics, the nature of candidates, the events of the campaign, political alienation, cultural orientations, or partisan identification." They found a strong relationship between a liberal–conservative proximity measure and the citizen's vote. Moreover, they observed fairly high correlations within clusters of issues, which they viewed as evidence of constraint, as well as substantial correlations between specific issues and the citizen's position on a liberal–conservative scale. Concluding that ideology had become much more relevant in influencing vote, the authors attributed this to the more distinctive alternatives offered by candidates in response to the social and political crises of the 1960s and 1970s. In the CPS report on the 1976 election, Arthur Miller and Warren E. Miller (1977) found that while the impact of party identification on vote choice had increased and the effect of issues declined, the levels of issue consistency and ideological thinking remained essentially unchanged from 1972. And in an analysis of the 1980 CPS surveys, Warren E. Miller and Merrill Shanks (1982) argued that voters' party identification, ideological self-classification, and assessments of Carter's performance were crucial factors in explaining vote choice. Moreover, citizen preferences for conservative changes in public policies on a number of issues also contributed importantly to the Reagan victory. Hence, analyses of three presidential elections suggest that ideological and/or issue considerations have played important roles in shaping vote choices.

Finally, additional research suggests that citizens' opinions exhibit constraint, at least within specific issue areas. For example, Paul Sheatsley (1966) has shown that generalized racial attitudes are closely related to opinions on specific race-related matters. Similarly, Page and Brody (1972) found a clear structure in citizens' responses to a series of questions about the Vietnam War. James Stimson (1975) found that constraint was highest over a set of issues for citizens with the greatest cognitive abilities, as measured by level of education and amount of political information. Other research (for example, Robert Lane, 1962) relying on more in-depth, intensive interviewing techniques has revealed greater consistency and coherence in citizens' attitudes. This raises the possibility that the sample survey approach may not be optimal for investigating constraint, mainly because people may not be able to articulate in a brief interview the kinds of considerations that enter into their evaluations of politics and because there may be insufficient probing to determine why people believe what they do. However, in-depth approaches may be suitable for answering questions different from those raised in the issue-voting controversy. Since the political stimuli and communications in the real world are not presented to voters in an in-depth fashion, the sample survey may be the more appropriate way to study citizen responses to an election campaign.

The Competence of
the Independent and the Floating Voter

It is clear that elections are won and lost in large part according to the behavior of Independents, the citizens who are most volatile in their partisan choice over successive elections, as seen in figure 3.6. This volatility in conjunction with the increase in the number of Independents discussed in chapter 3 makes the Independent citizenry a critical battleground for campaign strategists. It therefore becomes important to ascertain how informed and concerned Independents are; it would be extremely upsetting to many observers of American politics if election outcomes largely depended on blocs of uninformed voters.

As with the issue-voting literature, there is both a traditional and a revisionist portrait of the Independent voter. Before turning to these portraits, note that the relevant literature discusses different yet interrelated groups of voters. Some analyses focus on partisans versus Independents, while others concentrate on standpatters versus switchers, or floaters—that is, citizens who are consistent versus those who are inconsistent in their partisan choice over successive elections. While Independents are more likely to be switchers and partisans standpatters, there is certainly not a perfect overlap between the categories. For example, the partisan who temporarily defects from his or her party's nominee but returns to the fold at the next election is clearly a switcher, but certainly not an Independent. The reader should keep the distinction between switchers and Independents in mind as the relevant literature is discussed.

The American Voter summarizes the traditional view of the Independent very briefly as follows (p. 143):

> Far from being more attentive, interested, and informed, Independents tend as a group to be somewhat less involved in politics. They have somewhat poorer knowledge of the issues, their image of the candidates is fainter, their interest in the campaign is less, their concern over the outcome is relatively slight, and their choice between competing candidates, although it is indeed made later in the campaign, seems much less to spring from discoverable evaluations of the elements of national politics.

And concerning the floating voter, Converse (1970b) found that citizens who voted for different parties in 1956 and 1960 had lower levels of information than the stable voters. Thus, the standard image of the Independent and the floater is not very positive.

RePass (1971) has challenged *The American Voter* description of the issue awareness of the Independent. He discovered (p. 398) that Independents ranked between Republicans and Democrats with respect to the extent of their issue concerns; for example, 30 percent of the Independents mentioned four to six issues about which they were concerned, compared to only 15 percent of the strong Democrats. RePass's findings did not challenge *The American Voter* findings about involvement and participation.

RePass explained his findings of high issue concern among Independents by arguing that *The American Voter* may have used inappropriate measures (pp. 398–399):

> Conclusions about the Independent voter . . . were based upon responses to the open-ended questions that measured attitudes toward parties and candidates, not toward issues. The Independent is placed at a disadvantage in answering these questions—especially the questions about parties. . . . [R]esponses to these questions frequently reflect long-term cognitive

elements of party identification. Since most Independents have received few cues about parties in their socialization process, it is understandable that their references to parties would be deficient.

Furthermore, there is evidence (Philip Converse, 1974: 324, fn. 20) that if one excludes from analysis those Independents who are habitual nonvoters and therefore cannot influence election outcomes, the remaining Independents are just as involved and informed as the partisans, if not more so.

A more telling criticism of *The American Voter* description of the Independent is the failure to distinguish between Independent leaners and pure Independents. Chapter 3 noted that Independent leaners tend to vote like the partisans of the party to which they lean rather than mirroring the pure Independents. In a similar vein, there is a growing body of literature (Miller and Miller, 1977; Keith et al., 1977) that shows, among other things, that Independent leaners more closely resemble partisans than Independents in such areas as turnout, campaign attentiveness, civic involvement, and political knowledge. And concerning the conceptualization of politics, table 4.5 demonstrates that leaning Independents differ dramatically from pure Independents.

Note that only 12 percent of the pure Independents are classified as ideologues, compared to 21 and 33 percent of the Independent Democrats and Republicans. And fully 37 percent of the pure Independents are in the no-issue-content category, compared to only 20 and 23 percent for the leaning Democrats and Republicans. Perhaps pure Independents are penalized (see the

---

TABLE 4.5

The Relationship between Party Identification and Levels of Conceptualization, 1976 (in percentages)

Level of conceptualization	Party identification						
	Strong Democrat	Weak Democrat	Independent Democrat	Independent	Independent Republican	Weak Republican	Strong Republican
Ideologues	14%	15%	21%	12%	33%	26%	45%
Group benefits	48	35	32	18	11	12	10
Nature of times	26	30	27	33	33	30	28
No issue content	12	19	20	37	23	31	16
Total	100	99	100	100	100	99	99
Number of cases	340	584	281	344	244	354	222

SOURCE: John C. Pierce and Paul R. Hagner, "Conceptualization and Party Identification: 1956–1976," *American Journal of Political Science, 26:2* (May 1982), pp. 382, 385. By permission of the University of Texas Press and the authors.

RePass argument earlier) by a classification scheme based on evaluations of the political parties and candidates, but parties and candidates are the major actors in presidential elections. Finally, note that a higher proportion of leaners than strong partisans of each party are categorized as ideologues.[3] Surely the fact that a plurality of pure Independents have no issue content in their reactions to the candidates and political parties is a negative reflection on pure Independents.

Hence, the leaning Independents, who comprised about 66 percent of all Independents in 1988 (see table 2.1), are not the uninformed, uninvolved group depicted in *The American Voter*, although the pure Independents still bear a strong resemblance to the traditional portrayal. For example (as shown in table 4.6), 39 and 45 percent of the leaners in 1956 and 1988 had at least some college education, levels 7 and 2 percent higher than the figures for all citizens in those years. In contrast, only 28 and 30 percent of the pure Independents had some college education.

Returning to the floating voters, an ever-growing body of evidence suggests that the switching voters tend to move in response to genuine issue concerns and do not simply float randomly back and forth between the parties. In addition to the Key work cited earlier, Peter Natchez and Irvin Bupp (1970: 436–443) found that citizens who belonged to an issue public were more likely to change their partisan choice between 1960 and 1964. A similar conclusion was reached by Samuel Kirkpatrick and Melvin Jones (1974: 544–555) for 1964–1968 switchers *and* standpatters. That is, both stable and moving voters appeared to behave according to well-founded policy preferences. The SRC/CPS work on the 1968 election showed that 1964–1968 switchers, particularly 1968 Wallace voters, were clearly policy motivated (Converse, Miller, Rusk, and Wolfe, 1969: 1095–1101). Research on vote defection suggests a similar conclusion—namely, that defectors can be guided by policy concerns (Richard Boyd, 1969). Finally, a study of vote switchers in the 1980 and 1984 elections (Boyd, 1986) showed that their movement was in response to their

TABLE 4.6

Various Categories of Independents with at Least Some College Education, 1956 and 1988 (in percentages)

	1956	1988	Percent increase
Pure Independents	28%	30%	2%
Leaning Independents	39	45	6
All partisans and Independents	32	43	11

SOURCES: 1956 and 1988 SRC/CPS election studies.

issue positions, their economic well-being, and their views of the qualities of the candidates.

In summary, the contemporary research indicates that the floating voter can respond to issue considerations and that the leaning Independent is capable of making informed decisions. This is presumably good news for those who worry about elections being decided by blocs of uninformed, unconcerned voters. A more interesting implication is that there is a greater potentiality for issue-based politics than previously believed, mainly because of the weakening of partisan ties among the electorate. There may also be a better opportunity for an issue-oriented third party to appear or for the existing parties to realign on the basis of issues. In fact, this opportunity may be better now than at any time since the 1930s, even though the likelihood of such a realignment is low. Of course, any issue-based changes in the political system would require that candidates and parties articulate clear and coherent positions on *important* contemporary issues. Whether the political leadership is capable of fulfilling this requirement remains to be seen. Certainly the conduct of the 1988 presidential campaign did not inspire confidence.

Summary and Conclusion

The revisionist literature surveyed in this chapter generally revealed higher levels of issue awareness and ideological conceptualization. This was attributed to both methodological innovations and to genuine changes in the electorate brought on in part by the changed nature of politics in the 1960s and 1970s. However, any attempt to estimate the precise amount of issue voting or ideological sophistication must take into account a variety of conditions that can affect issue and ideological awareness. Hence, this chapter concludes by specifying some general conditions that influence the amount of issue voting.

Issue voting requires information, and the acquisition of information involves costs for the citizen. These costs are probably less for citizens with the cognitive skills (for example, education) that facilitate collecting and evaluating information. Thus, the increase in American educational levels may gradually lead to a citizenry better able to be informed about politics and elections.

The impact of educational trends, however, seems marginal at best. Probably the quickest way to reduce the information costs of citizens is for the parties and candidates to take distinct positions on issues and to campaign on the basis of those positions. Further, where parties offer meaningful choices on issues relevant to the population, citizens themselves will be more willing to incur the costs of being informed.

However, the incentives for the parties to take distinctive positions may not exist, even for issues that are points of contention at the elite level and among segments of the electorate. As Anthony Downs (1957: 117–122) argues, in a two-party system where most of the voters fall in the middle of the political spectrum, the wisest electoral strategy for the parties is to converge toward the center. If new issues arise that do not coincide with the existing lines of party cleavage, or if the existing issues that divide the parties assume new forms, then the parties may respond in a number of ways.

In one scenario the parties will try to incorporate the new or revised issues without upsetting the existing bases of party support. However, it may be impossible for the parties to handle these new issues without alienating some substantial segment of their existing support. In such a situation the parties may try to straddle or avoid issues, thereby making the information costs of voters very high.

Of course, where parties straddle an issue, a vacuum may exist, which can encourage the emergence of a third-party candidacy directed toward voters on the basis of issues. This development would reduce information costs and facilitate issue voting. Evidence for this scenario is provided by the formal work of Downs, who argues (pp. 125–127) that parties in a multiparty system are more likely to take distinctive positions, and by the empirical work of Converse, Miller, Rusk, and Wolfe (1969), who found that support for the third-party candidacy of George Wallace in 1968 was largely issue based, while the Nixon and Humphrey vote was primarily a party vote. Almost 50 percent of the citizens questioned said they liked Wallace because of his issue stands; only about 25 percent of the replies dealing with Nixon and Humphrey were concerned about issues. More specifically, Converse and his colleagues found that Wallace voters were far more uniformly hawkish, prosegregation, pro-police, and the like. In short, the authors argued (p. 1097) that "Wallace was a 'backlash' candidate, and there is no question but that the positions communicated to the public accounted for his electoral support in a very primary sense." The Wallace candidacy well illustrates the situation of an issue-based third party that makes it easy for voters to be informed on issues.

In conclusion, the important thrust of the revisionist literature is that citizens are capable of making issue-related vote decisions, especially when the candidates and parties fashion issue appeals to the electorate. Although the amount of issue voting may still not be impressively high, particularly with respect to classical democratic theory, it may be unreasonable to demand high levels of issue voting from citizens if the parties and candidates themselves do not present clearly stated choices.

However, some cautionary statements are necessary to keep people from drawing unduly optimistic conclusions about the competence and influence of the citizenry. It is clear that voters can come to voting decisions more easily when the candidates offer distinct alternatives. Moreover, it is easier to evaluate the candidate when voters are considering an incumbent seeking reelection. This is because the voters have had ample opportunity to judge the candidate's performance and person. Indeed, issue voting may be most prevalent when voters have an opportunity to evaluate retrospectively the performance of an incumbent administration.

The retrospective voting model is enjoying popularity among scholars of elections today. Its core element is that voters evaluate the performance of an incumbent administration and remove incumbents from office if the citizens are dissatisfied with that performance. The retrospective voting model has a number of attractive features. First, it casts the vote decision in a more rational, performance-based light and hence continues the effort begun by Key to redeem the competence of the American voter. At the same time, the demands placed on the individual voter by the retrospective model are not great. The voter has only to place the blame for bad times on the incumbent administration. There is no need for full and complete information or for a Downsian calculation of the relative payoffs that might result from various outcomes of the elections. Furthermore, many factors can be analyzed under the retrospective model. Most often economic issues may serve as the basis for retrospective voting, but other issues as well may certainly result in voting based on the performance of the incumbents.

The first reason cited for the attractiveness of the retrospective voting model is potentially too beguiling as political analysts look to salvage the voter's reputation and competence in democratic theory. One should be careful not to make too great claims for a democratic political system, even when it does satisfy the requirements of retrospective voting. Years ago Joseph Schumpeter formulated a procedural conceptualization of democracy (discussed at the end of chapter 1) that fits the retrospective model well. Schumpeter wrote (1950: 26): "The democratic method is that institutional arrangement for arriving at political decisions in which individuals acquire the power to decide by means of a competitive struggle for the people's vote." For Schumpeter, the key requirement of a democratic system was free and open competition among competing sets of elites. If this condition were met, then voters dissatisfied with the performance of the incumbents could oust them at the next election. For Schumpeter, the primary function of the citizens' vote was to produce a government that would have substantial discretion in formulating and instituting policies subject to the electorate's retrospective judgment at the next election. In this view elections are not prospective affairs in which voters give policy mandates to guide the victorious party. Instead, the policy consequences of an election are quite minimal and the role of the voter very limited. Thus, the retrospective voting model, which clearly fits under the Schumpeter perspective, should not be viewed too optimistically as the salvation of the individual citizen. The retrospective model and Schumpeter's procedural view of democracy do not require much competence on the part of the voters.

In contrast to the retrospective model is a prospective model in which citizens would be required to evaluate the various payoffs from the election of one party versus another and to choose appropriately among these payoffs. If such a model operated in the real world, then the rational independent citizen of classical democratic theory would truly have been resuscitated.

Moreover, with prospective voting, the possibility of electoral mandates and citizen influence is obviously enhanced, a sharp contrast to the retrospective model, in which the victorious candidate and party have pretty much of a free rein in how they address the problems that have proved the undoing of the previous incumbent administration. Hence, the retrospective model does not necessarily elevate the citizen to a position of great influence and competence, as its proponents might suggest. Citizens may select the government, but the policy implications of their votes, beyond a rejection of the incumbents, are difficult to ascertain.

Of course, even if citizens did vote prospectively, there would be no guarantee that their collective decision would constitute a mandate for particular public policies. It might be that the victorious candidate was supported by a coalition highly diverse in its issue concerns and preferences, so that it would be impossible to identify majority support on any particular issue. And even if the voters spoke predominantly with one voice, there still might not be any mandate translated into public policy, either because the victor misread the public or because political constraints (for example, the opposition party controlled the legislature) prevented the adoption and implementation of the mandated policies. Nevertheless, if citizens were indeed prospective in their voting behavior, the potential for citizen influence would be enhanced. But the ability to vote prospectively is not only a function of the skills and interests of the voters; it is also a function of the quality and clarity of the choices offered by the electoral system. The next two chapters will examine some of the factors affecting vote choice in presidential elections from 1952 to 1988.

Notes

1. The power of proximity measures is shown in the following example. The correlations between the respondents' own positions on Vietnam and the vote (as measured by Nixon vote versus non-Nixon vote, Humphrey vote versus non-Humphrey vote, and Wallace vote versus non-Wallace vote) were only –.03, .05, and –.03, respectively. When proximity items that measure the distance between the citizen's position and his or her perception of the candidates' positions are used, the correlations jump to .40, .43, and .36, respectively. See Beardsley (1973).

2. Prior to 1964, SRC/CPS issue questions presented respondents with a single position on an issue and determined support or opposition for the position along a five-point agree–disagree scale. For example, in 1960 the question on medical welfare was worded: "The government ought to help people get doctors and hospital care at low cost. Do you have an opinion on this or not? (If yes): Do you think the government should do this?" In 1964 SRC/CPS presented respondents with competing alternatives on an issue and asked them to choose between them. Hence, in 1964 the medical welfare question was worded: "Some say the government in Washington ought to help

people get doctors and hospital care at low cost; others say the government should not get into this. Have you been interested enough in this to favor one side over the other? (If yes): What is your position? Should the government in Washington help people get doctors and hospital care at low cost or stay out of this?" In 1968 these dichotomous choice items were expanded into seven category measures with labeled end points. Hence, the issue questions have been changed in major ways, mainly because the respondents' answers would be more valid when they were faced with a choice among alternatives. Because of the concern about measuring nonattitudes, issue items have been preceded by filter questions (for example, do you have an opinion . . . , have you been interested . . .) designed to screen out people without genuine attitudes. These filter questions have also changed over the years, and Bishop, Tuchfarber, and Oldendick (1978c) have shown that different filters result in substantially different numbers of people being included in the analysis. Hence, studies of issue consistency may not be truly comparable because of differently defined sets of respondents.

     3. As an aside, note that Republicans are much more likely to have an ideological orientation to politics, while Democrats are more oriented to group benefits. This may help explain why the GOP has problems expanding its base of support. One can speculate that Republicans' attachments to their party are more likely to be based on general agreement with philosophical principles that are not readily modified or compromised. Hence, attempts to broaden the base may be seen as threats to the purity of the party's traditional stances. But for Democrats, developing and maintaining a broad base is made easier by a dominant group-benefits outlook that enables political differences to be resolved by the provision of tangible (and symbolic) benefits to the groups making up the Democratic coalition. Although the numbers in table 4.5 refer only to 1976, the general pattern of results holds for other presidential election years as well.

CHAPTER 5

Issues and Candidates, 1952–1972

As discussed in Chapter 2, *The American Voter* identified six partisan attitudes that influence citizens' vote decisions— attitudes toward the Democratic and Republican candidates, attitudes toward the issues of domestic and foreign policy, attitudes toward the political parties as managers of government, and attitudes toward the groups involved in politics. These six attitudes achieved varying degrees of importance in the elections between 1952 and 1972, and thus this chapter's first task is simply to assess their impact on the parties' electoral fortunes over time. Discussion on each specific election will follow, highlighting the major factors that shaped the election outcome. (Chapter 6 will analyze the 1976, 1980, 1984, and 1988 elections.)

The Six Partisan Attitudes Over Time

ATTITUDES TOWARD THE CANDIDATES

Note that among the six partisan attitudes, attitudes toward the candidates have fluctuated the most with respect to the ups and downs of the Democrats and Republicans in elections between 1952 and 1972. Of course, it is not really surprising that attitudes toward candidates have varied so greatly. After all, the candidates are likely to be the unique and new elements in each election. But what is surprising is the fact that the parties have at times offered presidential candidates who were not highly evaluated by their own party members, let alone by Independents and the opposition. Figure 5.1 presents the mean evaluations of the major party presidential candidates between 1952 and 1972, as measured by the frequency of positive and negative comments offered about the candidates.

For all citizens the mean evaluations of the Democratic candidates were positive through 1964, slightly negative in 1968, and very negative in 1972. An even more telling fact is that the evaluation of McGovern in 1972 by Democratic identifiers was not positive but neutral, certainly a revealing comment on the weakness of the McGovern candidacy. Throughout this period Independents assessed three Democratic candidates positively (Stevenson in 1952, Kennedy in 1960, Johnson in 1964) and three negatively, while Republican loyalists were consistently negative toward the Democratic nominees, as expected, with Lyndon Johnson being the least unpopular Democratic candidate in Republican eyes.

Reactions to the Republican candidates by the entire citizenry and by Independents were uniformly favorable, with the major exception of Goldwater in 1964. Democratic assessments of GOP presidential candidates were generally more favorable than Republican evaluations of Democratic candidates; only in 1964 and 1968 were Democrats substantially negative toward the Republican nominees. Republican partisans, as expected, always ranked their candidates highly, with Goldwater receiving the weakest of these positive endorsements and Eisenhower, in 1956, the strongest.

Thus, evaluations of the major party candidates varied markedly. The interesting question is, "How did these assessments translate into vote outcomes?" Some research by Donald Stokes (1966), supplemented by findings presented by Michael Kagay and Greg Caldeira, helps address this question. Figure 5.2 shows the contribution to the Democratic and Republican vote totals due to the impact of candidate attitudes, while figure 5.3 summarizes the net impact of candidate attitudes on the vote division. Note that with the exception of 1964, attitudes toward the Republican presidential candidates always made a positive contribution to Republican vote totals; this tendency reached a peak in 1956, when the Eisenhower candidacy led to an almost 8 percent advantage for the GOP. Attitudes toward the Democratic candidates did not provide the same advantage for the Democrats as attitudes toward the Republican candi-

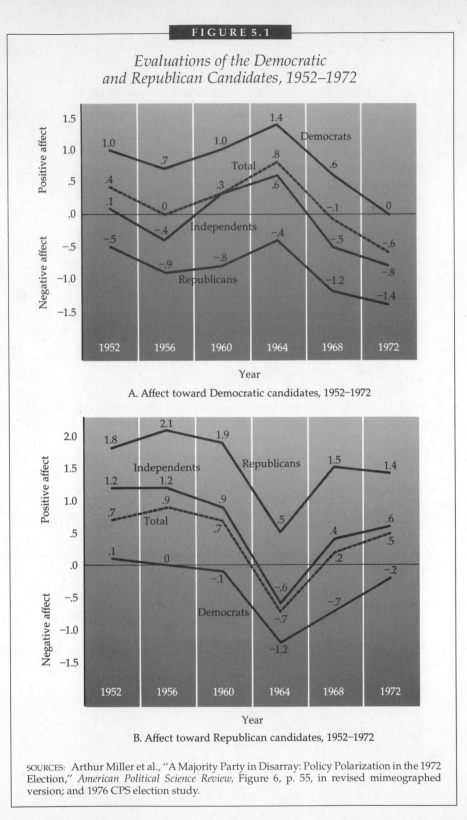

FIGURE 5.1

Evaluations of the Democratic and Republican Candidates, 1952–1972

A. Affect toward Democratic candidates, 1952–1972

B. Affect toward Republican candidates, 1952–1972

SOURCES: Arthur Miller et al., "A Majority Party in Disarray: Policy Polarization in the 1972 Election," *American Political Science Review*, Figure 6, p. 55, in revised mimeographed version; and 1976 CPS election study.

dates provided for the GOP. In fact, in three elections—1956, 1968, and 1972—
the net effect of assessments of the Democratic candidates was a gain in votes
for the GOP. While this Republican gain was tiny in 1956 and 1968, it exceeded
4 percent in 1972 and, in conjunction with the over 4 percent advantage
accruing to the GOP because of its own candidate, resulted in a net gain for
the Republicans of over 8 percent—the greatest net impact of candidates in
this era. The elections of 1952 and 1960 were characterized by the weakest net
impact of candidates. In these two cases both parties' nominees were evaluated positively and aided their own party's electoral prospects.

In summary, candidate evaluations have generally been a plus to Republican electoral fortunes. Further, Democratic party identifiers have generally
been less enthusiastic toward their party's candidates than Republican loyalists have been toward theirs (figure 5.1). Why is this the case? One speculative
but plausible answer is that the Democratic party is a more diverse, heterogeneous party. As a result, it finds it difficult to nominate a candidate with as

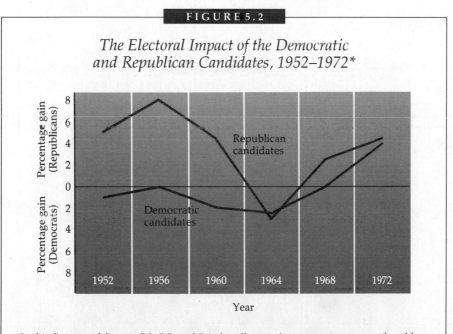

FIGURE 5.2

The Electoral Impact of the Democratic and Republican Candidates, 1952–1972*

*In this figure and figures 5.3, 5.5, and 5.6, the effect on the two-party vote attributable to
the attitudinal component in question is being measured. For example, the 1956 entry in
the above figure for Republican candidates indicates that the GOP received an advantage
of about 8 percent in the popular vote as a result of favorable attitudes toward Eisenhower.

SOURCES: Donald E. Stokes, "Some Dynamic Elements of Contests for the Presidency,"
American Political Science Review 60 (March 1966), Figure 3, p. 22; Michael Kagay and Greg
Caldeira, "Public Policy Issues and the American Voter, 1952–1972," unpublished paper;
and communication from Michael Kagay.

widespread appeal to Democratic loyalists as GOP nominees have to Republican followers. Perhaps there was no candidate that the Democrats could have nominated in 1972 who could have approached the popularity of Richard Nixon in the electorate at large, although there were probably Democratic candidates who would have been more attractive than McGovern to the Democratic rank and file.

Another reason for the GOP advantage in candidate evaluations might simply rest in the chance elements of politics, resulting in the Republicans nominating the more attractive, popular candidates. For example, if Robert Kennedy had not been assassinated in 1968, perhaps the Democratic party would have emerged from the Chicago convention with a stronger ticket. Likewise, if Hubert Humphrey had won the California primary over McGovern in 1972, perhaps a compromise or dark horse nominee would have been selected, thus enabling the Democrats to wage a more effective campaign. On the Republican side, if Rockefeller's narrow defeat by Goldwater in the California primary in 1964 had been reversed, the GOP would probably have nominated a compromise candidate such as Scranton, Lodge, or Nixon who would have been more popular with the various wings of the GOP.

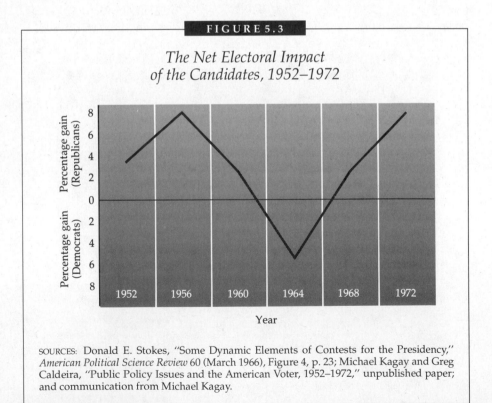

FIGURE 5.3

The Net Electoral Impact of the Candidates, 1952–1972

SOURCES: Donald E. Stokes, "Some Dynamic Elements of Contests for the Presidency," *American Political Science Review* 60 (March 1966), Figure 4, p. 23; Michael Kagay and Greg Caldeira, "Public Policy Issues and the American Voter, 1952–1972," unpublished paper; and communication from Michael Kagay.

Yet a third explanation for the Republican advantage in candidate evaluation at all elections except 1964 refers to the nature of the times and the impossibility of divorcing perceptions of the candidates from the political context in which nominees must compete. For example, twice—in 1952 and 1968—the Democratic party entered the election as the incumbent party under attack for a variety of reasons, including the state of the economy and unpopular land wars in Asia. While the Democrats were the incumbent party at these elections, their nominee was not the incumbent president. In both cases the president chose not to seek reelection, while a nonincumbent was saddled with the legacy of an unpopular administration. Under such circumstances it is difficult for voters to perceive the nominee very favorably, since in many voters' minds he is linked to the unpopular policies of the previous administration. Furthermore, in 1956 and 1972 the Democratic candidates (Stevenson and McGovern) had the unenviable task of challenging Republican incumbents (Eisenhower and Nixon) who were campaigning for reelection in part on the basis that they had solved many of the problems inherited from the previous Democratic administration. In view of the immense personal popularity of Eisenhower in 1956, perhaps there was no Democratic candidate who would not have suffered in popular evaluations. While Nixon's reelection did not seem assured in the middle of his first term, he was in a secure electoral position by the 1972 election, not only because of the Democratic nomination of McGovern, but also because of Nixon's ability, as the incumbent president, to structure situations for maximum political advantage. Note in this connection Nixon's well-timed, well-publicized trips to China and the Soviet Union as well as his stimulation of the economy by releasing massive funds prior to the election.

One thrust of this discussion is that much more enters into citizens' assessments of candidates than simply the candidate's personality, speaking style, and the like. Voters may like a candidate because of personal characteristics, policy views, or association with other positively evaluated elements of politics. It is useful to know which of these basic factors most influence citizen evaluations of candidates, for some important strategic considerations are involved. If feelings toward the candidates are mainly based on personality, then it behooves parties to nominate personally attractive candidates. But if policy considerations are also important components of candidate evaluations, then the candidates and parties must be concerned with fashioning optimal policy appeals as well as generating attractive candidate images. Of course, both policy and personality factors affect the way citizens evaluate candidates. This is because the two elements are not independent when the tendency of people to distort their perceptions of candidates and to rationalize their voting decisions is taken into account. Furthermore, a variety of situational factors, such as the kinds of appeals a candidate makes, affect whether people respond to the candidates primarily in personal or policy terms.[1] Still, researchers would like to know how the personality and policy components of candidate evaluations have varied over time. It would be expected that the personality aspects of candidate ratings undergo the widest fluctuations since such aspects are so idiosyncratic.

The work of Donald R. Kinder and Robert P. Abelson (1981) on the 1980 election uncovered two general dimensions of candidate evaluation—candidate competence and candidate integrity. Research by Samuel Kirkpatrick et al. (1974) examined various components of candidate evaluation. Kirkpatrick analyzed the responses to the SRC/CPS open-ended questions about candidate likes and dislikes and classified citizens' comments according to which aspect of the candidate they mentioned—personality, domestic policy stances, foreign policy positions, or suitability as an administrator of government. As shown in figure 5.4, the personality component of candidate rankings has varied the most over time, while the domestic policy aspect has always been pro-Democratic, even in 1972 when McGovern himself received highly nega-

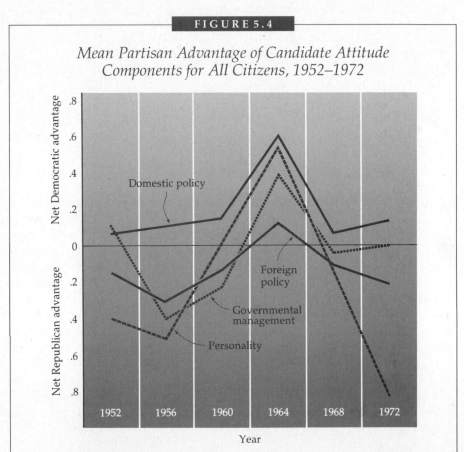

FIGURE 5.4

Mean Partisan Advantage of Candidate Attitude Components for All Citizens, 1952–1972

SOURCE: Samuel Kirkpatrick, William Lyons, and Michael R. Fitzgerald, "Candidate and Party Images in the American Electorate: A Longitudinal Analysis," paper presented at the annual meeting of the Southwestern Political Science Association, Dallas, March 28–30, 1974, modified from Figure 4.

tive ratings. This means that for many voters the issue positions they associated with McGovern were more popular than McGovern himself. Undoubtedly, this reflected a long-standing Democratic advantage in the electorate with respect to certain domestic policy programs, particularly matters of social welfare. The foreign policy component of candidate assessment favored the Republicans in all years except 1964, while the management component was more evenly divided. (Chapter 7 contains further discussion about the conceptual difficulties in sorting out the impact of candidate and issue attitudes.) In summary, it appears that different elements do enter into evaluations of a candidate, and that the personal characteristics of the nominee are able to affect election outcomes. Certainly, the very nomination of one candidate over another strongly determines the kind of campaign that will be conducted.

ATTITUDES TOWARD DOMESTIC AND FOREIGN POLICY ISSUES

Figure 5.5 shows the electoral impact of domestic and foreign policy attitudes between 1952 and 1972. Note that the era began and ended with a Republican advantage in the realm of foreign affairs, an advantage that disappeared only in the 1964 election because of the "collapse of the belief that the party under Goldwater was more likely to bring peace than were the Democrats under

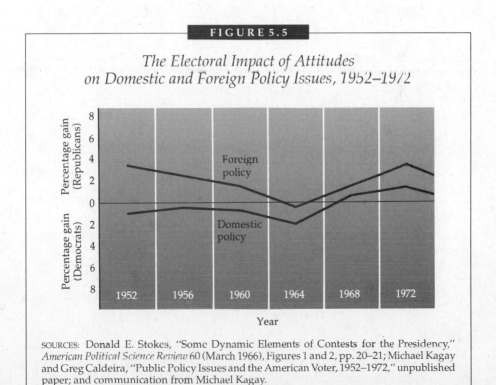

FIGURE 5.5

The Electoral Impact of Attitudes on Domestic and Foreign Policy Issues, 1952–1972

SOURCES: Donald E. Stokes, "Some Dynamic Elements of Contests for the Presidency," *American Political Science Review* 60 (March 1966), Figures 1 and 2, pp. 20–21; Michael Kagay and Greg Caldeira, "Public Policy Issues and the American Voter, 1952–1972," unpublished paper; and communication from Michael Kagay.

Johnson" (Donald E. Stokes, 1966: 21). This is a prime example of a situation in which the choice of a specific candidate can upset long-standing images of the parties. By 1968, the Republican advantage in foreign affairs returned as a result of the Democrats' responsibility for the Vietnam War, and by 1972 the GOP advantage returned to the peak achieved in 1952.

The domestic policy curve reveals a small but consistent advantage for the Democrats through 1964 and a lead for the Republicans in 1968 and 1972, as traditional New Deal social welfare issues gave way in part to new issues dealing with race, law and order, and other matters associated with social issues. Until 1964 the predominant domestic policy image of the parties was the association of Democrats with prosperity and Republicans with hard times. Stokes (1966: 21) writes that this association weakened with the prosperity of Eisenhower's first term, an experience that convinced many voters that the GOP was not inexorably linked with economic depression. But the Republican recession of 1958 in conjunction with the relatively good times of the Kennedy/early Johnson years served to strengthen the linkage between bad economic times and Republican occupancy of the White House.

ATTITUDES TOWARD PARTY PERFORMANCE AND GROUPS

This section considers the attitudes of citizens toward party performance and the groups involved in politics. As figure 5.6 indicates, there are fairly consistent party differences in how these two attitudinal components have influenced vote outcomes between 1952 and 1972. With the exception of the 1964 election, attitudes toward the parties' performances have favored the Republicans, although only in 1952 was this effect particularly strong. Attitudes toward groups, on the contrary, have consistently favored the Democratic party, with the most frequent positive comment referring to the Democrats as the party of the common man, in contrast to the image of the GOP as the party of the more privileged elements of society. Stokes (1966: 20–21) suggests that one reason for the decline in the Democratic advantage in this dimension in 1960 and 1964 was the association of the Democratic party with groups less popular than the common man, such as racial groups (blacks in 1964) and religious groups (Catholics in 1960). But even in 1968 and 1972, when racial themes were underlying currents in the campaigns and white resistance to black demands in a number of areas was increasing, the Democratic party maintained its favorable position with respect to group benefits.

The Candidates and Issues, 1952–1972

The previous section showed that the six partisan attitudes fluctuate in response to the conduct and content of campaigns. In addition, these attitudes represent the short-term forces at each election that help explain why the majority Democratic party was not victorious in all of the elections. This section will turn to a more explicitly political discussion of each election and try to make more politically meaningful the content of the six partisan attitudes. This section will consider the elections sequentially, beginning each discussion with a chart summarizing the effects of the six partisan attitudes. Finally, this section will analyze the issues, events, and candidates that gave meaning and shape to the partisan attitudes.

1952 AND 1956

This discussion will center around the 1952 and 1956 elections in order to facilitate comparisons across elections in which the major party candidate choices were identical. Figure 5.7 summarizes the impact of the six partisan attitudes across the two elections. Stokes and his colleagues describe figure 5.7 as indicating the following (1958: 382):

> The Republican victory of 1952 resulted from the great appeal of Eisenhower, from a pro-Republican attitude toward foreign issues, and from a strongly anti-Democratic response to the parties as managers of government. This combination of forces appears to have overwhelmed the favorable response to Stevenson, the substantial Democratic group appeal, and

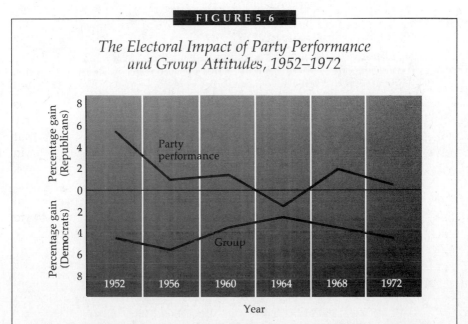

FIGURE 5.6

The Electoral Impact of Party Performance and Group Attitudes, 1952–1972

SOURCES: Donald E. Stokes, "Some Dynamic Elements of Contests for the Presidency," *American Political Science Review* 60 (March 1966), Figures 1 and 2, pp. 20–21; Michael Kagay and Greg Caldeira, "Public Policy Issues and the American Voter, 1952–1972," unpublished paper; and communication from Michael Kagay.

a pro-Democratic attitude on domestic issues. The Republican victory of 1956 seems to have resulted from somewhat different components. In the latter election, the force of Eisenhower's appeal seemed of paramount importance. The Republican cause was again aided by a favorable response to foreign issues. But with the corruption issue spent, the public's attitude toward the parties as managers of government contributed much less to the Republican majority. On the Democratic side, the appeal of Stevenson apparently was no longer more an asset than a liability to his party, and the party's advantage in domestic issues was greatly diminished. Only a strong Democratic group appeal appeared to reduce the size of the Republican majority in the latter year.

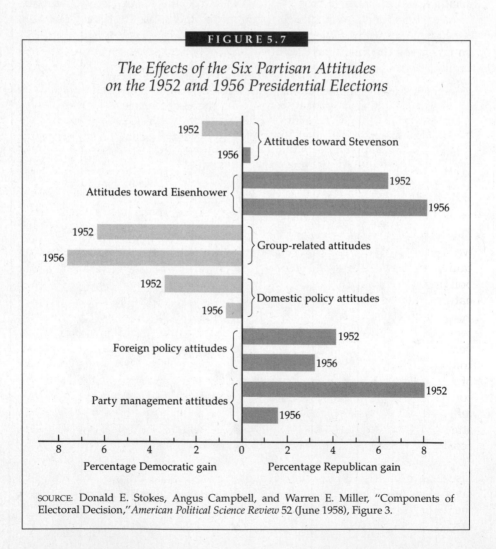

FIGURE 5.7

The Effects of the Six Partisan Attitudes on the 1952 and 1956 Presidential Elections

SOURCE: Donald E. Stokes, Angus Campbell, and Warren E. Miller, "Components of Electoral Decision," *American Political Science Review* 52 (June 1958), Figure 3.

The importance of party management and foreign policy concerns to the 1952 election outcome is reflected in the GOP's campaign theme that tagged the Democratic party as the party of "Corruption, Korea, and Communism." The issue of corruption and the extent to which it hurt the Democrats in 1952 may seem perplexing in retrospect since Stevenson and not Truman was the Democratic candidate in 1952. Nevertheless, in the 1952 campaign the Republicans emphasized the "mess in Washington" under the Truman administration, even though Truman himself was in no way implicated in the misdeeds of his aides. The misdeeds themselves pale in comparison to the Watergate-related offenses, but the repeated pattern of publicized misdeeds created the image of the Democrats as the party of mismanagement and corruption.

The Korean War was the dominant force behind citizens' evaluations of the parties on the issue of war and peace in 1952. The Republican advantage on this issue received a further boost when General Eisenhower said, in a campaign speech in Detroit less than two weeks before the election (Weisbord, 1966: 378):

> Where will a new Administration begin?
>
> It will begin with its President taking a simple, firm resolution. That resolution will be: To forego the diversions of politics and to concentrate on the job of ending the Korean war—until that job is honorably done.
>
> That job requires a personal trip to Korea.
>
> I shall make that trip. Only in that way could I learn how best to serve the American people in the cause of peace.
>
> I shall go to Korea.

This simple promise, despite its lack of any specific content as to how the war would actually be ended, and despite the fact that it was made late in the campaign after most voters had made up their minds how to vote, served to bolster the image of the GOP and Eisenhower as competent to handle the nation's foreign affairs.

Despite the tremendous amount of attention given the "communism issue" by the media and by political elites, the communist threat was not a very central concern to most Americans in 1952, at least in comparison to other concerns. The failure of the communism issue to penetrate the consciousness of the mass electorate suggests the need to keep in mind that hard-hitting controversy at the elite level about apparently earthshaking issues may not be reflected in the concerns expressed by average citizens, who are often more attentive to issues of more immediate relevance to their own social and economic situations.

While such factors as Korea, corruption, and the personal appeal of Eisenhower led to an impressive Republican victory in 1952, there were forces favorable to the Democratic party; namely, perceptions of the Democrats as the party of lower-status groups, the party of prosperity, and the party associated with the popular domestic policies of the New Deal and Fair Deal.

According to Stokes and his associates (1958: 372), these three favorable images carried over to the 1956 campaign, although Democratic advantages with respect to prosperity and domestic programs declined markedly as the country remained prosperous under a Republican administration that did not try to repeal the New Deal and Fair Deal.

There have probably been few campaign slogans that better expressed the sentiment of the electorate than the 1952 and 1956 theme of "I like Ike." As figure 5.7 indicates, the only pro-Eisenhower attitudinal component to increase in importance between 1952 and 1956 was attitudes toward Eisenhower himself. While references to Eisenhower's military accomplishments were quite common in 1952, by 1956 these comments were fewer, replaced by positive assessments of his personal qualities. Stokes and his coauthors state (1958: 378):

> It was the response to personal qualities—to his sincerity, his integrity and sense of duty, his virtue as a family man, his religious devotion, and his sheer likeableness—which rose sharply in the second campaign. These frequencies leave the strong impression that Eisenhower was honored not so much for his performance as President as for the quality of his person.

Thus, the 1956 election is commonly described as one dominated by the personality of Eisenhower, with issue concerns playing a minimal role. To be sure, the foreign policy crises of Suez and Hungary, which erupted shortly before the 1956 election, may have worked to the advantage of the incumbent Republican administration. Voters perceived it as more competent in foreign affairs and better able to maintain peace. Nevertheless, personality and not policy concerns were the more important determinants of the 1956 election outcome.

In summary, using terminology from chapter 1, the 1952 and 1956 elections represent deviating elections in which the minority Republican party was twice successful in electing its presidential candidate. Yet throughout the period the Democrats maintained their hold on the electorate's partisan loyalties, as shown in table 2.1, and kept control of the Congress for six of the eight Eisenhower years as many Democrats who had defected to Ike returned to their party for other contests. The major short-term forces resulting in departures from the normal vote in 1952 and 1956 were the immense popularity of Eisenhower in both elections and the government mismanagement issue in 1952. Between 1948 and 1952 the Republicans improved their presidential vote performance in almost all population groups and maintained and even increased these gains in 1956, with the major exception of the farm vote. Eisenhower's popularity was a short-term force that affected most segments of the population similarly. As discussion turns to the 1960 election, note that its outcome more closely reflected the normal vote, but it was influenced by a short-term force that differentially affected religious groups— John Kennedy's Catholicism.

1960

The most striking feature of the six partisan attitudes in 1960—as shown in figure 5.8—is their almost perfect balance: three favored the Democrats and three the Republicans, with the net impact of the six a toss-up. Of course, the 1960 election outcome reflected this closeness; Kennedy defeated Nixon by the very slim margin of 112,000 votes out of about 69 million votes cast. Because of the photo finish in the 1960 election, observers are prone to cite a number of factors critical to the election outcome. Commentators speculate about who would have won the election had Eisenhower begun campaigning for the Republican ticket sooner, had Nixon instead of Kennedy expressed symbolic opposition to the jailing of Martin Luther King, or had Nixon been in better physical shape for the first of the televised Great Debates. Since any of a number of influences might have tipped the election either way, such an influence might be labeled decisive. Still, a few factors that merit particular attention must be kept in mind. The first of these, quite simply, is the attitude of the voters toward the candidates. In retrospect, it may surprise many readers to learn that Nixon received more favorable evaluations than Kennedy, even though attitudes toward both candidates were positive. Since Kennedy's

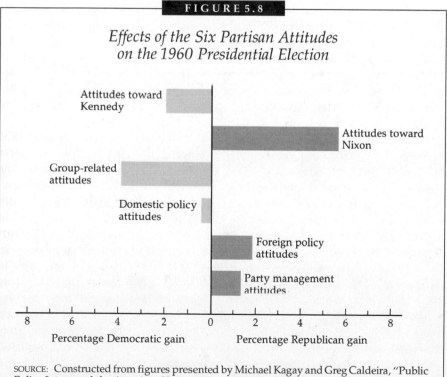

FIGURE 5.8

Effects of the Six Partisan Attitudes
on the 1960 Presidential Election

Attitudes toward
Kennedy

Attitudes toward
Nixon

Group-related
attitudes

Domestic policy
attitudes

Foreign policy
attitudes

Party management
attitudes

8   6   4   2   0   2   4   6   8

Percentage Democratic gain   Percentage Republican gain

SOURCE: Constructed from figures presented by Michael Kagay and Greg Caldeira, "Public Policy Issues and the American Voter, 1952–1972," unpublished paper.

Catholicism was a major factor in evaluations of him, the religious issue will be discussed first; then policy issues will be discussed; finally, discussion will center around the effect of the Great Debates on the election outcome.

The religious issue in 1960.   In 1928, the Democrats nominated as their presidential candidate Governor Al Smith of New York, a Catholic. Smith suffered an overwhelming defeat, losing many traditional Democratic states. His showing was cited as evidence that the American electorate was not ready for and would not accept a Catholic president. As Kennedy was contesting for the Democratic nomination in 1960, the impact of his religion became a central question, one which was presumably answered in the West Virginia primary, where the Catholic Kennedy easily defeated the Protestant Hubert Humphrey in an overwhelmingly Protestant state. Unfortunately, the West Virginia primary did not end the religious issue; once Kennedy won the Democratic nomination, this issue arose again and again, often taking very ugly forms.

Most observers today agree, and the evidence seems quite convincing, that Kennedy's Catholicism hurt him substantially in the popular vote. Converse, Campbell, Miller, and Stokes (1966: 92) estimated that throughout the nation the religious issue cost Kennedy about 2.2 percent of the popular vote, which translates into approximately 1.5 million votes. However, the effects of the religious issue were not uniform throughout the country; it is estimated that Kennedy's Catholicism cost him 16.5 percent of the two-party vote in the heavily Protestant South, while it resulted in a 1.6 percent gain outside the South. Thus, while religion may have hurt Kennedy in the popular vote, it may not have hurt him and may actually have helped him in the Electoral College vote, which he won by the sizable margin of 303–219 despite his small popular vote margin.[2] For example, although Kennedy's Catholicism cost him many votes in the South, this area was so heavily Democratic that the reduced Democratic vote totals enabled the GOP to carry only three states—Florida, Tennessee, and Virginia. Outside the South, Kennedy scored narrow victories in many states with large numbers of electoral votes and large numbers of Catholic voters. For example, Kennedy carried Illinois and its 27 electoral votes by a margin of less than 9,000 votes, or approximately 2/10 of 1 percent, and New Jersey with 16 electoral votes by 22,000 votes, or 8/10 of 1 percent.

The assertion that religion was an issue in 1960 does not mean that the candidates or parties themselves took stands on the matter or made it a focal point of the campaign. To the contrary, Kennedy and Nixon exercised considerable restraint and care in trying to prevent religion from emerging as an ugly, divisive issue. Nevertheless, religion was an important concern, as evidenced in a number of ways. For example, Philip E. Converse (1966b: 112–113) reports that more than half of the Protestants interviewed in the 1960 SRC election study spontaneously introduced the Catholic question, mainly in a negative fashion, suggesting its salience to many citizens.

More direct evidence is given by an analysis of the normal Democratic vote expected from Protestants and Catholics. While the normal Democratic vote among Catholics in 1960 was 63 percent, their actual Democratic vote was 80 percent. And the actual Democratic vote among white Protestants was about the same margin below normal. Finally, an examination of the voting behavior of Protestant Democrats and Protestant Independents of various degrees of religiosity, indicates that the greater the religiosity, the more marked were the departures from the expected Democratic vote. For example, Converse, Campbell, Miller, and Stokes (1966: 89) report that Protestant Independents who did not attend church split their vote almost 50–50 between Kennedy and Nixon, as expected. Among infrequent church attenders, Nixon received 61 percent of the vote; among frequent churchgoers, Nixon got 72 percent of the vote; and among regular church attenders, he received 83 percent of the vote.

Religion was an unusual issue in two respects—it had a substantial impact on vote choices and its impact did not depend on skilled exploitation of the matter by candidates. Religion was one of those few salient concerns capable of arousing many citizens even as the candidates themselves tried to ignore the matter. The novelist James Michener wrote of his experiences as Democratic county chairman in Bucks County, Pennsylvania, in 1960 and gave some vivid illustrations of the grass-roots passions that religion could arouse. Numerous anti-Catholic pamphlets were circulated, some of which Michener described as follows (1961: 91–92):

> One of the most impressive carried a cover showing a fat and apparently venal bishop on his throne, with "The Rest of Us" kneeling abjectly and kissing his foot.
>
> * * * * *
>
> One of the pamphlets . . . showed a trio of priests supervising the following tortures of Protestants: one victim was being crucified upside down; another was being hauled aloft by his hands twisted behind his back while weights were applied to his feet; a third was stretched prone while water was being forced into him.

Michener reported the following experience, which graphically illustrates the kinds of emotions and fears religion was capable of releasing (p. 293):

> In the bars in my district broken-hearted Republicans were saying, "In this election the decent people of America were swamped by the scum. It's really terrifying to contemplate the kind of people who are going to govern this nation." One man garnered a lot of laughs each Saturday by announcing, "Tomorrow attend the church of your choice . . . while you still have a choice."

At the national level the renowned Reverend Norman Vincent Peale misguidedly lent his presence to a conference devoted to such matters as the fitness of a Catholic to be president, thereby giving respectability to much of the anti-Catholic activity. This event and the obvious snowballing of religious propaganda led Kennedy to speak before the Greater Houston Ministerial Association on September 12. In discussing his view of the presidency and the relevance of his Catholicism, he said (Theodore H. White, 1961: 468):

But because I am a Catholic, and no Catholic has ever been elected President, the real issues in this campaign have been obscured—perhaps deliberately in some quarters less responsible than this. So it is apparently necessary for me to state once again—not what kind of church I believe in, for that should be important only to me, but what kind of America I believe in.

　　I believe in an America where the separation of church and state is absolute—where no Catholic prelate would tell the President (should he be a Catholic) how to act and no Protestant minister would tell his parishioners for whom to vote—where no church or church school is granted any public funds or political preference—and where no man is denied public office merely because his religion differs from the President who might appoint him or the people who might elect him.

While Kennedy's speech was received favorably by a previously skeptical if not hostile audience, it did not lead to the elimination of religious influences on citizens' candidate preferences.

The issues in 1960. Figure 5.8 indicates that domestic and foreign policy issues exercised relatively little influence on the election outcome. In fact, there was no consensus in 1960 as to which issues were crucial. Table 5.1 lists the

---

TABLE 5.1

The Five Problems Most Frequently Cited as Most Important in 1960

Problem	Party preferred on most important problem (percentage)			Total percentage	No. of cases	Percentage of electorate mentioning problem
	Democrats	No difference	Repub-licans			
Foreign affairs/ keeping peace	18%	33%	49%	100%	125	8.4%
Unemployment	72	24	4	100	102	6.8
Foreign affairs/no mention of peace	38	18	44	100	94	6.3
Keeping a position of strength	20	18	62	100	60	4.0
Negotiate with Russia	33	21	46	100	52	3.5

SOURCE: SRC 1960 election study. The table presents those five problems most frequently mentioned as the most important problem facing the nation. The percentages in the last column of the table are based upon all respondents who cited the problem, regardless of whether they could answer the question about the more preferred party.

five problems most frequently mentioned as most important in 1960, the table also indicates which party was perceived as preferable on each problem and the proportion of respondents mentioning the problem.

Note first that no problem is mentioned by as many as 10 percent of the respondents. Even though four of the five problems mentioned deal directly or indirectly with foreign affairs and national defense, their cumulative total barely represents one fifth of the electorate. This contrasts sharply with the 1968 and 1972 elections, in which 43 and 25 percent of the citizens asserted that Vietnam was the most important national problem. Further observe that in 1960 the issue of foreign affairs is cited in very general terms; there was no single, well-defined issue on which opinions had crystallized. This is not surprising in view of the various appeals made by the candidates. For example, on the question of which party could better deal with Khrushchev and the Soviet Union, the Republicans would point to Nixon's famous kitchen debate with the Soviet leader, while the Democrats would charge that the GOP had allowed our military capability and economic growth to falter, thereby making it more difficult for the United States to meet the Soviet challenge. Both candidates did their best to demonstrate that they would be firmer in dealing with the Communist bloc. The Democrats even charged the Eisenhower administration with allowing a "missile gap" to develop that threatened American security; after Kennedy became president, the missile gap mysteriously and quickly vanished.

Overall, matters of genuine public policy (as opposed to the religious issue) had little impact on the vote division in 1960. The strongest pro-Democratic force indicated in Figure 5.8 was group-related attitudes, and Kennedy on the campaign trail emphasized his ties to the Democratic party and the Democrats as the party of the average citizen. It was not unusual for Kennedy to include in his speeches such statements as the following (Marvin R. Weisbord, 1966: 411–412):

> Mr. Nixon and I represent two wholly different parties, with wholly different records of the past, and wholly different views of the future. We disagree, and our parties disagree, on where we stand today and where we will stand tomorrow. . . . Mr. Nixon and the Republicans stand for the past. We stand for the future. Mr. Nixon represents the Republican Party which has put up in recent years Mr. Dewey, Mr. Landon, Mr. Coolidge, Mr. Harding, Mr. Taft, Mr. McKinley. I represent the party which has run Woodrow Wilson and Franklin Roosevelt and Harry Truman and Adlai Stevenson.

Kennedy in general emphasized a mood, a need to sacrifice, a need to get the country moving again. As the candidate of the out party, he had greater leeway in going on the attack and challenging the GOP record of the previous eight years. As the Republican heir, Nixon both defended the record of the Eisenhower administration and promised to build on it. Despite their efforts to exploit the differences that existed between them, the candidates (particularly

Nixon in the first debate) often wound up in agreement on goals and therefore stressed differences in the means to achieve those goals. Evidently, these latter differences were not very salient to the electorate, and in many eyes the two candidates were Tweedledee and Tweedledum. Thus, the election outcome basically reflected the impact of partisanship as modified by the religious issue. This resulted in a Democratic vote somewhat lower than normal, but a Democratic victory nonetheless. Hence, the 1960 election was a maintaining election, one in which the party with the majority allegiance in the electorate captured the White House.

The Great Debates.   The Great Debates probably represent the high point in the use of television to bring the campaign to the electorate. The debates have become almost mythologized as the factor that led to Kennedy's victory; Kennedy himself is reported as saying, "It was TV more than anything else that turned the tide" (White, 1961: 353). Yet most of the available research indicates that the debates had little impact on vote choice, although that impact may have been sufficient to swing an election as close as the one in 1960.

In the debates, Kennedy and Nixon confronted one another, usually at the same studio, responding to questions from reporters and commenting on each ether's answers. This format reduced the opportunity for citizens to be highly selective in listening to the candidates; it took great effort to tune in one's preferred candidate and tune out the other. There were four debates, each devoted to various topics. Congress facilitated the debates by waiving Section 315 of the Federal Communication Act—the equal time provision; this action allowed the networks to give free time to the major party candidates without having to grant the same time to the numerous minor party contenders.

An examination of Gallup poll results just before and after the first 1960 debate indicates little net change in vote preferences. Just before the first debate, Gallup reported that Nixon was favored over Kennedy by a margin of 47 to 46 percent, with 7 percent undecided. After the first debate, Gallup found Kennedy favored by a margin of 49 to 46 percent, with 5 percent undecided (Elihu Katz and Jacob J. Feldman, 1962: 211). Thus, while it is tempting to conclude that Kennedy gained 3 percentage points because of his first debate performance, such a conclusion is risky since the observed changes could easily be accounted for by sampling error as well as by other political factors. The studies of the debates generally indicate that Kennedy "won," particularly the first debate, not because he won over many former Nixon partisans, but because he established himself as a credible, competent candidate to many citizens, including Democrats, who worried about his youth and supposed inexperience. Theodore White (1961: 349) reports that after the first debate Kennedy's crowds, already growing in size, became much larger and far more enthusiastic "as if the sight of him, in their home or on the video box, had given him a 'star quality' reserved only for heroes and movie idols." At the local level, Michener (1961: 127 128) reports that immediately after the first debate money and volunteers began streaming into campaign headquarters. Thus, one important effect of the debate may have been to rally the faithful, to increase the enthusiasm of Democrats toward the Democratic ticket.

Katz and Feldman (1962) reviewed numerous studies of the effects of the Great Debates and concluded that the first debate was won by Kennedy, the third by Nixon, while the second and fourth were even. They found that partisans tended to claim that their candidate had won the debate, although Republicans were more likely to say that Kennedy had won than Democrats were to say that Nixon had. The most ambitious research on the debates reviewed by Katz and Feldman was the four-wave panel investigation of the nation conducted by the Opinion Research Center (ORC). According to these surveys, the primary effect of the debates, especially the first, was to strengthen the commitment of partisans to their own party and its candidates. This was especially true of Democrats who had been less enthusiastic and convinced about Kennedy earlier in the campaign. Table 5.2 presents the results of the ORC surveys.

Note that only after the first debate was there a sizable advantage for either candidate. Also observe that nonviewers of the debates tended to be *less* stable in their evaluations than viewers. Katz and Feldman wrote (1962: 209):

> This is not as surprising as it sounds considering the fact that the non-viewers were far less interested in the election and far less committed to a candidate than the viewers. Previous election studies have shown that these are the people who are most open to influence, who are least likely to vote, and whose responses, in any case, are of dubious reliability.

In summary, most of the empirical research on the Great Debates argues that they changed few votes. Yet, as Katz and Feldman (pp. 211–213) point out, if people are asked whether the debates helped them make their candidate choice, they readily say yes. It is likely that most of this "help" is in the reinforcement of existing predispositions, and this may have been just what Kennedy needed to convince a sufficient number of Democrats that he was indeed a serious, legitimate candidate for the presidency. Perhaps, then, Kennedy was correct in his assertion that he could not have won without television.

1964

The landslide victory of the Democrats in 1964 is readily understandable, given the effects of the six attitudinal components depicted in figure 5.9. The Democrats were preferred on all six components, including such traditional Republican strengths as foreign affairs and government management. To run against the popular incumbent president, who had reassured the nation with his steady performance after the assassination of President Kennedy, the Republicans chose Senator Barry Goldwater of Arizona after a hotly contested,

TABLE 5.2

The Great Debates and the Stability of Attitudes
toward the Candidates, by Viewer and Nonviewer (in percentages)

	First debate		Second debate		Third debate		Fourth debate	
	Viewers	*Nonviewers*	*Viewers*	*Nonviewers*	*Viewers*	*Nonviewers*	*Viewers*	*Nonviewers*
Unchanged	58%	52%	65%	66%	73%	69%	70%	67%
Change to Kennedy	25	25	17	17	14	15	16	16
Change to Nixon	17	23	18	17	13	16	14	17
Net gain for Kennedy	+ 8	+ 2	–1	0	+ 1	–1	+ 2	–1

SOURCE: Elihu Katz and Jacob J. Feldman, "The Debates in the Light of Research: A Survey of Surveys," Table 11–7, p. 210. From *The Great Debates*, edited by Sidney Kraus (Bloomington, Ind.: Indiana University Press, 1962). Copyright © 1962 by Indiana University Press, Bloomington. Reprinted by permission of the publisher. The table entries represent the percentage of viewers and nonviewers whose attitudes toward the candidates changed or remained stable as measured along a nine-point scale.

relatively inconclusive series of primary battles that split the GOP along ideological lines. Because of the massive Republican defection from the Goldwater candidacy, Lyndon Johnson won in a landslide.

What is surprising about the 1964 election is the uncertainty in classifying it as either a maintaining, converting, or realigning election. On one hand, the majority Democratic party was victorious, and thus the election might be termed maintaining. On the other hand, the 1964 vote patterns differed dramatically from the results of the three previous presidential contests, raising the possibility that significant shifts in partisan allegiances were occurring. Thus, the following analysis of the 1964 election will focus on the candidates and issues as well as on the various interpretations of the election outcome.

The candidates and issues. Any discussion of the candidates and issues in 1964 must link the two, since Goldwater himself gave special meaning to many of the issue positions he espoused. The election outcome might be summarized with two campaign themes associated with Goldwater. The first was his promise to offer "a choice, not an echo." That is, Goldwater sought to stress his differences with the incumbent Democratic administration (as well as with

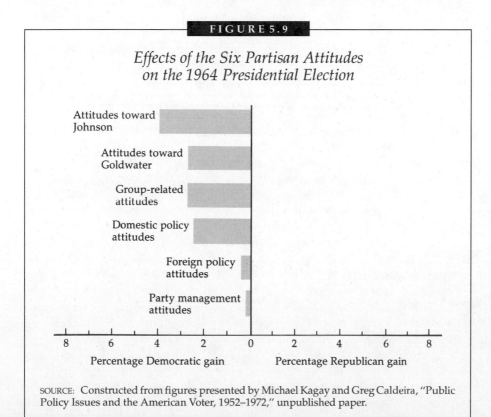

FIGURE 5.9

Effects of the Six Partisan Attitudes on the 1964 Presidential Election

SOURCE: Constructed from figures presented by Michael Kagay and Greg Caldeira, "Public Policy Issues and the American Voter, 1952–1972," unpublished paper.

previous GOP "me-too" candidates) on matters of general philosophy of government and specific issues. With respect to the former, Goldwater warned against the encroachment of government and the concomitant loss of freedom. Thus, he proposed to roll back the trend toward government intervention in society. In offering specific suggestions he made some careless comments about the possibility of making social security voluntary and selling the Tennessee Valley Authority to private interests. Hence, Goldwater, like previous Republican candidates, railed against the growth of the federal government, but unlike his precursors, he gave the impression that if elected, he would try to repeal many of the social programs of the New Deal and the Fair Deal. These positions, together with some careless statements about the use of nuclear weaponry, led many to revise the Goldwater slogan "In your heart you know he's right" to "In your heart you know he's right—far right." Goldwater was perceived as a reactionary by some and by others as a radical who would fundamentally alter the existing political and social arrangements between the people and the government. Undoubtedly, many of his issue positions, if stated more carefully by another candidate, would not have been so frightening to so many voters.

Goldwater's difficulties did not begin with the general election campaign, but in fact were a legacy of the Republican primaries and the GOP National Convention. The Republican primaries in 1964 were indecisive, with no contender having a consistently strong track record. In the first primary (New Hampshire), a write-in candidate, Henry Cabot Lodge of Massachusetts, defeated both Goldwater and Nelson Rockefeller of New York, the two major contenders, who represented the conservative and liberal wings of the GOP. In the last two primaries before the nominating convention, Rockefeller carried Oregon, while Goldwater narrowly defeated Rockefeller in the climactic California primary. But despite Goldwater's less than impressive showing in the primaries, he and his supporters were in a dominant position at the convention, in part because of superior groundwork and organization in the nonprimary states, which resulted in solid blocs of delegates for Goldwater, especially from the South. With Goldwater's nomination all but assured, the battle turned to the GOP platform, a highly conservative document that moderate and liberal Republicans wanted to modify. They proposed compromise planks on three key issues: a stronger, pro-civil rights plank (Goldwater had voted against the 1964 Civil Rights Act); a condemnation of extremist groups, such as the Ku Klux Klan, the Communist party, and the John Birch Society (the leader of which had called President Eisenhower a Communist dupe); and a statement that the president and not military field commanders should control the use of nuclear weapons (Goldwater had talked of giving field commanders discretion in the use of tactical or conventional nuclear weapons).

The moderates lost on all three issues, Goldwater won the nomination, and the stage was set for his acceptance speech, usually a statement that among other things is designed to bind the wounds of a divisive nomination

battle. Goldwater, however, did not mollify the moderates and instead exac
erbated the split with his now famous lines (Weisbord, 1966: 421):

> Anyone who joins us in all sincerity we welcome. Those, those who do not
> care for our cause, we don't expect to enter our ranks in any case. And let
> our Republicanism so focused and so dedicated not be made fuzzy and
> futile by unthinking and stupid labels.
>
> I would remind you that extremism in the defense of liberty is no
> vice!
>
> And let me remind you also that moderation in the pursuit of justice
> is no virtue!

In the context of the convention, this was a direct slap at the Republican
moderates and liberals, mostly from the Northeast, who in large part sat out
the presidential campaign.

What further hurt Goldwater was that many of the disgruntled Republicans did have someplace else to go—to Lyndon Johnson. Unlike 1960, when
Kennedy stressed that he was the nominee of the Democratic party, Johnson
in 1964 submerged partisanship to some extent as he tried to win over
Independents and Republicans to fashion an overwhelming victory. It was not
uncommon for Johnson to make such statements as the following (Kelley, 1966:
59):

> I am proud that I have always been the kind of Democrat who could work
> with my fellow Americans of the party of Lincoln and McKinley, Herbert
> Hoover and Dwight Eisenhower, Robert Taft and Everett Dirksen.

Moreover, the Democratic platform, written after the GOP fracas, included the
following planks designed to have widespread appeal to dissatisfied Republicans and worried Independents (Porter and Johnson, 1970: 642, 644–645, 649):

> Control of the use of nuclear weapons must remain solely with the highest
> elected official in the country—the President of the United States.
>
> *   *   *   *   *
>
> The Civil Rights Act of 1964 deserves and requires full observance by every
> American and fair, effective enforcement if there is any default.
>
> Resting upon a national consensus expressed by the overwhelming
> support of both parties, this new law impairs the rights of no Americans;
> it affirms the rights of all Americans.
>
> We condemn extremism, whether from the Right or Left, including
> the extreme tactics of such organizations as the Communist Party, the Ku
> Klux Klan and the John Birch Society.

Detailing the images of the candidates as ascertained in the SRC 1964
election study reveals that the controversies surrounding Goldwater were
widely visible to the mass public. Summarizing citizens' perceptions of the
candidates, Angus Campbell wrote (1966b: 260, 263):

> While Mr. Johnson's personal attributes did not stir unusual favor among
> the electorate, he profited greatly from his long experience and record as

a public official. He also drew favorable comment because of his association with the Democratic party and with the Kennedy administration. He was criticized as a "politician," "lacking in integrity," and associated with "immorality in government," these criticisms coming very heavily from the Republican partisans. . . . Mr. Johnson's stands on issues . . . were more frequently referred to than those of either candidate in 1960 and they were more commonly seen favorably than unfavorably.

. . . Mr. Goldwater was much more commonly spoken of unfavorably than favorably. While he was more often referred to as a man of integrity than Mr. Johnson, and less commonly as a "politician," in most other respects he suffered from the comparison. He was especially weak in the public assessment of his past record and experience. . . . His policy positions . . . drew an exceptional number of comments, most of them unfavorable.

Some of the more specific comments shed further light on the candidates' images. For example, 192 respondents said that Goldwater was impulsive, that he didn't think before he talked; only 1 person made this comment about Johnson. Similarly, 107 citizens thought that Goldwater was a fanatic or unstable; 1 individual thought the same of Johnson. With respect to the issue of social security, 177 people said they disliked Goldwater's stand; only 5 disliked Johnson's. More than 200 citizens said that Goldwater was too militaristic; 2 citizens offered that comment about Johnson (Campbell, 1966b: 261–262).

With respect to the issue of civil rights and the Civil Rights Act of 1964, there was widespread awareness of where the candidates stood. Civil rights was obviously a salient issue to many citizens, especially in the South, and it moved both Republicans and Democrats to desert their party's nominee. For example, about 25 percent of the strong and weak Democrats in the South, who thought the civil rights movement was being pushed too fast, voted for Goldwater; these defections constituted almost 20 percent of all southern Democrats (Campbell, 1966b: 272–273). This is not to say that civil rights was the only issue affecting the South. Philip E. Converse, Aage R. Clausen, and Warren E. Miller assert (1965: 330):

Beyond civil rights, Southerners reacted negatively to the Goldwater positions much as their fellow citizens elsewhere. Many Southern white respondents said in effect: "Goldwater is right on the black man, and that is very important. But he is so wrong on everything else I can't bring myself to vote for him." From this point of view, the civil rights issue did indeed have a powerful impact in the South; without it, the 1964 Goldwater vote probably would not only have slipped to normal Republican levels, but would have veered as elsewhere to the pro-Democratic side.

Even more dramatic than the movement of many white Southerners to the Republicans was the almost unanimous support given Johnson by black citizens. While Goldwater certainly did not seek racist support, his vote against the Civil Rights Act attracted many unreconstructed segregationists to his cause and repelled most black voters. There was substantial concern among Democrats about the potential problem of backlash—the negative reactions of white citizens to the social and economic gains made by blacks—and how it might affect the ticket's chances in November. Evidence for the existence of backlash had been provided by the strong showings made by Alabama Governor George Wallace, who entered three northern Democratic primaries—Wisconsin, Indiana, and Maryland—where he won 34, 30, and 43 percent of the vote. Wallace ran well in traditionally Democratic, white working-class neighborhoods, which raised the possibility that Goldwater might be able to fashion a majority by appealing to the South and West as well as to disgruntled urban workers—a coalition very similar to that envisaged by Democratic candidate William Jennings Bryan in 1896. The outbreak of riots in major urban areas added further fuel to the potentiality of backlash. But backlash never developed to any great extent because of Goldwater's unwillingness to exploit an overtly racial issue, the lessening of urban disorders as the presidential campaign began in earnest, and the cessation of black civil rights activities (partially under White House pressure) so as not to threaten the election of Johnson. Shortly after the Republican convention, Wallace decided not to run for president as a third-party candidate, leaving the field to Goldwater and Johnson.

In summary, there was little working for the Republicans in 1964, with the major exception of the race issue in the South, particularly the Deep South. Johnson and the Democrats, and it must be added, Goldwater himself, were successful in portraying Goldwater as outside the mainstream of American politics. Even when it appeared that a personal scandal involving a top-ranking Johnson aide might hurt the Democrats, two major international events occurred—the resignation of Khrushchev and the explosion of an atomic bomb by China—that served to turn the nation's attention away from thoughts of impropriety and toward the importance of firm but unimpulsive leadership in a dangerous nuclear age. The conservative majority was not to be in 1964.

Interpreting the 1964 election. Classifying the 1964 election is not as straightforward as one might think. Since the majority party won the election, it could be argued that it was by definition a maintaining election. But the actual vote patterns in 1964 differed substantially from those of previous elections that are classified as maintaining (1948 and 1960) and deviating (1952 and 1956). Of particular importance is the fact that the GOP ran best in the South in 1964 and worst in the Northeast, a pattern opposite to that of past elections. And within the South the Republicans ran best in the states where they had traditionally been weakest—the Deep South. Goldwater carried Mississippi, Alabama, South Carolina, Louisiana, and Georgia with margins ranging from 87 to 54 percent even as he was polling less than 40 percent of the vote throughout the nation. Moreover, the phenomenon of the South being more Republican in presidential voting than the non-South continued through the 1968 and 1972 elections but not in the 1976 and 1980 elections when Southerner Jimmy Carter was the Democratic nominee. In 1984 and 1988, the South was once again more Republican in its presidential voting than the non-South.

This reversal in traditional patterns has led some observers to argue that the 1964 election was a critical or realigning election. Gerald Pomper states this argument most directly (1972: 424–425):

> The central importance of the 1964 campaign lends support to the supposition that this election was a critical election, initiating a new political era in the United States, rather than the aberrant event it appeared at the time. A critical election, such as that of the New Deal, is one in which a deep and enduring cleavage in the electorate becomes evident. Characteristic of such elections is increased voter consciousness of policy questions, and the later electoral persistence of group divisions based on the policy questions raised in the critical election. These hallmarks of a critical period are evident in the upsurge of mass perceptions of party differences in 1964 and the persistence of these perceptions in 1968.

Yet Pomper himself recognizes that additional evidence, such as substantial shifts in party identification and the emergence of new issues, is needed to determine whether the 1964 election was indeed realigning. And the evidence relevant to party identification suggests that no major realignment took place. For example, a comparison of the distribution of party identification in 1964 and 1966 (see table 2.1) indicates a net drop of 6 percent in Democratic identification and a net increase of 1 percent in Republican identification. While these net figures may conceal additional gross change, they do not indicate any substantial shifts in partisan loyalties. A comparison of the 1964 and 1968 distributions of partisanship leads to the same conclusions.

An examination of the distribution of party identification nationally might conceal important regional differences. But even when examining the South and non-South separately, there is little evidence of any large number of changes in party affiliation. The proportion of Democratic identifiers did drop more in the South than in the non-South—10 percentage points versus 6; however, the net result was an increase in the number of Independents as the proportion of Republicans in both regions remained virtually unchanged. Additional evidence of stability (and hence no realignment) is provided by the 1966 election returns for gubernatorial and congressional races, which closely resembled the pre-1964, traditional voting patterns (Cosman and Huckshorn, 1968: 234–239).

What, then, can be concluded about the 1964 election? In the nation at large there was no major change in the strength of the parties; thus, the election might be classified as maintaining. In the South, however, there was a major change in voting behavior, though not in partisan affiliations. That change in voting behavior has continued at the presidential level, resulting in presidential Republicanism in the South. But at the state and local levels the South is still substantially Democratic. Events since 1964—for example, the 1984 and 1988 presidential outcomes in the South as well as the changed distribution of southern partisanship—suggest that in hindsight the 1964 election is better viewed as a realigning rather than a deviating election, particularly in the South. The 1964 outcome demonstrates how an issue—race—can dramatically upset traditional voting patterns when the parties offer distinctive choices on the issue. Chapter 11 returns to the question of whether the South has undergone realignment.

1968

The effects of the six partisan attitudes shown in figure 5.10 reveal that, in a two-party, two-candidate comparison, citizens gave a sizable advantage to the GOP in 1968. The Republicans enjoyed a slight to moderate advantage on all partisan attitudes except the group-benefits component. However, figure 5.10 tells only a part of the 1968 election story, since the race was a three-candidate contest, with George Wallace of the American Independent party challenging the major party candidates, Hubert Humphrey and Richard Nixon. Wallace's candidacy was certainly the preeminent feature of the campaign, and his presence contributed a second important aspect to the election, namely, the

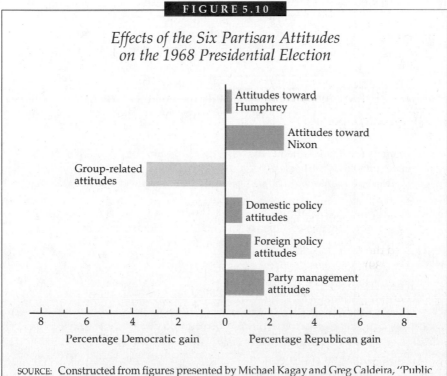

FIGURE 5.10

Effects of the Six Partisan Attitudes on the 1968 Presidential Election

Attitudes toward Humphrey

Attitudes toward Nixon

Group-related attitudes

Domestic policy attitudes

Foreign policy attitudes

Party management attitudes

8   6   4   2   0   2   4   6   8

Percentage Democratic gain   Percentage Republican gain

SOURCE: Constructed from figures presented by Michael Kagay and Greg Caldeira, "Public Policy Issues and the American Voter, 1952–1972," unpublished paper.

closeness of the outcome, given the huge early Republican lead. In discussing the 1968 election, the primary focus will be on the features just mentioned as well as on the issues raised during the campaign.

The resurgence of the Democrats.   The Democrats left their 1968 nominating convention in Chicago bitterly divided over the Vietnam War as well as the conduct of the convention itself. Hubert Humphrey, who was closely tied to the war policies of the Johnson administration, won the nomination over antiwar candidates in a strenuously fought struggle. The party was hurt further by the fact that its convention was held late in August; this occurred since the convention was scheduled when it was assumed that President Johnson would be the nominee. Hence, the Democrats had little time to heal their wounds and map strategies prior to the traditional Labor Day start of the campaign.

At one stage early in the campaign, Wallace was running a fairly close third to Humphrey in the public opinion polls, and there was much conjecture that Humphrey might even finish third in the Electoral College vote, given Wallace's presumed solid base of southern support. Humphrey's resurgence has been attributed to a number of causes. One is that many Democrats returned to the fold after toying with a Nixon or Wallace vote. This return was facilitated in the North by the activities of labor union leaders and Democratic party officials in portraying Wallace as an enemy of working people.

Lewis Chester, Godfrey Hodgson, and Bruce Page (1969) believe that it was Humphrey's September 30 Salt Lake City speech on Vietnam that marked the turning point in his campaign. After much debate among his aides, Humphrey carved out a position on Vietnam somewhat distinctive from that of President Johnson. The provisions of Humphrey's stance were as follows (Chester, Hodgson, and Page, 1969: 726):

> As President, I would be willing to stop the bombing of North Vietnam as an acceptable risk for peace, because I believe that it could lead to success in the negotiations and a shorter war. This would be the best protection for our troops.
>
> In weighing that risk—and before taking action—I would place key importance on evidence, direct or indirect, by deed or word, of Communist willingness to restore the Demilitarized Zone between North and South Vietnam.
>
> If the Government of North Vietnam were to show bad faith, I would reserve the right to resume the bombing.

This speech helped Humphrey establish his independence from Johnson, encouraged some Democratic doves to return to the ticket, and brought in badly needed campaign contributions.

The surge of Humphrey and the decline of Wallace were also facilitated by the vice-presidential candidates of the three parties. Wallace chose as his running mate General Curtis LeMay, former Air Force chief of staff. At the news conference announcing his candidacy, LeMay gave a series of responses to reporters' questions that indicated his readiness to use nuclear weaponry. Despite the effort of Wallace to minimize the impact of LeMay's statements, their effect was similar to that of similar statements made by Goldwater in 1964.

Nixon chose as his running mate Governor Spiro Agnew of Maryland, while the Democratic vice-presidential nominee was Sen. Edmund Muskie of Maine. Almost immediately, the competence and caliber of the two nominees became a campaign issue. Muskie was widely praised for his calm, forthright approach, his ability to handle protesters, and his overall performance. Agnew, however, became something of a campaign joke to many citizens, with his use of ethnic slurs and his assertions that "when you have seen one slum, you have seen them all" and "Hubert Humphrey is squishy soft on Communism." The Democrats did their best to exploit the vice-presidential issue, such as taking out full-page ads in newspapers that simply stated: "President Agnew?" Yet strategically Agnew may have been an excellent choice to appeal to southern conservative voters, thereby allowing Nixon to avoid blatant regional and ideological appeals.

On October 31, about one week before the election, President Johnson announced a halt to the bombing of North Vietnam and the commencement of peace talks the following week. Unfortunately for the Democrats, the South Vietnamese balked at this arrangement and Humphrey did not profit as much as he might have by the cessation of bombing. Theodore White (1969: 383), among others, believes that had these last-minute developments clearly indicated that peace was at hand, Humphrey would have won the election. Four years later Henry Kissinger would announce somewhat prematurely before the 1972 election that "peace was at hand" in Vietnam.

Discussion of the ebb and flow of the 1968 campaign has thus far focused mainly on Humphrey and Wallace and largely ignored Nixon. In part, this is because the Nixon campaign was primarily a holding action designed to protect the lead the Republicans enjoyed at the outset of the campaign; this description is supported by the fact that Nixon began the campaign with 43 percent of the vote in the polls and two months later received just that proportion from the voters. Political satirist Art Buchwald (1968) described a conversation between the "old" Nixon and the "new" Nixon that humorously reflected the GOP campaign:

> The "New" Nixon said, "Sit down, Dick, and listen carefully. This is a unique election situation. We don't have to attack the Democrats because they're going to make mincemeat out of each other. In order for Humphrey to get anywhere in the election he's going to have to attack Lyndon Johnson's policies in Vietnam. Then to defend himself Lyndon Johnson is going to have to attack Hubert Humphrey. Gene McCarthy will attack both of them, and all we have to do is sit back and talk about crabgrass in the United States."

In a more serious vein, *New York Times* journalist James Reston (1968) criticized Nixon for evading the issues. Reston wrote:

The Vietnam issue is probably the best illustration of the point. Mr. Nixon is exploiting it very shrewdly. He is simply saying it's a mess, which it obviously is, and holding Vice President Humphrey and the Democrats responsible for it.

He is certainly not telling us how to get out of it. He is merely refusing to discuss it on the ground that this might interfere with the Paris peace talks, and meanwhile putting out campaign TV ads showing dead American soldiers on the battlefield while a voice cries it is time for new leadership.

As the campaign drew to a close, there was increasing evidence that Nixon's campaign performance was hurting him among voters; Rowland Evans and Robert Novak (1968) reported that, based on polling conducted by the Oliver Quayle organization, "the caution with which Richard M. Nixon has pursued his meticulously planned campaign has backfired into a deepseated and probably ineradicable public belief that he is ducking the issues."

On Election Day the Republicans held on to eke out a narrow victory. Wallace carried only Alabama, Mississippi, Georgia, Louisiana, and Arkansas, while Nixon comfortably carried the Electoral College vote even as he and Humphrey almost evenly shared the popular vote. The only southern state carried by the Democrats was Texas, as a three-way split in the vote enabled Humphrey to squeak through. As in 1964, the Democrats ran best in the Northeast.

The Wallace candidacy and the issues.   The presence of George Wallace in the 1968 presidential contest marked the first serious third-party challenge since the four-candidate race of 1948. While Wallace ultimately received only 13.5 percent of the popular vote and 46 electoral votes, these figures should not detract from the importance of his candidacy. Certainly Wallace's presence hurt the Republican ticket, resulting in an election closer than it would have been otherwise. Evidence for this assertion is provided by a survey cited by Daniel Mazmanian (1974: 71), which found that "Wallace supporters overwhelmingly favored Nixon when forced to decide between the two major-party candidates; 58 percent chose Nixon, and 22 percent Humphrey." Converse and his colleagues (1969: 1090–1092) found that while Wallace voters tended to be Democrats (68 percent in the South and 46 percent outside the South), many of them preferred Nixon over Humphrey and would probably have so voted had Wallace not been running. They concluded that in a two-candidate contest Nixon would have run somewhat stronger.

As mentioned in chapter 4, the Wallace vote, in contrast to that for Humphrey and Nixon, was largely issue based, the crucial issues being Vietnam, law and order, and civil rights. In contrast to the evaluations by the citizenry of Humphrey and Nixon, evaluations of Wallace were fairly closely related to citizens' own issue stances. One reason for this was that there was far less ambiguity about where Wallace stood on the issues. More than 66 percent of the citizens saw Wallace as favoring the use of all available force to solve the problem of urban unrest, while almost 50 percent saw Wallace as favoring a complete military victory in Vietnam. Assessments of the positions of Humphrey and Nixon on urban unrest ranged over the spectrum of alternatives, with Humphrey viewed as more toward the liberal end of the continuum and Nixon as more toward the conservative end. On Vietnam, there were scant differences in popular perceptions of the stands of Humphrey and Nixon, in part because (as discussed in chapter 4) the two candidates took very similar stands.

The widespread agreement on Wallace's issue stances obviously reflects the clarity of his stands. For example, the American Independent party platform was unusually straightforward, as far as party platforms go, on a number of issues as indicated in the following passages (Porter and Johnson, 1970: 702, 715–716):

> We have seen them [the courts], in their solicitude for the criminal and lawless element of our society, shackle the police and other law enforcement agencies; and, as a result, they have made it increasingly difficult to protect the law-abiding citizen from crime and criminals. This is one of the principal reasons for the turmoil and the near revolutionary conditions which prevail in our country today....
>
> * * * * *
>
> We will then require the establishment of firm objectives in Vietnam. Should negotiations fail, and we pray that they will not fail, these objectives must provide for a military conclusion to the war. This would require the military defeat of the Vietcong in the South and the destruction of the will to fight or resist on the part of the government of North Vietnam.

And Wallace himself uttered a number of graphic campaign statements that left absolutely no doubt as to where he stood; for example, demonstrators, protesters, and the like received the following warning from Wallace: "The first anarchist who lies down in front of my automobile when I become President, that's the last automobile he'll ever want to lie down in front of."

Overall, there was substantial agreement in the electorate about what constituted the most important issues, although there was much less agreement as to the party best able to handle the problem. As table 5.3 indicates, only five issues account for almost 66 percent of the problems mentioned as most important, a situation that differs dramatically from the elections discussed previously. The Democrats enjoyed an advantage on civil rights and poverty, while the Republicans were preferred on Vietnam, public disorder, and Negro riots. Note that among those respondents who mentioned the specific problem of Negro riots, rather than the more general problem of public disorder, preference for Wallace rose to 17 percent. A poll reported by Theodore White (1969: 364) showed that more than 50 percent of all Americans thought that Wallace would handle the problem of law and order in the way it was supposed to be handled.

The racial overtones to many of the issues, which are reflected in the 1968 voting patterns, cannot be ignored. For example, about 97 percent of black

TABLE 5.3

The Five Problems Most Frequently Cited as Most Important in 1968

Problem	Party preferred on most important problem				Total percentage	Number of cases	Percentage of electorate mentioning problem
	Democrat	No difference	Republican	Wallace			
Vietnam	23%	40%	35%	2%	100%	584	43%
Public disorder	11	41	44	4	100	117	8
Civil rights/general	39	34	22	5	100	67	5
Poverty	49	30	19	2	100	59	4
Negro riots	17	26	40	17	100	47	3

SOURCE: SRC 1968 election study. The table presents those five problems most frequently mentioned as the most important problem facing the nation. The percentages in the last column of the table are based on all respondents who cited the problem, regardless of whether they could answer the question about the most preferred party.

citizens voted for Humphrey and the remaining 3 percent for Nixon. Among whites, the Democrats received about 35 percent of the vote, the Republicans 52 percent, and Wallace 14 percent. This 62 percent difference (97–35) in support for Humphrey by racial groups is a much greater difference than that associated with social class (Converse, Miller, Rusk, and Wolfe, 1969: 1085, fn. 4).

Beyond the obvious racial differences in support for Wallace, there were some noteworthy patterns among other demographic groups. Most surprising was the fact that Wallace ran best among the youngest age groups. Converse and his associates (1969: 1103) report that Wallace received 13 percent of the vote cast by citizens under thirty years of age and only 3 percent from citizens over seventy, with a regular decline in support from the intermediate age groups. The explanation given for this finding was that young people have weaker attachments to the party system and therefore are more susceptible to the appeals of a third-party candidate. Furthermore, the authors point out the fallacy of assuming that the young age groups are a homogeneous, politically liberal, college-educated collection of citizens. Certainly one implication of the age-level differences in support for Wallace is that prospective third-party candidates might look to the large bloc of uncommitted, Independent young citizens as the most likely sources of support.

As expected, Wallace ran best in rural areas and in the South, where he garnered more than 50 percent of his popular vote and all of his electoral votes. Among religious groups, Wallace ran best among Protestants; among partisan groups, he ran best among Independents and weakest among Republicans. There was a tendency for males to be more supportive of Wallace than females, and there was a pattern of greater Wallace strength among less-educated citizens. Finally, Wallace received greater support among union members than among nonunion members; in particular, his poorest showing among occupational groups came in the professional and business category (Converse et al., 1969: 1101–1102; *Gallup Opinion Index*, December 1968, p. 5).

Popular evaluations of Wallace clearly reflect his greater attractiveness to southern whites and Independents and his lesser appeal to nonsouthern whites and blacks and partisans. For example, the most frequent reason given for liking Wallace was his stand on the law and order issue, which was mentioned by almost 20 percent of Independents and 16 percent of white citizens but only 1 percent of blacks. The personal characteristics of Wallace most frequently commended were his integrity and outspokenness, each of which was cited by 5 percent of all citizens and even by 2 percent of the black respondents.

Yet the preponderant image of Wallace was a negative one, particularly among blacks. The most common hostile comments offered by blacks about Wallace centered not on his personal attributes but on his issue stances. More than 25 percent of all blacks disliked Wallace's civil rights stand and his general association with blacks; a much smaller proportion of blacks expressed dissatisfaction with his law and order stand. Almost 33 percent of black citizens said there was nothing at all about Wallace that they liked. Overall, about 10 percent of all citizens volunteered that Wallace was a bigot and racist, and at least 5 percent of the population said that Wallace was impulsive, fanatical, dictatorial, and lacking in integrity.

Interpreting the 1968 election. The Wallace candidacy was significant because of what it had to say about the possibilities of realignment. It demonstrated that millions of voters can be attracted to a third party when the two major parties are perceived as offering unsatisfactory alternatives on important issues. Yet it also suggests the vulnerability of a third-party candidate to attempts by a major party to co-opt its positions. To illustrate, one might argue that an independent candidacy by Wallace in 1964 would not have been nearly as successful since Goldwater offered a distinctive alternative to Johnson on the issues of race, and law and order. Furthermore, while Wallace attracted many voters because of the clarity and extremity of his positions, he also repelled many voters. As discussed previously, a candidate may be "right" on one issue but wrong on many others. This is especially critical for a third-party candidacy that does not have a natural partisan source of support to rely on. As an attempt to win the presidency, the Wallace candidacy fell far short. But if Wallace was attempting to serve as a broker resolving an Electoral College deadlock in favor of the candidate who promised the most, he came a lot closer to success than many observers realize. Certainly the Wallace candidacy showed that many traditional Democrats, especially in the South, were upset by the policies and priorities of the national Democratic party and its nominees, and presaged the growing Republican strength in the South in the elections of the 1980s.

1972

Figure 5.11 clearly shows the reasons for the Nixon landslide in 1972. According to the effects of the six partisan attitudes shown, the Democrats enjoy an advantage only for group-related attitudes. Perhaps the surprising feature of the 1972 election is the shallowness of the GOP victory; even as Nixon was capturing the White House, the Democrats gained two Senate seats and one governorship and lost only a scattering of House seats. This suggests that the presidential election was more a rejection of McGovern than an endorsement of the GOP. The very low voter turnout in 1972 further suggests that the voters were not wildly enthusiastic about the choices available to them.

The Nixon landslide is all the more surprising since, throughout 1971 and even into 1972, it appeared that Nixon would face a tough battle for reelection because of the nation's economic difficulties and the continued American involvement in Vietnam, albeit at a sharply reduced level. For example, in a trial run among Nixon, Muskie, and Wallace in February 1972, the Gallup poll found that Nixon held a scant 43–42 percent advantage over Muskie among registered voters, with 10 percent for Wallace and 5 percent undecided. Hence, the major focus on the 1972 election concerns how the minority party won an overwhelming victory.

The campaign. McGovern began the campaign even further behind than Humphrey had been in 1968, but unlike Humphrey he was never able to close the gap substantially. The first Gallup survey after the conventions showed Nixon leading McGovern 57 to 31, with 12 percent undecided, and the actual November vote of 61–39 did not differ much from the early poll results. Some observers argue that the Democratic ticket—in fact, any Democratic ticket—was doomed once the crippling of Governor Wallace prevented even his consideration of a third-party candidacy. The effect of Wallace on the parties' fortunes is demonstrated by what happened in the hypothetical Nixon–Muskie race cited previously when Wallace was not a third-party candidate; in such a contest, Nixon easily defeated Muskie by a margin of 52 to 41, with 7 percent undecided.

As in 1968, the Democrats left their convention a divided party in 1972. Many traditional sources of Democratic support, such as labor, were alienated by the McGovern nomination and the proceedings surrounding it. And later,

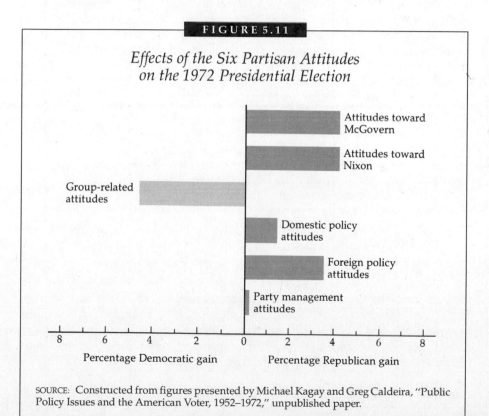

FIGURE 5.11

Effects of the Six Partisan Attitudes on the 1972 Presidential Election

SOURCE: Constructed from figures presented by Michael Kagay and Greg Caldeira, "Public Policy Issues and the American Voter, 1952–1972," unpublished paper.

when McGovern tried to make peace with disenchanted Democrats, such as Chicago Mayor Richard Daley, he received flak from ardent supporters who saw him as behaving like the traditional politicians they had opposed.

In the postconvention period, when the candidates should have been gearing up for the general election, the McGovern candidacy suffered two serious jolts from which it never recovered. The first was the disclosure that the Democratic vice-presidential nominee, Senator Thomas Eagleton of Missouri, had been treated for mental exhaustion on a number of occasions. McGovern compounded the problem by his vacillation on the issue; his statement of 1,000 percent support for Eagleton was soon followed by dropping Eagleton from the ticket. McGovern's credibility was also lessened by the Salinger affair. Pierre Salinger had talked with North Vietnamese peace negotiators in Paris at McGovern's request, but upon Salinger's return, conflicting public statements were issued by McGovern and Salinger as to whether McGovern had actually suggested the meeting.

McGovern was further hurt by his campaign's openness. The great accessibility of McGovern and his staff to the press guaranteed that all quarrels and disputes within his organization would eventually be made public. This resulted in the appearance of the McGovern organization as fragmented and McGovern as an ineffective leader. The accessibility was so great that newspaperman Timothy Crouse, upset by the isolation of the Nixon campaign, complained about the McGovern organization (1973: 361–362):

> It is one thing for a candidate to see the press frequently and answer their questions honestly, which McGovern tried to do, thereby providing an admirable contrast to the reclusive Nixon. However, it is another thing for a campaign staff to talk openly about its problems, feuds, and discontents. That is the political equivalent of indecent exposure, and the McGovern staffers indulged in it with a relish that bordered on wantonness. While the Nixon people, by keeping their mouths tightly shut, managed to keep the lid on the largest political scandal in American history, the McGovern people, by blabbing, succeeded in making their campaign look hopelessly disorganized and irresponsible.

Meanwhile, the Republican campaign was running smoothly (with the exception of the Watergate arrests) according to plans laid out months earlier. Nixon ran as the incumbent president and not as the candidate of the Republican party; in fact, his campaign was run not by any GOP committee but by his own specially created organization, the now infamous Committee for the Reelection of the President (CREEP). Nixon kept his overt campaign activities to a minimum and relied heavily on surrogate campaigners to bring the attack to McGovern. And since the McGovern campaign never got off the ground, Nixon was never forced to step down from his "above the battle" posture.

The issues.   Table 5.4 shows the five issues most frequently cited as the most important problems confronting the nation. Vietnam and inflation are obviously the most important concerns, with the GOP enjoying an advantage on each. Yet an average of almost 50 percent of the citizens saw no difference between the parties on the five issues, which may seem surprising, given that the 1972 election is commonly described as one in which one candidate (McGovern) regularly took extreme issue positions. This apparent paradox is readily resolved when we distinguish between the candidate's position and the party's position.

George McGovern was widely perceived as being to the far left on the political spectrum. This perception was probably encouraged by the California primary debates, in which Humphrey aggressively attacked McGovern's issue positions, particularly his plans for defense cutbacks and his $1,000-a-person welfare program. While McGovern did not unqualifiedly endorse "amnesty, acid, and abortion," as charged by his political opponents, his campaign rhetoric—his comparison of Nixon to Hitler, his offer to beg the North Vietnamese for the return of American prisoners of war, and the like—helped create the image of McGovern as an extremist. Evidence for this is provided by Arthur H. Miller and his associates, who found that citizens saw Nixon as closer to their own preferred issue positions than McGovern on eleven out of fourteen issues studied. Only on the questions of urban unrest, inflation, and ecological pollution was McGovern seen as closer to the citizens' positions, while on such issues as Vietnam, amnesty, campus unrest, marijuana, and desegregation, Nixon was viewed as closer to the citizens' preferences.

TABLE 5.4

The Five Problems Most Frequently Cited as Most Important in 1972

| | Party preferred on most important problem | | | | | |
Problem	Democrat	No difference	Republican	Total percentage	Number of cases	Percentage of electorate mentioning problem
Vietnam	21%	39%	40%	100%	201	26%
Inflation	24	44	32	100	104	14
Drugs	14	59	27	100	44	6
Crime	17	55	29	101	42	6
Civil rights/general	31	44	26	101	39	5

SOURCE: CPS 1972 election study. The table presents those five problems most frequently mentioned as the most important problem facing the nation. The percentages in the last column of the table are based on all respondents who cited the problem, regardless of whether they could answer the question about the most preferred party.

A normal vote analysis conducted by Miller and his colleagues (1973) showed how voters' stances on issues related to their vote decisions. For example, among voters who opposed amnesty, McGovern received only 22 percent of the vote, a full 28 percent below the normal Democratic vote. Similarly, among voters who favored a military victory in Vietnam, the normal Democratic vote was 49 percent, yet McGovern received only a scant 15 percent. And among voters who favored heavy penalties for marijuana usage, McGovern's 30 percent of the vote was fully 24 percent lower than the normal Democratic vote (p. 21). While McGovern received slightly more than the normal Democratic vote among citizens who favored amnesty, the legalization of marijuana, and immediate withdrawal from Vietnam, the number of citizens who took the extreme liberal position on these and other issues was usually small, which meant that the gains that McGovern received from citizens in these categories did not begin to balance the losses he suffered from more conservative citizens. Miller and his associates further show that the effects of issues on vote choices are even more pronounced when citizen perceptions of the candidates' stances are directly incorporated (pp. 24–28). Peter Natchez summarized the issue difficulties that McGovern encountered and how these difficulties interacted with his more general image problem (1974: 5):

> People—75 percent of them—thought that McGovern's ideas were "far out" and "impractical." He was thought to be a liberal by 31 percent; another 31 percent took him for a radical. (In contrast, only 17 percent of the electorate described themselves as liberal, and only 1 percent as radical.) The two weaknesses of George McGovern's candidacy, his "indecisiveness" and "extremism," fed on each other; his indecisiveness created an aura of impracticality around the issue positions he was trying to develop; his search for the right issues made him seem indecisive.

Watergate.   The notable point about the issues listed in table 5.4 is the one issue that does not appear there—Watergate. For a variety of reasons McGovern was unable to exploit Watergate as an issue damaging to the GOP. One reason is that the full dimensions of Watergate, especially the cover-up, were not clear by Election Day. Much of the Watergate story, however, had been reported prior to the election. *Washington Post* reporters Carl Bernstein and Bob Woodward wrote numerous stories about illegal or questionable activities of high-level Nixon aides. For example, they wrote in early October 1972 that the Watergate break-in was only a small part of a Republican plan of sabotage and spying headed by Donald Segretti. They also reported that the president's personal attorney, Herbert Kalmbach, was one of the five persons authorized to make payments to Segretti out of a secret fund. And shortly before the election, Bernstein and Woodward charged that the president's closest and most powerful aide, H. R. Haldeman, controlled a secret fund for political espionage and sabotage.

Thus, a significant part of the Watergate story was known prior to the election, and the question arises as to why the scandal had so little effect. One compelling explanation is that the sources of the Watergate news, such as the *Washington Post,* the *New York Times,* and George McGovern, were not viewed as impartial, trustworthy sources. Instead, they were seen as biased and out to "get" the president with innuendos and unproven charges. Presidential press secretary Ron Ziegler repeatedly referred to the Watergate stories as character assassination, guilt by association, shabby journalism, and the like, and even characterized the *Washington Post* as an agent of the McGovern campaign. Evidently many citizens agreed with Ziegler's characterizations, and thus the sources of most of the Watergate information were not credible to many citizens. The administration did its best to portray the *Washington Post* as a part of the liberal eastern establishment that was not to be believed. And McGovern himself was seen as a biased source since he had a direct interest in the election outcome as well as severe credibility problems of his own.

Other reasons given for the minimal impact of Watergate were that citizens viewed the matter as politics as usual, the Republicans had not done anything that the Democrats had not done in the past. Perhaps the partial exposure of the Watergate scandals led to this view; perhaps if the full story had been disclosed by Election Day, citizens might have responded differently. The Watergate story, however, was still unfolding as the election drew near, and it was submerged by the developments in the Vietnam peace negotiations and Henry Kissinger's dramatic statement that peace was at hand.

The images of the candidates. Overall, McGovern was not a very popular candidate. His mean thermometer rating was a cool 49 compared to a relatively warm 66 for Nixon. His presumed major advantage—a reputation for integrity and honesty—was quickly eroded by the Eagleton and Salinger fiascoes. A poll reported in *Newsweek* and summarized in part in table 5.5 shows the image problems that McGovern faced.

It is ironic that 40 percent of citizens would use the phrase "sticks to principles" to describe the Nixon presidency after Nixon had established peacetime wage and price controls, pursued a policy of détente with the Soviet Union, and established diplomatic contacts with the People's Republic of China. All of these policies were pursued in clear contradiction to Nixon's previous record and promises in these areas. Yet it was McGovern whom few people saw as sticking to principles because the issues on which McGovern vacillated, such as Eagleton, Salinger, and welfare reform, were simpler to comprehend, especially as the media were able to show clearly conflicting statements uttered by George McGovern within a relatively short time. Certainly the media's coverage of Nixon's foreign policy initiatives did not focus on the inconsistency of Nixon's present policies with past Nixon stands, but instead emphasized the boldness and imagination of the Nixon foreign policy maneuvers. (Chapter 9 will discuss the role the media play in structuring the public's perceptions of events.)

Interpreting the 1972 election. Some observers have claimed that the 1972 vote marked the end of the Democratic coalition of the New Deal era. There is evidence both to support and to refute this assertion, depending upon the perspective taken. It is clear that McGovern ran poorly among traditional sources of Democratic strength. For example, he received less than a majority of the vote among manual workers, members of labor union families, and Catholics; among Southerners, he received less than 33 percent of the vote. He ran strongest among blacks and Jews, though his percentages here (about 87 and 67 percent) were lower than the comparable figures for Humphrey in 1968 (*Gallup Opinion Index,* December 1972, pp. 8–10). Thus, it does appear that the New Deal coalition fell apart. From another perspective, however, McGovern ran better among components of the New Deal alliance (except for the South) than he did among groupings not considered a part of the Roosevelt coalition. The problem for McGovern was that he ran poorly among all population segments—so that even as his support coalition resembled the New Deal alliance, his level of support was so much lower than that given to previous Democratic candidates that he suffered a lopsided defeat.

Arthur H. Miller and his colleagues (1973: 35) have argued that the 1972 outcome is best explained by recourse to ideology and issues and that the

TABLE 5.5

Evaluations of Nixon and McGovern as President (in percentages)

Which of these words or phrases describe Richard Nixon's conduct of the presidency? Which would describe George McGovern's?	Nixon	McGovern
Sticks to principles	40%	17%
Strong, forceful	34	17
Thinks things out slowly	34	8
Tries to be fair	30	22
Good judgment	30	11
Forward-looking	29	26
A moderate	24	9
Puts country's interest ahead of politics	27	13
Too much of an opportunist	12	14
Weak, uncertain	7	10
Makes snap decisions	9	18
Biased, unfair	6	5
Poor judgment	11	17
An extremist	3	20
Too much of a politician	24	19

SOURCE: *Newsweek,* August 28, 1972, pp. 17–18. Copyright 1972 by Newsweek, Inc. All rights reserved. Reprinted by permission.

"effects of party identification [were] for the first time in at least 20 years slightly less potent in determining voting behavior than [were] issue attitudes." Without claiming that a realignment occurred in 1972, they point out that the potential for realignment is great so long as citizens' issue preferences and the parties' issue positions do not coincide. Yet, the evidence for realignment is at best spotty. As mentioned earlier, the outcomes of the nonpresidential races were generally favorable to the Democrats. An examination of the 1972 congressional and gubernatorial voting by elements of the New Deal coalition shows solid Democratic support. To illustrate, Catholics cast 65 percent of their vote for Democratic House candidates, 55 percent for Democratic Senate candidates, and 60 percent for Democratic gubernatorial candidates. The comparable figures were 62, 53, and 67 percent for labor union families and 69, 60, and 59 percent for Southerners. Thus, there were substantial differences in support for the Democratic party from the top to the bottom of the ticket.

Any pro-Republican realigning effects that the 1972 election may have had were probably canceled by the Watergate revelations and the economic difficulties of the mid-1970s. As these issues occupied center stage, voters became less concerned about the social issues associated with the McGovern candidacy. The 1974 election was a Democratic sweep, and particularly notable was the strong showing that the party made in the South, where many of the GOP gains of previous elections were wiped out. And, of course, in the 1976 presidential contest, the South returned home to support its native son, Jimmy Carter.

Notes

1. Goldie Shabad and Kristi Andersen (1979) show that women are not more personality oriented and less issue oriented than men in their evaluations of the presidential candidates.

2. This speculation is supported by the simulation work of Ithiel de Sola Pool, Robert P. Abelson, and Samuel Popkin, who estimated that Kennedy's Catholicism gained him 22 electoral votes even as it was costing him about 1.5 million popular votes. See Pool, Abelson, and Popkin (1965: 115–118).

The Carter, Reagan, and Bush Elections— 1976 to 1988

With the exception of the 1976 outcome, the presidential elections between 1976 and 1988 resulted in solid to landslide Republican victories. The election of George Bush in 1988 guaranteed the longest consecutive GOP control of the White House since the 1920–1932 era. In 1976 and 1980 the nation witnessed what had been a rare occurrence, namely, the defeat of an incumbent President. Ford, of course, was an unelected incumbent, but Carter's loss was the first for an elected incumbent since Herbert Hoover's unsuccessful reelection effort in 1932.

One similarity between the 1976 and 1980 elections is how the respective nominees obtained their parties' nominations. In both years the incumbent president had to withstand a serious intraparty challenge to deny him the nomination, the effect of which was to leave the party divided as it entered the general election. Ford in 1976 won a narrow majority of the delegates at the GOP nominating convention, yet it was clear that the hearts of many Republican activists belonged to Reagan. Carter faced a similar situation in 1980, his major opponent being Senator Edward Kennedy. Although Carter had a sizable delegate lead over Kennedy, the contention between the two candidates continued through the convention; the efforts made at demonstrating party unity at the end of the convention were far from convincing.

For the out party in 1976, 1980, 1984, and 1988, the situation was very different. Carter, Reagan, Mondale, and Dukakis all began their nomination quests against a large field of opponents. But early in the primary season, the field had been narrowed substantially. Carter, Reagan, and Dukakis captured their respective nominations well before the national conventions, with the result that the Democratic conventions of 1976 and 1988 and the Republican convention of 1980 were veritable love-ins in which party harmony dominated. In 1984, Mondale's battle for the Democratic nomination continued somewhat longer, although the Democrats enjoyed a surprisingly harmonious convention in San Francisco.

Yet another similarity between the 1976, 1980, and 1984 elections is the role of economic issues and evaluations of the performance of the incumbent president in shaping the election outcomes. Both Ford in 1976 and Carter in 1980 suffered from public perceptions that they had mishandled the economy and from doubts about their competence and performance as leaders. By way of contrast, Reagan in 1984 benefited from the public's evaluations of him on these topics. Indeed, a similar interpretation may be assigned to all three elections; namely, that retrospective evaluations of the performance of the incumbent presidents were a major determinant of the election outcomes. This point will be developed later in the chapter.

The 1984 election was a rerun of 1980 in the sense that Reagan faced Carter in 1980 and Carter's vice-president—Mondale—in 1984. In both years the GOP scored impressive victories—by 10 percent in 1980 and 18 percent in 1984, with overwhelming Electoral College majorities each time. Some observers viewed the 1988 contest as yet another rerun—Reagan's vice-president, George Bush, faced the "liberal" governor of Massachusetts, Michael Dukakis. The magnitude of the successive Republican victories fueled much speculation about a GOP realignment.

Hence, this chapter will examine the issues and candidates that shaped the general election outcomes in 1976, 1980, 1984, and 1988. With the exception of a discussion of the Jackson candidacy in 1984 and 1988, and Super Tuesday in 1988, emphasis will be on the general election campaigns. (Chapters 9 and 10 will explain the paths by which the candidates secured their nominations.) A final concern of this chapter will be to evaluate the alternative interpretations given to the election outcomes, particularly for 1980 and 1984.

1976

INTRODUCTION

Had any political analysts predicted in 1972 that Gerald Ford and Jimmy Carter would be the 1976 presidential nominees and that Ford would be running as the incumbent president, they probably would have had their credentials (as well as their sanity) challenged. The Republicans won a landslide victory in 1972, a victory that many observers thought foretold the emergence of a Republican majority. But the era of Republican dominance was not to be—as Richard Nixon and Spiro Agnew left office in disgrace and the unelected incumbent Ford failed in his bid to keep the presidency in Republican hands. The 1976 election provided evidence of continuity and change, the continuity arising from the restoration of a Democratic voting majority similar to the New Deal coalition, and the change represented by dramatic alterations in the presidential selection process. These changes included the increased importance of the primaries and the mass media as well as the advent of public financing of presidential campaigns—developments that enabled an unknown candidate like Carter to capture the nomination in the first place.

THE COURSE OF THE CAMPAIGN

Unlike the Democratic conventions in 1968 and 1972, the Democratic convention in 1976 was characterized by harmony and unity, while the GOP gathering was marked by rancor and divisiveness. Carter had clinched his nomination early, thereby allowing the Democrats to stage a very orderly convention, which was viewed positively by the television audience. In contrast, the Republican contest between Ford and Ronald Reagan continued right up to the convention, with Ford's victory not secured until the eve of the balloting. Although the Republicans managed a convincing display of unity on the last night of their convention, with the appearance of Reagan on the podium and the selection of Robert Dole as the vice-presidential nominee, Ford clearly began his general election effort as the heavy underdog. After the Democratic convention Carter had an amazing 33 percent lead over Ford in the Gallup poll[1] and going into the traditional Labor Day kickoff of the campaign, his lead was a substantial 18 percent (see table 6.1). The remainder of the campaign witnessed Carter trying to maintain his lead and Ford attempting to get the GOP effort rolling.

By late September and early October, Ford had dramatically closed the gap on Carter, an improvement largely attributed to Ford's performance in the first debate on September 23 and to Carter's interview with *Playboy*. In this interview Carter talked of lust and adultery, used graphic language in discussing his own views of morality, and spoke highly critically of Lyndon Johnson. The interview received substantial media coverage and served to reinforce doubts about Carter's presidential qualifications.

Throughout this period the candidates stressed very different campaign themes. Carter ran as the anti-Washington outsider who had not been a part of the mess in Washington and talked of streamlining and reorganizing government. Ford adopted a "rose garden" strategy, which had him campaigning from the White House itself, where he signed bills and made major announcements before the television cameras and in general acted "presidential." Carter's anti-Washington theme was a continuation of his nomination campaign in which he ran against the government in Washington and the traditional power brokers in the Democratic party.

Just as his campaign seemed to be moving into high gear, Ford committed a major gaffe in the second debate, when he claimed that Eastern Europe was not under Soviet domination. Compounding the error, Ford and his advisers failed to clarify his statement immediately, so that for days after the debate the Ford campaign was on the defensive. Eventually the Ford campaign moved back on track and narrowed the gap, but Carter held on to win 51 percent of the two-party vote on Election Day, a far cry from his 20 to 30 percent lead in the polls in the summer. The individual state results as well as the national outcome were close; in twenty-seven states the losing candidate got

---

TABLE 6.1

The Standing of Carter and Ford
over the Course of the Campaign (in percentages)

Date	Carter	Ford	Other	Undecided	Total
June 25–28	53%	36%	2%	9%	100%
Democratic convention					
July 16–19, 23–26	62	29	2	7	100
August 6–9	57	32	3	8	100
Republican convention					
August 20–23	50	37	3	10	100
August 27–30	54	36	2	8	100
First debate					
September 24–27	51	40	5	4	100
September 27–October 4	47	45	2	6	100
Second debate					
October 8–11	48	42	4	6	100
Mondale–Dole debate					
October 15–18	47	41	4	8	100
Third debate					
October 22–25	49	44	3	4	100
October 28–30	48	44	3	5	100
Final poll	46	47	3	4	100

SOURCE: Extracted from *Gallup Opinion Index*, No. 137, December 1976, p.13.

at least 47 percent of the two-party vote. Although there was no major third party or Independent candidacy on the scale of the Wallace effort in 1968, the presence of former Democratic Senator Eugene McCarthy on the ballot in thirty states may have kept Carter's margin down in some states and caused him to lose others. For example, Carter carried Ohio by only 11,000 votes as McCarthy was polling 58,000. Carter lost Oregon by only 1,700 votes, with McCarthy receiving over 40,000 votes. Overall, relatively small changes in the popular vote totals could have changed the Electoral College outcome dramatically.

THE ISSUES AND CANDIDATES

Although Carter and Ford did discuss issues, it is not unfair to assert that both candidates attempted to make their own qualities and personality the major theme of their campaigns. Carter emphasized his leadership abilities, promising to reorganize the government and make it more efficient. He also stressed his trustworthiness and his intention to restore morality to government and promised never to lie to the American people. Ford emphasized his integrity and decency and portrayed himself as having earned the trust of the American people by returning honesty to government after the Watergate scandals. When the candidates discussed issues, they often employed very subtle nuances of meaning. Carter was particularly skillful at this, a factor that earned him the label of being fuzzy on the issues.

Both Carter and Ford received similar overall positive ratings from the electorate, but the components of their positive evaluations differed sharply. According to Arthur H. Miller and Warren E. Miller (1977: 99), Carter was judged positively because of his personal leadership and his association with Democratic ideology and positions on domestic issues. Ironically, Carter's lack of a national record and his status as a relative unknown made it easier for voters to view him primarily in terms of his Democratic affiliation. But for Ford the positive evaluations were linked more to characteristics of the candidate himself; Ford was seen as more reliable, more decisive, and more competent in terms of previous public service.

Despite the emphasis on the personal qualities of the candidates, there were important issues in 1976, and these tended to work in favor of the Democrats. Table 6.2 presents the problems most frequently cited as most important by Americans in 1976. Note that economic problems topped the list, with unemployment and inflation running first and second, and that the Democrats enjoyed a slight to substantial advantage on all five of the issues. Certainly the one issue that Carter hammered home constantly was Republican mismanagement of the economy. Hence, one might wonder how the election outcome could have been so close, given the Democratic advantage on these salient issues and the overall Democratic advantage in the electorate. Figure 6.1 provides a partial answer.

According to figure 6.1, four of the six attitudinal components had scarcely any impact whatsoever on the vote division. In contrast are the group-related attitudes and the opinions of Ford. The former, a traditional Democratic strong point, favored the Democrats once again in 1976; voters were more likely to see the Democrats as the party of people like themselves. And attitudes toward Ford moved the vote in a pro-Republican direction to a much greater extent than attitudes toward Carter moved the vote in a Democratic direction. As Election Day approached, the economy seemed to be improving under Ford's leadership and the economic issues that were expected to benefit the Democrats lost some of their impact. Miller and Miller (1977: 109) summarized the 1976 election as "incumbent performance versus partisan ideology," with the latter narrowly emerging victorious.

According to journalist Jules Witcover (1977: 685), Ford attributed his close election loss to the "Nixon issue," particularly Ford's pardoning of Nixon. Although the pardon per se was not a continual source of debate in the campaign, there is some evidence that it might have tipped the vote outcome (as might many other issues and campaign events). Miller and Miller (1977: 73–74) show that approval versus disapproval of the Nixon pardon was associated with vote choice even when the effects of party identification were considered. For example, among the 28 percent of Republican identifiers who disapproved of the pardon, 30 percent voted Democratic, compared to only 8 percent of Republicans who favored the pardon. Likewise, among the 25 percent of Democrats who supported the pardon, 44 percent voted for Ford, compared to a Ford vote of only 12 percent among Democrats who opposed

---

TABLE 6.2

The Five Problems
Most Frequently Cited as Most Important in 1976

| | Party preferred on most important problem | | | | | Percentage of electorate mentioning problem |
Problem	Democrat	No difference	Republican	Total percentage	Number of cases	
Unemployment	49%	44%	7%	100%	668	33%
Inflation	30	48	22	100	452	22
Economics (general)	35	47	18	100	217	11
Fuel shortage/ energy crisis	44	50	6	100	112	5
Crime/violence	18	77	4	99	93	5

SOURCE: CPS 1976 election study. The table presents the five problems most frequently mentioned as the most important problem facing the nation. The percentages in the last column of the table are based on all respondents who cited the problem, regardless of whether they could answer the question about the most preferred party.

the pardon. The real effect of the pardon may have occurred long before Election Day. The pardon was overwhelmingly disapproved by Americans, and after Ford granted it, his popularity plummeted. The pardon may have depleted much of the goodwill and admiration for Ford apparent when he assumed the presidency, although in 1976 Ford was still widely perceived as a person of integrity and honesty despite the unpopularity of the pardon.

A comparison of the important issues in 1972 and 1976 (tables 5.4 and 6.2) suggests one reason the Democrats were able to oust an incumbent president. In 1972 social and lifestyle issues, such as the Vietnam War and drugs, were of great importance to the electorate. Moreover, these were issues on which Democrats were deeply divided, with large blocs favoring opposite policy alternatives. Hence, a Democratic nominee risked losing substantial support from his party's adherents should he favor one side on an issue. This, of course, is what happened to McGovern in 1972. Because his stands on a number of salient social issues were perceived as liberal, many Democrats voted for Nixon. The key point about 1976 is that while Democrats were just as divided as ever on these issues (Miller and Miller, 1977: 38–42), these divisions did not hurt the party at the polls. One reason for this was the lessened salience of social issues for the voters in 1976. And

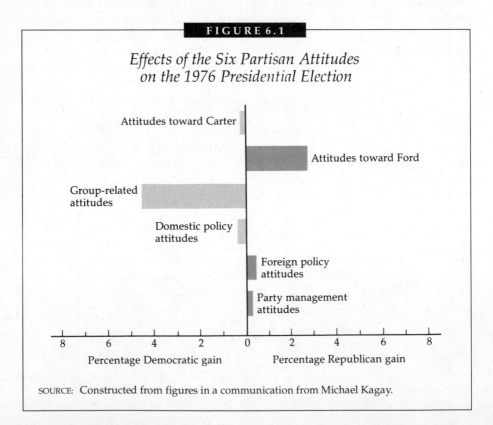

FIGURE 6.1

*Effects of the Six Partisan Attitudes
on the 1976 Presidential Election*

Attitudes toward Carter

Attitudes toward Ford

Group-related attitudes

Domestic policy attitudes

Foreign policy attitudes

Party management attitudes

Percentage Democratic gain   Percentage Republican gain

SOURCE: Constructed from figures in a communication from Michael Kagay.

this lessened salience can be attributed to the economic problems that occupied people's attention and to the fact that the candidates did not talk about social issues.

Party identification made a comeback in its impact on vote choice in 1976. Overall, the proportion of defections was down substantially from 1972; almost 85 percent of citizens with a party affiliation remained loyal to their party. Yet this does not mean that citizens were automatically following an unthinking partisan loyalty. Instead, the dominant issues in 1976 coincided nicely with the traditional stances and images of the parties and thereby made partisanship a more useful cue for vote choice than it was in 1972. Although the growth of Independents seemed to level off in 1976 (see table 2.1), there is little reason to believe that the parties were in a stronger position in 1976 than in 1972. Popular perceptions of the utility of elections and political parties remained at low levels (see figure 1.1), and evaluations of the parties continued to decline.

THE DEBATES[2]

Like the 1960 Kennedy–Nixon debates, the Carter–Ford debates were not debates per se, but rather press conferences in which both candidates were present to answer reporters' questions and to comment on their opponent's replies. As such, the debates were media events, whose coverage may have been more consequential than their actual content. There were three debates between the presidential candidates and one between the vice-presidential candidates. Viewership was high, with Nielsen ratings indicating that almost 90 percent of the electorate had seen some part of the debates and that 72 percent of all households had turned on the first debate. Prior to the debates, many studies indicated that citizens looked forward to the debates to learn where the candidates stood on issues and to obtain help in making their vote choice. Many observers expected the debates to play a critical role, particularly since more voters in 1976 than in previous elections were undecided as to their vote choice later into the campaign (see table 10.1).

Yet it appears that the debates had relatively little impact on the final outcome. According to a CBS poll (Warren J. Mitofsky, 1977) 10 percent of the voters gave as a reason for candidate choice the fact that the candidate impressed them during the debates; but a survey after the third debate found that only 3 percent of the respondents claimed to have changed their vote preference as a result of the debates. Polls taken after the debates generally agreed that Ford "won" the first debate, Carter the second and third, and Mondale the vice-presidential debate.

Voter reactions to the debates were highly influenced by the media coverage accorded them. Despite the fact that the debates had much issue content, the primary focus of subsequent media coverage was on who won, how the debates would affect the campaign, and related questions that reflect the horse race mentality (a topic that will be discussed in chapter 9). One study

(Lang and Lang, 1978) found that citizens whose reactions to the first debate were measured four to seven days after the event were much more likely to state that Ford had won than citizens whose evaluations were obtained immediately after the debate. The authors argue that the former group was swayed by media coverage of later polls that declared Ford the winner. The power of the media to structure people's judgments of political events was demonstrated clearly in the second debate, in which Ford uttered his Eastern Europe misstatement. A poll done immediately after the debate found Carter a narrow victor; but as Ford received critical media coverage over the next several days for his mistake, later polls showed that citizens viewed Carter as the overwhelming winner. Hence, "winning" a debate may be less a function of the candidate's actual performance than of media interpretation of that performance.

Generally, citizens responded to the debates in terms of their own predebate preferences and partisan predispositions. That is, people tended to claim that their preferred candidate was the winner. For example, a Roper poll (Roper, 1977) conducted immediately after the first debate found that 70 percent of predebate Ford supporters thought Ford had won and that only 8 percent thought Carter had won. Likewise, 55 percent of predebate Carter supporters thought their candidate had won, compared to only 13 percent naming Ford as the victor.

Overall, the debates seemed to have little impact on vote intention. Carter's big margin over Ford had dropped substantially prior to the first debate, and it declined further after the debate; but there is little direct evidence linking the decline to the debate. Some learning of the candidates' issue positions was attributable to the debates, but there is little evidence that this affected the vote. One study (Abramowitz, 1978) suggested the opposite causal sequence—namely, that voters moved toward the issue positions espoused by the candidate they initially favored. That is, candidate preference influenced issue stance and not the reverse. Sears (1977) summarizes the major effect of the debates as crystallizing and reinforcing prior preferences, with little real change in vote intention because of the debates. It may be that both Ford and Carter performed well enough to erase any lingering doubts that their partisans might have harbored about their competence, intelligence, and experience.

As a final point, it is questionable whether the media coverage of the debates did justice to them. Despite the high issue content of the debates, television and newspaper coverage focused disproportionately on the question of who won. In addition, there is some evidence that postdebate media commentary critical of the debates resulted in more negative evaluations of the worth of the debates on the part of citizens. And certainly the media emphasis on who won so structured citizen viewing and discussion of the debates that people became more concerned with the horse race aspect than the issue content of the debates. (Media coverage of the presidential selection process is discussed more fully in chapter 9.)

INTERPRETING THE 1976 ELECTION

According to the classification scheme described in chapter 1, the 1976 election is a maintaining election, one in which the majority party (defined in terms of psychological attachments) was actually victorious at the polls. Not only did the Democrats win, but it appears that they enjoyed considerable success in reconstructing the New Deal coalition. However, as Arthur H. Miller (1978: 146–150) cautions, the support garnered by Carter differed in a number of important respects from the Roosevelt coalition. For example, while Carter and FDR both ran strongly in the South, Roosevelt's southern base consisted of solid support from white voters in the presence of a negligible black electorate. Carter's southern base, in contrast, consisted of minority support from white voters in conjunction with overwhelming support from a vastly expanded black electorate. In addition, although Carter ran well among Catholics, a traditional pillar of the New Deal coalition, religious differences in party support were actually less in 1976 than they had been in earlier elections. Between 1952 and 1972 the average Democratic vote among Protestants and Catholics was 39 and 61 percent, a difference of 22 percent. In 1976 this difference was halved as Carter won 46 percent of the Protestant vote and 57 percent of the Catholic ballots (*Gallup Opinion Index,* December 1976, pp. 3–4). Thus, Carter's support did not have as distinctive a religious hue as that normally associated with the Roosevelt coalition.

Overall, the 1976 outcome yields little evidence of partisan realignment. Instead, it seems more reflective of traditional voting patterns. Discussion of realignment grows in importance when viewing the 1980 election. Reagan's strong showing, GOP gains in other races, the apparent rejection by the electorate of Democratic and liberal policies, and other factors have led many observers to speculate whether the 1976 election might simply have been a temporary aberration in the ultimate creation of a Republican majority.

1980

THE COURSE OF THE CAMPAIGN

In 1980 the attitudes of citizens toward the candidates were extremely volatile. This was particularly so for Jimmy Carter, who was expected to have an uphill struggle against Massachusetts Sen. Edward Kennedy for the Democratic nomination. Public opinion in the fall of 1979 showed Kennedy as the strong favorite among Democrats for the party's nomination. But by early 1980 Carter had become favored. This development was attributed to the following events: (1) the seizure of American diplomats by Muslim fundamentalists in Iran at first rallied popular support for Carter as the incumbent president; (2) the Soviet invasion of Afghanistan also tended to tilt public support toward Carter; and (3) Kennedy had a disastrous television interview with Roger

Mudd during which Kennedy had a hard time articulating why he should be the Democratic nominee. In addition, Kennedy was put on the defensive concerning his behavior about ten years earlier when he drove a car off a bridge on Chappaquiddick Island, and a young woman in the car drowned.

Nevertheless, evaluations of Carter had again declined by the end of the primary season. As a result, Kennedy was able to defeat Carter in five of the eight primaries held on the last day of the primary season, including the important primaries in California and New Jersey. A series of national polls conducted by CBS News and the *New York Times* clearly documented these swings in Carter's popularity. In October 1979, 31 percent of Americans approved of Carter's performance, 49 percent disapproved, and the rest were undecided. By January 1980, Carter's popularity had soared, with 52 percent approving his performance and 30 percent disapproving. But by the end of the primary season, Carter's standing had plummeted once again; 30 percent of Americans approved his performance, and 60 percent disapproved. Nevertheless, Carter had acquired enough delegates to assure himself a first-ballot victory at the Democratic convention.

The volatility of voters' reactions to the candidates continued throughout the summer, but during the fall preferences seemed to stabilize as a small margin separated Carter and Reagan in the polls from mid-August until the final poll (see table 6.3). The most dramatic trend throughout this period was the continued decline in support for John Anderson, the Independent candidate, a decline that probably reflected the return of voters to their party and the popular belief that a vote for Anderson would be wasted.

Throughout the general election campaign, there were minor spurts and surges by Carter and Reagan, often in response to gaffes and miscalculations by the other candidate. Early in the campaign Reagan made a number of misstatements that the Carter organization quickly exploited; in particular, Reagan's comment that Carter had begun his campaign in the birthplace of the Ku Klux Klan was skillfully rebutted. In late September and early October the Carter campaign began using very harsh words to describe Reagan and his policies. This was done in an attempt to focus voters' attention on Reagan and away from Carter, who did not want the election to become a referendum on his performance. Carter's popularity had dropped sharply, because voters were upset by the state of the economy and the continuing hostage crisis in Iran. Hence, it seemed to be good strategy to go on the attack against Reagan. To Carter's misfortune, however, the media focused less on the merits of Carter's accusations and more on their tone. The issue quickly became the meanness of Carter and the nastiness of his campaign tactics. For a while a Carter attack on Reagan's policies was viewed as additional evidence of Carter's meanness. Needless to say, this temporarily set back the Carter effort.

The Carter organization began complaining publicly that Reagan was getting a free ride from the media. Shortly thereafter, the press and television began a series of in-depth analyses of Reagan's positions that suggested that some of the issue stances held by Reagan during the general election were not consistent with positions he had espoused in the past. By mid-October Carter was once again leading narrowly in the public opinion polls, with momentum seemingly on his side.

At this stage the Reagan strategists, seeing that their candidate was not moving up in the polls, made a critical decision to debate Carter in a head-to-head confrontation in late October. In retrospect, strategists for both parties agree that this was the critical event of the campaign—the Carter–Reagan debate accounted for much of the last-minute surge in Reagan support.

There were a number of risks for Carter in agreeing to debate. Given his flawed performance as the incumbent president, the debate would be a prime opportunity for the challenger to go on the attack. Probably the most telling point of the debate occurred in Reagan's closing comments, in which he said:

> Next Tuesday is Election Day. Next Tuesday all of you will go to the polls, will stand there in the polling place and make a decision. I think when you make that decision, it might be well if you would ask yourself, are you better off than you were four years ago? Is it easier for you to go and buy things in the stores than it was four years ago? Is there more or less unemployment in the country than there was four years ago? Is America as respected throughout the world as it was? Do you feel that our security is as safe, that we're as strong as we were four years ago? And if you answer all of those questions yes, why then, I think your choice is very obvious as to whom you will vote for. If you don't agree, if you don't think that this

---

TABLE 6.3

The Standing of Carter, Reagan, and Anderson over the Course of the Campaign (in percentages)

Date	Carter	Reagan	Anderson	Other/ undecided	Total
Mid-June	35%	33%	24%	8%	100%
Late June	32	37	22	9	100
Mid-July	34	37	21	8	100
Republican convention					
Early August	29	45	14	12	100
Democratic convention					
Mid-August	39	38	13	10	100
Mid-September	39	39	14	8	100
Mid-October	44	40	9	7	100
October 25–26	45	42	9	4	100
Carter–Reagan debate					
October 29–30	43	44	8	5	100
Final poll	44	47	8	1	100
Actual election result	41	51	7	1	100

SOURCE: Constructed from various issues of *Gallup Opinion Index*.

> course that we've been on for the last four years is what you would like to
> see us follow for the next four, then I could suggest another choice that you
> have (*Congressional Quarterly Weekly Report*, November 1, 1980, p. 3289).

These words probably crystallized voter frustration with an incumbent president plagued by lingering domestic and foreign policy crises.

Another advantage of debating for Reagan was the opportunity debating gave him to dispel perceptions that he was uninformed and reckless, particularly on matters of foreign policy, and war and peace. Throughout the debate Reagan appeared as the calm, informed person of reason who gently chided Carter each time Carter attacked him. Certainly the debate did much to reassure voters about Reagan's competence to be president. In mid-1983 it became known that the Reagan camp had improperly obtained a copy of the briefing book used by Carter to prepare for the debate. Although the briefing book was undoubtedly helpful to the Reagan team as it coached its candidate for the debate, it is not likely that the Reagan camp's possession of the briefing book affected the outcome of the debate in any significant way.

Hence, an election that seemed to be close turned into a near landslide on Election Day. According to the pollster George Gallup, Reagan's huge victory reflected one of the most dramatic shifts ever observed in voters' preferences in the last week of a campaign. Abramson, Aldrich, and Rohde (1982: 55–56) argue that the polls indicating a close contest were probably accurate when conducted; they simply did not capture many of the last-minute changes. Yet even when the polls were indicating a close popular vote contest, the prospects of a Reagan victory seemed high because of the arithmetic of the Electoral College. Reagan had a fairly solid base of support west of the Mississippi River and was making inroads in parts of the country like the South and the industrial Midwest in which a Democratic candidate had to run well in order to win nationally. As the election turned out, both the popular vote and the Electoral College vote reflected an impressive Reagan victory. Yet earlier in the campaign it had seemed possible that the winner in the popular vote might be the loser in the Electoral College vote.

THE CANDIDATES AND ISSUES

Figure 6.2 presents an evaluation of the Democratic and Republican candidates in 1976 and 1980. Note that both Reagan and Carter were relatively unpopular candidates in 1980 in comparison to Ford and Carter in 1976, with Carter's evaluation dropping more sharply between 1976 and 1980 than the decline from Ford to Reagan. These negative evaluations of the candidates in 1980 help explain why each nominee tried to make the other candidate the issue and why Carter did not want the election to turn into a referendum on his presidency.

Figure 6.3 shows the effects of the six partisan attitudes on the 1980 election outcome. Note that the net effect of the candidates was negligible; this simply reflects the overall lack of enthusiasm for both nominees. Also observe that domestic policy attitudes, which in the past had often been a Democratic strength, were a strong Republican advantage, as were foreign policy attitudes. One surprising aspect of figure 6.3 is that overall the components are relatively balanced and give little indication of the magnitude of the Reagan victory. One reason is that the effects of the Anderson candidacy, which most observers believe hurt Carter more than Reagan, are ignored. Another reason is that the components do not sufficiently take into account the salience of the specific factors that each component comprises. The election of 1980 was an issues election, with the economy (inflation/unemployment) dominant in the domestic policy realm and Iran preeminent in foreign policy. And as shown in table 6.4, the Republican party was strongly preferred on these issues. Indeed, on every issue listed in table 6.4, including unemployment, which had been a traditional Democratic strength, voters opted for the Republican party. Table 6.4 makes it clear that the record of the Carter administration with respect to the economy and the hostage crisis was a tremendous liability to carry throughout the campaign.

INTERPRETING THE 1980 ELECTION

The interpretation of the 1980 election has been a controversial topic among politicians and pundits, although political scientists have reached a fairly broad consensus as to what the election signified. For obvious reasons Repub-

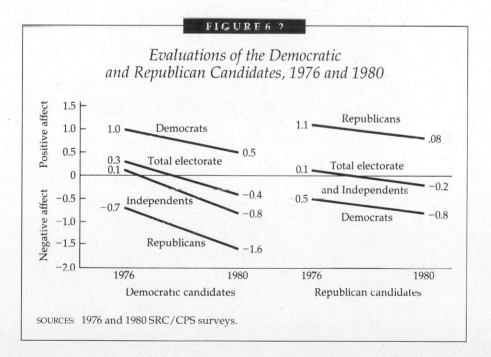

FIGURE 6.3

Evaluations of the Democratic and Republican Candidates, 1976 and 1980

SOURCES: 1976 and 1980 SRC/CPS surveys.

licans and conservatives prefer to view the election as a mandate for a shift to rightist public policies and as a realignment of American politics that would result in the domination of electoral politics by a conservative majority. In addition to the presidential outcome, conservatives point to the GOP capture of the U.S. Senate and Republican gains of more than thirty seats in the House as evidence that the Reagan victory was part of a conservative tide and not simply a rejection of Jimmy Carter. Finally, conservatives point to the gains in party identification made by the GOP in the early months of the Reagan administration as additional evidence that fundamental shifts in partisan allegiances were occurring.

Democrats and liberals, in contrast, prefer to interpret the election as a rejection of Jimmy Carter because of his handling of the economy and the hostage crisis. They attribute the Democratic congressional losses to Reagan's coattails or to Carter's negative effect on the rest of the Democratic ticket. Democrats and liberals also cite the surge in Democratic affiliations in late 1981 and the Democratic congressional advances in 1982 as evidence that there was no inexorable conservative tide sweeping the country.

Which of these two contending interpretations is better supported by the evidence? Political scientists clearly opt for the second interpretation, namely,

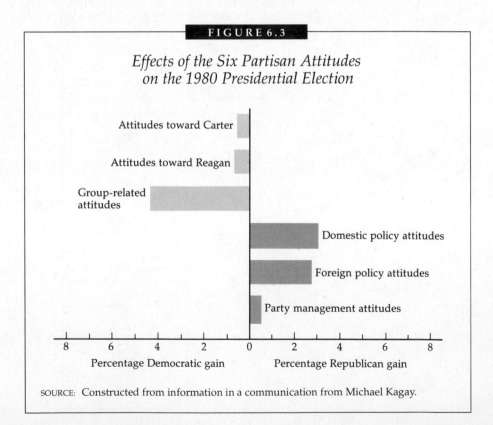

FIGURE 6.3

*Effects of the Six Partisan Attitudes
on the 1980 Presidential Election*

Attitudes toward Carter

Attitudes toward Reagan

Group-related
attitudes

Domestic policy attitudes

Foreign policy attitudes

Party management attitudes

| 8 | 6 | 4 | 2 | 0 | 2 | 4 | 6 | 8 |

Percentage Democratic gain   Percentage Republican gain

SOURCE: Constructed from information in a communication from Michael Kagay.

that the 1980 election was a rejection of the Carter presidency and not a mandate for conservative public policies. Political scientists described the election outcome as a negative retrospective judgment of the performance of the Carter administration. Since voters were dissatisfied with that performance, they chose to oust the incumbent. This is not to say that the public remained as supportive of liberal programs and an activist national government as they had been in the past. Indeed, there is evidence that on a number of issues, including whether the federal government had become too powerful, there were sizable shifts in opinion in the conservative direction. Warren E. Miller and J. Merrill Shanks (1982) distinguish between the individual decision to vote for Reagan or Carter versus the collective vote outcome. They argue that negative evaluations of Carter's performance were more important than any conservative tide in explaining individual vote choice, although citizen desires for conservative changes in certain policy areas helped shape the aggregate vote outcome. They conclude that there was no electoral mandate for the economic program the Reagan administration subsequently submitted to Congress.

Other scholars are more emphatic in rejecting a mandate–realignment interpretation of the 1980 election and in opting for an explanation based on unsatisfactory presidential performance. Paul R. Abramson, John H. Aldrich, and David W. Rohde (1982: 141–158) argue that retrospective evaluations of Carter's performance, especially in the economic sphere, accounted for his defeat. Gerald M. Pomper also rejects a realignment interpretation. He points out that features typical of a realigning election, such as increased turnout, differential vote shifts among groups within the electorate, and the presence of a highly popular victorious candidate, were not present in 1980. His analysis of the vote on the basis of ideology and partisanship revealed very similar

TABLE 6.4

Five Problems Most Frequently Cited as Most Important in 1980

| Problem | *Party preferred on most important problem* | | | | | *Percentage of electorate mentioning problem* |
	Democrat	*No difference*	Republican	*Total percentage*	*Number of cases*	
Inflation	6%	42%	52%	100%	413	32%
Iran hostages	12	54	34	100	180	15
Unemployment	18	56	26	100	107	9
National defense	5	33	62	100	79	6
Economy	8	31	61	100	36	3

SOURCE: 1980 CPS election study.

patterns in 1976 and 1980 and did not reflect any basic shift in partisan attachments. William Schneider (1981), Arthur H. Miller and Martin P. Wattenberg (1983), and Douglas A. Hibbs, Jr., (1982) all see the 1980 election as a repudiation of the Carter administration. Everett Carl Ladd, Jr., (1981) reached a similar conclusion and argued that it is difficult to bestow a mandate today, given the continued dealignment and increased volatility of American politics.

Polls conducted immediately after the 1980 election provided little evidence that Reagan had received a mandate at that time. A CBS News poll found that the reasons most often given for voting for Reagan were a general belief that it was time for a change, a widely shared perception that Carter had done a bad job, and a feeling that the economy was in poor shape. Clearly, all these reasons are examples of a negative reaction to the incumbent's performance. In this same poll, almost 40 percent of Reagan's voters chose him because they did not like the other candidate. Moreover, a plurality of the sample thought that there were no important differences in what the parties stood for, a belief that undermines any interpretation of the election as a clear choice between liberalism and conservatism. In fact, only 50 percent of the sample regarded Reagan as a conservative; the rest thought he was a moderate or a liberal or had no opinion.

An ABC News Election Day exit poll yielded similar results. Almost 50 percent of the respondents described Carter as a weak leader, while 33 percent said he would not get things accomplished. Other polls showed that there was little to no increase in the proportion of citizens calling themselves Republicans or conservatives. On many issues voter attitudes had remained fairly stable, often on the liberal to moderate side of the issue, particularly with respect to lifestyle matters. Voters may have become more conservative on certain issues, but on others their views remained essentially the same as they had been four years earlier. Hence, it is difficult to find support for a mandate–realignment interpretation in all of these studies. Clearly, evaluations of Carter's leadership and performance played the major role in the election of Ronald Reagan.

THE GENDER GAP

Carter ran poorly in 1980 among many of the traditional components of the Democratic coalition (see table 3.6). Nevertheless, his support coalition still resembled the traditional New Deal groupings. There was, however, one feature of the 1980 vote that represented a departure from past voting patterns, namely, the fact that men and women differed markedly in their presidential vote preference. Most surveys of the 1980 electorate showed Reagan leading Carter by about twenty percentage points among men but by less than 8 percent among women. For example, the CPS national election survey showed men preferring Reagan over Carter by 56 to 36 percent, while women opted for Reagan by a much smaller 48 to 43 margin. Although differences in presidential voting by sex had shown up in previous presidential elections (for example, 1964, 1968, and 1972), the 1980 differences were larger in magnitude and seemingly more enduring.

Thus was born the gender gap, and since 1980 the gap has manifested itself in a variety of ways. The gap was evident in the 1982 congressional elections; polls conducted by CBS, NBC, and ABC all showed that women were more likely than men to support Democratic congressional candidates, the average difference being about 5 percent *(Public Opinion,* December–January, 1983, p. 4). Arthur H. Miller and Oksana Malanchuk (1983) also observe a gender gap in the 1982 congressional elections. They found that women voted about 6 percent more Democratic than men in all congressional districts taken together, but in districts without an incumbent running the gender gap increased to 16 percent.

The gender gap has also appeared in ratings of the performance of the president. Typically, Reagan's approval was 8 to 10 points higher among men than among women, a difference much more pronounced than that observed for previous presidents. In a similar fashion, the gender gap is now also observed in the distribution of party identification. According to Kathleen Frankovic (1982) and Miller and Malanchuk (1983), a gap in partisanship developed in the early 1980s, so that the party preferences of men are now measurably different from those of women. For example, Frankovic found that women were about 8 percent more Democratic than men in 1982.

The gender gap also showed up in the 1984 presidential election and the 1986 congressional elections. The CBS News/*New York Times* general election exit poll in 1984 showed men voting for Reagan over Mondale by a 61 to 37 percent margin while women supported Reagan by the lesser margin of 57 to 42 percent. The ABC News exit poll indicated a somewhat larger gap; men supported Reagan over Mondale by 62 to 38 percent, women by only 54 to 46 percent. In the 1986 U.S. House elections the ABC News exit poll found men voting 53 to 47 percent in favor of the Democrats and women voting 58 to 42 percent Democratic. The CBS News/*New York Times* exit poll revealed a 51 to 49 percent Democratic advantage among men and a larger 56 to 44 percent Democratic lead among women. Both polls found a gender gap with respect to party identification. The ABC News poll found that 41 percent of the men identified themselves as Democrats and 37 percent as Republicans, while 48 percent of the women called themselves Democrats and only 33 percent identified themselves as Republicans. In the CBS News/*New York Times* survey men divided evenly between the Democratic and Republican parties (36 to 36 percent), while women preferred the Democrats by a margin of 43 to 33 percent. Finally, the ABC News poll showed a marked gap in which party was seen as best able to handle the problems most important to citizens; men preferred the GOP by a 56 to 44 percent margin, while women chose the Democratic party by a 53 to 47 percent margin.

Depending on which surveys are examined, the gender gap in the 1988 presidential campaign ranged from 4 to 10 percent. For example, in the

American National Election Studies survey, Bush and Dukakis split the female vote, but Bush carried the male vote by about 56 to 43 percent. Earlier in the campaign, the gender gap was much larger. Bush did a good job of stressing issues such as education and child care, and that helped reduce the gap. Dukakis was not very effective in reinforcing his initial strong support among women. Finally, the results of the 1990 midterm elections also revealed a modest gender gap. In the exit poll conducted jointly by the major television networks and the major newspapers, the gap ranged from 5 points in voting for the U.S. House and the governorships to 8 points in U.S. Senate contests.

Finally, the gender gap is also evident in attitudes on public issues. In its April–May 1982 issue, *Public Opinion* reviewed a vast collection of public opinion surveys, dating back to 1948, to discover the historic dimensions of the gender gap. In general, there were scant differences in men's and women's political attitudes from the late 1940s through the mid-1970s, the major exception being issues related to the use of force. Women were more likely to reject the use of force, either in foreign affairs (for example, fighting an all-out nuclear war or living under communist rule) or in domestic policy (for example, capital punishment). By the late 1970s, however, gender differences in new issue areas had arisen and differences on the force dimension had increased.

Public Opinion discussed compassion and risk dimensions, and confidence in the political system. Various polls indicate that the position of women is more compassionate than that of men on a variety of issues. For example, 73 percent of women, compared to 61 percent of men, endorsed the position that the government should work to substantially reduce the income gap between rich and poor. On the risk dimension, women were less likely to favor risking environmental pollution by relaxing environmental standards. With respect to confidence in the system, women seemed more pessimistic about the country's future and more likely than men to assert that the country was in serious trouble.

Hence, there seems to be a gender gap, and the question becomes: What is the source of the gap, and what is its future? Miller and Malanchuk (1983) analyzed the gender gap in the 1982 election and found that demographic variables, such as age, education, and work status, did not account for the observed differences. In addition, personal economic anxieties also failed to account for the gap even though women were particularly vulnerable to recession and to policy decisions of the Reagan administration. Instead, according to Miller and Malanchuk, women seemed to be affected more by "a compassionate concern for the welfare of people in general" (p. 18) than by their own financial situation. Why women were more compassionate was a question not directly addressed by the authors, but one plausible explanation would refer to distinct socialization experiences of women that may produce more nurturant and concerned persons.

Frankovic (1982) also analyzed the sources of the gender gap and found that many likely explanatory factors, such as age, education, economic status, and even one's position on women's issues, did not account for male–female differences. Two factors that did help account for gender differences in voting behavior were attitudes on war-and-peace issues, an area in which men and women have differed for years, and attitudes on the environment, a new area of difference between the sexes. Gilens (1988) agreed in part with Frankovic; Gilens found that the gap in Reagan's performance ratings in 1982 was affected by military and defense policy attitudes as well as social welfare and economic concerns. Other issues such as women's rights and the environment and demographic differences contributed little to explaining the gap.

Many questions remain unanswered about the gender gap, including its durability and its significance. Some observers view the gap as a transitory phenomenon, a short-term response to the politics of the Reagan administration. (Some of the studies cited previously would seem to belie this notion.) Other observers recognize the gap, but argue that it is less important than other cleavages observed in voting behavior—for example, racial, religious, and socioeconomic cleavages. It seems to me that the gender gap is a significant political phenomenon for at least two reasons. Efforts to account for male–female differences on the basis of other demographic differences between the sexes have generally failed; men and women seem to differ genuinely on certain political matters. Conover (1988) argued that feminism accounted for much of the gender gap in public opinion. She concluded that the gender gap is less a difference between all men and all women than a gap between men and *feminist* women, women who identify themselves as feminists. On almost every issue she examined, Conover found a gap between men and feminist women, but none between men and nonfeminist women.

Second, the gender gap is significant because politicians believe it to be so. Typically, the gender gap is considered to be an opportunity for the Democratic party and a problem for the GOP. The usual question raised is why the Republican party does less well among women. But the reverse question could also be asked—why is the Democratic party doing less well among men? This is the perspective taken by Daniel Wirls (1986), who argues that the gender gap is the result of differential movement by men and women away from liberal values and the Democratic party. He asserts that the gender gap was created by a greater shifting of men than of women to the GOP and conservative positions; hence, the Republican party has been the beneficiary rather than the victim of the gender gap.

One final point is worth stating. Although there is a gender gap, there is not a monolithic, liberal, women's voting bloc. Indeed, as mentioned earlier, although women were less likely to vote for Reagan than were men, a majority of women in 1980 and 1984 did support Reagan. Linda Bennett (1986) argues that one reason for this is that women tend not to identify with their gender in a political sense. However, Arthur Miller, Anne Hildreth, and Grace Simmons (1986) argue that women are increasingly making the link between their own social situation and the world of politics, and that increased politicization among women can be expected in the future. To the extent that an increased and unified gender consciousness occurs among women, the prospects for a women's voting bloc will be enhanced.

1984

THE COURSE OF THE CAMPAIGN

As table 6.5 shows, Reagan consistently led Mondale in the polls. Thus an election that in 1983 seemed to be closely contested by the Democrats ended up as a landslide reelection for President Reagan. Perhaps no Democrat could have beaten Reagan, since the economy was performing well and the president had a strong reputation for integrity, leadership, and competence. Nevertheless, Mondale's prospects were made poorer by the process through which he secured the Democratic nomination. He was seen by many as the candidate of special interests, especially of organized labor, a charge repeatedly leveled by his main Democratic challenger, Gary Hart of Colorado. Mondale was often depicted as pandering to the various Democratic constituency groups, and his selection of U.S. Representative Geraldine Ferraro of New York as his running mate was seen by some critics as additional evidence of Mondale's catering to various societal groups.

After an unusually harmonious Democratic convention in San Francisco, in which Ferraro's selection both unified and energized the Democratic party for the general election campaign, the Mondale effort immediately encountered problems. These difficulties destroyed any momentum that the convention might have generated. The business dealings and tax returns of Ferraro's spouse came under fire. Although Ferraro was ultimately credited for her handling of the situation, the Democratic team lost critical weeks and enthusiasm during the summer.

Thus, at the traditional Labor Day start of the general election campaign, most polls showed Reagan leading Mondale by twenty percentage points. Probably the major source of excitement during the campaign was the two presidential debates and the one vice-presidential encounter. In the first debate, the president performed poorly, raising publicly the question of whether his age was catching up to him. As is typical of campaign events in general, the public's reaction to the first debate was much influenced by the media's reporting. A *New York Times*/CBS News poll of Americans conducted right after the debate showed Mondale the victor by a narrow 9 percent margin. But as the media focused on the president's weak performance over the next few days, a later *New York Times*/CBS News poll showed Americans thought Mondale won the debate by a 66 to 17 margin, with the rest calling it a tie.

Because of the first debate, the Mondale campaign gained a bit of momentum, the gap between the candidates narrowed slightly in some polls, and attention turned to the second presidential debate and to the question of whether the president would have another bad night. Fortunately for the Reagan campaign, the president was in better form. Pundits unanimously agreed that Reagan had done well enough in the second debate to dispel any of the concerns about his capacity for office raised by the first debate. The Reagan–Bush team held onto its big lead and scored a smashing victory on Election Day.

THE CANDIDATES AND THE ISSUES

An examination of the issues deemed most important by Americans in 1984 and the party they thought would do a better job on these issues (see table 6.6) might lead to expectations of a closer outcome than actually occurred. On two of the five issues—unemployment and nuclear war—the Democratic party was favored, while the GOP was favored on the other three. However, a comparison of the five most important issues in 1984 with those in 1976 (table 6.2) and 1980 (table 6.4) indicates that there was no dominant issue or two in 1984 as there had been in the previous two elections. In 1976 unemployment was cited by 33 percent of Americans as most important, followed by 22 percent who mentioned inflation, while in 1980, 32 percent cited inflation and

---

TABLE 6.5

The Standing of Reagan and Mondale over the Course of the Campaign (in percentages)

Date	Reagan	Mondale	Other/don't know
June 6–8	53%	44%	3%
June 22–25	55	38	7
June 29–July 2	51	43	6
July 6–9	54	38	8
July 13–16	53	39	8
Democratic convention			
July 27–30	53	41	6
August 10–13	52	41	7
Republican convention			
September 7–10	56	37	7
September 21–24	58	37	5
September 28–October 1	55	39	6
First Reagan–Mondale debate			
October 15–17	58	38	4
Second Reagan–Mondale debate			
October 26–29	56	39	5
Final poll	57	39	4

SOURCE: Extracted from *Gallup Report*, Number 230, November 1984, p.5.

9 percent unemployment. Certainly inflation and unemployment are the two pocketbook issues that hit closest to home to Americans, yet they were mentioned as the most important problem by only 16 percent of Americans in 1984. This low total obviously reflects the economic recovery of 1983 and 1984 and the concommitant rise in President Reagan's popularity throughout this period. Thus an ABC News Election Day exit poll showed that 49 percent of the electorate felt they were better off financially than they had been four years ago; 84 percent of this group voted for Reagan. Among the 31 percent of the voters who were in the same financial shape as four years earlier, 56 percent supported Reagan. Only among the 20 percent of voters who said they were worse off did Mondale run strongly, winning 85 percent of their vote.

The issue mentioned most often in table 6.6 was the deficit, yet this proved to be a source of frustration to Mondale and the Democratic party. Americans who thought the deficit was the most important problem preferred the GOP by an almost two to one margin as the party better able to handle the deficit despite the fact that the national debt had nearly doubled during Reagan's first term. In his acceptance speech at the Democratic convention, Mondale pledged to seek a tax increase to help reduce the deficit. This stance was quickly turned against him as Reagan promised no tax increases, arguing that the deficit could be managed by economic growth and spending cuts.

After the economy, Reagan's major advantage rested not in specific issues but in the feeling of pride and confidence he fostered in his fellow citizens. Certainly this was tied to the economic recovery, but it also went beyond that—to a reaffirmation of American values and patriotism of which the president was the embodiment. One set of Reagan's commercials—"It's morning again in America"—depicted Americans at work and play, feeling good about themselves and their country. The Olympic Games in Los Angeles

---

TABLE 6.6

Five Problems Most Frequently Cited as Most Important in 1984 (in percentages)

| Problem | Party preferred on most important problem | | | | | Percentage of electorate mentioning problem |
	Democrat	No difference	Republican	Total percentage	Number of cases	
Deficit	20%	43%	37%	100%	337	18%
Unemployment	33	48	19	100	206	11
Nuclear war	35	44	22	101	148	8
Prevent war	21	49	30	100	122	7
Inflation	16	49	36	101	84	5

SOURCE: CPS 1984 election study.

became another outlet for the surge in national spirit. Thus, the message of the Republicans and Reagan was one of optimism and opportunity. It was left to the Democrats and Mondale to be the messengers bearing the bad news about those left behind by the economic recovery, about the spiraling arms race, and about the huge federal deficit. As is often the case with the bearer of bad tidings, the messenger was rejected.

Because of Mondale's traditional liberal position and the popular perception of him as the candidate of special interests, he was perhaps not the strongest opponent to challenge an incumbent president in a time of prosperity. Adding to Mondale's woes was the president's advantage in the personal characteristics of leadership and competence. Even on issues in which citizens disagreed with the president, a substantial proportion still supported Reagan's reelection.

One issue that arose at this time and may be a harbinger of future conflict for the political parties was the role of religion and religious leaders in politics. Reverend Jesse Jackson and the black churches were major actors in the Democratic nomination contest. In the general election the role of the religious right in shaping the Republican platform and aiding the Reagan candidacy became a source of controversy. The candidates talked about the separation of church and state, abortion, and other religious matters. Raising the specter of certain religious groups using the government to impose their view of morality on others, Mondale affirmed his belief in the strict separation of church and state. Reagan decried the effort to separate religion and religious values from politics. Although religion per se probably influenced few votes directly, there were strikingly different voting preferences among different religious groups. Unlike most blocs of voters, Jews were weaker in their support of Reagan in 1984 than in 1980, a shift in part attributed to Jewish concerns about attempts to Christianize America by using the GOP as the vehicle for this objective. Overall, Jews favored Mondale by a two to one margin; Catholics preferred Reagan by about a three to two margin; white born-again Protestants chose Reagan by a four to one margin; and other white Protestants supported Reagan by a more than two to one split (Clymer, November 25, 1984).

THE JACKSON CANDIDACY

Although Jesse Jackson was not the first black presidential contender, his candidacy was the first to receive sustained and serious attention. The Jackson effort violated many traditional rules of presidential selection, particularly with respect to its staying power in the face of few outright electoral victories. As the initially large Democratic field was winnowed down, the Jackson candidacy remained alive, along with Hart's and Mondale's, long after the demise of the Glenn, Cranston, Hollings, Askew, and McGovern efforts. Jackson received almost 20 percent of the total vote cast in Democratic primaries, won two primaries outright (District of Columbia and Louisiana), and obtained more than 25 percent of the vote in four other states (New York,

Tennessee, Maryland, and North Carolina). Although Jackson received a smaller percentage of convention delegates than popular votes (a source of complaint on his part), he did receive almost 500 delegate votes for president at the Democratic convention and delivered a major prime-time address.

Jackson attempted to build a multiracial, multiethnic "Rainbow Coalition," although the coloration of his core support group was heavily black. His candidacy was marked by controversy because of his relationship to the demagogic and anti-Semitic black Muslim leader, Louis Farrakhan, and because of Jackson's own comments about Jews. The Jackson candidacy accomplished much. First, it demonstrated that a black candidate could win substantial support, albeit primarily from black citizens. Nevertheless, that served notice on the Democratic party that it must remain attentive to the needs of blacks and minorities. Clearly the Jackson candidacy tried to pull the Democratic party to the left in its policies and programs, an electoral position that generally was not supported by moderate and conservative white Democrats. Hence, the Jackson effort pointed up the diversity of the groups comprising the Democratic coalition and the difficulty faced by the party and its nominee in building and maintaining a coalition that can win both the nomination and the general election.

It seems clear that had Jackson not been in the race, Mondale would have clinched the nomination earlier and perhaps been in a stronger position in the general election. Mondale was forced to tread a fine line in dealing with Jackson's candidacy. Too much accommodation to Jackson might lose Mondale the support of moderate and conservative Democrats; too confrontational an approach might alienate a critical part of the Democratic coalition—black voters.

Finally and most fundamentally, the Jackson candidacy raised the issues of race relations and class conflict in American society. His candidacy sought the support of a diverse set of citizens, including the impoverished underclass and liberal critics of American domestic and foreign policy. The Jackson candidacy tried to demonstrate that while it might be "morning again in America," it was not so for all of the nation's citizens.

INTERPRETING THE 1984 ELECTION

As happened with the 1980 election, there has been controversy about how to interpret correctly the 1984 election. Conservatives claim that the election was a mandate for continuing and expanding a conservative agenda, while liberals dismiss the election outcome as simply a reflection of the president's personality and leadership style.

It seems clear that the election was not a classical mandate for at least two obvious reasons. One is that the president himself did not articulate any coherent agenda to which the voters might respond. Without such an agenda, it is difficult to demonstrate popular support for a set of policy objectives. More important, on many issues a plurality and even a majority of citizens disagreed with the president. Yet in a number of cases, a substantial proportion of citizens who disagreed with Reagan's stance supported him for reelection.

If the election was not a mandate for conservative policies, what was it? Probably the best way to view it was as a referendum on the incumbent administration. Voters asked themselves if they were satisfied with the Reagan administration and resoundingly answered yes. Or, to use a different termi-nology, the voters made a retrospective evaluation of Reagan's first four years and decided that a second term was in order. Clearly the core elements in this positive evaluation were the solid performance of the economy and the president's leadership traits.

One final question remains about the 1984 election: Did it consolidate a Republican realignment that had begun in 1980 or even earlier? Certainly the 1984 results once again emphasized the Electoral College advantage enjoyed by the GOP in presidential elections. So long as the Republican party enjoys solid support in the states west of the Mississippi and is able to carry the South handily as it has done in recent years, the prospects for the Democratic party to secure an Electoral College majority and win the presidency are highly problematical. At the individual level, a number of polls conducted in 1984 showed the GOP almost wiping out the Democratic advantage in party identification. In terms of voting behavior, young citizens in 1984 supported the president more than older citizens. Hence, the future seems bright for the GOP as this young cohort matures and replaces the more Democratic older cohorts. However, the Iranian arms scandal and growing doubts about the future of the economy have resulted in a resurgence of Democratic party loyalties. And the Democratic recapture of the U.S. Senate by a surprisingly large margin in 1986 also diminished talk of a GOP realignment. In 1988, the GOP captured the White House for the third consecutive time and for the fifth time in the last six elections, thereby raising once again the question of whether a Republican realignment had occurred.

1988

THE COURSE OF THE CAMPAIGN

The 1988 presidential campaign was dismaying, not because it was unduly negative, but because it was often irrelevant to the issues facing the United States. The agenda of the general election was dominated by the Bush cam-paign, which skillfully defined Michael Dukakis as an out-of-the-mainstream liberal with respect to core values and concerns of the American people. Thus, the Bush campaign focused heavily on the Willie Horton incident, the Pledge of Allegiance, and Boston Harbor but said little about the developing savings and loan crisis, the budget deficit (except for the slogan "Read my lips, no new taxes!"), or the profound political and economic upheavals going on in the

Soviet Union and throughout the Eastern bloc nations. Horton had committed a rape in Maryland while on a furlough from prison in Massachusetts and became the focal point of the GOP effort to portray Dukakis as soft on crime. The fact that Horton was black and brutalized a white family gave added drama to this story. Likewise, the fact that Dukakis had vetoed a bill mandating recital of the Pledge of Allegiance in Massachusetts provided Republican operatives the chance to subtly and not so subtly raise questions about Dukakis's core values and patriotism. Moreover, the "Boston Harbor" ads run by the Bush campaign did a marvelous job of turning attention from the weak environmental record of the Reagan-Bush administration to environmental problems of Governor Dukakis's own backyard.

The effort to brand Dukakis as an extreme liberal was successful, in part because of the brilliance of the Bush campaign team, which included media and strategy wizards Roger Ailes and Lee Atwater. Indeed, Buchanan (1991) showed that much of what Americans learned about Dukakis over the course of the campaign came from Bush campaign commercials. The ineptitude of the Dukakis campaign's response to the Republican attacks also contributed to Dukakis's defeat. For weeks, Dukakis allowed himself to be a punching bag as Bush defined Dukakis and liberalism for the American people. Dukakis lamely tried to argue that the election was about competence, not ideology, and gave Bush free rein to define the terms of the campaign debate. Too often when Dukakis did try to counter the Bush attacks, his response was weak and legalistic (as on the Pledge of Allegiance controversy) and failed to recognize the emotional impact of the issues Bush had raised. Probably the epitome of Dukakis's inability to comprehend the emotional dimensions of issues occurred at the beginning of the second debate when CNN reporter Bernard Shaw asked Dukakis (an avowed opponent of the death penalty) how he would feel about the death penalty for someone convicted of the rape and murder of his wife. Dukakis responded in a very calm and legalistic fashion, repeating his opposition to capital punishment and displaying no passion or emotion about the hypothetical situation that Shaw had presented. Almost every observer of the debate agreed the Dukakis should have expressed some gut-level, impassioned reactions and then repeated the reasons for his opposition to capital punishment. It was not until the last two weeks of the campaign that Dukakis identified a theme—populism—that stirred his audiences and allowed him to go on the attack. Dukakis resurrected traditional appeals and images of the Democratic party as the party of the working man. Dukakis emphasized that he was on the side of the working- and middle-class citizens in contrast to his opponent, who favored the rich. Dukakis's class-based appeals had some effect as the actual Bush margin was less than predicted in the polls, and many key states were decided by relatively narrow margins. Nevertheless, this populist appeal was a little too late; the Bush campaign had done the superior job of defining the issues and the candidates.

Table 6.7 presents the standing of the candidates over the course of the campaign. Note that a Dukakis lead of 14 percent in early June had shrunk to

6 percent in early July as the Bush campaign went on the attack early. But after the Democratic convention, the Dukakis lead ballooned to 17 percent, a margin that vanished after the GOP convention. As the campaign moved into October, the Bush lead widened, which gave rise to many horse race stories that argued that Dukakis could not win. Buchanan's (1991) content analysis of media coverage in the 1988 campaign showed that across multiple media more than 36 percent of all stories between September 8 and November 8 focused on the campaign horse race. And when one looked at broadcast news separately, the percentage of horse race stories was even higher, approximately 60 percent on CBS, NBC, and ABC; 66 percent on CNN; but "only" 39 percent on PBS. Probably the most publicized piece of broadcast horse race journalism occurred on ABC News the evening before the second debate. In a fifty-state review of the likely Electoral College outcome, the ABC report showed that the Dukakis campaign was in even worse shape than had been indicated by the popular vote projections in the public opinion polls. This ABC analysis in turn generated many other stories about the dim prospects for the Dukakis campaign.

THE CANDIDATES AND THE ISSUES

An analysis of the issues cited by Americans as most important in 1988 and of the preferred party on those issues (see table 6.8) helps explain the comfortable

TABLE 6.7

The Standing of Bush and Dukakis over the Course of the Campaign (in percentages)

Date	Bush	Dukakis	Other/undecided
June 10–12	38%	52%	10%
June 24–26	41	46	13
July 8–10	41	47	12
Democratic convention			
July 22–24	37	54	9
August 5–7	42	49	9
Republican convention			
August 19–21	48	44	8
September 9–11	49	41	10
First presidential debate			
September 27–28	47	42	11
October 7–9	49	43	8
October 21–23	50	40	10
Final poll	53	42	5

SOURCE: The *Gallup Report*, Number 278, November 1988.

GOP victory. Note that the issue cited as the most important issue facing the nation was the budget deficit. This is somewhat surprising since both candidates studiously avoided saying much about the issue, Bush claiming that economic growth would resolve the problem and pledging no new taxes, and Dukakis vowing to first go after tax cheats and stating that tax increases would be a last resort. Note that a majority of Americans thought there was little difference between the parties on this issue, but among those who did have a preference, it was almost two to one in favor of the GOP. Hence, a stronger Dukakis emphasis on the deficit might not have been sound election strategy.

The next most cited issue was drugs, but neither party enjoyed much of an advantage on this issue. The final three issues—unemployment, housing, and poverty—were all problems in which the Democrats were much preferred over the Republicans. But relatively few Americans named these three concerns as being the most important ones facing the nation; therefore, there was little Democratic gain on these issues. The absence of any foreign policy issues in table 6.8 as well as the scant reference to unemployment and inflation (which did not even make the top five list) suggest that the GOP had the themes of peace and prosperity going for it in 1988.

The Bush strategists recognized that although peace and prosperity were popular legacies of the Reagan administration, there were some features of the Reagan record that were potential liabilities. In each case, the Bush campaign got out in front on these issues and neutralized subsequent Dukakis attacks. In particular, Bush boldly claimed that he wanted to be the environmental president. Bush put Dukakis temporarily on the defensive with his strong criticisms of the condition of Boston Harbor. The Bush strategists also realized that the Reagan record on education and child care could hurt them, so they had Bush present carefully crafted proposals on these topics and vow that he

---

TABLE 6.8

Five Problems Most Frequently Cited as Most Important in 1988 (in percentages)

	Party preferred on most important problem					Percentage of electorate mentioning problem
Problem	Democrat	No difference	Republican	Total percentage	Number of cases	
Deficit	15%	57%	28%	100%	491	30%
Drugs	19	69	13	101	210	13
Unemployment	46	40	14	100	77	5
Housing	44	44	12	100	61	4
Poverty	39	56	5	100	61	4

SOURCE: CPS 1988 election study.

wanted to be the education president as well. Thus, the Bush effort tried to anticipate and neutralize Democratic attacks on certain issues. With peace and prosperity favoring the Republican ticket, the remaining factor that could strongly affect the election outcome was the leadership attributes of the candidates.

Early in 1988, many Democrats were secretly rooting for George Bush to win the GOP nomination. They believed that Bush would be seen as weak on the characteristics of leadership. The wimp factor, his unusual mannerisms, and unfavorable comparisons to Ronald Reagan led many Democrats to argue that Bush was not "presidential" and could therefore be beaten by a strong Democratic nominee, even during a time of peace and prosperity. Early in the general election campaign, Dukakis was seen as that candidate, a perception reflected in the polls showing Dukakis in the lead. But much of this early advantage was squandered as Dukakis, who was a newcomer on the national political scene, allowed the Bush campaign to define him to the American public. Before long, it was Dukakis who was seen as weak, and personally unappealing, while the nation got to see the new, strong and tough, yet personable and caring George Bush. Thus, the Bush campaign was very successful in drawing a negative portrait of Dukakis on both personal and policy grounds.

The plight of the Dukakis campaign was typified by the contrast between and the reactions to the vice-presidential candidates. Bush shocked political observers by picking as his running mate Dan Quayle, a relatively obscure U.S. Senator from Indiana. Shortly after his selection, Quayle came under fire because of the use of family influence to get into the National Guard during the Vietnam War, his mediocre college performance, and the general impression that he was a spoiled rich kid who had things handed to him throughout life. The controversy surrounding Quayle reached a frenzy with commentators speculating whether Bush would drop him from the ticket. In contrast, Dukakis's selection of Texas Senator Lloyd Bentsen was widely praised, even though the two men differed substantially on certain issues. The comparison between Bentsen and Quayle came to a head in the vice-presidential debate when Bentsen uttered his now famous lines in response to Quayle's comparing himself to President Kennedy: "Senator, I knew Jack Kennedy. Jack Kennedy was a friend of mine. Senator, you're no Jack Kennedy." Public opinion polls conducted after the debate showed Bentsen to be the big winner.

Yet the contrast between the vice-presidential candidates did not benefit the Dukakis campaign as much as might be expected. Indeed, in some ways, Bentsen's overall performance served to diminish Dukakis's standing as a would-be president; many observers, including some Democrats, wished that Dukakis and Bentsen could change positions on the Democratic ticket. The bottom line for many citizens was that when one voted, one voted for a president and not a vice-president. And on the presidential comparison, Dukakis came up short in the view of many citizens.

THE NOMINATION CAMPAIGNS IN 1988

The nominating system in 1988 once again witnessed great change, the major thrust being grouping many southern primaries on the same date to create a southern regional primary relatively early in the primary system. Moderate and conservative Democrats were tired of the Democratic party nominating liberal candidates who would then get clobbered, especially in the South, on Election Day. Because the South was seen as more hospitable territory for moderate candidates, the southern regional primary on "Super Tuesday" was created. Unfortunately for Democratic proponents of the plan, Super Tuesday did not work exactly as planned. The southern results did have the intended benefit of promoting the candidacy of Tennessee Senator Albert Gore, who had not contested the earlier Iowa precinct caucuses and the New Hampshire primary. But the other two winners on Super Tuesday were Michael Dukakis and Jesse Jackson. And as subsequent primaries moved back to the north and the west, Gore was quickly eliminated, leaving the contest to Dukakis and Jackson. Jackson's presence made Dukakis seem less liberal than he was and perhaps set the stage for the Bush campaign to define the real Dukakis later in the campaign. Moreover, the Jackson candidacy in 1988 enjoyed even more success than in 1984, so that Jackson was a major player at the Democratic convention. Indeed, Jackson was the focal point of the convention for its first three nights, which hurt the Dukakis candidacy in the long term, particularly as the issue of Jackson's role in the Dukakis campaign remained a topic of controversy.

On the Republican side, Bush had the nomination wrapped up by Super Tuesday. But the Bush campaign got off to a very rocky start in the Iowa precinct caucuses, where he finished third behind victorious U.S. Senator Bob Dole and evangelist Pat Robertson. The next contest was the New Hampshire primary, a make or break state for Bush. In a preview of what was to come in the general election, Bush campaigned sharply against Dole and won the primary. From then on, Bush had clear sailing to the nomination.

INTERPETING THE 1988 ELECTION

George Bush's victory in 1988 was the third consecutive GOP presidential victory and the fifth in the last six elections. Once again the South went solidly for the Republican ticket, thereby demonstrating the difficulty Democrats have in putting together an Electoral College majority based upon an industrial, large-state strategy. Certainly Bush benefitted by popular evaluations of the Reagan administration and perceptions of Bush as the heir to Reagan. Positive retrospective evaluations of the performance of the Reagan administration and lack of confidence in what the Democrats and a Dukakis administration had to offer certainly contributed much to Bush's win. Moreover, Bush profited by the changed distribution of partisanship in the United States, especially the growth of Republican party identification among white citizens, particularly in the South. Hence, the three presidential elections of the 1980s show that the GOP has become the dominant party in presidential politics.

Yet one is hesitant to say that a classical realignment has occurred because growing GOP strength is still not reflected in many other election outcomes. Indeed, despite Bush's sizable victory in 1988, the Democrats actually gained seats in the House and Senate. In fact, in the three most recent congressional elections, 1986, 1988, and 1990, the Democratic party has gained in all of them. And although Bush was clearly the heir to Reagan, he did try to distance himself from the Reagan administration in a number of specific policy areas, such as the environment and education, and did not espouse the strident anti-government philosophy so prevalent in the Reagan years. Hence, many conservatives felt uncomfortable with Bush and the directions in which he might try to move the GOP. Meanwhile, the Democratic party demonstrated once again in 1988 that its heterogenous composition and the primary- and caucus-based nominating system make it difficult to produce a nominee with widespread appeal to the disparate party faithful and to Independents. The future of the political parties and the question of realignment will be discussed further in the last chapter.

Notes

1. This margin was artificially inflated by the fact that the Republican nominee had not yet been selected, and that the Carter–Mondale ticket had just gotten the traditional boost in the polls that presidential candidates get immediately after their nomination. Moreover, many Ford and Reagan supporters claimed that they would vote for Carter should their own candidate not win the GOP nomination, a situation that further increased Carter's lead. Most Reagan supporters returned to the fold and supported Ford, although in election postmortems many Ford backers expressed the view that Reagan himself could have worked much more strenuously for the Republican ticket.

2. Parts of this discussion of the debates are based on review essays by David O. Sears (1977), Stephen H. Chaffee (1978), and Sears and Chaffee (1979). In addition, two books that contain many of the major studies of the 1976 debates are available; see Sidney Kraus (1979) and George F. Bishop, Robert G. Meadow, and Marilyn Jackson-Beeck (1978).

Candidates & Elections

CHAPTER 7

Elections: From Citizens to Candidates

This chapter has two major aims: to summarize briefly the relative importance of issues, candidates, and party identification on vote choice and to discuss the linkages between these determinants of the vote and the conduct of campaigns. Unfortunately, there are a number of difficulties in determining the precise and unique effects of party identification, issues, and candidates on vote choice. One problem is that party identification and issue and candidate attitudes may be so interrelated that it is not possible to assess their separate effects. For example, many voters viewed Carter in 1980 as a weak and ineffective leader. This description of Carter would appear to be a candidate-centered attitude, yet its underlying rationale may be dissatisfaction with the economy, an issue concern. As another example, Philip E. Converse and his colleagues (1970: 42, fn. 4) report that one negative comment often made about Goldwater in 1964 was that he was "impulsive." Yet it was not entirely clear whether the impulsiveness resided in the candidate or in the policies he espoused. In a similar vein, party identification may have a strong issue component to it, particularly for those persons who identify with a party largely because of issues and ideology. For such people a "party" vote may in actuality be an issue vote.

Evaluations of candidates often have a strong issue and partisan component that may be indistinguishable from candidate qualities. This notion is supported by the research of Herbert F. Weisberg and Jerrold G. Rusk (1970), who found that the contenders for the presidential nominations in 1968 were evaluated in both partisan and issue-related terms. Contenders such as Humphrey and Nixon, who had been on the national scene for some time and who were considered national leaders within their respective parties, were evaluated primarily in partisan terms; that is, Democratic identifiers tended to evaluate Humphrey positively and Nixon negatively, while the reverse held for Republican identifiers. The partisan component was weaker and the issues relatively more important for such challengers as Rockefeller, Romney, and McCarthy, who in 1968 were somewhat out of step with their respective parties, in part because of the issue positions they espoused. And with respect to a candidate such as Wallace, who rejected the two major parties, issue positions were a strong determinant of evaluations.

Yet another problem in assessing the impact of candidates, issues, and party identification is that their effect on vote choice may be both direct and indirect. For example, in the diagram of the vote decision (figure 7.1), party identification has a direct impact on vote choice as well as an indirect impact via its effect on issue attitudes and candidate attitudes. Likewise, issue attitudes have a direct effect on vote choice and an indirect effect operating through candidate attitudes.

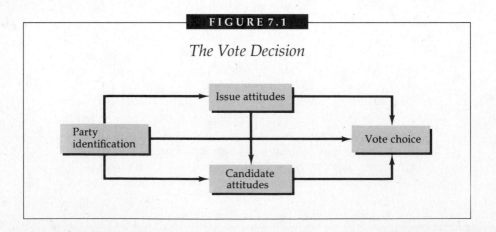

FIGURE 7.1

The Vote Decision

Hence, the total effect of any variable on vote choice includes its direct and its indirect effects. In the accompanying diagram the indirect effect of party identification on vote choice is a function of the assumption that partisanship affects issue and candidate attitudes, and not the reverse. Some scholars argue that the diagram should be made more realistic by allowing linkages from issue and candidate attitudes back to party identification, a linkage from candidate attitudes back to issue attitudes, and even linkages from vote choice to the other variables. Examples of such research are discussed in the next section of this chapter.

A final difficulty in assessing the impact of issues on vote choice is that they can have both a short-term and a long-term effect on elections. While the impact of issues in any specific election may be relatively unimportant, the long-term effect may be very consequential. As Richard Boyd argues (1969: 510):

> The impact of issues, while rarely great at any single moment, accumulates over a period of time. Overall, issues may outweigh candidates in affecting the outcome of elections, for issues have the capacity to alter the greatest single determinant of a vote, party identification.

The Impact of Candidates, Issues, and Party Identification

When one examines how political scientists have viewed presidential elections since 1952, one observes both continuity and change. The continuity is represented by the repeated finding attesting to the importance of candidate evaluations throughout this era. Even in the 1950s when stronger party loyalties were prevalent in the electorate, candidate evaluations were a very important factor in determining the election outcomes (Schulman and Pomper, 1975; Hartwig, Jenkins, and Temchin, 1980). Indeed, Eisenhower, the candidate of the minority party, could not have been elected in 1952 and 1956 had he not enjoyed a substantial advantage in popular evaluations of himself versus his opponent. In contrast, the importance of party identification as a factor influencing the vote has gradually diminished in the past four decades as the extent and intensity of party loyalties have weakened. Nevertheless, partisanship remains an important factor in presidential campaigns.

The importance of issues has fluctuated the most over the 1952 to 1988 period. Issues were of greatest importance in 1964, 1972, and 1980, elections characterized by distinct alternatives. In those elections (especially the first two), voters widely viewed one of the candidates as offering a clear ideological choice—Goldwater in 1964 and Reagan in 1980 providing a conservative alternative, and McGovern in 1972 providing a liberal option. In the other elections citizens often did not perceive the issue stances of the candidates to be very different, and candidate attitudes and partisanship played a more prominent role in vote choice. For example, in 1976, both candidates—Carter and Ford—were relatively new to the national scene, both were unassociated with specific policy positions, and both chose to emphasize aspects of their personality and character as reasons to vote for them.

Thus, the importance of candidate attitudes provides continuity across presidential elections that were very diverse in many ways. It is the candidates who are most likely to be the "new" elements in any election. Hence, the nomination of an attractive candidate (however that is defined) is crucial for electoral success. That is, it is extremely difficult in any single election to dramatically alter the existing patterns of partisan allegiances or to change the generalized images of political parties; the one element most susceptible to change is the perception voters have of the candidates. The ability of the Bush campaign in 1988 to redefine Michael Dukakis for the American electorate exemplifies the potential short-term volatility of candidate images, especially for candidates who had not previously been prominent on the national scene.

Recent analyses of presidential elections reflect the importance of candidate evaluations. Political scientists have increasingly come to view elections as candidate-dominated choices in which the effects of other variables, such as party identification and issue attitudes, are channeled through candidate evaluations. Moreover, candidate, issue, and partisan attitudes are increasingly viewed as having mutual or reciprocal effects on each other in contrast to the simple situation depicted in the diagram on page 200. For example, Gregory B. Markus and Philip E. Converse (1979) argue that the major effect of issue preferences, candidate personality, and party identification is to jointly shape candidate evaluations, which in turn directly affect vote choice. Likewise, Benjamin I. Page and Calvin C. Jones (1979) see comparative candidate evaluations as the most immediate determinant of the vote decision; these evaluations in turn are influenced by issue considerations and party identification.

Donald R. Kinder and Robert P. Abelson (1981) analyzed the trait judgments made by a sample of citizens about the 1980 presidential contenders and found that citizens evaluated the candidates along the two general dimensions of competence and integrity. In their general vote model, candidate competence and integrity along with positive and negative affect toward the candidates were the most immediate determinants of the vote decision. The effects of policies, party identification, and national economic conditions were indirect, channeled through appraisals of the candidates. Miller, Wattenberg, and Malanchuk (1986) elaborated on the Kinder and Abelson work and argued that the criteria of competence, reliability, and integrity were enduring ones that had structured candidate evaluations over the 1952–1984 period. Hence, Miller and his colleagues assert that the standard treatment of candidate evaluations as "idiosyncratic responses to superficial criteria" must be revised. They propose a reconceptualization in which candidate assessments are based primarily on perceptions of how the candidate will perform, or has performed, in office. For Miller and his colleagues, candidate-based voting has a rational foundation; it is not simply a gut reaction to a candidate's personality or appearance.

Thus, for many analysts of elections the candidates have become the central phenomenon of presidential campaigns. And elections themselves are increasingly viewed as retrospective evaluations of how the incumbent has performed in his or her first term. If there is no incumbent seeking reelection, then elections are viewed as prospective assessments of how the candidates will perform should they win office. In 1988, Bush was not the incumbent, but came from the incumbent administration. Hence both retrospective and prospective evaluations affected the election outcome. Bush benefited from positive feelings toward the Reagan administration and also from comparative assessments of him and his opponent. The impact of issues and party identification will vary, depending on the political climate. For example, when salient issues arise that are not readily linked with the stances of the two major parties, issues will play a greater role in vote choice and party identification will play a lesser one. But when issues that traditionally separate the parties dominate in an election or when there are few issues, partisanship will play a more prominent role. In contrast to the variability of party identification and issues, candidate evaluations will remain important in most elections. This is particularly the case in view of the heavy media emphasis on the candidates as they seek the presidency. Thus, the remainder of this book will focus on elections from the perspective of the candidate.

From Citizens to Candidates

Voting patterns and the importance of party loyalties and issues in elections are often explained by referring to the "nature of the times." But a nature-of-the-times explanation is incomplete. Issues do not arise out of nowhere, and their ultimate resolution is not a foregone conclusion. Instead, the positions and behaviors of candidates and parties significantly determine both the development and the outcome of controversies over issues. Specific candidates may emerge in times of crisis, and the stance of the candidates will determine in part voter perceptions of the seriousness of problems. For example, one might speculate that if Senator Eugene McCarthy of Minnesota had not challenged President Johnson's renomination in 1968, the depth of anti-Johnson sentiment among Americans might never have been uncovered. As a result, the nation might instead have had a Johnson–Nixon–Wallace race in 1968. And what if George Wallace had chosen not to run in 1968? Would the internal contradictions in the Democratic party have produced another Wallace? Would the choices offered to the electorate in 1968 have been more distinctive or less so?

The point is that the behavior of political elites does make a difference in the alternatives available to the electorate and in the response of the electorate to these alternatives. In fact, the very selection of a candidate may introduce issues and concerns into an election that otherwise would not have impinged upon the voter's consciousness. For example, the selection of John Kennedy as the Democratic nominee in 1960 introduced the question of religion into the campaign and affected the votes of millions of citizens. Similarly, certain candidates possess characteristics that facilitate or hinder their ability to make specific kinds of appeals to the electorate. Another example is the failure of the Democrats to make more of an issue of the Watergate scandal in the 1972 presidential election. Some observers point out that George McGovern, the Democratic nominee, was not the best candidate to exploit this issue—partly because of his highly strident campaign style and partly because of his being tagged as a radical. Moreover, certain candidates may be more appropriate, that is, have a greater chance of success, under certain circumstances. One might argue that Lyndon Johnson accurately read the mood of the electorate after Kennedy's assassination by emphasizing continuity, consensus, and centrism. In contrast, Barry Goldwater misread the electorate's mood when he offered distinctive alternatives; he suffered accordingly. Because of the Watergate revelations and White House scandals in 1973 and 1974, the country was more receptive in 1976 to an inexperienced politician who emphasized his own personal virtues. Outspoken candidates will probably fare better in times of severe stress in the society because their outspokenness will reflect concerns about which the citizens of that time are highly conscious. For example, it's difficult to imagine the electorate in 1964 being as congenial to George Wallace as the 1968 electorate was. In short, voters do not respond to an inert environment that only includes issues and candidates. The candidates themselves have tremendous opportunities to fashion appeals to the electorate, thus moving millions of voters and challenging the existing bases of partisan loyalties. This is clearly demonstrated by the skillful exploitation of the "hot button" issues by the Bush campaign in 1988.

This is not to say that candidates have complete flexibility in formulating appeals to the electorate and in staking out issue positions. The very process of obtaining the presidential nomination imposes commitments and constraints on a candidate that may structure his or her campaign behavior in the general election. For example, Hubert H. Humphrey's presidential campaign in 1968 suffered from the close association that many voters perceived between Humphrey and the unpopular policies, particularly on the Vietnam War, of the Johnson administration. It was not until the September 30 Salt Lake City speech that Humphrey successfully moved some distance from the administration's positions. Yet Humphrey probably could not have broken from the Johnson policies much earlier even had he wanted to, since Humphrey's strategy to win the Democratic nomination bypassed the primaries and relied on party chieftains, labor bosses, and others to deliver blocs of delegates to him. Had Humphrey moved too fast and too far from the

Johnson administration, he would have lost delegate strength in states, especially in southern and border states, that were more supportive of Johnson's policies and less receptive to the protest candidacies of McCarthy and Robert Kennedy.

In a similar vein, George McGovern's presidential campaign was constrained by his nomination strategy of winning delegates in both primary and nonprimary election states by relying on an extensive organization of volunteer workers attracted to his candidacy largely on the basis of issue concerns. Given the coolness of many Democratic party workers to his candidacy, McGovern could not afford to disillusion his enthusiastic supporters by waffling on certain key issues. In the general election, however, McGovern paid dearly for keeping the faith. Many voters, including many Democrats, saw him as a radical who was out of the mainstream of politics and the Democratic party. Carter, in contrast, forged a more diverse support coalition during the primaries that was not centered on one key issue. Hence, he had greater flexibility in shifting ground and making peace with the various segments of the Democratic party. Of course, Carter's postnomination task was made easier by the widespread belief that he would win in November. Reagan in 1980 was quite skillful and successful in expanding his base of support from the primary season to the general election. The presence of an unpopular incumbent made it easier for Reagan to moderate his positions, but even so he received some unflattering media coverage because of his inconsistencies.

McGovern's difficulties illustrate a general political rule of thumb, namely, that the primary-election electorate may differ markedly from the November electorate. This means that tactics appropriate for the primaries may be inappropriate and even disastrous for the general election. Moreover, the McGovern and Carter primary and general election campaign strategies point up the crucial difference in the structure of political competition in the two elections: the primaries are often multicandidate elections in which only a plurality of the vote is needed for victory, while the presidential contest is usually a two-candidate, majority-winner race.

Another constraint on candidates and parties is their goals, particularly with respect to the election outcome. If the major goal of a candidate or party is to win the election, then the desire for victory may limit the kinds of issue positions that a candidate or party can or should take. For example, it might be argued that Senator Goldwater's disparaging comments about social security and the Tennessee Valley Authority in 1964 were electorally foolish statements in view of the public's attitudes on these matters, no matter what Goldwater's own principles were. Candidates or parties whose major goal is not electoral success have greater freedom to espouse relatively unpopular issue positions.

While the number of cases in which presidential candidates have not had victory as their primary goal is small, there have been instances in the past fifty years in which other goals became important. For example, there were four main contenders for the presidency in 1948, and two of them—Strom

Thurmond heading the Dixiecrats and Henry Wallace leading the Progressives—had no realistic chance of winning. Instead, their primary goal was to affect the policy orientation of the Democratic party; the Dixiecrats wanted to maintain the status quo on race-related matters while the Progressives preferred a more liberal Democratic party. The electoral process was the means by which the Dixiecrats and Progressives hoped to influence the future of the Democratic party. If each group had been able to siphon off enough votes from President Truman, the party's nominee, so that he would lose, then the Dixiecrats and Progressives felt that in the future the Democratic party would not be able to ignore or offend certain blocs of voters—that is, if it hoped to win elections. Similarly, some observers argue that some of Goldwater's chief supporters in 1964 were more concerned with seizing control of the Republican party than with winning the election.

Anthony Downs (1957: 127) has discussed this notion of future-oriented parties whose initial goal is not electoral success but gaining influence over the existing party system. Downs distinguishes between two types of newly created parties—those designed to win elections and those designed "to influence already existing parties to change their policies, or not to change them." The best contemporary example of the latter is the Conservative party in the state of New York. While it has scored some important electoral successes, notably the election of James Buckley as U.S. Senator, it was originally created to influence the policy directions of the New York Republican party, which many conservatives viewed as too liberal. Hence, the Conservative party was formed to run candidates who, it was hoped, would garner sufficient votes to ensure the defeat of the Republican candidate, thereby demonstrating to the GOP leadership that it must return to conservative principles in order to win elections.

The Wallace candidacy in 1968 may be interpreted to some extent along these lines, especially given Wallace's post-1968 move back into the Democratic party. Even when it was clear that Wallace could not win in 1968, his plea "to send a message to Washington" was an attempt to influence the policy positions of the Democratic and Republican parties. His warning that the Democratic party must not repeat its mistakes of 1968 and 1972 (mainly nominating candidates who were too liberal) was a not too subtle threat to the party that if it fails to move toward the center, it may have a Wallace challenge on its hands, perhaps in the form of a third-party candidacy or perhaps in other forms. The point is that candidates and parties that are not first and foremost concerned with winning have greater flexibility and freedom in ranging over the political landscape.

Other constraints faced by candidates and parties are the existing opinions and preferences that citizens have on political affairs. While the campaign may in part be an effort to educate the public and move it in certain directions, there are issues on which the public is very immovable, and the candidate who fails to recognize this may suffer. Goldwater's comments about social security are an example of this situation. On the other hand, the shift by liberal

Democrats toward a position of opposition to busing reflects a pragmatic (some might say unprincipled) view that the busing issue is not an issue that the white public is willing to listen to or to be educated about. The busing issue illustrates a common occurrence in electoral politics, namely, the perceived need to compromise or even capitulate on certain issues in order to be around to fight the good fight on other issues. Whether such behavior represents political pragmatism at its best or political expediency at its worst is left to the judgment of the reader. Clearly, the specific issues involved are likely to influence any conclusions.

Finally, while the actual means of conducting campaigns impose limitations, those same means can also provide opportunities for candidates to appeal to the electorate. For example, the heavy reliance today on public relations firms, especially firms skilled in television and the other media, allows a prospective candidate to ignore the party organization and traditional routes of political advancement. Instead, the candidate can go directly to the public by emphasizing those personal characteristics and stances on issues more likely to work to the candidate's advantage, especially when the pollsters and focus group experts have identified the most advantageous issues and characteristics. On the other hand, because of the pervasiveness of the national media—especially television—candidates find it virtually impossible to present blatantly different appeals in different regions of the country. What a candidate says on the stump in New England, for example, will be reported in the South on the evening news.

Thus, subsequent chapters focus on the candidates and the campaigns through which the candidates make their appeals to the citizenry. While citizens are limited in their electoral choices in part by the alternatives offered by the candidates, the candidates themselves are constrained by a number of factors, including the issue and partisan preferences of the citizenry. Hence, our analysis of elections must include an investigation of the interactions between citizens and candidates, interactions that are largely confined to the actual political campaigns. Therefore, chapters 8 and 9 will focus on the changes in the conduct of presidential campaigns that have occurred since 1952, stressing the likely consequences of these changes for election outcomes and for the political system. Chapter 10 will consider the strategic aspects of capturing a presidential nomination and campaigning for president.

CHAPTER 8

The Campaign Financing, Recruitment, and Nomination of Presidential Candidates

Campaign Financing

When Gerald Ford became president in an unusual way—through the forced resignation of Richard Nixon because of the Watergate scandal—political commentators observed one bright note in an otherwise gloomy situation: at least the new president would not be beholden to wealthy contributors or special interest groups that had helped elect him. What a sad commentary on the disrepute into which campaign financing had fallen! To many citizens, financing electoral campaigns had become a national disgrace that only major reforms could remedy. People frequently expressed the belief that no one gave sizable contributions to a candidate without expecting something in return.

This cynical viewpoint was reinforced by reports of ambassadorships for sale, charges of increases in dairy price supports in exchange for campaign contributions, and the like. Thus, as the Watergate affair and its assorted manifestations unfolded, public attitudes moved markedly toward support of such reforms as public financing of national elections and campaign spending ceilings. After much prolonged debate, Congress in late 1974 passed, and the president signed, a major campaign reform measure, the provisions of which governed the 1976, 1980, 1984, and 1988 elections. Technically, the reforms passed in 1974 were amendments to the Federal Election Campaign Act of 1971. Since 1974 the campaign finance laws have been amended in important ways both in 1976 and in 1979.

Two basic issues involved in campaign financing are the amount of money the candidates spend and the way in which they raise it. It is common-place to cite the tremendous increase in campaign costs, even allowing for the effects of inflation. Table 8.1 shows the costs of presidential general elections from 1932 to the present. Note in particular the huge amounts of money spent by the winning *and* the losing candidate in 1972. The sharp decrease in expenditures in 1976 reflects the impact of the 1974 reforms that limited candidates to spending no more than $21.8 million in public funds, assuming that they qualified for and accepted public funding.

Although the dollar amounts in table 8.1 may seem large, some observers argue that the amount of money spent is less relevant than who spends it and how it is raised. Moreover, given the central role of elections in democratic politics, people argue that election campaigns should not be unduly restricted in scope by too severe limitations on the amounts of money that can be spent. Some observers claim that the actual amount of money spent is relatively small, given, for example, the great expenditures made to advertise commercial products. Herbert E. Alexander notes that inherent features of election campaigns inevitably raise costs. For example, he states that "political costs tend to be high because the political season is relatively short and intensity must be high for each candidate just before an election." He further states that candidates "are not just in competition with each other, but also are in competition with commercial advertisers possessed of large budgets" (Alexander, *New York Times* offprint). In short, it necessarily costs a lot to attract the voters' attention.

THE COSTS OF RUNNING FOR PRESIDENT

Table 8.2 indicates the total nomination and general election spending by party for the five most recent presidential elections. Observe in table 8.2 that the nomination competition for the out party—the Democrats in 1972, 1976, 1984, and 1988 and the Republicans in 1980—was substantially more expensive than the corresponding contest within the incumbent's party. Nevertheless, even with incumbent presidents in the White House, the Republicans in 1976 and the Democrats in 1980 had costly nomination struggles. In 1984, no Republicans challenged President Reagan's nomination; nevertheless, almost $35 million was spent in the prenomination period. In 1988, nomination costs soared as both parties had multicandidate struggles for the nomination.

Since millions of dollars are spent to win the presidency, the next question is, "How are these dollars allocated?" The answer is simple; the largest chunk goes to the media, particularly television air time and production costs. It has been estimated that the nominees in 1976, 1980, 1984, and 1988 spent about half of their public subsidy on advertising, mainly through television. In fact, the proportion of general election spending devoted to the electronic media has increased steadily since 1960, the major exception being 1972, when both nominees had ample dollars and therefore could spend money on other

---

TABLE 8.1

The Cost of Presidential
General Elections, 1932–1988

Year	Republican		Democratic	
1932	$ 2,900,052	Hoover	$ 2,245,975	Roosevelt*
1936	8,892,972	Landon	5,194,741	Roosevelt*
1940	3,451,310	Willkie	2,783,654	Roosevelt*
1944	2,828,652	Dewey	2,169,077	Roosevelt*
1948	2,127,296	Dewey	2,736,334	Truman*
1952	6,608,623	Eisenhower*	5,032,926	Stevenson
1956	7,778,702	Eisenhower*	5,106,651	Stevenson
1960	10,128,000	Nixon	9,797,000	Kennedy*
1964	16,026,000	Goldwater	8,757,000	Johnson*
1968	25,402,000	Nixon*	11,594,000	Humphrey
1972	61,400,000	Nixon*	30,000,000	McGovern
1976†	23,186,641	Ford	24,600,000	Carter*
1980‡	46,565,818	Reagan*	32,944,670	Carter
1984‡	77,300,000	Reagan*	71,100,000	Mondale
1988‡	93,600,000	Bush*	106,400,000	Dukakis

*Indicates winner.
†The Ford total includes $1.4 million spent on his behalf by the Republican National Committee. The Carter total includes $2.8 million spent on his behalf by the Democratic National Committee. Public funding was first used in presidential campaigns in 1976.
‡The 1980, 1984, and 1988 totals include public funding; independent expenditures for and against candidates; and expenditures by national, state, and local party committees.
SOURCES: The 1932–1976 figures are extracted from Table 1–1 in Herbert E. Alexander, *Financing Politics*, 2d ed. (Washington, D.C.: Congressional Quarterly Press, 1980). The 1980 figures are constructed from press releases (November 29, 1981, and February 21, 1982) issued by the Federal Election Commission. The 1984 figures are from Herbert E. Alexander and Brian A. Haggerty, *Financing the 1984 Election* (Lexington, Mass.: D.C. Heath and Company, 1987), Table 7–1, p. 331. The 1988 figures are from Herbert E. Alexander, "Financing the Presidential Elections, 1988," paper presented at the annual convention of the International Politicial Science Association, September 8–10, 1989.

TABLE 8.2

Nomination and General Election Spending
in 1972, 1976, 1980, 1984, and 1988 by Party (in $ millions)

	1972		1976		1980		1984		1988	
	Democratic	Republican	Democratic	Republican	Democratic	Republican	Democratic	Republican	Democratic	Republican
Nomination	32.6	3	46.3	25.7	35.6	63.2	83.8	34.9	114.6	94.0
General election	30	61.4	24.6	23.2	32.9	46.6	71.1	77.3	106.4	93.6

SOURCES: Herbert Alexander, *Financing Politics*, 2d ed. (Washington, D.C.: Congressional Quarterly Press, 1980), Tables 5–1 and 5–2; Federal Election Commission, *Record*, March 1982, pp. 5–7; and Herbert E. Alexander and Brian A. Haggerty, *Financing the 1984 Election* (Lexington, Mass.: D.C. Heath and Company, 1987), Tables 3–4 and 3–5, pp. 86–87; Herbert E. Alexander, "Financing the Presidential Elections, 1988," paper presented at the annual convention of the International Political Science Association, September 8–13, 1989.

aspects of the campaigns. But because of the spending limits inherent in public funding, the candidates must channel the bulk of their resources into television, which is the most effective way to send their messages to the electorate when there is a limited supply of dollars. This means that nonmedia activities to contact voters, such as storefront headquarters and campaign paraphernalia, have become much less common in recent presidential campaigns. This, in fact, has been a major complaint arising from the 1974 reforms.

CAMPAIGN FINANCING REFORM

The problems of campaign financing that confronted presidential candidates in the prereform era are reflected in the following comments of Hubert Humphrey (*New York Times,* October 13, 1974, p. E18):

> Campaign financing is a curse. It's the most disgusting, demeaning, disenchanting, debilitating experience of a politician's life. It's stinky, it's lousy. I just can't tell you how much I hate it. I've had to break off in the middle of trying to make a decent, honorable campaign and go up to somebody's parlor or to a room and say, "Gentlemen, and ladies, I'm desperate. You've got to help me. . . ."
>
> And you see people there—a lot of them you don't want to see. And they look at you, and you sit there and you talk to them and tell them what you're for and you need help and, out of the twenty-five who have gathered, four will contribute. And most likely one of them is in trouble and is somebody you shouldn't have had a contribution from.

In response to the rising costs of politics and the abuses uncovered in the Watergate investigations, Congress passed the Federal Election Campaign Act Amendments of 1974, which was signed into law by President Ford with some misgivings in October 1974. Prior to the 1974 act, the most recent efforts at campaign finance reform were the Revenue Act of 1971 and the Federal Election Campaign Act of 1971. The Revenue Act was an attempt to generate public contributions to campaigns by allowing citizens to take a tax credit or deduction on their donations. The act also had a tax checkoff provision that would allow citizens to specify on their income tax return that one dollar of their tax money be used to subsidize presidential campaigns. Under the threat of a Nixon veto, this provision did not take effect until after the 1972 campaign. There had been a similar provision in the Presidential Campaign Fund Act of 1966, but it was repealed the following year.

The tax checkoff plan in the 1971 Revenue Act is a good example of how difficult it is to institute reforms that simultaneously achieve a number of desired goals without leading to any unintended consequences. For example, one provision of the law stated that a candidate must choose between public and private financing. Yet might this not impose unconstitutional restrictions on citizens who want to give money to a candidate who has already opted for public financing? George Thayer (1973: 291) suggested one possible unintended consequence of the checkoff plan. He argued that state and local party organizations were likely to atrophy further if the responsibility of fund raising was taken from them. Furthermore, there were biases built into the checkoff plan that favored the two major parties; nominees of minor parties could receive public monies only if they received between 5 and 25 percent of the vote. Even then, the amount they would get would be only 25 percent of the major party amount (Delmer C. Dunn, 1972: 56).

The major features of the 1971 Campaign Act were to provide for a thorough disclosure of campaign contributions received after April 7, 1972, and to limit the amount of money that could be spent on media advertising. The massive fund raising conducted by the Nixon campaign prior to the April 7 deadline certainly violated the spirit of the law, though not the letter. The 1971 law was quickly attacked on a number of grounds, one simply being that its enforcement was not very strict. A more fundamental objection was to the philosophy underlying the statute: was the simple disclosure of the sources of a candidate's funds a sufficient safeguard to reduce the influence of wealth on politics, or were more direct controls on spending and contributions needed?

Prior to the reform efforts of the 1960s and 1970s, the two most important statutes governing presidential campaign financing were the Federal Corrupt Practices Act of 1925 and the Hatch Act of 1940. The 1925 law required financial reports from any committee seeking to influence presidential campaigns in two or more states and prohibited corporate contributions (Herbert E. Alexander, 1972a: 78). This was a weak law; expenditures by committees confined to one state did not have to be reported, nor did primary election gifts. Yet even this weak law helped Common Cause force disclosure of the pre–April 7 contributions to the Nixon campaign.

The Hatch Act limited individual contributions to any political committee to $5,000 and limited total spending by a committee to $3 million per year. The parties and candidates got around the law by decentralizing financing to state and local committees, particularly in states with weak to nonexistent reporting requirements, and by creating many theoretically separate national committees, each of which was allowed to spend $3 million. Thus, in 1968 there were such committees as Arts and Letters for Humphrey–Muskie, Business for Humphrey–Muskie, Citizens for Humphrey, Citizens for Humphrey–Muskie, United Chiropractors for Humphrey–Muskie, Veterans for Humphrey–Muskie, and many more. A related reason for the proliferation of committees was that donors could avoid the gift tax by giving up to $3,000 each to a large number of committees rather than a lump sum to one committee. Thus, Stewart Mott, a major McGovern financial backer, divided his contributions among a large number of committees, just as Richard Mellon Scaife gave his million dollars to the Nixon campaign in the form of $3,000 checks to the requisite number of committees (*Dollar Politics*, p. 69).

The above discussion should make it abundantly clear that the campaign financing laws prior to 1974 were easily circumvented and permitted many serious abuses. The 1974 reforms addressed the problems of excessive expenditures and improper fund-raising practices. With respect to the former, the law set limits of $10 million per candidate for the primary elections and $21.8 million for the 1976 general election for candidates who received public funding. Built into the law were automatic cost-of-living adjustments in these ceilings to take into account the impact of inflation. Thus, for the 1980 election the spending limits were approximately $14.7 million for the primaries and $29.4 million for the general election; for the 1984 election they were $20.2 and $40.4 million; and for 1988 they were $23.1 and $46.2 million. Legal, accounting, and compliance costs and the costs of fund raising are not included in these limits. Hence, candidates actually spend more than the limits.

In order to receive public funds during the primary season, candidates have to demonstrate their credibility by first raising on their own $100,000 in amounts of $5,000 or less from twenty or more states with contributions under $250. In 1988, if a candidate met these conditions, then he or she was eligible for matching public funds for each dollar collected from private contributions under $250 up to a total of $11.55 million in public monies. Thus, up to half of the $23.1 million that candidates could spend during the primary season could come from public funds. But, as exemplified by John Connally of Texas in 1980, candidates could refuse public funds in the primaries and thus not be subject to the spending limits.

Candidates who accepted public funding in the primaries had to abide not only by the overall spending ceiling but also by individual state ceilings calculated according to the number of voters in the state. Most important, candidates could not spend the maximum amount in every state since, if they did, they would quickly exceed the overall limit. In 1988 the overall limit was $23.1 million, but the sum of the separate state ceilings was almost $70 million. Therefore, candidates had to allocate their resources very carefully and sometimes they had to play games in order to meet the technical requirements of the law. For example, New Hampshire, with the first primary, is a state where candidates want to spend more than the full amount allowed ($461,000 in 1988). A variety of ploys were used to increase New Hampshire spending. Television time was purchased on Massachusetts television stations (which cover New Hampshire) and charged against the Massachusetts ceiling. Campaign workers often stayed overnight in Vermont or Massachusetts so that their lodging costs would not count against the New Hampshire ceiling. Some New Hampshire campaign events were structured as fund raisers since fund-raising costs were exempt from the spending limits.

Public funding is also provided in the general election for the major party candidates. Candidates who choose to reject public funding are not subject to the general election expenditure limits. If candidates accept public money for the general election, then they cannot raise or accept private contributions except to help defray the costs of complying with the campaign finance laws. The source of all public funds to be spent on the campaign is the Presidential Election Campaign Fund, monies that citizens designate on their income tax returns for use in presidential elections. In 1976, 1980, 1984, and 1988, both major party nominees accepted public funding.

Minor party candidates can get public money only if they received at least 5 percent of the popular vote in the previous election. The amount of money received by minor party candidates is proportional to their vote strength in relation to the vote totals of the major party candidates. Thus, in 1980 John Anderson received about $4.2 million in public funds *after* the election. For a new minor party to qualify for *postelection* public funding in 1992, it must be on the ballot in at least ten states, provide certain guarantees to the Federal Election Commission prior to the election that it will comply with features of the campaign finance law, and receive at least 5 percent of the vote. Had John Anderson run again in 1984 as a minor party candidate, he would have been eligible to receive general election public funds *prior* to the election, since he had been a candidate of a political party in the previous election and had received at least 5 percent of the vote.

Clearly, the primary and general election spending ceilings for candidates who accept public financing address concerns about the rising costs of campaigns. But they do not address the problem of huge contributions coming from wealthy donors. Hence, the campaign finance laws also provided for limits on the amounts that individuals and groups are allowed to contribute to candidates; these limits are summarized in table 8.3. Note that individual contributions to a candidate are restricted to $1,000 for each primary, runoff, and general election, with an annual limit of $25,000. Candidates receiving public funds in the general election cannot accept private contributions, and candidates getting public monies in the primaries receive matching public dollars of up to $250 per contribution. These limits have effectively eliminated large private contributions to candidates. Even candidates who reject public funding are limited to accepting individual contributions no larger than $1,000. Some observers have argued that these contribution limits should be increased, that a contribution of $1,000 in 1974 is worth less than $400 in 1991 because of the effects of inflation.

Presidential candidates may also receive financial support from their party's national committee in the general election; in 1988 this amount was limited to $9.2 million, a limit that rises with inflation. The Federal Election Campaign Act Amendments of 1979 tried to encourage state and local political party participation in the presidential race by exempting certain activities from the spending and contribution limits. Since then, state and local party committees have been allowed to spend unlimited monies on volunteer voter registration and get-out-the-vote drives and on campaign materials associated with genuine volunteer activities, such as brochures, yard signs, pins, bumper stickers, and leaflets.

These 1979 amendments, admirable in their intent to encourage party-building activities, have generated controversy since they have opened up the possibility that monies not collected under federal laws might find their way into the presidential campaign. Thus, huge contributions from wealthy donors and from corporations, all of which are legal in some states, might end up in the presidential contest. Such funds, which are referred to as *soft money*, are raised by state and local party committees. Supposedly such monies pay for the state and local share of the party-building activities that are encouraged by the 1979 amendments. Clear distinctions are not being made, it would seem, between the national shares versus the state and local shares. Moreover, the national parties have been playing a major role in assisting the state and local parties to raise funds that would not be legal under federal laws but are acceptable under state statutes. The soft money loophole could result in large amounts of impermissible funds entering the presidential campaign. Alexander (1989) estimated the amount of soft money in the 1988 campaign at $45 million, divided almost evenly between the parties.

There is one other potentially important source of money for presidential candidates, namely, independent expenditures. According to the Federal Election Commission, an independent expenditure is "one made for a communication which expressly advocates the election or defeat of a clearly identified candidate and which is not made with any direct or indirect cooperation, consent, request or suggestion or consultation involving a candidate or his/her authorized committee or agent." Because there is no limit on the amount or frequency of independent expenditures, they represent a major loophole in the campaign finance laws that can undermine financial parity between the major party candidates. Thus in 1984, more than $16 million in independent expenditures was raised during the primaries and general elec-

---

TABLE 8.3

Contribution Limits

	To each candidate or candidate committee per election	To national party committee per calendar year	To any other political committee per calendar year	Total per calendar year
Individual may give	$1,000	$20,000	$5,000	$25,000
Multicandidate committee may give*	5,000	15,000	5,000	No limit
Other political committee may give	1,000	20,000	5,000	No limit

*A multicandidate committee is a political committee with more than fifty contributors that has been registered for at least six months and, with the exception of the state party committees, has made contributions to five or more federal candidates.
SOURCE: Federal Election Commission, *The FEC and the Federal Campaign Finance Law*, p. 4.

tion on behalf of the Reagan campaign, compared to only about $1 million for the Mondale effort. Fortunately for the Democrats, little of this $16 million benefited the Reagan campaign directly; most of it was eaten up by the operating and fund-raising costs of the sponsoring organizations. In 1988, independent expenditures amounted to $10.1 million, with most of the money devoted to supporting Bush or opposing Dukakis. In the 1974 version of the campaign finance reforms, independent expenditures were prohibited, but this provision was ruled unconstitutional by the U.S. Supreme Court.

The 1974 reforms have undergone a series of legal challenges. A disparate group of citizens and organizations, including former Senator James Buckley, former Senator Eugene McCarthy, Stewart Mott, the New York Civil Liberties Union, and the American Conservative Union, brought suit against the 1974 law on the grounds that it deprived the plaintiffs of freedom of speech and association, of the right to petition for redress of grievances, of the right of privacy, and of due process of law and discriminates invidiously against them, all in violation of the First, Fourth, Fifth, Sixth, and Ninth Amendments to the Constitution. (*Congressional Record,* January 28, 1975, p. 51106). The plaintiffs argued that the disclosure requirements of the law violated their right to privacy and that the contribution ceilings limited their freedom of speech and association and their right to petition for redress of grievances.

The Supreme Court issued its decision on the constitutionality of the 1974 campaign finance law in January 1976, shortly before the start of the primary season. It upheld the contribution limits on individuals and organizations and the public financing of presidential campaigns. It struck down all expenditure limits, except for presidential candidates who accepted public funding, and invalidated the restriction on independent contributions made on behalf of a candidate so long as the donors were giving without the knowledge and encouragement of the candidate. The Court also declared the Federal Elections Commission (FEC) to be improperly constituted. As originally established, the FEC was composed of six members appointed by Congress and two appointed by the president. The Court ruled that only the president had the power of appointment; but to avoid confusion, it let stand previous actions of the FEC and gave Congress ample time to reconstitute the commission. However, Congress delayed in reestablishing the FEC, so that on March 21, at the height of the primary season, the commission was no longer able to disburse matching public funds to eligible candidates. Needless to say, this created a major hardship for the candidates, particularly for Udall and Reagan, who were unable to make strong efforts in certain states because of the lack of money. In the Federal Election Campaign Act Amendments of 1976, Congress reestablished the FEC as a six-member board appointed by the president and subject to Senate confirmation. Finally, in 1985, the Supreme Court struck down the last major restriction on independent expenditures when it ruled that PACs could make unlimited independent expenditures rather than be bound by the $1,000 contribution limit. Hence, the current legal situation is that unlimited independent expenditures by individuals and PACs are allowable in the presidential contest. The question becomes whether most independent expenditures are truly independent.

As is the case with many reforms, the consequences of the campaign finance law were both anticipated and unanticipated. The 1976, 1980, 1984, and 1988 contestants for the nominations met the eligibility requirements for matching public funds fairly readily. Included in the 1976 group was Ellen McCormack, a single-issue (antiabortion) candidate for the Democratic nomination. In fact, the ease with which candidates were qualifying for matching funds, and the frequency with which no longer viable candidates were able to draw public funds, led Congress in the 1976 amendments to the financing law to require that presidential candidates who withdrew from the nomination campaign had to return unspent federal funds. In addition, federal support to a candidate who won less than 10 percent of the vote in two consecutive primaries in which he or she ran was automatically cut off, although provisions were made whereby a candidate could reestablish eligibility.

Although the requirements for obtaining matching public funds in the primary season were not particularly burdensome to candidates, they did serve a screening function, namely, as a test that, if passed, bestowed an extra measure of legitimacy on a candidacy. Candidates attempt to establish their eligibility for matching funds quickly so as to provide evidence that theirs is a serious candidacy. Hence, the campaign finance law has had the unintended effect of further lengthening the presidential season. In fact, if candidates can establish their eligibility early and begin the caucus and primary season with their matching funds in hand, then they will be able to plan and budget ahead and not have to devote extensive time and effort to fund raising. Moreover, the candidate with contributions already collected is not as much at the mercy of the early primary results. In the past many candidates have found themselves without financial backing after an unimpressive showing in New Hampshire or some other early primary.

The campaign finance laws governing the creation and activities of PACs have fostered a new development in presidential campaigning. Four 1980 Republican contenders—Ronald Reagan, Robert Dole, George Bush, and John Connally—formed PACs to raise and distribute funds to GOP candidates in the 1978 election, thereby hoping to gain support in their quest for the presidential nomination (Rhodes Cook, 1979). Reagan's PAC, Citizens for the Republic, contributed over $500,000 to Republican U.S. House and Senate candidates in 1978. In the past, would-be presidential candidates often campaigned on behalf of fellow party members, but the direct provision of campaign funds is very new. The use of candidate PACs has continued in subsequent elections.

The actual experience with the campaign finance laws suggests some additional consequences for the general election campaign. The law certainly reduced spending in the presidential race from the bloated levels in 1972, but it also lessened the visibility of the campaign as the spending limit resulted in a scarcity of campaign buttons, bumper stickers, and other paraphernalia.

With the limited funds available, the candidates' media campaigns received top priority and as a result the organizational effort within states suffered.

In a related vein, the limited funds served to alter the relationship between the national campaign organization and the state and local party organizations. In previous elections the candidate's national organization often was able to contribute money to the state and local organizations, thereby creating a common electoral bond by promoting the entire party ticket and providing the national ticket with some leverage over state and local efforts. There was little such money available in 1976, 1980, 1984, and 1988, especially for the Democrats, thereby reinforcing the trend to candidate-centered presidential contests. In many cases the national ticket itself looked to the state and local levels for financial and other support, which often did not materialize.

The reforms have spawned new job opportunities for lawyers and accountants, who today are indispensable components of a presidential campaign. The reforms have also given rise to a cottage industry devoted to uncovering loopholes in the law. One of the more imaginative efforts occurred in 1980, when various artists donated to the Kennedy campaign works of art valued at several hundred thousand dollars that the campaign then sold for a tidy profit. This did not violate the individual contribution limit of $1,000 since the Federal Election Commission views the time and effort of artists as volunteer labor to the campaign and assigns a monetary value only to the materials used to produce the art.

The future of campaign finance reform is unpredictable; there will probably be changes in the law resulting from new congressional decisions or future court rulings. Certainly there is a need to raise the amount of money provided in the general election beyond the inflation factor built into the law. In areas such as television ads, costs are rising more rapidly than inflation. There have been legal challenges against provisions of the law dealing with the treatment of third parties in such areas as eligibility and disclosure requirements. Moreover, even if the basic statutes remain unchanged, there are no guarantees that presidential candidates will opt for public funding in future contests. And the Supreme Court's ruling allowing unlimited independent expenditures on behalf of a candidate could undermine the major thrust of the finance reforms and leave political authorities once again with the problem of designing a better campaign finance system. Because of soft money and independent expenditures in 1988, general election spending for each party was far in excess of the $46.1 million in public funding and the $8.3 million in allowable national party spending.

The Recruitment of Presidential Candidates

In 1976 former Georgia Governor Jimmy Carter captured the Democratic presidential nomination, while in 1980 former California Governor Ronald

Reagan captured the Republican presidential nomination. These two events marked the return of the governorship as a source of presidential candidates. Prior to those events, the breeding ground of presidential hopefuls between 1952 and 1972 had been, as a rule, the U.S. Senate and the office of the vice-president rather than the nation's governorships. Between 1952 and 1972 the only presidential and vice-presidential nominees to have been governors were Adlai Stevenson (of Illinois) and Spiro Agnew (of Maryland). Every other nominee, with the exceptions of General Eisenhower, William Miller (Goldwater's 1964 running mate), and Sargent Shriver (McGovern's second 1972 running mate), had served in the U.S. Senate; and Nixon, Johnson, and Humphrey followed their Senate service with a vice-presidential incumbency prior to running for president. Carter's 1976 success once again sensitized observers to the governorship as a springboard to the presidency.

Carter's capture of the nomination is important, not because it represented the success of a former governor, but because it signified that this could be done by an outsider with little previous political experience and scant national recognition. His accomplishment was made possible by expanding the primaries as the means of selecting delegates to the national nominating conventions (see the next section of this chapter), the media coverage given to the primaries (see chapter 9), and the campaign financing reforms discussed earlier. Hence, the lesson of 1976 is that serious aspirants for the presidency can come from diverse political backgrounds, and this has been reflected in the diverse fields that have sought presidential nominations since then. In 1988, both parties had varied fields of contenders that included members of the U.S. House and U.S. Senate, governors, religious figures, and others.

The critical issues facing the nation may help determine what kinds of experience are desired in a presidential candidate. For example, if foreign policy crises are uppermost in voters' minds, then a candidate with limited national and international experience may not be considered very favorably. Carter's claim in 1976 that he was an outsider without Washington connections may have worked to his advantage because the citizenry was upset with big government and the Watergate scandals. By mid-1979, as energy and economic problems became acute and as Carter was continually frustrated by an independent Congress, many observers viewed his lack of prior Washington experience as a liability rather than an asset. For the future, it seems likely that presidential aspirants will continue to come from varied backgrounds, although the visibility of and the significance attached to the vice-presidency, U.S. senators, and governors suggest that they will be better springboards than other positions.

The traditional political lore argued for the strength of the governorship and the weakness of the Senate and the vice-presidency as springboards for a presidential bid. For example, Louis Harris (1959: 364–365) summarized a number of reasons why governors were believed to have an advantage over senators in quests for the presidential nomination, including the following: senators were frequently not real political powers in their home states, while governors were; legislators were forced to go on record on controversial issues more often than governors; and senators and vice-presidents tended to get hidden behind the scenes, while governors were often highly visible.

The traditional advantages and disadvantages of senators and governors have been turned around by changes in the nominating process that, in turn, are related to broader changes in the American political system. Peabody and Lubalin (1975: 44–45) argue that geographic considerations in the selection of presidential nominees are less important than they once were, that it has become much more important for a potential nominee to have widespread national appeal rather than just a special appeal to one or two key states. This in turn has led to increased reliance on the mass media to develop name recognition nationwide, to widespread use of public opinion polls to measure candidate popularity, and to contesting many primaries to demonstrate popularity and win delegate support. And as the proportion of convention delegates chosen in primaries increased along with the number of primaries, the need to demonstrate one's national appeal became even more pronounced.

The extended period over which presidential nomination bids are now contested helps explain some of the advantages of senators over governors in seeking the presidency. The six-year term of office gives senators more time to plan their presidential bids and allows them more opportunities to run in a year when their Senate seats are not up for election, thereby guaranteeing their continuation as senators should their presidential quest fail. Governors, on the other hand, have two- or four-year terms of office, which do not provide as much electoral security for the upwardly mobile governor. Note in this regard that Carter in 1976 and Reagan in 1976 and 1980 were no longer governors when they sought their party's nomination; hence, each had the flexibility to campaign full time. In contrast, when Jerry Brown challenged Carter's renomination in 1980, he did so as the incumbent governor and therefore was of necessity absent from California frequently, which was a source of criticism. In 1984 Walter Mondale, unlike his chief challenger Gary Hart, did not have to worry about attending to the duties of office. In fact, the current nomination system has put a premium on being a *former* elected officeholder. The unemployed politician will be able to devote full time to campaigning in the drawn-out selection process, in contrast to the elected official, who must be attentive to the responsibilities of his or her current office. Thus Howard Baker in 1984 and Gary Hart in 1986 chose not to seek reelection to the U.S. Senate in order to enhance their 1988 presidential prospects. And even though Dukakis in 1988 succeeded in winning the Democratic nomination as the incumbent governor of Massachusetts, his need to tend to state business was seen by many observers as a detriment to his presidential campaign.

A final advantage that senators have enjoyed over governors in recent years is that they are at the hub of a national communication network in Washington, D.C., whereas many state capitals receive little national media coverage. To the extent that possessing national appeal aids one in winning the nomination, senators often begin the race with a head start. Senators can often receive coverage on the nightly news shows simply by conducting hearings on some controversial public issue, while governors are more hard-pressed to attract media attention; state problems will be less interesting to a national audience and to the national networks. Since the public views the president as paramount in the conduct of foreign policy, would-be presidents must establish their credentials in this area, and senators are in a much better position to accomplish this than are governors. An appointment to the Senate Foreign Relations Committee and the almost obligatory fact-finding trip abroad, complete with an audience with Soviet leaders, serve to establish the senator's expertise in foreign affairs. Nevertheless, governors have become more skillful in promoting themselves and their states and have joined the international travel circuit through trade missions and the like. And as the locus of innovation and ideas moved from Washington to the state capitals in the 1980s and 1990s, the governorship as an incubator of presidential nominees received more media attention. Finally, the sequential nature of the primary system and the horse race emphasis given the process by the press and television allow an unknown candidate of any political background to develop a popular following.

The Nominating System

INTRODUCTION

The presidential nominating system has undergone major change, particularly since 1968, and even as this chapter was written, one year before the first presidential primary in 1992, developments were still occurring. Certainly the major change in the nomination process has been the change in the number of states employing the primary election to select delegates to the nominating conventions. In 1972 there were twenty-three Democratic presidential primaries, including that of the District of Columbia, an increase of six over the 1968 figure. In 1976 there were thirty presidential primaries, while in 1980 the number rose to thirty-one, dropped to twenty-five in 1984, and rose to thirty-eight in 1988. About 61 percent of Democratic convention delegates were selected in primaries in 1972, a figure that climbed to 73 percent in 1976 and 1980, dropped to 54 percent in 1984, and increased to 67 percent in 1988.

Table 8.4 presents the delegate selection schedule for 1988 and indicates which states have used primaries to select democratic convention delegates in recent years. Note that sixteen states held their primaries on March 8, including fourteen southern and border states. Also note that many of these states had moved their primary up to March 8—Super Tuesday—in order to create the southern regional primary discussed in chapter 6.

Looking ahead to 1992, there will likely be less juggling of the primaries' dates and fewer changes in the rules governing them, a marked contrast to the radical rules changes witnessed between 1972 and 1984. An example of how the rules had been repeatedly changed is the matter of winner-take-all primaries. The Democratic party conducted its 1976 primaries under a set of rules that, among other things, banned winner-take-all primaries and required that at least 75 percent of duly elected delegates be elected from districts no larger than congressional districts. The elimination of winner-take-all primaries was adopted to prevent a repetition of the 1972 California primary outcome in which George McGovern won a narrow popular vote victory over Hubert Humphrey yet received California's entire bloc of 271 delegates, the largest at the convention. The intent of the 1976 Democratic rules was to guarantee that a state's delegates were allocated according to the candidates' demonstrated strength in the state. There were, however, important loopholes in the 1976 rules, the most significant of which allowed winner-take-all primaries within any district (congressional or otherwise) in which delegates were directly elected. Hence, a candidate could still win all or most of a state's delegates with only a small plurality of the vote, thereby undermining the move to proportional representation.

In 1980 the loophole primary was banned (except for Illinois and West Virginia) and delegates were to be allocated to candidates in proportion to their showing, assuming that the candidate achieved a certain threshold of support. For delegates selected at state conventions and for at-large delegates in primary states, the state parties were allowed to establish a threshold of between 15 and 20 percent. For district delegates in primary states, the threshold would be determined by dividing 100 by the number of delegates elected in the district, with the proviso that the maximum threshold would be 25 percent. Hence, if a district elected five delegates, the minimum percentage of the vote required to win a delegate would be 20 percent. For 1984, the rules changed again. The Hunt Commission (a Democratic reform commission) said that states could keep proportional representation if they wished, but they could also adopt a bonus plan that would give the top vote getter in each district an extra delegate. More important, the loophole winner-take-all primary at the district level was once again allowed. Because most states in 1984 established a threshold of at least 20 percent, complaints arose that this was unfair to candidates who were not among the top vote getters. Hence, for 1988 the Democrats adopted a 15 percent threshhold, although supporters of Jesse Jackson wanted the threshhold abolished entirely. As a concession to Jackson, the Democratic convention in 1988 modified the rules for 1992 to guarantee that the allocation of delegates more closely mirrors the popular vote cast in the primaries.

Another repeated target of rules changes has been the timing and scheduling of primaries. Because the primary season had become so lengthy and enervating and because the early caucus and primary states, such as Iowa and New Hampshire, had gained undue influence, the Democrats compressed their primary season into a three-month period, with only Iowa and New Hampshire allowed to conduct their delegate selection outside this period. For

TABLE 8.4

The 1988 and the 1984 Primary and Caucus Schedules and the List of States Which Had Primaries in 1980, 1976, 1972, 1968, 1964, and 1960

State	1988 date	1984 date		1980	1976	1972	1968	1964	1960
Hawaii (R)	Jan. 27	Mar. 13	C						
Michigan (R)	Jan. 29–30	Mar. 17	C	x	x	x			
Iowa	Feb. 8	Feb. 20	C						
New Hampshire	Feb. 16	Feb. 28	P	x	x	x	x	x	x
Minnesota	Feb. 23	Mar. 20	C						
South Dakota	Feb. 23	June 5	P	x	x	x	x	x	x
Maine (R)	Feb. 26–28	Mar. 4	C						
Maine (D)	Feb. 28	Mar. 4	C						
Vermont	Mar. 1	Apr. 24	C*	x	x				
South Carolina (R)	Mar. 5	Mar. 17	C						
Wyoming	Mar. 5	Mar. 10	C						
Kansas (R)	Mar. 5	Mar. 24	C						
Alabama	Mar. 8	Mar. 13	P	x	x	x	x	x	x
Arkansas	Mar. 8	Mar. 17	P	x	x	x	x	x	x
Florida	Mar. 8	Mar. 13	P	x	x	x	x	x	x
Georgia	Mar. 8	Mar. 13	P	x	x				
Hawaii (D)	Mar. 8	Mar. 13	C						
Idaho (D)	Mar. 8	May 24	C*						
Kentucky	Mar. 8	Mar. 31	C	x	x				
Louisiana	Mar. 8	May 5	P	x	x				
Maryland	Mar. 8	May 8	P	x	x	x	x	x	x
Massachusetts	Mar. 8	Mar. 13	P	x	x	x	x	x	x
Mississippi	Mar. 8	Mar. 17	C						
Missouri	Mar. 8	Apr 18	C						
Nevada (D)	Mar. 8	Mar. 13	C						
North Carolina	Mar. 8	May 8	P	x	x	x			
Oklahoma	Mar. 8	Mar. 13	C						
Rhode Island	Mar. 8	Mar. 13	P	x	x	x			
Tennessee	Mar. 8	May 1	P	x	x				
Texas	Mar. 8	May 5	P	x	x				
Washington	Mar. 8	Mar. 13	C						
Virginia	Mar. 8	Mar. 24–26	C						
Alaska (D)	Mar. 10	Mar. 15	C						

State	Date		Type							
South Carolina (D)	Mar.	12	C							
	Mar.	17	C	×						×
North Dakota (D)	Mar.	14	C							
	Mar.	18–28	C*	×	×					×
Illinois	Mar.	15	P	×	×	×	×	×	×	×
Kansas (D)	Mar.	19	C	×						
Wyoming (R)	Mar.	19	C							
	Mar.	10	C							
Puerto Rico	Mar.	20	P	×	×	×	×	×		
Michigan (D)	Mar.	26	C	×	×	×	×	×	×	×
	Mar.	17	C	×						
Connecticut	Mar.	29	P	×	×	×	×	×		
	Mar.	27	P							
Colorado	Apr.	4	C							
	May	7	C							
Wisconsin	Apr.	5	P	×	×	×	×	×	×	×
	Apr.	7	C*							
Arizona (D)	Apr.	16	C							
	Apr.	14	C							
Utah (R)	Apr.	18	C							
	Apr.	25	C							
New York	Apr.	19	P	×	×	×	×	×	×	×
Vermont (D)	Apr.	19	C	×	×					
	Apr.	24	C							
Utah	Apr.	25	C							
	Apr.	23	C							
Pennsylvania	Apr.	26	P	×	×	×	×	×	×	×
Vermont (R)	Apr.	26	C	×	×					
	Apr.	24	C*							
Ohio	May	3	P	×	×	×	×	×	×	×
	May	8	P							
District of Columbia	May	3	P	×	×	×	×	×	×	×
	May	1	P							
Indiana	May	3	P	×	×	×	×	×	×	×
	May	8	P							
Nebraska	May	10	P	×	×	×	×	×	×	×
	May	15	P							
West Virginia	May	10	P	×	×	×	×	×	×	×
	June	5	P							
Delaware (D)	May	16	C	×	×					
	May	14	C							
Oregon	May	17	P	×	×	×	×	×	×	×
	May	15	P							
Idaho	May	24	P	×	×	×	×	×	×	×
	May	24	C*							
California	June	7	P							
	June	5	P							
Montana	June	7	P	×	×					
	Mar.	25	P							
New Mexico	June	7	P	×	×					
	June	5	C							
New Jersey	June	7	P	×	×	×	×	×	×	×
	June	5	P							
North Dakota (R)	June	14	P							
	Mar.	18–28	C*	×	×					×
Alaska (R)	June	17	C	×						
	Mar.	15	C							

P—denotes a primary election state.

C—denotes a caucus state that usually concludes with a state convention.

*—Nonbinding primary held, delegates selected by caucus process. The date is for the caucus.

In 1964 Texas did not have a primary law, but the GOP held a nonbinding presidential preference poll. For the 1960–1980 period, an (X) indicates that the state held a presidential primary. It should be noted that the 1988 calendar is more likely to be correct for the Democratic party than for the Republican party.

SOURCES: Constructed from information presented in Congressional Quarterly Weekly Report, May 19, 1972, p. 952, and November 24, 1979, p. 2661; Guide to 1976 Elections (Washington, D.C.: Congressional Quarterly, Inc., 1977), pp. 26–32; and National Journal, July 16, 1983, pp. 1484–1489, and August 13, 1983, p. 1683; Congressional Quarterly Weekly Report, June 2, 1984, p. 1317 and June 16, 1984, p. 1443; Congressional Quarterly Weekly Report, August 29, 1987, p. 1992.

1988 the Democrats kept this three-month period (from the second Tuesday in March to the second Tuesday in June), but allowed Iowa, Maine, and Wyoming to begin their caucuses somewhat earlier and also allowed New Hampshire to hold its primary up to two weeks earlier.

The Democrats have also regularly modified their rules to influence what kinds of persons will be chosen as convention delegates. Prior to 1972 the typical convention delegate was a middle-aged white male with an upper-status background. One of the reforms adopted by the Democrats after their 1968 convention—the so-called establishment of quotas—urged the adequate representation of minorities, women, and young people on state delegations, a move that resulted in sharp increases in black, female, and youth participation at the 1972 convention (see table 8.5). Since 1972 the Democrats have backed off from their quota requirements and, instead, have issued affirmative action guidelines for state parties to follow to assure adequate representation of different groups at the national convention. However, with respect to women, the Democrats have an equal division rule requiring state delegations to the national nominating conventions to be composed equally of men and women. The Republican party has taken some weak and tentative steps to make its convention more open and diverse by calling for "positive action," but it has not come up with any serious ways of enforcing these recommendations. Nor are there any sanctions against state parties that fail to put into effect such positive action.

One other area in which the Democrats changed their rules for 1988 was to increase the number of superdelegates—elected officials and party leaders who will automatically be delegates to the nominating convention. Over 15 percent of the seats will be filled by superdelegates who comprise all members of the Democratic National Committee, all Democratic governors, and 80 percent of all Democratic members of Congress. This represents a major increase in participation by the party professionals; for example, whereas in 1980 only about 15 percent of congressional Democrats attended the convention as delegates, 80 percent attended in 1988. One impetus for this change was a growing recognition that party officials are central to political parties and to the process of governing. Some influential Democrats also thought that the political savvy of the party elites might be of value to the convention as it made its weighty decisions about nominees and the platform.

In conclusion, note that although the reform movement has been of particular concern to the Democratic party, it has also affected the GOP. Many of the Democratic changes required the enactment of state laws, and this procedure also affected GOP procedures. Nevertheless, Democrats and Republicans can still employ markedly different procedures within the same state. For example, the California primary for Republicans in 1976 was winner-take-all, so that Ford's 34.5 percent of the vote (versus Reagan's 65.5 percent) won Ford no delegates. On the Democratic side, proportional allocation of delegates was required, so that Carter's 20.4 percent of the vote (compared to Brown's 59 percent) won Carter sixty-seven delegates. In some states the two parties select their delegates on different dates and use very different procedures.

SELECTING THE DELEGATES

As mentioned previously, the reliance on primary elections to select delegates to the nominating conventions has fluctuated tremendously since 1968. Primaries became popular partly because of the rhetoric surrounding them. According to such hoopla, primaries are the most democratic way to choose delegates. In addition, the extensive coverage of primaries in the mass media has contributed to the fascination with primaries. This same coverage is not given to other means of selecting delegates such as caucuses (with the exception of Iowa), state party committees, and state conventions. Certainly primary elections have the elements of drama, excitement, and ease of understanding that attract media attention. And many states moved to a primary between 1968 and 1976 because it was easier to comply with Democratic party rules under a primary system than under any other method of delegate selection.

Frank Sorauf (1972: 271–272) has described four types of presidential primaries: (1) those that involve the election of unpledged delegates, with no presidential candidates on the ballot; (2) those that involve an expression of presidential preference only, with no delegates elected; (3) those that combine the first two types of electing delegates pledged to presidential candidates; and (4) those that involve a presidential preference poll and a separate election of delegates. Beyond these four basic types, the primaries differ in several important respects. In some states a candidate must give his or her consent to be placed on the ballot, while in other states every conceivable candidate is included on the ballot. This means that some primaries give a better indication of the relative popularity of various candidates, suggesting that strategic concerns play a central role in the decision as to which primaries to contest. In some states delegates are only nominally pledged to a candidate, while in other states delegates are required by law to take a pledge of loyalty to the candidate and to continue to support the candidate through multiple ballots unless formally released from their commitment. In some states all delegates are elected in the primary, while in other states delegates are chosen via the primary election and the state convention. And finally, in states that use only the primary to select delegates, the delegates may be elected from a variety of geographic units, including state legislative districts, congressional districts, and even the state at large. In short, there are many variations in primary elections that the prospective candidate must be aware of to wage an effective campaign.

While the number of delegates elected in state and district conventions has decreased in the past two decades, a substantial bloc of delegates are still chosen in this manner. Lacking the spectacle of the primaries, those conventions were largely ignored by the media, although not by the savvy candidate. Even though Goldwater's primary election track record in 1964 was far from impressive, his nomination was assured by his success in securing delegates at state conventions (and by his California primary victory). After President Johnson's decision not to seek reelection in 1968, Hubert Humphrey announced his presidential candidacy too late to contest most primaries, a strategically fortunate situation for him. Humphrey scored his major delegate successes in nonprimary states.

In recent years the caucus–convention system of delegate selection has received rather more attention. Largely this development is due to the lessons of 1964 and 1968 as well as to the Iowa caucus–convention system. This procedure initiated the process of delegate selection and provided the first direct sounding on the relative standing of candidates on the basis of direct voting. As will be shown in chapter 9, reporting the Iowa caucus results became a political event in itself; the caucus results took on more importance than they merited. By mid-1985 prospective nominees for 1988 were already at work in Iowa! Yet with the exception of Iowa, convention states still receive little media coverage.

Since state and district conventions were so much less visible than primary elections, it was easier to manipulate and structure them for particular political purposes. In response to their 1968 experiences, the Democrats adopted a set of reforms designed to make the state conventions more open and representative. Delegates could not be selected until the calendar year of the nominating convention; this rule prevented the early selection of delegates at a time when most citizens were not yet attuned to presidential politics. State parties were required to publicize the time, place, and rules of all party meetings, to hold meetings in accessible places, and to provide as much information as possible about the presidential preferences of the persons seeking to be delegates to the national convention. Formerly, party organizations often held the conventions under a veritable veil of secrecy, which resulted in very limited participation in the delegate selection process.

THE ALLOCATION OF DELEGATES

Each party has its own formula for determining how many votes each state and territory will have at the nominating convention. The formulas take into account the population of the state and the partisan success of the party within the state at previous elections. In addition, the Republican rules provide bonus convention votes to those states with Republican presidential, congressional, and gubernatorial election victories.

Unlike the Republicans, the Democrats have often modified their delegate apportionment methods since 1952. Their current formula gives each state "three times its number of electoral college votes plus additional votes based on the average vote for the party's presidential ticket in the past three elections" (Parris, 1972: 30). This formula resulted in 1976, 1980, and 1984 conventions with over 3,000 votes; in fact, each time the Democrats changed their rules, the number of convention votes increased. In 1988 the Democrats had their largest convention ever, with 4,162 delegates while the GOP convention had about half that number.

THE CHARACTERISTICS OF DELEGATES

Observers have taken an interest in the characteristics of convention delegates, assuming that delegates with different backgrounds and different experiences would, in fact, behave differently at national conventions. But this seems to be a questionable assumption for delegates voting for presidential nominees because many delegates are morally if not legally bound to vote for a particular candidate. Of course, delegates are likely to have greater discretion over certain other activities at conventions, for example, over fights about platform and credentials rights. Prior to the 1972 convention, for instance, there was much speculation that McGovern would not be able to keep his delegates united on disputes over the platform and credentials. This was because many of his delegates were new to conventions, highly motivated by issue concerns, and unlikely to accept discipline. While this did not occur, it does suggest how background characteristics may plausibly be related to behavior.

Table 8.5 shows the demographic background and previous convention experience of delegates. The table entries are based on different sample surveys conducted of convention delegates, which is why the results are not identical across studies. Note that the proportion of women delegates has risen dramatically since 1968; for the Democrats, women currently comprise about 50 percent of the delegates because of the party's equal division rule. The proportion of young delegates appears to have declined after reaching a peak in 1972. For the Democrats, 1972 was the peak year because of the existence of quotas for young people.

The delegates' experience at previous national conventions has also interested political observers. It is argued that conventions dominated by newcomers are likely to be unpredictable and disorderly affairs, in contrast to conventions dominated by political veterans. Loch K. Johnson and Harlan Hahn (1973: 148) report that between 1944 and 1968, the average Republican convention had 65.1 percent inexperienced delegates and the average Democratic convention 63.7 percent. As shown in table 8.5, the proportion of newcomers to the 1972 Democratic convention increased to about 84 percent because of the rules changes adopted by the party and because of the attractiveness of the McGovern candidacy to citizens not normally involved in partisan and presidential politics. Demonstrating the effect of previous convention experience on convention behavior is difficult. Johnson and Hahn (1973: 161) did uncover a pattern between 1948 and 1968, which indicated that experienced delegates were more likely to support seasoned candidates and that inexperienced delegates were more likely to support political newcomers to presidential politics. Note that in 1988, the percentage of first-time delegates was at a low because of the presence of the superdelegates, experienced party officials, and elected officials.

One final characteristic of delegates has received increased attention: is the delegate's outlook on politics that of an amateur (that is, of a purist) or that of a professional? Participation of an amateur, or purist, in politics is based mainly on pragmatic issue concerns; the amateur judges candidates according to their stands on issues. In contrast, the professional is motivated by more traditional party concerns, such as the need to win elections; hence, candidates are judged on how well they can unify the party and win the election. From this basic difference in outlook follow a number of other differences; for example, the professionals are more willing to compromise on issues, since issues are not their central concern, while the amateurs are more willing to contest issues to the bitter end, no matter what the consequences are for party unity. Obviously, a convention dominated by purists concerned only about issues and principles might not be the optimal setting for producing a winning ticket. Yet a convention dominated by party regulars may not be a productive setting for confronting controversial issues that are in need of some resolution.

TABLE 8.5

Distribution of Demographic Groups among Convention Delegates, 1968, 1972, 1976, 1980, 1984, and 1988

	1968	1972			1976		1980		1984	1988
		NPE*	CPS†	CBS‡	CPS†	CBS‡	CPS†	CBS‡	CBS‡	CBS‡
Democrats										
Women	13%	42%	44%	40%	38%	33%	53%	49%	50%	52%
Blacks	6	16	7	15	5	11	7	15	18	21
Under 30	4	24	19	22	15	15	14	11	8	4
College +	—	56	70	57	70	64	66	65	71	73
First convention	—	83	86	83	75	80	76	87	71	62
Republicans										
Women	17	34	39	29	34	31	32	29	44	37
Blacks	2	5	2	4	1	3	1	3	4	3
Under 30	9	8	8	8	7	7	7	5	4	4
College +	—	58	62	—	63	65	63	65	63	68
First convention	—	66	81	78	82	78	73	84	—	59

*Data are based on responses to the 1972 delegate study, interview portion. Reported in Jeane J. Kirkpatrick, *The New Presidential Elite: Men and Women in National Politics* (New York: Russell Sage Foundation, 1976).
†Center for Political Studies, 1981 convention delegate study.
‡CBS News/*New York Times* delegate surveys.
SOURCE: Barbara Farah, "Convention Delegates: Party Reform and the Representativeness of Party Elites, 1972–1980," paper presented at the annual meeting of the American Political Science Association, New York City, September 3–6, 1981, Table 2, p. 4, and Steven V. Roberts, "Delegates 'Feel Good' About Candidate," *New York Times*, August 24, 1984, p. A10.

A convention dominated by professionals may produce a ticket and platform so bland that it will be difficult to mobilize the thousands of volunteers needed to conduct a full campaign.

Studies of the 1968 and 1972 Democratic conventions found that the amateur–professional distinction was related to the candidate preference of delegates, with amateurs favoring more issue-oriented and liberal candidates. For example, John W. Soule and James W. Clarke (1970: 89) report that the most typical supporter of Eugene McCarthy in 1968 was the liberal amateur, while the strongest support for Humphrey came from conservative professionals. Similarly, in an investigation of the 1972 convention, Denis G. Sullivan and his associates (1974: 124) found that the centrist candidates, such as Humphrey, Muskie, and Jackson, tended to be supported by professionals, while the more ideologically extreme candidates, such as Wallace and McGovern, were much more likely to be supported by purists. Overall, purists at the 1972 convention overwhelmingly favored McGovern, while professionals preferred the candidates of the center. In a similar vein, Jeane J. Kirkpatrick (1976) found that the supporters of the centrist candidates in 1972 emphasized the role of the convention in unifying the party and putting forth a winning ticket, while the Wallace and McGovern delegates were much more likely to cite the importance of correct issue positions, party reform, and the like.

Studies of the 1976 convention delegates found distinctive orientations among supporters of Reagan versus Ford (Roback, 1977a, 1977b) but scant differences among Carter delegates versus backers of other Democratic contenders (Jackson, Brown, and Brown, 1978). Reagan delegates were far more likely than Ford loyalists to cite support for their candidate's positions on issues and ideology as the reason for their participation in the convention. Compared to the Ford delegates, the Reagan backers were more likely to cite matters associated with political purposes and programs as their incentive for becoming active in the party; they were less likely to cite material rewards and solidarity. Fortunately for Ford, many supporters of Reagan's programs also valued highly party loyalty and victory in the election. At the Democratic convention there were only modest differences between the political orientation of Carter delegates and of supporters of other candidates. Because the differences were slight, the task of achieving party unity after the convention was much easier.

THE NOMINATING CONVENTIONS

The nominating conventions have a number of functions, the foremost being nominating the presidential and vice-presidential candidates, drafting a platform, and running the party in the interelection period via the national committee. Certainly nominating the presidential candidate is the focal point of the convention; yet in recent years this decision has largely been settled prior to the convention. Donald Matthews (1974: 54) points out that since 1936 the leading candidates at the beginning of the primary season have invariably won their party's nomination, the major exceptions being the failure of the early Democratic front-runner, Senator Edmund Muskie of Maine, to win the 1972 nod and the rise of Jimmy Carter from obscurity to win the nomination in 1976. Table 8.6 indicates the open-and-shut nature of the nominating conventions. This table shows the number of candidates who received more than 10 percent of the convention vote and the number of ballots required to select a presidential nominee since 1952. Note that the only nomination to go beyond the first ballot was that of Stevenson in 1952.

There was much speculation in late 1975 that the 1976 Democratic convention would break the pattern of recent conventions and require numerous ballots and extensive convention bargaining to select a nominee. This speculation was fueled by the absence of an obvious front-runner, by the presence of many candidates in the race, and by the Democratic delegate selection rules banning winner-take-all primaries. Yet not only were there no multiple ballots, but the nominee was effectively decided far in advance of the convention. How did this happen? Certainly Jimmy Carter started early, worked hard, adopted a shrewd strategy, and put together the needed resources. Yet this is only a partial explanation of how Carter emerged from the pack of candidates to secure the nomination early. The focus of media coverage and the role the media play in winnowing candidates must also be examined. As will be seen in chapter 9, the primaries and caucuses, particularly the early ones, receive extensive coverage, which serves to establish front-runners, create momentum, and eliminate candidates. Carter's early successes in Iowa and New Hampshire were certainly notable, but they were not of such significance as to thrust him to the head of the pack. After all, Carter came in second in the Iowa precinct caucuses with 29.1 percent of the vote, compared to 38.5 percent for uncommitted delegates. And in the highly fragmented New Hampshire primary, Carter "won" with 28.4 percent of the vote, compared to 22.7 percent for Udall, 15.2 percent for Bayh, 10.8 percent for Harris, and a scattering of votes for other candidates. How can these showings be considered so impressive that Carter was thrust to the forefront? The answer is that the media treated them as consequential—and they therefore became so. As Thomas E. Patterson (1977a) has demonstrated, the media's focus on winners resulted in Carter getting a disproportionate share of media coverage because of his early successes, and this in turn made him better known than his opponents in subsequent primary states. Patterson labeled the phenomenon *winner-take-all journalism* and showed that in the critical two-month period between February 23 and April 27, Carter got 43 percent of the network evening news coverage given to Democratic presidential contenders, 59 percent of the *Time* and *Newsweek* space, and 46 percent of the coverage in selected newspapers.

The fact that the nominee is most often determined prior to the convention does not mean that conventions are unexciting and lack controversy. Of course, McGovern's nomination in 1972 would have been more problematic had the challenge to his California delegates ultimately proved successful.

Credentials contests, such as the California challenge, and disputes over the party platform can generate substantial excitement and conflict. Eisenhower's nomination in 1952 certainly depended on the disposition of a number of credentials fights. Moreover, losing candidates and causes often attempt and sometimes are successful in altering the party's platform. Reagan in 1976 and Kennedy in 1980 left their imprint on their parties' platforms. In 1964 moderate Republicans unsuccessfully turned their efforts toward modifying the GOP platform once it became clear that Goldwater had clinched the nomination. Likewise, Democratic doves in 1968 made a major effort to get a Vietnam plank to their liking, while recognizing that Hubert Humphrey's nomination was virtually assured. In 1960 Nelson Rockefeller considered a challenge to the nomination of Richard Nixon and eventually focused his efforts on the party platform, which resulted in the famous "Compact of Fifth Avenue," in which Nixon pushed for platform changes desired by Rockefeller. At the 1988 Democratic convention, Jesse Jackson successfully pushed for a formal vote on a number of controversial issues even as Dukakis was assured of victory in the nomination battle.

Some of the more significant deliberations of the convention take place behind the scenes in the presence of a small number of party elites. The

---

TABLE 8.6

The Number of Ballots and the Number of Candidates Polling 10 Percent of the Votes in the Democratic and Republican Conventions, 1952–1988

| Year | Democratic conventions | | Republican conventions | |
------	Candidates over 10 percent	Number of ballots	Candidates over 10 percent	Number of ballots
1952	4	3	2	1
1956	2	1	1	1
1960	2	1	1	1
1964	1	1	2	1
1968	2	1	3	1
1972	3	1	1	1
1976	3	1	2	1
1980	2	1	2	1
1984	3	1	1	1
1988	2	1	1	1

SOURCES: Frank J. Sorauf, *Party Politics in America*, 2d ed. (Boston: Little, Brown, 1972), Table 1, p. 293; accounts of the 1972 election; *Guide to 1976 Elections* (Washington, D.C.: Congressional Quarterly, Inc., 1977), pp. 14–15; and *Congressional Quarterly Weekly Report*, July 19, 1980, p. 2067, and August 16, 1980, p. 2437 and 1984 *CQ Almanac*, p. 68-B.

selection of the vice-presidential nominee is such an activity; the selection process is best described as haphazard. The usual procedure is for the vice-presidential decision to be made by the successful presidential nominee in consultation with his or her staff and a broad range of party elites. This means that the decision is often made under extreme time constraints by an exhausted candidate and staff. This is the explanation given for the Eagleton fiasco in 1972; the McGovern staff simply did not have the opportunity to do an extensive investigation of Senator Eagleton's background. Normally the presidential nominee's choice for vice-president is routinely ratified by the convention delegates, although there was opposition to both parties' vice-presidential selection in 1968 and 1972. In rare cases, the determination of the vice-presidential candidate is left to the convention at large; Adlai Stevenson in 1956 allowed the Democratic convention to choose his running mate. The process by which Carter selected Mondale as his running mate in 1976 was much more thorough and deliberate than is normally the case. In 1980 there was a flurry of excitement at the GOP convention as rumors spread that Reagan was planning to select former president Ford as his vice-presidential running mate. Reagan finally acted to quell these rumors and announced his selection of George Bush. In 1984, Mondale announced his selection of Ferraro early, while in 1988, Bush surprised the Republican convention with the selection of U.S. Senator Dan Quayle as his running mate.

REFORMING THE NOMINATION SYSTEM

At present, there is much dissatisfaction with the nomination system and especially with the state presidential primary elections. Those in favor of the primaries point out that these elections allow citizens to participate in the nomination process, thus increasing the public's interest in politics. Those opposed criticize the primaries on personal, political, and philosophical grounds. On personal grounds they argue that primaries require too much time, energy, and money; in this way the primaries effectively rule out candidates who do not have ample funds or are unwilling to subject themselves to the indignities associated with primary contests. As mentioned in chapter 1, the primary system has become an endurance contest. Its critics question whether candidates should have to endure such a trial by fire. On the other hand, proponents of the primary system argue that it enables voters to determine if the prospective nominee has the strength and fortitude to stand up to the rigors of being president; the grueling pace of the primaries is said to be a proper test of a candidate's ability to be president. Yet other observers have argued just the opposite, claiming that the endurance contest aspect of the primaries has little to say about a candidate's fitness for the presidency.

Another set of critics of the primaries focus on how to interpret the results of an election. They argue that for a variety of reasons the primaries do not indicate accurately the voters' preference for candidates. For example, not all candidates participate in a primary. Because many candidates may compete in a primary, the victor may be a plurality winner who is not preferred (and may even be opposed) by a majority of the party faithful.

In addition, the representativeness—or its lack—undermines our ability to interpret the outcome of a primary election. For example, in a study of eleven contested presidential primaries between 1952 and 1968, Austin Ranney (1972: 23–24) found a mean turnout rate of 39 percent, some 30 points below the general election average. The low turnout in many primaries clearly increases the probability of an unrepresentative electorate. Examining the 1968 New Hampshire and Wisconsin primaries, Ranney (1972: 36) concluded that the electorates were demographically unrepresentative and to a lesser extent atypical in their issue and candidate preferences. In a study of competitive presidential primaries in 1976, Ranney (1977: 22–26) found a mean turnout rate of only 28 percent, again raising the possibility of an unrepresentative electorate. In contrast, Geer (1988) and Norrander (1989a, 1989b) argue that primary voters were reasonably representative of their parties' potential and actual supporters in the general election and, more importantly, that the composition of the primary electorate did not in any major way bias the outcome of the process. The general thrust of their argument is that one should not blame the primary system for producing unrepresentative and unelectable nominees for the general election.

The New Hampshire primary is a useful target for questioning the significance of primary results. As the first presidential primary, it has become crucial and has the power to make or break candidates. Certainly Muskie's relatively unimpressive (though victorious) showing in New Hampshire signaled the beginning of his decline as a viable candidate. Yet, should the voters of New Hampshire, a lightly populated, relatively unurbanized state, have so much power? In particular, should fewer than 100,000 Democratic voters in New Hampshire be in such a crucial position when these Democrats are unrepresentative of Democrats nationally? Compounding the atypicality of New Hampshire was the presence of now deceased publisher William Loeb and his influential newspaper, the *Manchester Union Leader*. Loeb did his best to hurt the Muskie candidacy and apparently was successful in holding down Muskie's margin in Manchester, where his paper had its greatest circulation.

Another problem with the primaries is the criteria used to interpret the results and the effects of these interpretations on the selection process. Obviously, it was highly newsworthy when the heavy underdog McGovern managed to win 37 percent of the New Hampshire vote in 1972, as against only 46 percent for the heavy favorite, Muskie. Yet the fact is that Muskie did win the primary. But the candidate who is designated the front-runner by the media incurs risks because the media may evaluate the candidate's performance in terms of how strongly he or she has won rather than in terms of whether the candidate has won or not. Thus, the media widely interpreted Muskie's weaker than expected showing in New Hampshire as a major setback to his candidacy.

The point here is that the results of primary elections receive their significance from the standards used in interpreting them. Different standards may affect the future course of political events in different ways. For example, the coverage of the McGovern candidacy in 1972 may have served to promote his chances. That is, since McGovern was not expected to do well, his relatively strong though nonwinning performances in a number of states were widely viewed as victories. It was not until late in the primary season that the press began dissecting the McGovern campaign as closely as it had others. Likewise, Ford's winning, but weak, performance in the New Hampshire primary in 1976 was made more impressive by media interpretations grounded in the expectation that Ford would actually lose. (This will be discussed further in chapter 9.)

A final problem with the primaries is that the system itself is not neutral but highly manipulable; it can help some candidacies and hurt others. As suggested earlier, the scheduling of primaries is of strategic importance; an early loss can be devastating, just as an early victory can be uplifting. What would have happened in 1976 had western states been first on the primary schedule? Would Californian Jerry Brown or Idahoan Frank Church, or both, have entered the contest earlier, and would their possible early victories have established them as the leading candidates? Finally, it is clear that victories (or losses) are not equivalent, given the serial nature of the primaries. An early loss (for example, New Hampshire) or a late loss (for example, California) is probably more damaging than a loss in the middle of the primary season. The primary system as a decision-making procedure is not neutral; instead, it bestows benefits on certain candidacies, thereby influencing the outcome of the process.

Numerous reforms of the primary system have been suggested that would alleviate certain shortcomings and worsen others. The most commonly mentioned alternative to the present primaries is a national primary in all fifty states. To prevent the possibility of a victorious candidate who has only a small plurality of the vote, most proposals for a national primary include a runoff provision between the top two vote-getters should no candidate get 40 percent of the vote.

The national primary certainly eliminates the possibility of any single state's primary (or caucus) being given undue weight. It also permits a broader, and possibly more representative, participation of citizens in the candidate selection process. And a national primary shortens the campaign period, thereby making life more civilized for the candidates. Yet the national primary has some obvious drawbacks. One is that it raises the specter of three national elections—primary, runoff, and general—which would require substantial resources. Furthermore, it is likely that only candidates who are already well known will have a reasonable chance of victory in a national primary. By eliminating the serial nature of the present primary system, the national primary rules out the possibility of some obscure candidate (such as McGovern in 1972 or Carter in 1976) rising from obscurity to win the nomination. A national primary would prevent candidates from "testing the waters"; instead, a candidate would have to enter full force or not at all.

Proposals have also been made for regional primaries and for clusters of primaries on the same date in geographically diverse states. Each of these proposals is designed to avoid some of the pitfalls of the national primary while retaining some of the better features of the existing primary system. For example, a set of grouped primaries would maintain the sequencing features of the present system and allow a candidate to enter one set of primaries before having to decide on the remainder. None of these proposals seems likely to much reduce campaign costs.

John C. Geer (1986) has offered an intriguing set of reform proposals to avoid the possibility that the primaries might yield nominees unpopular with their own partisans and unable to win the general election. First, Geer advocates that delegates be awarded in close proportion to the primary outcome. Second, he proposes preference voting in which citizens are allowed to "rank order" the competing candidates; that is, voters could indicate their first choice, their second choice, and so on among a field of candidates. Finally, he urges allowing Independents to participate in party primaries. He argues that these changes would provide a better test of a candidate's electability. But the prospects for his reforms, particularly for preference voting, seem remote at best.

While such proposals for primary election reforms would affect both parties identically, other reform efforts have proceeded differently in each party. The Democrats have taken the more dramatic steps. After their bitter 1968 convention they created two reform commissions, one on party structure and delegate selection, headed by Senator McGovern, and one on rules, headed by Representative James O'Hara of Michigan. After a year of deliberations, the McGovern commission issued a list of eighteen guidelines for delegate selection, many of which have been mentioned previously. The intent of the reforms was to make the convention more representative and to open up the political process to people who had traditionally not participated.

The issue of representation with respect to national party conventions is a tricky one. For example, critics in 1968 lamented that the nominees selected in the conventions (Humphrey and Nixon) were unrepresentative relics of the old politics. In fact, nationwide polls of *all* citizens indicated that Rockefeller was more popular than Nixon and that McCarthy was preferred over Humphrey. But among Democrats and Republicans only, Humphrey and Nixon were the respective favorites. Thus, the conventions in 1968 adequately reflected the desires of the partisans of each party.

Since the issue of representation also extends to the characteristics of the convention delegates, some critics argue that both parties' delegates were unrepresentative, being mainly white, middle-aged males. Thus, one of the McGovern commission reforms was the now infamous quotas for women, youth, and blacks; it was assumed that these groups had interests that only their own members could represent. The rationale for providing quotas for these three groups and not for others was in part that blacks, youth, and women had been traditionally underrepresented; but this did not satisfy those groups that were without the protection of quotas.

The McGovern reforms, especially opening the delegation selection process through quotas, seemed to answer the question as to whether greater loyalty was owed to one's party or to one's group. Examining the 1972 Democratic delegation from California, William Cavala (1974: 40) concluded that it was very difficult to select delegates on the traditional basis of service to the party and that the delegates finally selected had only a distant relationship to the state and local campaign effort. Cavala (1974: 42) concluded that the new rules "hindered the efforts of the eventual winner to mount an effective electoral campaign." It seems clear that in the choice between issue purity and electoral success, the rules resulted in an emphasis on the former.

However, since 1972 the Democratic party, through the Mikulski, Winograd, and Hunt commissions, has backed away from some of the McGovern–Fraser rules changes. As mentioned earlier, quotas have given way to affirmative action. The creation of a superdelegate status at the 1984 and 1988 conventions reserved for party officials and officeholders, reflects a different perspective on party service and party leadership than that which characterized the 1972 convention. F. Christopher Arterton (1978) has analyzed the consequences of party reform. He notes that the presidential selection process has become nationalized as more and more decisions are taken away from the state political parties. Moreover, state party leaders are no longer central actors at conventions; state interests have given way to candidate-centered coalitions. The delegates themselves have less flexibility in their convention behavior as primary and caucus results bind them to a particular candidate. Overall, Arterton concludes that the rules changes have made it difficult for the party establishment to control who gets the nomination; certainly McGovern and Carter were not the candidates preferred by party leaders. The ongoing controversy over Democratic party rules reflects the inherent strain between concerns about participatory values and party loyalty. Citizens whose main priority was participation probably viewed the McGovern–Fraser reforms very positively as new participants became involved in the presidential selection process, even if they were more committed to the welfare of a particular candidate than to the political party itself. Citizens more concerned about the party per se probably saw the modifications of the McGovern–Fraser rules since 1972 as steps in the right direction. Questions of party reform and the future of political parties will be discussed further in the last chapter.[1]

Note

1. For a discussion of the normative and descriptive aspects of party reform, see Austin Ranney (1975), William Crotty (1977, 1978), and Nelson W. Polsby (1983).

CHAPTER 9

The Media and Presidential Politics

Television and Presidential Politics

Presidential candidates often follow hectic campaign schedules, at times campaigning on the same day in cities separated by thousands of miles. In contrast, it is clear that most voters do not experience the campaign firsthand but instead follow it through the media—television, radio, newspapers, and magazines. Television, of course, has become *the* medium through which campaigns are conducted. This section will describe the patterns of media usage in presidential elections, present a brief history of the uses of television in contests for the presidency, and focus on two effects television has had on presidential politics—*systemic effects* and *individual effects*. The former refer to the consequences of television for the presidential nomination and election process, while the latter refer to the more subtle impact of television on the average citizen.

PATTERNS OF MEDIA USAGE OVER TIME

The most dramatic development in media usage patterns has been the increased reliance on television as a source of information about presidential campaigns. In 1952, when television ownership in the United States was not widespread, about 36 percent of Americans said that television was their most important campaign information source, followed closely by radio (32 percent) and newspapers (26 percent), with magazines trailing far behind (6 percent). By 1960, when television ownership was nearly universal, reliance on television had increased to 65 percent, while the proportion of citizens citing radio as their most important medium had dropped to 6 percent; newspapers and magazines held fairly steady at 24 and 5 percent respectively. Today the patterns very closely resemble those of 1960: about 66 percent of Americans claim that television is their most important source of campaign information, about 25 percent cite newspapers, and the rest are split between magazines and radio. Only for information about local politics do newspapers enjoy a sizable advantage over television in terms of citizen confidence and reliance.

Table 9.1 gives a more complete picture of the patterns of media usage by indicating the percentage of Americans who have used each of the various media as sources of campaign information since 1952. Note that most Americans claim to use television for campaign information, with newspapers running a strong second; radio and magazines are less frequently used. While table 9.1 charts the basic patterns of usage, the information presented is quite

TABLE 9.1

The Frequency of Media Usage, 1952–1988* (in percentages)

Medium	1952	1956	1960	1964	1968	1972	1976	1980	1984	1988
Newspapers	79%	68%	80%	78%	75%	57%	73%	71%	77%	64%
Radio	70	45	42	49	41	43	45	47	45	31
Magazines	40	31	41	39	36	33	48	35	35	25
Television	51	74	87	89	89	88	89	86	86	95

*The table entries are the percentage of respondents in each year who reported using each of the media as a source of campaign information. If one discounts respondents who said they relied on television very little, then the percentage of television users in 1988 drops to 80.

SOURCES: SRC/CPS election studies.

crude in that one has little sense of the extent of reliance on each medium or of the kind of information that each medium provides. For example, when a person claims that television is his or her most important source of information, this does not tell us whether it is political advertisements or public affairs documentaries or the evening news programs that are most important for the person. The amount and quality of information conveyed by a partisan spot commercial should be appreciably lower than that provided by an hour-long documentary. Thus, to gain a more detailed perspective on citizens' media reliance, table 9.2 shows the number of media employed by citizens as sources of campaign information. While the number of media is itself a crude indicator of the richness of the information obtained by citizens, it nevertheless yields some insight into the diversity of information available to citizens.

Note that, according to table 9.2, there is a measurable proportion of citizens who do not follow the campaign in any of the four media. This result is a bit startling, given how readily a citizen was classified as a media user. That is, the respondent need only claim to have employed the medium once (for example, watched one campaign show on television) in order to be coded as a user of that medium. The number of citizens who rely on all four media has been above 13 percent in all elections except 1988. The most noteworthy point of table 9.2 is that with the exception of 1988 about 50 percent of the citizenry relies on two or fewer media and the other 50 percent on three or four. Citizens who depend on one or two media most frequently cite television and newspapers.

While a detailed analysis of the characteristics of various media users is beyond the scope of this book, note that educational level is closely related to certain types of media exposure and not to others. In particular, reliance upon magazines and newspapers covaries with the level of education. Thus, more highly educated citizens are more likely to cite the print media as a source of campaign information. Television exposure, however, has not been related to education in recent elections except that television is more likely to be the only way that people with lower levels of education follow the campaign. And these low involvement/low information citizens are of great importance to the electoral process because they often comprise a large portion of the crucial swing vote (Cundy, 1989). Before television became widespread, there was a moderate relationship between television reliance and education since the early owners of television sets tended to be disproportionately wealthy and highly educated.

Hence, television is the preeminent source of campaign information, a situation upsetting to some observers because of the limited ability of television to present in-depth coverage of news stories. The half-hour national evening news programs must of necessity distill from a large number of stories those that are most newsworthy. And the stories selected for presentation must be condensed into a few minutes, thereby making it difficult to place the story in a broader context or to present the full range of relevant details. Some readers of the *New York Times*, overwhelmed by the amount of information presented in the paper, have facetiously modified the paper's slogan from "All

TABLE 9.2

The Number of Media Used by Citizens, 1952–1988* (in percentages)

Number of media	1952	1956	1960	1964	1968	1972	1976	1980	1984	1988
None	6%	8%	5%	3%	4%	5%	5%	5%	6%	10%
One	14	19	13	12	15	21	15	16	13	29
Two	30	32	28	30	32	33	23	30	31	33
Three	35	28	35	36	34	27	34	32	32	21
Four	15	13	19	19	14	13	23	17	18	7
Total	100	100	100	100	99	99	100	100	100	100
Number of cases	1,646	1,741	1,808	1,449	1,341	1,108	2,378	1,408	1,937	2,040

*The table entries are the percentages of citizens in each year reporting that they used the specified number of media. The percentages for 1988 are not strictly comparable since the wording of some questions had changed.

SOURCES: SRC/CPS election studies.

the News That's Fit to Print" to "All the News That Fits We Print." All the same, major newspapers are far more able than television to devote substantial space to stories that give both background and analysis.[1] Television, on the contrary, is much less able to analyze and editorialize, to provide context and evaluation. Yet television network news is more analytical and interpretive than the wire services, such as UPI, which tend to present straight factual reports (Michael J. Robinson and Margaret Sheehan, 1983).

The more important point is that the only reality many events have for people is what is presented on television. Blume (1985, p. 2) asserts that "the nightly news, for all practical purposes, *is* the electoral process. In this culture, if something is not on the TV nightly news, it didn't happen, it doesn't exist, it's invisible." The presence of both a video and a narrative component is very powerful in shaping citizens' judgments of an event. Just, Neuman, and Crigler (1989) argue that televised messages may be more memorable because they provide what newspapers cannot—moving pictures and animation—which facilitates storage and retrieval of information by citizens. As Kurt Lang and Gladys Engel Lang (1968: 297) point out, "The televised event, however inauthentic and unrevealing, becomes the actuality." The television camera need not tell it as it is; there is ample opportunity for staging events to achieve maximum effect, as in a televised campaign rally during which the camera pans only on the enthusiastic supporters of the candidate, thereby giving the impression of widespread warmth toward the candidate. And once an image, however inaccurate, has been transmitted, it is extremely difficult to correct that image later on.[2]

Thus, citizens rely most heavily on the medium that is least able to present detailed information about issues and candidates. This is not to say that television, particularly news reporting, is biased, only that it is incomplete. In a systematic study of network news coverage of the 1972 campaign, C. Richard Hofstetter (1976) found very little evidence of any partisan bias on behalf of a party or a candidate.[3] This contrasts markedly with newspaper editorial endorsement policies, which have overwhelmingly favored the Republican presidential candidates, with the exception of Goldwater in 1964. At times, the partisan biases of newspapers spill over from the editorial page to the news columns themselves. *The Manchester Union Leader*, New Hampshire's largest newspaper, was renowned as an outlet for the views of its right-wing publisher, William Loeb, now deceased. The *Union Leader* is influential in New Hampshire because of the absence of statewide television stations and in presidential politics because of the crucial position of New Hampshire as the first state to hold a presidential primary.[4] Loeb's vendetta against Senator Muskie in 1972 (including scurrilous attacks on Muskie's wife and the publication of fabricated letters accusing Muskie of uttering ethnic slurs against Franco-Americans, an important voting bloc in New Hampshire) undoubtedly played a significant role in unraveling the Muskie candidacy.[5] In the 1976 Republican primary in New Hampshire the *Union Leader* covered Ford more negatively than Reagan (Loeb's preferred candidate) in both news reports and editorials (Eric P. Veblen and Robert E. Craig, 1976), and in 1980 the paper strongly favored Reagan over his competitors in the GOP primary.

The absence of widespread partisan bias in television does not alter the fact that the medium is poorly suited to provide citizens with a full, detailed, and accurate description of political events.[6] Paradoxically, this failure of television is one reason for its effectiveness, since it forces citizens to fill in the partial picture presented by television according to their own predispositions. That is, television is a "cool medium": there is substantial audience involvement in completing the partial images depicted by television. The potential consequences of this situation as well as a more general analysis of television's effects will be discussed after a brief discussion of the history of television in presidential campaigns.

A BRIEF HISTORY OF TELEVISION IN PRESIDENTIAL CAMPAIGNS[7]

An intriguing feature in the evolution of television in presidential campaigns has been its close association with the career of Richard Nixon. Nixon's famous "Checkers" speech in 1952 provided one of the earliest indications of television's political power. Nixon had been accused of profiting from a political slush fund, and there were demands that he be removed as the vice-presidential candidate on the Republican ticket. To counteract the criticisms, Nixon gave a speech on national television that was described by Marvin R. Weisbord in the following manner (1966: 181–182):

> The broadcast proved Nixon a cool performer in an extremely ticklish situation. His fund, he said earnestly, was not secret; no money went for his personal use; no favors were granted in return for contributions. In a firm voice he recited his life story—the poor boy who had worked his way through college, married, gone off to war, returned to law practice, and run for Congress. He listed everything he owned—from a 1950 Oldsmobile to GI life insurance, and paid homage to his wife's "respectable Republican cloth coat". . . .
>
> Americans nodded in sympathy as Nixon bared his life, his finances, his affection for the wife and daughters flanking him on stage, and the family's affection for another gift they had received, a black and white cocker spaniel named Checkers. "I just want to say this, right now, regardless of what they say about it, we are going to keep it."

Nixon's speech was television at its melodramatic best, and his closing appeal for support was answered by thousands and thousands of letters and telegrams. The impact of the speech provided an early indication of how candidates might use television effectively.

The year 1952 also witnessed the advent of the televised spot commercial in politics. The spot was a very short ad designed to convey a basic point or image without going into depth on issues or providing much information. One commercial showed General Eisenhower being asked, "Mr. Eisenhower, what about the high cost of living?" The general responded, "My wife, Mamie, worries about the same thing. I tell her it's our job to change that on November 4" (Rubin, 1967: 34). Note that this spot does not say anything specific about how the problem will be solved; it simply conveys the image that the candidate is sincerely concerned about the issue. The use of spot commercials has been particularly upsetting to those observers who believe that the function of the campaign is to inform the electorate. Since that time spot commercials have been part of political campaigns, and they are often very useful vehicles for creating distorted, simplistic images of issues and candidates. In 1964 the Democrats used a very controversial spot commercial that portrayed a little girl picking daisies, followed by pictures of a nuclear explosion; this was followed by the reassuring statements of Lyndon Johnson about the need for nuclear responsibility. Obviously this spot was a blatant scare tactic designed to increase voters' fears of Senator Goldwater.

The Kennedy–Nixon television debates, discussed in chapter 5, are widely viewed as an example of the best that television has to offer politics. It was estimated that between 70 and 75 million Americans saw the first debate, with audiences of over 50 million for the other three. The Carter–Ford debates in 1976, the Carter–Reagan debate in 1980, the Reagan–Mondale debates in 1984, and the Bush–Dukakis debates in 1988 also enjoyed large audiences, although they did not attain the prominence of the 1960 debates.

The 1968 election witnessed a more sophisticated use of television in the Nixon campaign. In the primaries television was successfully used to change Nixon's image from that of an untrustworthy loser to that of a confidence-in-spiring winner. Commercials portrayed Nixon as a warm person with the skills to manage the nation's affairs, especially in the realm of foreign policy. And in the general election, the basic television strategy was to have Nixon appear in staged, controlled settings, answering prepared questions before carefully selected audiences. The home viewer would see in these televised sessions a confident Nixon fielding questions from a highly enthusiastic audience. Nixon avoided, until the very end of the campaign, any appearances on spontaneous televised interview programs, such as "Face the Nation" and "Meet the Press." Longstanding concerns about the ability of the media and media experts to market candidates were reemphasized by a book entitled *The Selling of the President 1968*, which presented a behind-the-scenes description of the marketing of Richard Nixon. The following comments by Roger Ailes, the producer of the staged Nixon television shows, epitomize the marketing approach to packaging candidates (McGinniss, 1969: 103):

> Let's face it, a lot of people think Nixon is dull. Think he's a bore, a pain in the ass. They look at him as the kind of kid who always carried a bookbag. Who was forty-two years old the day he was born. They figure other kids got footballs for Christmas, Nixon got a briefcase and he loved it. He'd always have his homework done and he'd never let you copy.
>
> Now you put him on television, you've got a problem right away. He's a funny-looking guy. He looks like somebody hung him in a closet

overnight and he jumps out in the morning with his suit all bunched up and starts running around saying, "I want to be President." I mean this is how he strikes some people. That's why these shows are important. To make them forget all that.

The 1972 election was unusual in that television's major impact came in its "normal" coverage of political events rather than in any paid advertising campaigns. The immediacy with which television brought home George McGovern's inconsistencies on such matters as Eagleton's nomination and welfare reform was probably more devastating to McGovern's chances than any well-orchestrated advertising campaign. Likewise, the televised coverage given to Nixon's historic trips to China and the Soviet Union served to improve his political prospects by showing him as president while the various contenders for the Democratic presidential nomination were portrayed as politicians. The power of a president to dominate the broadcast media by foreign travel, dramatic announcements, and the like means that an incumbent president seeking reelection has a tremendously important resource at his or her disposal. Certainly the pinnacle of televised political drama was reached in 1974. The live broadcast of the select Senate committee's Watergate investigation and of the House Judiciary Committee's impeachment hearings captured the attention of the electorate and helped set the stage for Nixon's resignation.

THE EFFECTS OF TELEVISION

Introduction. The question of the effects of the mass media, particularly television, has given rise to numerous controversies and differences of opinion. Some observers have praised the mass media for widely disseminating information about public affairs, thereby presumably facilitating the development of the informed, independent citizenry of classical democratic theory. Other observers have asked whether television debases or perverts the political process and have worried about the power of television and the other media to manipulate and mold the preferences and opinions of a naive public. For example, Page and Shapiro (1988) suggest that the threat to the democratic political process comes from elite manipulation and control of American information systems rather than from any deficiencies on the part of citizens. They argue that abundant information is not necessary for vote choice *if* accurate information is available. They then assert that there are corporate, nationalistic, capitalistic, and elite biases in the information provided to citizens. While these worries have often been expressed in unnecessarily alarmist terms, they do represent genuine concerns about the consequences of television for American politics. Unfortunately, it is difficult to talk in a rigorous and systematic fashion about the effects of television in many areas because the appropriate evidence does not exist or is incomplete and contradictory. This situation occurs because many of the effects of the media are long-term and indirect rather than short-term and direct. As Joseph Klapper observes (1960:

8): "Mass communication *ordinarily* does not serve as a necessary and suffi cient cause of audience effects, but rather functions among and through a nexus of mediating factors and influences." This means that an ambitious research program examining many factors over an extended time is required to determine the effects of the media. For now, one is forced in part to speculate about the effects of the television, buttressing arguments wherever possible by appropriate evidence. Two broad classes of television effects can be identi fied—consequences for the political system at large, such as change in the presidential nomination system, and consequences for the individual citizen, such as the acquisition of political information. While this distinction between systemic effects and individual effects breaks down at times, it provides a useful organizing framework for discussion.

Television and the political system. Harold Mendelsohn and Irving Crespi (1970: 297–298) have identified four interrelated changes in American politics brought on in part by television:

1. It has altered the processes of nominating candidates at party conven- tions.
2. It has altered campaigning.
3. It has altered traditional party structures and functions.
4. It has helped encourage questioning of the traditional ways of choos- ing and electing candidates, and, as a consequence, will aid in usher- ing in the new politics of the future.

With respect to the second of the changes cited, it is now commonplace to describe presidential campaigns as being conducted primarily through the medium of television, with the planning and execution of the campaign largely in the hands of media experts and public relations and marketing specialists. This means that the party professional is no longer the central figure in the campaign and that the party organization is no longer the major source of campaign information. And with the development of computerized, direct mail fund-raising techniques, often aided by televised appeals, the party organization has become less important in another area traditionally within its domain.

Robert Agranoff (1972: 43) notes that the typical media campaign hurts the political party since media campaigns are designed to support a single candidate—not an entire ticket. The Nixon reelection campaign in 1972 is probably the preeminent example of this. In its concern to win an overwhelm- ing victory, the Nixon reelection team was careful not to antagonize potential Democratic defectors to Nixon by trying to elect the entire GOP ticket. The Nixon campaign was run, not through the Republican National Committee, but through the President's own personal organization—the Committee to Re-elect the President (CREEP).

Agranoff has also identified some positive changes in campaigning brought about by the electronic media. Certainly it is possible for greater numbers of citizens to follow campaigns today. And it is possible for voters to get a deeper, more personal insight into both candidates since the massive flow of information in presidential campaigns makes it less likely that selective processes could occur whereby partisans psychologically "tune out" the opposition candidate.

Yet the prominence of television has some serious negative consequences, the most obvious one being the need to package the candidate, which results in the campaign being a merchandising enterprise rather than an effort to inform the citizenry. The 1968 Nixon campaign is the classic marketing effort, while the 1988 Bush effort shows how the strategic selection of issues in conjunction with effective television commercials can shape candidate images and attractiveness. Another obvious consequence of the heavy reliance on television is the need for candidates who can at least minimally master and exploit the medium by projecting an attractive image. While this need not mean that George Washington or Abraham Lincoln would be unelectable candidates in the United States today, it does imply that the savvy candidate and his or her advisers will attempt to exploit the properties of television. And one such property is that television requires high involvement by the audience to complete the partial image that it conveys: this is what Marshall McCluhan (1964: 229) means when he calls television a "cool," or low-intensity, medium. This characteristic of television leads to an emphasis on audience participation and on the campaign as drama and may, in combination with Americans' weak ideological leanings and low political interest, create conditions conducive to significant media influence.

Another effect of television is on the day-to-day conduct of the presidential campaign. Today campaigns are geared to the television coverage they will receive; rallies are scheduled early in the day so that televised news reports will be ready for the nightly news programs. Candidates' speeches are designed to provide headlines for news broadcasts, and the rallies themselves are organized to create the image of enthusiastic support for the candidate. This concern for how the campaign will come across on television leads Mendelsohn and Crespi (pp. 281–282) to talk of the pseudo campaign.

There are some more subtle, more speculative systemic effects of television on American politics. If previously the political party via the machine, patronage, and constituent services served as a major link between citizens and government, today television provides that link by being the major source of information about the activities of government, particularly at the national level. The tenor of the news and information conveyed by television, however, tends to be negative, focusing on the shortcomings and failures of governmental actors. Thus, while serving as a link between citizens and government, television may serve to increase the distance between the two. Graber (1987) suggests that the networks may present more reports critical of the political establishment in order to "demonstrate that they are not pandering to the powers that be" (p. 558). The political party, on the other hand, may have served to bring government closer to the people since it was often a dispenser of direct rewards to the citizenry. Similarly, the political party often served as a unifying force, organizing a disparate variety of interests into some fairly unified whole. Television in certain ways may serve as a unifying force as it depicts the common concerns confronting citizens, but it may also exacerbate the differences that divide citizens by bringing controversies directly into the home. Thus, television's contribution to the demise of the political party may have some broader ramifications in society.

A number of observers have discussed the potential impact of television's coverage of "bad news." Michael Robinson (1972) has argued that when television news programs show two public institutions in conflict, both institutions suffer in citizens' evaluations and citizens' feelings of political effectiveness may drop. Gary L. Wamsley and Richard A. Pride (1972) argue in a similar vein that television news may be creating a citizenry that is more cynical and negative about politics, which in the long run may set the stage for dramatic system upheavals. They write (1972: 449–450):

> It seems reasonable to assume that members of a political system are supportive of that system and see it as legitimate to the degree that it is perceived to be: effective in solving problems, efficient in doing so, morally right in its conduct, and responsive and/or solicitous of citizen welfare. *It is a possibility* that the characteristics of TV news . . . result in a sum total of *effects* that is denigrative of political system authority symbols rather than supportive. It should be noted this is *not* necessarily the same thing as imputing "bias" to TV news. It is rather to say that . . . TV news [may] present the authority figures of the American political system in more of a negative light than a positive one. If this possibility is affirmed by thorough research, the incredibly difficult task of analyzing effects would only have begun. But it is *possible* that the characteristics of TV news, when combined with some relatively new conceptions of impact, effects, and audience characteristics, could lead to conclusions that are quite contrary to those complacently held for so long. Certainly the need is clear to view TV news with a new, scholarly skepticism, for it may hold a far more important place in the flow of political information than social scientists have assumed up to now.

As Wamsley and Pride admit, their argument is highly tentative and in need of confirming evidence.[8] In fact, a study by Garrett O'Keefe (1980) partially contradicts the Wamsley and Pride notion. O'Keefe finds that greater media (newspaper and television) reliance is associated with more positive political attitudes and values. Nevertheless, the possible negative effects of television on citizens' views of their political system remain a significant topic for research. And as Graber (1987) notes, negative media coverage could arise from several sources: reporting mainly adverse factual material, interpreting stories in a negative light, or actually selecting more negative stories in the first place.

The potential for television to set the issue agenda and determine the kinds of issues of concern to citizens and candidates may be related to increasing levels of cynicism. Byron Shafer and Richard Larson (1972) argue that television brings home to citizens information about a variety of issues, such as law and order, political protests, and deviant lifestyles, that otherwise would not have impinged on their consciousness. In so doing, television creates issues and concerns that otherwise would not exist. For example, residents of very safe neighborhoods express considerable fear about personal safety, undoubtedly because of television news coverage of crime in other localities.

Shafer and Larson argue that longer and more detailed news shows would help alleviate the tendency of television to oversimplify and create issues, but they further argue that the problem will not be solved until the current definition of what constitutes news is changed (1972: 16):

> The definition which almost all working journalists use—"outstanding deviations from civil norms"—exacerbates the problem of too many deviant, intrusive, incomprehensible minorities. On the other hand, if "news" were defined in a more outcome-oriented way—"events of importance to sizeable number of viewers"—actors who are merely novel or strident, but in no way influential in others' lives, would no longer fill the screen so copiously.
>
> The first to disappear would be those who are news only because the cameras record them. A news program ought to *reveal* what happened, not *create* the happening. Events which legitimately comprise news may affect more lives if the cameras arrive, but they would have impact beyond a few central actors even without publicity. With an outcome-oriented definition, events staged to manipulate the journalist's view of news as anything sufficiently outrageous would disappear.

Note that the suggestions of Shafer and Larson would result in more tranquil, more positive news programs, which perhaps would weaken the cynicism-producing effects of television cited by Robinson and Wamsley and Pride. Perhaps their suggestions might also lead to unjustifiably optimistic news broadcasts if decisions were made to systematically exclude bad news on the pretext that it did not fit the definition of news.

The work of Maxwell E. McCombs and Donald R. Shaw (1972) provides more rigorous evidence of the media's role in setting the agenda. They found that the issues emphasized in 1968 by the press and evening news shows in Chapel Hill, North Carolina, had a strong correlation with the issues the citizens themselves considered important. Likewise, Funkhouser (1973) found a relationship between media coverage of an issue and the tendency of citizens to cite the issue as being important to the country. However, when citizens were asked about the important problems confronting them directly, they referred to issues different from those that were the focus of media coverage. Hence, Funkhouser argued that the issues people mention in response to general questions about what issues are important are simply those that they have heard about on the media and not necessarily those that are meaningful to them, thereby weakening any claims for the agenda-setting function of the media. The work of Michael B. MacKuen (1979, 1981) supports Funkhouser. MacKuen found that the issue concerns of Americans tended to mirror media content, although in the area of economics, public concerns did not depend upon media coverage of economic matters.

Krosnick and Kinder (1990), in their study of priming and the Iran Contra affair, found that respondents' changes in their evaluations of President Reagan were directly related to changes in media focus after the scandal broke. The theory of priming holds that when people are asked to assess presidential performance, they mention those aspects that are most accessible to them. Since most people rely on the media for political information, it follows that those items that the media give greater attention to will be the ones the public uses to evaluate presidential performance. By focusing on certain matters and ignoring others, the media will affect the bases upon which citizens evaluate the president. Similarly, Iyengar (1987) found that how people explained national issues affected their judgment of presidential performance and that their explanations in large part depended on how television presented those issues. For example, when television covered a story by a "particular-victim" approach, citizens tended to see the issue not as national in scope, but instead very individualistic, thereby making it less likely that the president would be seen as responsible for the issue.

While the evidence for the cynicizing effects and agenda-setting function of television is not yet definitive, these notions nevertheless remain highly plausible, with major implications for the future shape and stability of the political system. Over the long run, the media, especially television, may define the basic issues society must confront. And given the extensive coverage of bad news, American society may be faced with a series of issues and crises, each of which contributes to a further decline in confidence in political institutions and authorities. How the media determine what to cover will become increasingly important. Schram (1987) contends that the networks have used the results of public opinion polls to decide which issues to emphasize in news coverage during presidential campaigns. Those issues, in turn, become the ones that viewers told pollsters were the most important ones facing the nation. Thus, according to Schram, networks "confused adequate coverage of the issues with telling the public about the things people had told the poll takers they already knew" (p. 96). In the more immediate future, television's agenda-setting property may affect voting behavior by determining the issues upon which voters base their choices. According to Entman (1989), media decisions as to which issues to cover or ignore can influence citizens' attitudes toward the candidates and thus their vote decisions. The work of Michael J. Robinson and Cliff Zukin (1976) may have provided some evidence that television created the "social issue" of the late 1960s and 1970s. They found that in 1968 reliance on television for political information was associated with a positive evaluation of George Wallace, the candidate who most exploited the social issue.

Television and the citizen.   Evidence about the effects of television and other media on the individual citizen, particularly in a voting situation, is much more thorough and convincing than evidence dealing with the systemic effects discussed earlier. The one potential effect of television of greatest interest to students of elections is its influence on citizens' vote choices. The two classic studies of the impact of the campaign and the mass media on citizens' candidate preferences are *The People's Choice* and *Voting.* While both works predate the major introduction of television into presidential contests, the findings of both are important, if for no other reason than that they have become a part of the standard folklore about campaigns. According to the most frequently cited finding of both studies, the mass media and the campaign mainly reinforce the voter's initial predispositions and attitudes rather than change attitudes. For example, Paul Lazarsfeld and his colleagues (1968: 101–104) found that very few residents of Erie County, Ohio, changed their vote intentions between May and October 1940. A similar result was reported in the Elmira, New York, study of the 1948 election: 96 percent of citizens who expressed a partisan preference in both August and October remained stable in their vote intention. And in the last month of the campaign, only 5 percent of the respondents changed their vote intentions (Berelson, Lazarsfeld, and McPhee, 1954: 16).

Thus, it appeared from these early studies that the campaign and the mass media had little effect on citizens' preferences. And the voters who did change their preferences over the course of the campaign tended to be those voters who were less interested in the election and less exposed to campaign communications. A number of reasons were given for the primacy of the reinforcement effect. Of particular importance was selective exposure, that is, the tendency of individuals to expose themselves primarily to communications sympathetic to their beliefs. Such exposure would obviously have the effect of reinforcing rather than altering predispositions. Another factor cited for the prominence of reinforcement effects was the political homogeneity of the primary and secondary groups to which the individual belonged; interaction with like-minded individuals is likely to reinforce one's own attitudes.

Thus, the classical view of the campaign and the media is that both make relatively little difference to the election outcome; reinforcement means that the election turned out the way it would have if there had been no media communications or campaign. This conclusion, however, is in need of some important caveats and modifications, particularly about the importance of the media. First of all, reinforcement is an important (though perhaps not dramatic) effect that should be credited to the media. Moreover, reinforcement implies that there exist initial predispositions to be strengthened, and these initial attitudes are most often partisan loyalties. But as partisanship becomes weaker and the number of Independents grows, there will be less opportunity for reinforcement, and therefore the media may have a greater effect on campaigns. The work of Gary Jacobson (1974) supports the notion that the media will be more important where voters have weaker predispositions, less information, and more uncertainty. Jacobson found that broadcast campaigning was more effective in nonpresidential elections, especially primary elections where voter information was low and party identification was not available as a basis of vote decision.

Another criticism of the findings on the reinforcement effects of the campaign and the media focuses on the evidence used to support the selective exposure process. Reviewing a number of studies on selective exposure, David O. Sears and Jonathan L. Freedman (1967) conclude that the evidence is far from convincing and that in many cases people actually expose themselves to information contrary to their existing beliefs. One might expect the tremendous amount of information available in presidential contests to overcome any tendency toward selective exposure. Moreover, in the current era of television domination, where viewers are often exposed to political communications simply because the television set is turned on to regular programming, the extent of selective exposure may be quite limited; in such a situation, inadvertent learning may occur (Neuman, Just, and Crigler, 1988).

A final criticism of the classical research on campaigns is that it predates the era of television; findings based on the print media and radio may not be applicable to television. While more recent evidence indicates that on the average only about 33 percent of citizens make their candidate selection during the actual campaign, this does not mean that the media are ineffective in influencing vote decisions. The fact that about 66 percent of citizens have made their vote decisions by the end of the nominating conventions may mean that the media play their crucial role early. The many Democrats who decided early in 1972 that they would not support the McGovern candidacy certainly received information from the media that helped shape their decisions. Thus, while the media change relatively few preferences during the actual campaign, they still are influential in providing citizens with information and images upon which to base precampaign vote decisions and in structuring alternatives and depicting potential candidates throughout the interelection period. Certainly Mondale entered the 1984 general election campaign with negative images of his candidacy that arose in part from the nomination campaign and its coverage in the media.

Much of this research focuses on the general election campaign, although some data exists about the effects of the media during the primary season. Also, recent work is more sophisticated in how it views the media; it not only talks about distinctive media, such as television, radio, and newspapers, but distinguishes among different types of content within a medium. For example, recent research on television has been careful not to treat the medium as a single entity; instead, it has explicitly recognized that there are different types of political television, such as the nightly national news shows, public affairs documentaries, and televised political commercials. The current research is also more sophisticated in how it conceptualizes media effects in the context of a campaign. Thus, recent studies analyze not only media influences on vote choice but also more subtle effects in such areas as information acquisition and agenda setting. Finally, the recent work takes a more realistic and complex view of how media effects occur. Rather than simply assuming that identical media content affects different people in the same way, the current research argues that, to assess media effects, one must be sensitive to the recipients of the media messages as well as to the messages themselves.

One prominent approach along these lines has been labeled the *uses and gratifications approach;* it emphasizes not what the media do to people, but how and why citizens use the media. This approach argues that the effects of a campaign medium on voters will depend on the motivations that voters have for following the medium. For example, the uses and gratifications approach claims that the effect of the debates on viewers depends not only on the viewers' predispositions, such as party identification, but also on why viewers watched the debates in the first place. People who watched the debates for their entertainment value might respond to them very differently from people who watched for other reasons, such as the desire to acquire information about the candidates or the need to be a good citizen by watching the debates.

Like the classical studies, contemporary research finds little direct effect of the media on vote preference. With respect to issue awareness, however, Thomas E. Patterson and Robert D. McClure (1976: 49, 116) and Patterson (1980: 156–159) found that regular viewing of network news had no effect on the voter's issue awareness but that viewing political commercials was associated with higher voter awareness of candidates' issue stances. Political advertising actually had more issue and information content to it than did the nightly network news shows. Hofstetter, Zukin, and Buss (1976: 11) supported this finding somewhat; they found that exposure to network election specials and to political advertising was more highly correlated with richness of issue perceptions than was exposure to network news programs. M. Timothy O'Keefe and Kenneth G. Sheinkopf (1974) disputed the information-producing effects of political advertising. They argued that even though the political use of television in 1972 involved longer and more informative ads than the short ads used in previous elections, viewers did not see the television ads as important information sources. Moreover, O'Keefe and Sheinkopf concluded that no matter what their length, the television ads served mainly as image builders rather than information sources. The contradiction between their findings and those of Patterson and McClure can be reconciled by the notion of the inadvertent audience. While it may be true that O'Keefe and Sheinkopf's respondents did not consciously view political commercials as important information sources, they were nevertheless acquiring information from these commercials unknowingly. Spot commercials come on during regular programming, so that many viewers who might not ordinarily tune in political programming accidentally end up watching political commercials and learning from them. A study of spot commercials in the Wisconsin and Colorado gubernatorial races in 1970 supports this notion (Bowen, Atkin, Nayman, and Sheinkopf, 1972); the authors found that specific information, such as candidates' qualifications and issues stands, rather than more general images, was learned from the ads.

Patterson and McClure (1976: 67–68) uncovered no effect of television news shows on the candidate images of committed voters. Among the undecided voters exposed to television, images of Nixon and McGovern changed very little until *after* the decision was made about which candidate to support. Hofstetter, Zukin, and Buss (1976: 10) agreed with this finding in part, claiming that exposure to news programming "appeared to have increased the total amount of imagery about the candidates, but failed to influence the nature of this imagery." McLeod, Glynn, and McDonald (1983) compared the effects of television to the effects of newspaper reliance on the ways in which people made their vote choices in 1980. In general, the authors found that television-reliant voters were much more likely than newspaper-reliant voters to base their vote choice on candidate imagery, particularly for the major party candidates.

Content analyses of the network evening news shows indicate that such shows pay little attention to the issue stands and qualifications of the candidates. Instead, it is the hoopla, the rallies, the noise and the excitement that are covered; network news treats the general election campaign like a horse race. For example, Patterson and McClure (1976: 31) reported that about 60 percent of the time a presidential candidate was shown on camera in 1972, he was shown in a crowd scene. They charge (1976: 144) that the networks maintain the charade of the horse race with the active cooperation of the candidates, who gear their campaigns to this kind of media coverage, a point elaborated upon in the second part of this chapter. Likewise, Patterson (1980) finds that in magazines and newspapers and on the national network evening news broadcasts, the "game" of politics receives much more coverage than the substance of politics, particularly during the primaries and conventions and less so during the general election (see table 9.3). Michael J. Robinson and Margaret Sheehan (1980) present evidence that the national networks improved their coverage of issues in the 1980 general election. Whereas about 67 percent of the television news stories during the 1980 primaries dealt with the horse race and game of politics (in contrast to 64 percent found by Patterson in 1976), by October issue coverage outweighed the horse race emphasis. In the 1984 general election Maura Clancy and Michael J. Robinson (1985) found that television news stories on campaign issues were more common than horse race pieces. One reason for this finding was the lopsided nature of the Reagan–Mondale contest; there was not much of a horse race to cover.

This finding about the increased coverage of campaign issues in 1984 must be tempered by a recognition of what campaign issues are—topics of contention that the candidates stress to further their campaigns. There is no guarantee that the campaign issues emphasized by the candidates will have much relevance to the serious problems facing the country. This certainly was the case in the 1988 Bush campaign, which featured such issues as Willie Horton and the Pledge of Allegiance but remained largely silent on many of the real issues confronting the United States.

Numerous studies (Patterson, 1989; Hershey, 1989; Buchanan, 1991; Lichter, Amundson, and Noyes, 1989) have demonstrated the inadequacies of media coverage of genuine policy issues in the 1988 campaign. In a content analysis of *Time* and *Newsweek*, Patterson found that 32 percent of the stories dealt with the horse race aspects of the campaign, while another 28 percent dealt with campaign issues (such as prison furloughs and flag fealty); only 17 percent focused on policy issues. Hershey found that almost 67 percent of the campaign coverage in the newspapers she analyzed focused on campaign strategy. Even the Lichter, Amundson, and Noyes study, which came to the media's defense, showed that of the top ten story topics on the network news in 1988, 24 percent dealt with the (often phony) campaign issues, another 24 percent with strategy and tactics, 20 percent with policy issues, and 12 percent with the horse race. In the most comprehensive empirical analysis of the 1988 campaign, Buchanan found that 36 percent of the campaign stories in various media focused on the horse race, another 21 percent on candidate conflicts, while less than 10 percent dealt with policy issues. In short, media coverage of the 1988 campaign was dismal. In discussing the paucity of issues coverage in 1988, Hershey commented (p. 100):

TABLE 9.3

News Coverage of Substance and Game during the 1976 Primary, Convention, and General Election Periods (in percentages)

Period	Network evening newscasts	Erie Times/ News	Los Angeles Herald- Examiner	Los Angeles Times	Time/ Newsweek
Primaries					
Game	64%	64%	62%	59%	62%
Substance	24	26	24	28	24
Other	12	10	14	13	14
Total	100	100	100	100	100
Conventions					
Game	58	59	55	52	54
Substance	29	28	28	33	31
Other	13	13	17	15	15
Total	100	100	100	100	100
General election					
Game	51	52	51	42	46
Substance	35	36	36	42	41
Other	14	12	13	16	13
Total	100	100	100	100	100

SOURCE: Thomas E. Patterson, *The Media Election* (New York: Praeger Publishers, 1980), Table 3.3, p. 29.

The problem is not just the difficulty of the issues. The problem lies in the structure of incentives for candidates and reporters to deal with these issues. The 1988 campaign suggested that there are no incentives at present for campaigners and the media to address the tough problems of governance; the incentives all lead toward the use of symbols, and the creation of artificial drama through the emphasis on polls and strategic moves. The question remains whether it is possible to create different incentives: forces encouraging campaign debate that enrich voters' choices among candidates. For when the 1988 presidential campaign came down to a choice between Willie Horton and the Pledge of Allegiance, the only people enriched were the campaign consultants.

Two studies have detailed media effects during the primary season. Patterson's (1980) study of the 1976 presidential campaign examined popular awareness of the candidates, perceptions of the candidates' prospects for winning the nomination, and images of the candidates over the course of the campaign. Patterson found that the level of awareness concerning many of the candidates was very low before the primaries. Recognition increased mainly for one candidate, Jimmy Carter, whose early successes generated media coverage, which in turn helped him win later primaries. The work of Scott Keeter and Cliff Zukin (1983) on the 1976 and 1980 campaigns confirms some of Patterson's findings. Using NES/CPS, CBS/*New York Times*, and New Jersey Poll surveys, Keeter and Zukin found relatively little learning and minimal increases in knowledge about the candidates in 1980. The learning that did occur was mainly about two candidates—Bush and Anderson—who enjoyed some early successes in the primary season. The authors argue that citizens learn about victorious candidates through media reports. They note that losing candidates almost always fall in the popularity polls, while winners gain, although the latter effect is conditioned by how the media report their victories.

The Patterson, and Keeter and Zukin studies show that there is a strong relationship between media coverage and awareness of the candidates during the primary season. More important, candidate awareness has electoral pay-offs; citizens are unlikely to vote for a candidate of whom they are unaware. Hence, the inordinate coverage given to the victor, particularly in the early primaries and caucuses, provides a tremendous advantage to his or her candidacy. Table 9.4 shows how skewed the coverage given to the contestants can be. Note that the first-place finisher received the bulk of the media coverage. And since Carter in 1976 was the first-place finisher in many of the early delegate selection contests, he benefited from a huge volume of publicity.

Although Patterson argues that newspaper coverage is a more effective way of achieving higher public awareness, the importance of television cannot be downplayed, particularly with respect to reporting the early primaries and caucuses. For example, an analysis by Robinson of the coverage patterns of "CBS Evening News" found a heavy emphasis on Iowa and New Hampshire that increased over time. In 1972, 1976, and 1980, there were nineteen, thirty-four, and thirty-three stories, respectively, on the New Hampshire primary and two, five, and twenty-three stories on the Iowa precinct caucuses. The states that held their delegate selection contests in the first month of the season averaged eighteen stories apiece on "CBS Evening News"; the states that held their contests in May averaged only two stories each. Thus, the early primaries and caucuses receive substantial coverage, and the winner of these early contests gets a major boost in public awareness of his or her candidacy.

In contrast to recent studies of television, recent studies of newspapers have identified surprisingly strong effects on information levels and vote choice. Patterson and McClure (1976: 51) discovered that people who read the newspaper regularly became much better informed about the campaign. Patterson (1980) found that newspapers were far superior to television in conveying issue information to citizens. Four studies have indicated that newspaper endorsements have a direct effect on vote choice. Robert S. Erikson (1976: 217–218) analyzed the effect of newspaper shifts in partisan endorsements between 1960 and 1964 on the Democratic presidential vote. Among other things he found that in counties with a single major newspaper the 1964 vote was 5 percent more Democratic if the paper supported Johnson over Goldwater. He speculated (1976: 220) about the long-term impact of the Republican press, arguing that the cumulative effect of newspaper endorsements over time may be important. Two studies by John Robinson also demonstrate the importance of newspaper endorsements on vote choice. In one study Robinson (1972) found that perception that a newspaper supported one candidate over the other was associated with a vote advantage of about 6 percent for the preferred candidate, an effect most pronounced among respon-

---

TABLE 9.4

Weekly News Coverage of the 1976 Democratic Candidates, Depending on Their Order of Finish in That Week's Primary (in percentages)

Position candidate finished in	Network evening newscasts	Erie Times/ News	Los Angeles Herald-Examiner	Los Angeles Times	Time/ Newsweek
First place	59%	58%	52%	60%	62%
Second place	17	18	29	19	14
Third place	16	16	17	15	13
Fourth place	8	8	2	6	11
Total	100	100	100	100	100

Based on average for the thirteen primary weeks of 1976.

SOURCE: Thomas E. Patterson, *The Mass Media Election* (New York: Praeger Publishers, 1980), Table 5.1, p. 45.

dents with weaker party loyalties. In the other study Robinson (1974) found that there was a correlation across five presidential elections between presidential endorsements made by newspapers and the vote choice made by readers of these newspapers, if relevant other variables were taken into account. In a study of gubernatorial and U.S. Senate voting, Steven L. Coombs (1981) found that newspaper editorial endorsements had marked effects on vote choice, particularly for citizens with less intense partisan feelings.

If newspaper endorsements do affect vote choice as this research suggests, then Republican presidential candidates can expect to have an advantage on Election Day. Despite Spiro Agnew's complaints about the liberal, Democratic press, the editorial policy of newspapers is heavily Republican. For example, a 1984 survey (Thimmesch, 1984) of 714 daily newspapers showed 394 endorsing Reagan, 76 Mondale, and the rest "uncommitted" or "no endorsement." The Reagan newspapers had 51 percent of the circulation, while the Mondale backers had 22 percent. In 1988, Bush enjoyed a similar advantage even as fewer newspapers chose to endorse in the presidential contest. This Republican edge is typical; only in 1964 did newspapers give more support to the Democratic candidate. In that year Johnson was endorsed by 440 dailies and Goldwater by 359. Even when a candidate is supported by a newspaper, the endorsement may not be a ringing one. For example, one less than enthusiastic endorsement that Ford got was from the *Manchester Union Leader;* publisher William Loeb, a Reagan enthusiast, said that the 1976 election was a choice between "stupid" (Ford) and "shifty" (Carter). He wrote, "Better the fool we know than the devil we don't." In 1980 the *New York Times* endorsement (October 26, 1980, p. 18E) of Carter began:

> The old joke still applies. Someone chases a voter down an alley, points a gun to his head and demands an answer: "Carter or Reagan?" After thinking for a moment, the voter replies, "Shoot."

It ended with:

> What a choice, says Johnny Carson: between fear of the unknown—and fear of the known. Neither man personifies our ideal candidate. But that does not mean there is no difference or that the choice is unimportant. There is a difference; it is important; and we choose Jimmy Carter. Ronald Reagan is the better salesman; Jimmy Carter keeps dropping his sample case on his own foot. But it contains better goods.

The Media and the Presidential Selection Process[9]

INTRODUCTION

This section will focus on how the media affect the presidential selection process, which is viewed as comprising three stages—the primary season, the national nominating conventions, and the general election campaign. The greatest attention will be given to the preconvention period, where the media's impact is most substantial. I will argue that in covering the primaries, the media are not neutral but actually affect the outcome of the process. This media intrusiveness is not due to any systematic bias or conspiracy on the part of reporters and television commentators but instead reflects the structural aspects of news reporting as well as the ambiguities and complexities of the primary season.

There is a paradox in analyzing media effects across the three stages of presidential selection. If it is indeed the case that media impact is greatest in the primary season, it is also the case that empirical evidence on this first stage is weaker than information on the later stages. Hence, this discussion of media effects in the primary season must of necessity be more speculative.

THE PRIMARY SEASON

Introduction. On a priori grounds the impact of the media might be expected to be greatest during the primary election phase of the presidential selection process. This is because of the ambiguity and complexity inherent in the primaries, which facilitate media influences and intrusiveness. For example, primary elections are often multiple-candidate contests, so that standards of victory may not be as clear as they are in the general election and the nominating conventions. Over the primary season, unlike the general election, the structure of competition shifts, with candidates declaring themselves in and dropping out, thereby making the comparative interpretation of a series of elections more problematic. Furthermore, despite the apparent confusion that the Electoral College adds to the general election, the variety of primary arrangements—binding versus nonbinding, delegate contests versus beauty contests, winner-take-all versus proportional allocation of delegates, popular vote versus delegates won, and so on—represents a level of complexity that literally invites media interpretation and misinterpretation. Finally, the amount of information available about the candidates is low during the primary season, especially early in the season, so that what the media choose to emphasize can affect the candidate's fate. This is particularly the case since party identification cannot serve as a cue for candidate choice in a partisan primary.

Some theoretical perspectives on mass communications also argue for the greater impact of the media during the primaries as opposed to the later stages. There is an ongoing debate as to whether candidate images are perceiver-determined or stimulus-determined. The former view (Sigel, 1964) argues that citizens' candidate images are filtered by their own predispositions, such as party identification, and that selective processes help maintain cognitive consistency. The stimulus-determined position (McGrath and McGrath, 1962; Baskin, 1976) asserts that citizens' images of candidates are more directly a function of what they actually see or read about the contenders.

Although there is evidence supporting both sides, perceptual defenses are lower during the primaries than during the general election, hence images of the candidates formed during the primary season, especially early in the season, are more likely to be stimulus-determined. In the general election, as people have more information about the candidates and as the perceptual screen function of party identification comes into play, images may be less stimulus-determined. In a related vein, given the low information levels characteristic of primaries, the media, even if they do not create or alter attitudes directly, can determine the grounds (for example, issues, personality) on which people choose between the candidates, an agenda-setting effect.

In summary, primary elections tend to be less well-defined phenomena that allow substantial leeway in media reporting and interpretation. It is difficult to demonstrate empirically that media coverage of primary election outcomes and of presidential preferences in opinion polls is necessarily good or bad for the candidates or can generate bandwagon effects, although recent studies are suggestive. J. R. Beniger (1976) found that a candidate's standing in the preference polls had little or no effect on changes in his or her standing in subsequent polls, although preference poll position contributed directly to primary election success. Beniger's results also indicated that success in the primary election led to an improvement in a candidate's poll standing, especially for Democratic candidates in the early primaries. This finding was supported by Collat, Kelley, and Rogowski (1976). In a study of the 1976 nominations, Aldrich, Gant, and Simon (1978) argued that primary election results affected campaign momentum in poll standing, contributions, and media attention. With respect to Carter's candidacy, they found that Carter's early successes in Iowa and New Hampshire led to great increases in media coverage, popular support, and eventually financial contributions. The authors concluded that early success was vital in the presidential selection process as early setbacks caused media, contributors, and voters to look elsewhere. This conclusion was supported by the work of Patterson (1980) and Keeter and Zukin (1983), discussed earlier.

A more intriguing aspect of this research is the evidence it presents that recent primary election campaigns have differed from the traditional patterns. Writing about nomination contests between 1936 and 1972, Beniger (1976) identified only three genuine horse races—the Democratic contests in 1960 and 1972 and the Republican race in 1964. Likewise, William H. Lucy (1973) observed that between 1936 and 1972, only once—in 1972—in twenty cases did the presidential contender leading in the last preprimary Gallup poll lose primaries and permanently lose the poll lead. Although this had occurred only once in thirty-six years, it happened again in 1976, when Jimmy Carter overcame an initial low standing in the polls to capture the Democratic nomination, and in 1988. Why has the traditional pattern of open-and-shut nomination campaigns, in which the early leaders ultimately emerged victorious, been broken three times in the last nineteen years? One answer is certainly the proliferation of primaries, which has resulted in popular election of an overwhelming majority of delegates, and another answer is the manner in which the media cover the primaries. The following discussion will show by example how the media can affect the course of the primary process. A list of examples obviously does not constitute compelling proof of the intrusiveness of the media, but the cases to be discussed are thought-provoking. The discussion will focus on three interrelated themes—the complexity of the primaries, the games candidates play, and the news-reporting emphasis.

The complexity of the primaries.   The primaries are complex in many ways, one being that they are often multiple-candidate contests. At times the field of declared candidates is only a small subset of the total number of prospective nominees. The media play a very prominent role here in determining which of all the potential candidates are serious and viable. David Broder (1976: 215–217) cites one role of reporters in presidential politics as being that of the talent scout who decides which candidates merit genuine consideration as presidential aspirants. The power of this screening function is detailed very insightfully by Timothy Crouse (1973: 39, 194–199), who describes how the press gave careful scrutiny to George Romney in 1968, ultimately overplaying his "brainwashed" comment and destroying his credibility as a candidate. Whether Romney merited such treatment is not central here. What is crucial is that in the same period when Romney was undergoing intensive scrutiny, Richard Nixon was enjoying a free ride from the press because he was maintaining a low profile. After the press was through with Romney, Nixon's path to the White House was made easier. Likewise, the candidacy of Sargent Shriver in 1976 was hurt by the heavy media emphasis on his being Ted Kennedy's brother-in-law, which led observers to wonder whether Shriver was a stalking horse for Kennedy. Had Shriver's past governmental experience (for example, ambassador to France, Peace Corps director) been the focus of media coverage, he might have been viewed as a more credible contender.

A more important aspect of the presence of multiple entrants in primaries is that standards of victory are less obvious than they would be otherwise. Where more than two candidates are vying, the simple majority criterion may have little utility and the media may establish their own tests of candidate performance. Passing these tests may indicate that a candidate is running strongly, but the question arises as to why one test is chosen and not others. For example, the Florida primary in 1976 was deemed crucial to Jimmy Carter's hopes. According to the media, Carter had to beat George Wallace to establish himself as a serious contender. But why did Carter have to win, particularly since the Jackson candidacy in Florida was likely to hurt Carter more than Wallace? As an alternative test, how about simply a strong showing by Carter in Florida, especially since Wallace had swept the Florida primary in 1972? In 1980 New Hampshire became a key test for Reagan after his unexpected defeat in Iowa; fortunately for Reagan, he passed the test handily.

The standards established by the media allow for an interpretation of events at some variance from what actually occurs. The classic example of this was the 1972 New Hampshire Democratic primary, in which Edmund Muskie "failed" to get the magic 50 percent of the vote needed to give his candidacy a boost, even though he defeated his chief rival, George McGovern, by a margin of 46 percent to 37 percent. James Perry explained how the 50 percent standard gradually emerged as the media consensus, beginning with a story by David Broder on January 9 (nearly *two* months before the primary) in which Broder wrote, "As the acknowledged front-runner and a resident of the neighboring state, Muskie will have to win the support of at least half the New Hampshire Democrats in order to claim a victory" (Perry, 1973: 85). According to Perry, television newsmen picked up the 50 percent figure and thereby managed to infuse drama into a race whose outcome was largely a foregone conclusion. Perry (1973: 86) attributed part of Muskie's problem to a preprimary poll showing Muskie with 65 percent of the vote. Despite the instability and unreliability of many preprimary polls (Burns W. Roper, 1975), the 65 percent and later the 50 percent mark became an albatross on the Muskie candidacy. In the first four primaries in 1972, Muskie won New Hampshire with 46 percent of the vote and Illinois with 63 percent, while Wallace carried Florida with 42 percent and McGovern carried Wisconsin with 30 percent. Yet it was the McGovern candidacy that was building and Muskie's that was collapsing when Wisconsin voted. Certainly media coverage of the New Hampshire primary hastened the downfall of the Muskie candidacy.

It is clear that the results of primaries and caucuses are interpreted in light of how candidates are "expected" to perform and that these expectations are generated by the candidates and the media. Winning and losing are often determined by whether the candidate ran better or poorer than expected. The results of the Iowa Democratic precinct caucuses in 1984 illustrate well the importance of expectations. A precaucus, front-page story in the *Washington Post* titled " 'Expectations' the Big Foe" (Peterson and Sawyer, 1984) included the following assertions:

> Front-runner Walter F. Mondale carried the heaviest burden of expectations into the Iowa precinct caucuses, the first contests of the presidential season.
>
> Mondale has held a 2-to-1 lead in polls here since December, and strategists for his rivals have said that anything less than 50 percent of the caucus vote would be a setback for him and possibly benefit one or more of his opponents. . . .
>
> * * * * *
>
> Expectations for Sen. John Glenn (D-Ohio), once predicted to give Mondale a stiff challenge here, have fallen through the floor. Glenn's standing has dropped steadily in polls here. And his strategists said that they expect him to get no more than 15 to 20 percent of the vote. Yet, to meet "expectations," Glenn needs to finish second in Iowa.
>
> For the rest of the eight-man Democratic field, Iowa and the New Hampshire primary a week from Tuesday essentially are survival contests.
>
> Their goal is not to win either contest, but to do "better than expected." This has resulted in a long and confusing "expectations" game, with candidates trying to set expectations for one another.

Sen. Gary Hart (D-Colo.) today joined in this game with relish before leaving for New Hampshire.

First, he tried to raise the expectations of his opponents. He said that Sen. Alan Cranston (D-Calif.) had "rolled all the dice here, and he's got to do well," and that Glenn has "got to run second here, or it's a serious setback. If Glenn runs fourth, he's in very serious trouble."

Meanwhile, in an interview and during a news conference, Hart tried to lower expectations for his performance in Iowa.

"If I come in fourth or better, I will feel good," Hart said. "I think Cranston made a serious mistake saying he'd come in third here because what does he do if he doesn't? He's way down in New Hampshire, and I don't think he's prepared to follow up in a serious way for any kind of showing in any state."

When the caucus votes were tallied, Mondale came in first with slightly less than half the vote, Hart finished second with about 15 percent of the vote, and Glenn came in sixth with about 5 percent. According to news media accounts, the real news from Iowa was not Mondale's victory since he was expected to do well. Instead, the significant outcomes were Hart's unexpected good showing and Glenn's unexpected poor performance. Hart received substantial positive press for his showing, while the Glenn campaign was widely criticized. Tom Brokaw opined on NBC News:

> Senators Hart and Glenn traded places in Iowa. Hart moved up to number two. Glenn became an also-ran. The effect of this surprising reversal is already being felt in their campaigns. (Adams, 1984)

Moreover, even though Mondale won Iowa handily, in the week between the Iowa caucus and the New Hampshire primary his share of the NBC and CBS news coverage went down sharply as the media were captivated by the new star—Hart—on the scene (Adams, 1984). Thus, it was the second place finisher in Iowa who benefited most by the way the media reported and interpreted the results of the caucus. In 1988, the Bush candidacy was almost derailed by his unexpected third place showing in Iowa. Dole finished first as expected, but Pat Robertson's status as runner-up surprised observers and generated much coverage for his campaign.

Roper (1975) has called for reform of media coverage of primaries, but his message has not been heeded. And of all primary coverage, that given to New Hampshire is most in need of reform. As the first state to hold a presidential primary, New Hampshire is of course critical to the presidential selection process. Its importance is heightened, however, by the inordinate media attention given to it. Michael Robinson (1978) found that of the network news stories devoted to the first eight primaries in 1976, fully 30 percent focused on New Hampshire. Moreover, media emphasis on New Hampshire increased substantially between 1972 and 1976 (Robinson, 1977: 83). Hence, the New Hampshire results, as interpreted by the media, are extremely influential in promoting or undermining a presidential candidacy. On the day before the 1976 New Hampshire primary, Walter Cronkite opined on the evening news that anything less than 55 percent of the Republican vote for Ford should be construed as a setback for the incumbent president. Luckily for Ford, this standard was not universally adopted. (In fact, other standards more favorable to Ford were adopted, a matter elaborated on in a later discussion of the games candidates play.)

Primary success, poll standing, and the ability to raise money and attract volunteers are all interrelated. The quest for the presidential nomination is in part a psychological battle, and the media can be very influential in unwittingly creating a psychological climate beneficial to one candidate. Morris Udall complained in April 1976 that Jimmy Carter had profited from an "orgy of publicity." Although Udall's complaint must be taken with a grain of salt, given his own aspirations, his comments (Louis Cannon, 1976) nevertheless get to the heart of the issue:

> Never underestimate the importance of momentum in these presidential elections. We all said we weren't going to let New Hampshire do it to us again, and New Hampshire did do it. We all said that the Iowa caucus was not that important, and the press made it that important. . . . Once that avalanche starts down the ski slope, get out of the way. . . .
>
> The people want winners and losers and if you make 27 points in a football game and I make 26, you're called a winner and I'm called a loser.

Similar complaints were uttered by some of the aspirants for the Republican nomination in 1980. In an interview with Katherine Evans of the *Washington Journalism Review,* Ron McMahan, press secretary to Sen. Howard Baker, a 1980 GOP contender, criticized the media:

> The Big Mo [momentum] was the most significant news story of the Republican primaries. As a result of the surprise Bush win in Iowa, practically all the media, and especially television, spent most of their time covering the Big Mo, the momentum of George Bush, and just shut the rest of us out—Baker and Connally and Crane and others. As far as determining the final outcome of the primary elections, the fact that the Big Mo hit, and there were five weeks between Iowa and New Hampshire when only Reagan and Bush were getting coverage, while Baker and Connally and Crane and others were not, [meant that] the media determined that they were the two viable candidates.
>
> Unless Senator Baker were to say something that was either controversial or demagogic or unreasonable, which he doesn't tend to do, he wasn't going to make the evening news.
>
> By the time the debates in New Hampshire happened, for all practical purposes, Baker, Connally, and Crane were already out of it because they hadn't received enough coverage to become credible candidates. (September 1980, p. 31)

McMahan's complaints were echoed by Connally and Dole, who felt that their candidacies had been hurt by a scarcity of coverage. Support for their criticisms is provided in table 9.5, which indicates how much coverage each

TABLE 9.5

ABC, CBS, and NBC Evening News Coverage
of the Candidates, July 1, 1979, to March 10, 1980*

Week	Anderson Number of stories	Total time in minutes	Baker Number of stories	Total time in minutes	Bush Number of stories	Total time in minutes	Connally Number of stories	Total time in minutes	Crane/Dole Number of stories	Total time in minutes	Kennedy Number of stories	Total time in minutes	Reagan Number of stories	Total time in minutes
July 1–7											2	2:27		
8–14							1	4:06			1	1:13		
15–21											3	12:08		
22–28											4	5:33		
August 29–4			1	0:11					1	1:00	2	1:01	1	0:11
5–11							1	0:10	3	3:06	4		1	2:51
12–18														
19–25			1	0:20					1	0:20	3	3:01		
September 26–1	1	0:19												
2–8											6	10:57	1	0:32
9–15			2	2:06							9	10:51		
16–22											12	10:12		
23–29			1	0:55			1	1:43			7	10:20	1	0:13
October 30–6											1	1:10		
7–13							4	4:57			5	15:11	1	0:51
14–20					1	0:15	2	0:35			6	6:30		
21–27							1	0:20			6	5:00		

November														
28–3			5	9:16			2	7:12			10	15:45		
4–10					1	0:55					10	16:27		
11–17							1	6:52			2	0:36	5	15:40
18–24	1	6:47									1	1:53		
25–1			1	0:16					1	5:15	7	5:25	1	0:26
December														
2–8					1	6:38					12	14:42		
9–15	2	0:28					3	3:56			4	6:45		
16–21	1	2:38			2	6:30					5	4:21		
January														
3–5			1	0:30			1	0:30						
6–12							1	1:32			4	7:52	1	0:09
13–19			1	6:26	1	0:35					9	14:06	1	0:35
20–26			1	0:12	14	13:34	1	0:12			14	23:04	12	15:14
February														
27–2					1	0:34	3	4:49			9	17:32	5	5:09
3–9			1	2:17	4	1:34	1	0:10			9	11:41	8	10:25
10–16			2	6:11	3	5:07			2	2:08	11	16:55	1	:30
17–23	1	1:15	1	1:30	9	5:54	2	1:15			4	8:55	8	7:56
March				0:20			2	3:10						
24–1	3	1:18	2		10	13:13					14	19:37	15	16:18
2–8	19	18:17	3	4:20	11	6:33	2	1:43	1	0:19	18	17:41	13	8:25
10					2	1:30	2	4:30			4	4:50	4	4:04

*Monitoring of television evening news from the daily *New Digest*, American Enterprise Institute. (Figures for all three networks are not available for November 12, 22, and 23 and December 22 through January 2; and for "ABC World News Tonight," July 9, October 19, December 3, and January 16–17.)

SOURCE: *Washington Journalism Review*, July–August 1980, p. 21.

of the candidates (excluding Carter) received on the ABC, CBS, and NBC evening news programs from July 1, 1979, to March 10, 1980. Note that in the critical period from late January through early March, Baker, Connally, Crane, and Dole received relatively little attention. In contrast, Kennedy was the object of extensive coverage even in the summer of 1979, prior to his declaration of candidacy; the media devoted much time to the question of whether Kennedy would run and followed very closely activities related to a draft Kennedy movement.

The media make the primaries a sporting contest, most often a horse race, where winners and losers must be identified even if there are no clear victors. Given the emphasis on outcomes, the question of how to define winning and losing still remains. If the media had decided on delegates won as the standard, instead of popular vote pluralities, then the early Democratic primaries in 1976 and 1980 would not have seemed so definitive and certainly would not have given the Carter candidacy so much impetus. As it is, the media began to emphasize delegates won in coverage of the later primaries, so that even as Carter began to lose more contests, his losses were offset by news reports emphasizing his delegate gains and his inexorable march to a delegate majority.

The notion that the media need to identify winners and losers can be extended to say that winners and losers must be individuals and not such undefined entities as "uncommitteds," that is, delegates pledged to no specific candidate. In fact, throughout 1976—beginning with the precinct caucuses in Iowa in January and culminating with the New Jersey primary in June—the performance of the uncommitteds was reported in, at best, questionable ways. Even though the uncommitteds won in Iowa with 37 percent of the vote, compared to 28 percent for Carter and 13 percent for Bayh, press attention focused on Carter. Elizabeth Drew (1976a: 133) reported that as a result of his Iowa "victory," Carter was interviewed on the "CBS Morning News," while NBC's "Today Show" and ABC's "Good Morning America" also ran segments on Carter. On the "CBS Evening News," Walter Cronkite said that Iowa voters had spoken, "and for the Democrats what they said was 'Jimmy Carter.' " Yet given the amount of time that Carter spent in Iowa, his performance might have been portrayed as less impressive. Perhaps the media had no significant political interpretation of the victory of the uncommitted in Iowa, beyond stating that it was a function of oddities in the delegate selection rules; but the victory of the uncommitted in New Jersey was a far different matter, a point to be developed shortly.

Given the increase in the number of primaries since 1968, an additional problem that the media must address is what primaries to stress. Rick Stearns, deputy campaign manager for McGovern in 1972, claimed (May and Fraser, 1973: 97) that the McGovern strategy was based on the assumption that primaries significant in the past would continue to be so viewed by the press in 1972. Hence, the McGovern camp stressed the Wisconsin primary and won it; but as Stearns himself said (May and Fraser, 1973: 97), there was no other reason than press inertia that "Wisconsin should have been the watershed for the McGovern campaign that it was; the Wisconsin primary fundamentally was not that important."

An additional complication associated with the increased number of primaries was that, since 1976, more than one major primary occurred on the same day, whereas in previous years the major primaries had unfolded in a nice temporal and geographic sequence starting in New Hampshire, moving to Wisconsin, and concluding in Oregon and California. Hence, the media had more difficult decisions to make about which primaries to stress, and it is not entirely clear that they made the right choices. For example, the Wisconsin and New York primaries in 1976 occurred on the same day. Even though the Wisconsin contest allocated many fewer delegates than did the New York contest (274 versus 68), Wisconsin received the lion's share of media attention. This may have been due to Wisconsin's traditional importance, or to the widespread feeling that since Henry Jackson was expected to win in New York, this made that race less exciting and less newsworthy. Perhaps Wisconsin was a simpler story to report since it entailed only two major candidates *and* a straightforward popular vote contest. Likewise, the Oregon primary was held on the same day as five other primaries in 1976. Oregon became the featured primary because it was deemed the most competitive race; Kentucky, Arkansas, and Tennessee were conceded to Southerner Jimmy Carter; Idaho to native son Frank Church; and Nevada to neighbor Jerry Brown. But even though Oregon was the most competitive race among Carter, Church, and Brown (as a write-in), it is arguable whether this made it the most newsworthy race, except for the fact that it most closely resembled the horse race that the media seem to emphasize. The mentality underlying this view of news is illustrated by *Washington Post* columnist Ed Walsh (1976: A6) who wrote that the California primary "appeared to lose some of its luster as polls continued to show Reagan a solid favorite to take the state's 167 delegates." With this kind of reporting, a victorious candidate will gain greater mileage by defeating a rival in a hotly contested race that is in doubt to the end rather than in a convincing victory that has been evident some time prior to the actual voting.

An excellent example of how expectations of candidates' performance and multiple primaries on the same day can influence media coverage of primaries occurred in 1984. On May 8 four states—Ohio, Indiana, Maryland, and North Carolina—held primaries. Hart defeated Mondale in Ohio and Indiana by less than 1 percent of the vote, while Mondale defeated Hart by 5 percent in North Carolina and 18 percent in Maryland. In terms of delegates won, Mondale increased his already sizable lead over Hart by more than ninety delegates. What interpretation should be given to the results of these four primaries?

One possible interpretation is simply to call the four contests a draw— Mondale won two, Hart won two—and conclude that little was changed in the nomination struggle in which Mondale was leading Hart. A second possible interpretation is to declare Mondale the victor since he won his two primaries by bigger margins than Hart won his, and Mondale also added significantly to his delegate lead. However, neither of these interpretations was the dominant one. Instead, the media emphasis was on Hart's impressive performance. What made it impressive, of course, was the expectation that Mondale would win all four states. Thus, *Washington Post* reporters David Broder and Bill Peterson (May 9, 1984) began their analysis story of these four primaries with the following paragraph:

> The voters of Indiana and Ohio gave Gary Hart two crucial hairbreadth victories yesterday that revived his faltering bid for the Democratic presidential nomination and assured that the battle will go on until the final round of primaries in another four weeks. (p. A1)

Needless to say, the Hart campaign welcomed this interpretation; the Mondale camp would certainly have preferred the following hypothetical analysis:

> Mondale's two sizable victories yesterday and his two narrow losses moved him closer to the Democratic nomination and made his nomination all but inevitable.

The interpretation given to the May 8 primaries provided a temporary boost to the Hart campaign and guaranteed the continuation of the Democratic warfare for another month. The point is not whether this or some other interpretation is correct, but simply that the perspective adopted by the media can affect how the presidential selection process unfolds. There could have been much opportunity for media intrusiveness in reporting the outcome of Super Tuesday in 1988. Fortunately, the results were sufficiently clear to prevent this. Bush swept to an overwhelming victory on the Republican side, while Dukakis, Gore, and Jackson each won a number of states.

Super Tuesday of the 1976 primary season best illustrates the problem that multiple and complex primaries conducted on the same day pose for the media. On June 8 California, New Jersey, and Ohio held primaries that, on the Democratic side, selected 540 delegates, more than 33 percent of the total needed for nomination. How would these primary results be interpreted? Which state outcome would be viewed as most significant? In retrospect, it was Ohio—not California and New Jersey—that proved critical. Carter's victory in Ohio was widely seen as locking up the nomination for him. But why Ohio? Was Super Tuesday such an unqualified success for the former Governor of Georgia?

The *New York Times* front-page story about New Jersey on the day before the primary read, "Carter Victory Is Forecast in Jersey Vote Tomorrow." On primary day, R. W. Apple's front-page story was entitled, "Carter Appears near Goal in Last 3 Primaries Today." On Wednesday the *Times* headline was, "Ford and Carter Lead in Votes in Jersey and Ohio; California Leaning to Brown and Reagan." The front-page headline in the *Times* on Thursday proclaimed, "Carter Seems Due to Win on First Ballot," while on page 43 was a story entitled "Humphrey—Brown Victory in Jersey Is Called Futile."

How could an anticipated Carter victory in New Jersey that turned into an overwhelming delegate loss (eighty-three for uncommitted, twenty-five for Carter) be given so little attention? At one level the New Jersey story did deserve less attention since the fact that Carter picked up over 200 delegates on Super Tuesday, even while being thumped in California and New Jersey, may have been the major story of the day—it put Carter so much closer to the nomination. But in terms of the popular appeal of the candidates, the Ohio results should have been balanced by the New Jersey and California outcomes, yet they were not. Why was this the case?

A part of the answer is the inability or unwillingness of the media to handle complexity. An NBC television reporter argued that Ohio was the real test, since there was a native son on the California ballot and in New Jersey there were uncommitted delegates, which made interpretation difficult and confused the issue. This, however, is no explanation, simply an admission that Ohio was more congenial to media coverage. It could be convincingly argued that front-runner Carter's loss in New Jersey to an uncommitted delegate slate (widely advertised as supporting Humphrey and Brown and opposing Carter) was truly the significant outcome of the day. Yet this was evidently too complicated to explain to readers and viewers. The New Jersey outcome was further complicated by a nonbinding beauty contest as well as the delegate selection vote. The fact that Carter won the former easily against token opposition and lost the latter decisively made the New Jersey story even more difficult to report. The lesson of all this is that the media seek excitement and simplicity—a point further developed later in this chapter.

The games candidates play.   While the media may inadvertently misinterpret primary results because of reasons inherent in media coverage, politicians try to manipulate the media to advance their own ends. As Elizabeth Drew (1976b: 89) notes, "A classic problem for candidates is how to inflate their prospects in order to attract allies and followers without creating a standard against which they can be measured unfavorably." This helps explain how the front-runner status hurt Muskie but not Carter. Muskie was a strong front-runner who was expected to do well, while Carter was a weak one who, each time he ran well, surprised observers with his strength. By the time Carter started to lose primaries to Brown and Church, he was so far out in front that it did not matter much. As Roper (1975: 29) notes, a candidate's goal is to run better than expected and, hence, the incentive, especially for underdog candidates, is to poor-mouth their own prospects so that the eventual results appear more promising.

An excellent example of successful media manipulation was Gerald Ford's quest for the Republican nomination in 1976. Despite the bungling attributed to the Ford campaign staff, the Ford operatives were more skillful than the Reagan camp in manipulating the media to their own ends. Late in the New Hampshire primary race, the Reagan forces leaked a poll showing their candidate 8 percentage points ahead. This was a tactical mistake since it created expectations of a Reagan win, against which Ford's narrow victory was seen as impressive. Ford's 51 percent of the vote was not interpreted as a weak showing for an incumbent president despite Cronkite's aforementioned judgment that an incumbent president should be able to get at least 55 percent. Clearly, the Reagan strategy should have been one of publicly hoping for 40 percent of the vote—and then New Hampshire might have served as Reagan's springboard to the nomination. Thus, Reagan got less help from his 48 percent of the New Hampshire vote in 1976 than McGovern got from his 37 percent in 1972.

The Ford partisans skillfully manipulated the New Hampshire results in subsequent primaries. In Florida they were aided by Reagan's campaign manager, who had predicted a two-to-one Reagan victory. After New Hampshire the campaign manager lowered his estimate to a 55 percent Reagan win. This allowed the Ford forces to claim a 12 percent gain and the ever-important momentum, while preserving their underdog status, a tactic that almost perfectly follows Drew's advice. Had the president lost narrowly in Florida, the Ford people might have been successful in portraying this as a moral victory even as the Reagan camp was unsuccessful in claiming New Hampshire as a moral victory. As it turned out, Ford carried Florida with about 53 percent of the vote, a victory heralded by the media as impressive in view of prior expectations of a Reagan win in Florida.

After Reagan's string of primary successes in Texas, Indiana, Nebraska, and elsewhere, the Ford campaign was very skillful in setting up the Michigan primary as one that the president might lose. It is hard to demonstrate that Ford was ever in any serious trouble in Michigan; yet successfully conveying that impression served to inflate the significance of his Michigan win and thereby put his campaign on the right track again. In retrospect, it is interesting to note that an incumbent president's victory in his home state was accorded much more importance than his challenger's home-state victory.

A final example of successful game playing is the claim by Mayor Richard Daley of Chicago that a Carter victory in Ohio would mean that Carter "will walk in [to the nomination] under his own power." Daley had picked Ohio as decisive, and it was. The question is, Which came first? Was Ohio always crucial, and was Daley simply recognizing a fact? Or was Ohio crucial because Daley said so? If the latter, then this helps explain why Ohio and not California and New Jersey received the most attention on Super Tuesday. The preprimary polls in Ohio indicated that a substantial Carter victory was in the making. Thus, it appears that Daley ably manipulated the media to put himself in the position of kingmaker.

Media manipulation by candidates can affect the outcome of the primary process. Imagine what the outcome would have been if the Reagan people in New Hampshire had been more savvy and understated their expectations. Or imagine what would have happened if Mayor Daley had said that New Jersey and not Ohio was the ball game. Had California and New Jersey been described as major Carter setbacks instead of second-place finishes, would people have been so eager to jump on the Carter bandwagon the next day? Again, the point is that politics is in part a psychological game and the side that can set the standard of performance adopted by the media has a tremendous advantage. To the extent that the media are successfully manipulated by the candidates, the media are playing an intrusive role in presidential politics.

Candidates can manipulate the media in ways other than setting standards of performance. A blatant example occurred on the day of the Wisconsin primary in 1980, when the White House scheduled an early morning news conference to announce a possible breakthrough in the hostage crisis. Many observers viewed the event as a cynical ploy by the Carter campaign team to enhance its electoral prospects in Wisconsin and thereby rebound from its defeat in the New York primary the previous week. Despite their skepticism, the media had to cover the news conference since the hostage crisis was such a central concern to Americans. It turned out that no breakthrough was imminent, but the Carter candidacy enjoyed positive (albeit short-lived) media coverage at an important juncture in the campaign.

A more subtle example of how a skillful candidate can use the media occurred in the Republican primary in New Hampshire in 1980. Bush and Reagan were scheduled to participate in a debate in Nashua from which the other Republican contenders were excluded. When the four excluded Republicans showed up at the debate hall, Reagan quickly seized the initiative and invited them to participate. The moderator of the debate objected, to which an indignant and eloquent Reagan replied, "I paid for this microphone." The subsequent television coverage given this event showed Reagan to be a decisive, eloquent, and fair-minded leader. What would have happened if Bush had been as quick and skillful as Reagan in exploiting the situation?

The news reporting emphasis. How the media report the primaries can greatly influence their outcome. As mentioned earlier, the dominant perspective that news reporting takes on the primaries is that of the horse race, with emphasis on who's winning and who's losing, who's closing fast and who's fading. James M. Perry (1973: 10) blames the "who's ahead" mentality in part on Theodore White's books on presidential elections. White, of course, had the advantage of writing after the winner's identity was already known. Reporters following the primaries as they occur do not have this luxury, yet they may get so hooked on the importance of proclaiming "who's ahead" that they put themselves in untenable positions, as was done when they awarded the nomination to Muskie before any of the primaries had been held in 1972. As David S. Broder observes (1976: 217), the handicapper role of reporters may mislead readers into believing that a candidate's current standing necessarily predicts his or her final standing accurately.

The horse race mentality is, of course, encouraged by the need to attract readers and viewers. A horse race is by definition an exciting event—with identifiable winners and losers. And as Collat, Kelley, and Rogowski (1976: 34) point out, journalists tend to agree in their judgment of who is ahead since "they see the same polls, read the same things, and talk to the same people." This results in a certain homogeneity in news reporting about the viability of candidates and can make the media more influential in winnowing candidates. The focus on who is winning even shows up on election night coverage of the primaries, where the networks often seem to be in a race among themselves to be the first to call the outcome of the primary.

It has also been argued that the horse race emphasis reflects the competence of political reporters to cover politics and their inability to cover government. Charles Peters (1976: 56) described political reporters as knowing "much about the process of being elected and little about what the government does or how it could be improved." This means that coverage of what the candidates actually stand for and what they plan to do often gets overwhelmed by the concern for winning and losing, a phenomenon that also occurs in the general election campaign. The policy positions of candidates are often inadequately reported.[10]

An excellent example of the horse race emphasis occurred in the "CBS Evening News" coverage of the Reagan and Carter campaign visits to Columbus one week before the Ohio primary in May 1980. It was Carter's first "officially" political trip of the 1980 primary season. Both candidates held rallies in downtown Columbus during the noon hour at locations six blocks apart. It was not surprising that a major theme on the "CBS Evening News" was the relative size of the crowd that each candidate attracted. Lesley Stahl reported that Carter had the larger crowd, but that Reagan had the edge in enthusiasm. Stahl's report also emphasized the visually attractive setting of each candidate's rally; Gerald Rafshoon was shown collecting footage of the Carter rally for use in future Carter commercials. Other themes stressed in Stahl's report were the advance work done to put together the rallies and the modes of transportation used by the candidates. Issues were a very small part of the CBS coverage despite the fact that both candidates' remarks had substantial issue content. An interesting sidelight was that the coverage of the candidates' visits by the local CBS affiliate was much more issue-oriented. This was probably because the local station could devote much more air time to the story and therefore was able to cover the substance as well as the horse race and the hoopla.

The horse race mentality can be very intrusive. Few people would want to bet on a candidate identified in the media as a loser. The interaction among media coverage, poll results, and primary outcomes can generate interpretations and prophecies that assume a life of their own and act to promote the prospects of one candidate over another.

The phenomenon of pack journalism (Crouse, 1973) may affect media coverage in major ways. For example, at times reporters may simply not know what sort of focus to give to a story and may therefore follow the lead of an influential journalist. The classic example of this occurred in 1972 when journalists were perplexed about how to interpret the results of the Iowa precinct caucus. According to Crouse (1973: 85), when R. W. Apple wrote as his lead for Iowa that McGovern had made a surprisingly strong showing, the other journalists picked up the story and reported the same theme back to their papers. Elizabeth Drew (1976a: 127) reported a similar occurrence in Iowa in 1976. Apple had written a story that Carter was doing well in Iowa, and this story itself became a political event "prompting other newspaper stories that Carter was doing well in Iowa, and then more newspaper, magazine, and television coverage for Carter than might otherwise have been his share."

THE CONVENTIONS

In discussing the effect of the media, especially television, on the nominating conventions, three targets of impact can be identified: the procedural and structural arrangements of the conventions, the delegates to the conventions, and the home viewers of the conventions. About the first, it should be noted that conventions today are events staged for television. Since 1952 conventions have been streamlined to be more attractive to the television audience. For example, Judith Parris reports (1972: 150) that whereas the 1952 Democratic convention totaled ten sessions that lasted over forty-seven hours, the 1968 convention consisted of just five sessions that ran less than twenty-nine hours. Although in 1972 McGovern gave his acceptance speech at three o'clock in the morning eastern time, convention activities, such as the nominee's speeches, are usually scheduled to reach the largest possible audience.

If the effect of television on conventions was simply one of streamlining and scheduling, then it would be difficult to argue that television is intrusive in any negative or harmful sense. Unfortunately, television's effects go beyond routinely shaping the convention. For example, the Democrats in 1976 were concerned that the American public should perceive their convention as a harmonious and orderly affair. They believed that their raucous and conflictual conventions of 1968 and 1972, as portrayed to the American public via television, were major factors contributing to their 1968 and 1972 defeats. Hence, the 1976 Democratic convention adopted a rule that minority reports on the platform, rules, and credentials had to have the support of 25 percent of the members of the appropriate committee to be brought before the full convention; only 10 percent had been required in the past. Certainly this rule change was an attempt to avoid televised divisiveness, to minimize the prominence of fringe elements, and to keep the convention on schedule. In 1988, the Democrats worked hard to present a televised image of the party as united and capable of governing.

Although making minority reports more difficult may not be the optimal way to achieve full airing of issues, it is easy to sympathize with party professionals who are concerned with what the citizen at home sees of the conventions on television. The Republicans in 1964 and the Democrats in 1968 and 1972 left stormy conventions as seriously divided parties, and all three lost in November. It is an empirical generalization that the nominee selected at the convention should gain ground in the polls right after the convention, yet McGovern actually lost ground in the postconvention polls conducted *before* the Eagleton affair. It appears that the vast majority of Americans are not enthralled by conventions characterized by conflict and rancor and are unsympathetic to parties and candidates whose conventions appear to be dominated by groups alien and threatening to the average citizen.

David L. Paletz and Martha Elson (1976) have presented one of the few systematic analyses of the aspects of conventions that television emphasizes. Their quantitative analysis of NBC's coverage of the 1972 Democratic convention demonstrated that violence and fringe elements were not given undue coverage and that there was no bias for or against McGovern. In their qualitative analysis of NBC coverage, however, Paletz and Elson came to a different conclusion. They argued that the predominant impression left by NBC's coverage of the Democratic convention was one of conflict and disorder. They attributed this, not to any deliberate bias on the part of reporters, but to the norms and procedures of television news reporting. For example, they argued that the media interpret fairness to mean getting all sides. But as Paletz and Elson point out (1976: 122):

> It [getting all sides] can make the "Stop McGovern Movement" seem as strong as the "Elect McGovern Movement" whether it is or not. Moreover the technique may actually create the impression of sides that do not really exist to a substantial degree among the delegates as a whole. It certainly increases the elements of conflict and drama.

Furthermore, when reporters do portray divisiveness, they do not do so in ways suggesting that it represents a healthy discussion of issues but in ways suggesting that it symbolizes bitterness and hostility. Cliff Zukin (1979: 19–22) presents evidence about the effects of perceived conflict from the perspective of viewers of the 1976 conventions. He found that people had negative images of the Republican convention, with many of these images centering on the style of the convention and the behavior of the delegates. He argued that the conflict associated with the hotly contested Ford–Reagan battle resulted in more negative evaluations of the Republican convention.

What Paletz and Elson are saying is that television distorts the conventions for reasons inherent in news reporting. Warren Weaver (1976) points out that in a dull convention, television, unlike newspapers, which can cut back convention column space, must fill the time. To accomplish this, television may seize upon an inconsequential story and blow it out of proportion. Weaver asserts that reports of anti-Carter dissension at the Democratic convention in 1976 received much more attention than they deserved for just this reason.

The networks are in competition to attract viewers, and this seems to be reflected in their readiness to push any story. If substantial coverage is given to an inconsequential story, it may be elevated to a matter of genuine importance. This is reflected in the eagerness with which the networks in 1976 seized upon the alleged bribing of two Ford delegates from Illinois; the television coverage was replete with interviews with representatives of both sides, heated charges and denials, and the like. On the CBS convention coverage, Cronkite himself said very dramatically that this might be the kind of issue that could shake delegates loose. It seems that the direct effect of this kind of reporting is to generate excitement and that the indirect effect is to increase the level of conflict and make party unity more difficult to achieve. The CBS preconvention program on the GOP gathering (held in Kansas City) was entitled "Kansas City Showdown," which captures the media emphasis well. Just as the primaries are infused with drama, so are the conventions.

With Reagan's nomination assured prior to the 1980 GOP convention and with no serious platform, credentials, or rules fights likely to occur, only the selection of Reagan's running mate promised to provide any suspense. The television networks and Reagan himself did their best to generate excitement about the vice-presidential choice. Floor reporters asked any and every Republican about his or her vice-presidential preference and were not at all hesitant about repeating the latest unsubstantiated rumor on the airwaves. This speculation was harmless until the possibility of the Reagan–Ford dream ticket emerged. Walter Cronkite reported that rumors of Ford as Reagan's vice-president had been circulating all day. Then the camera turned to floor reporter Dan Rather, who indicated that Ford and Reagan had met during the day and discussed the circumstances under which Ford would agree to be Reagan's running mate. The camera then returned to Cronkite and his guest in the anchor booth—Gerald Ford. After some probing from Cronkite, Ford stated that he might consider running but that he did not want to go back to Washington as a figurehead vice-president. This interview energized the GOP convention and spawned even more rumors and speculation. An hour later Cronkite reported:

> CBS has learned there is a definite plan for the nominee of this party, Ronald Reagan, that the former president of the United States, Gerald Ford, will be his selection as a vice-presidential running mate, an unparalleled, unprecedented situation in American politics. They are going to come to this convention tonight to appear together on this platform to announce that Ford will run with him.

The other networks reported similar stories and rumors. The first story announcing that George Bush and not Ford was the running mate was not aired until ninety minutes later. Reagan himself went to the convention to quell the Ford rumors.

This incident illustrates how the media can move beyond reporting the news to actually generating the news in the first place. Dan Nimmo and James E. Combs (1983) view the situation as one of pack journalism run amok. Although the media deserve a major share of the blame, politicians and candidates like Ford who are willing and able to exploit the media for their own purposes must share some of the responsibility for the excesses of the reporting. Sometimes television simply blows it, as evidence by the misinterpretation of the South Carolina delegation's challenge at the 1972 Democratic convention, which led some people to believe that the McGovern candidacy was in trouble when just the opposite was the case. At the 1968 Democratic convention Sander Vanocur and John Chancellor were responsible for a Kennedy-for-president boom that electrified the convention but was simply not accurate (James M. Perry, 1973: 171).

How intrusive the media might be at a deadlocked or close convention in which events are unfolding rapidly and television is the major source of information for the delegates is a matter for speculation. On the second night of the Republican convention in 1976, before the test vote on the critical rule 16-C (on vice-presidential selection) had occurred, the television networks fanned an uproar over alleged comments by Ford campaign manager Rogers Morton. He was cited in an Alabama newspaper, to the effect that Ford would write off the "Cotton South." Morton claimed to have said that certain southern states would be difficult for Ford to carry because of Southerner Carter heading the Democratic ticket but denied that these states had been written off. Nevertheless, newsmen confronted the Mississippi delegation with the "fact" that Ford was writing off the South. Earlier in the day, the Mississippi delegation had invoked the unit rule by a very narrow margin of 31–28 to support Ford's position on 16-C and thereby cast all 30 votes against the rule. When Morton's alleged comments became known, the Reagan forces wanted the Mississippi delegation to caucus again in the hope of changing two votes and breaking the unit rule and perhaps converting some Ford supporters. The intrusiveness of the media became absurd here. Dan Rather offered to lead Rogers Morton across the convention floor so that he might meet with the Mississippi delegation. Mike Wallace provided the Mississippi Reagan delegates with a CBS trailer in which to caucus. No votes were changed as a result of all this, but it should suggest how the media can sometimes forget that they are there to report the news, not to play an active part in generating it.

THE GENERAL ELECTION

The general election campaign is a better defined situation than the primaries, with the presidential choices narrowed down to two serious candidates. Hence, the chances for media intrusiveness are less at this time than during the primary season. Nevertheless, the opportunities for media manipulation and game playing by the candidates as well as misdirected coverage by the media remain substantial in the general election. Because the empirical studies reviewed earlier generally indicated weak media effects on vote choice, is concern about media manipulation in the general election warranted? One response is that successful manipulation of the media by a candidate may serve to alter the course of campaigns in ways not readily amenable to quantitative investigation. This can be illustrated by Richard Nixon's reelection campaign in 1972.

The Nixon camp recognized the structural aspects of news reporting and ran a campaign designed to take advantage of these features. Nixon campaigned as president from the White House, while surrogate campaigners carried the Republican message on the stump. As Jules Witcover notes (1973: 24–25), the absence of Nixon from the campaign trail resulted in intensive scrutiny of McGovern. Every little flaw in McGovern's campaign, every squabble among his advisers, received substantial media attention because of the availability of the McGovern camp to the media. McGovern was covered as a candidate striving for office, while Nixon was treated as the incumbent president above the political fray. Witcover argues (1973: 26) that even if Nixon had campaigned more, he would probably have kept himself insulated from press questioning, with the result that the accessible McGovern campaign would still have been subjected to intensive and critical scrutiny. Ford's Rose Garden strategy in 1976 was a variant on the 1972 Nixon effort, although Ford was more accessible to the media than Nixon had been.

Ben Bagdikian (1973) points out that the Nixon campaign strategy led to news coverage that effectively served as Nixon propaganda in many instances. One procedure that contributed to this was *twinning*—giving both sides of a story equal coverage even when they did not deserve comparable treatment. McGovern himself complained about this (Ryan, 1976: 8):

> Let me register one beef from my own campaign. There were times when we would have a great rally where local leaders would tell us, "This is the biggest crowd we've ever seen at Cleveland Airport!" Or: "This is the biggest crowd we've ever had at Post Office Square in Boston!" I would turn on the television set later to see the enormous throng, and well, there *would* be a 15-second spot of me addressing this crowd. Then, under some kind of curious interpretation of the equal-time rule, since Nixon was not campaigning, they would pick up some guy along the fence who would say, "I think McGovern stinks."
>
> And this would be the way the program would end—or "McGovern said this, but a disgruntled former Democrat interviewed by our roving reporter said this." And then they had some jerk get up and say that I was too radical for him or that I couldn't make up my mind on the issues. What the viewer was left with was a final negative image. It happened repeatedly during the campaign.

Bagdikian (1973: 11) did not blame Nixon for adopting the strategy that he did, arguing that this was standard behavior for a heavily favored incumbent. Instead, he criticized editors and publishers who allowed the Nixon camp to get away with such conduct. The point, however, is that a candidate could count on the networks and newspapers to try to present balanced coverage even when only one candidate was actively campaigning. Given the lesson of 1972, the media were more alert to the problem and devised some responses in 1976. For example, in response to Ford's Rose Garden strategy, television reporters in 1976 often concluded their stories with the phrase "with the Ford campaign at the White House" so that viewers would recognize Ford's actions and the media coverage of them as part of his campaign. A similar situation held in 1980 as Carter attempted a Rose Garden strategy;

again, the media were alert to this ploy. However, the media encountered another problem, a challenger who was largely inaccessible to the media except in controlled settings. Reagan aids did their best to shield their candidate from any impromptu interactions with reporters lest he make any verbal blunders and gaffes, a strategy that was repeated in Reagan's reelection campaign. How the media should handle such a situation raises the question of the proper role of reporters and journalists. Is it simply to record the campaign? If so, then the media may be the vehicle of skillful candidates. Or should media personnel evaluate as well as record? This latter role is certainly controversial, opening up news organizations to charges of bias and threats of political and economic reprisals.

Candidates are skillful in recognizing that news personnel need to file stories even when little hard news exists. Candidates can take advantage of this fact by constructing media events that project desired images without much hard content. Patrick Buchanan (1976) described an excellent example of this phenomenon, the media coverage of Jimmy Carter's extended stay in Plains, Georgia, after winning the Democratic nomination. Each day reporters would issue a report from Plains on who visited the candidate or how the softball game went. The television viewer was treated to pictures of Carter greeting fellow Democrats, Carter playing softball, Carter going to church, and the like. The question, of course, is whether all this merited any coverage. It is not the fault of the Carter camp that this occurred; its contribution was simply to recognize that the media needed "news" and to provide tidbits and scenes designed to show the candidate in the best possible light. There is an obvious response available to the media to counter such behavior, and that is simply not to report such activities. But this would require a redefinition of what constitutes news as well as a restructuring of the media incentives that encourage this type of news coverage. Unfortunately, it seems that the candidates have the upper hand. It is hard to imagine the media ignoring a speech designated by the president as major, which in fact turns out to be a rehash of existing policy. But the media can do much more than they do in providing context and background.

Certainly the television networks do not have to cover the "photo ops" provided by the candidates. In recent elections, especially in the Reagan and Bush campaigns, the use of staged events in visually stimulating settings—photo opportunities—has ballooned. Often there is little of substance in these events, but television treats them as newsworthy. The campaign strategists cannot be blamed for trying to generate favorable coverage of their candidates, but surely the media can recognize these pseudo-events for what they are and be restrained in their coverage of them. Television can also be criticized for its use of ever shorter sound bites. The candidates will of course provide the pithy quotable comments that they hope the media will use, but the media can refuse to play that game. Adatto (1990) notes that the average length of sound bites for Nixon and Humphrey in 1968 was 42.3 seconds; by 1988, the average statement by Bush and Dukakis on the network news shows had dropped to 9.8 seconds. Sound bites have become shorter because of the media's better technological capability to edit candidates' statements and because the candidates themselves try to give the media the short, quotable statement. But whatever the reasons, surely the quality of campaign debate is not enhanced by a system in which brevity and catchiness are rewarded.

The horse race coverage of the general election is commonplace, although, as discussed earlier, not as prevalent as in the primary season. Nevertheless, campaign events are regularly interpreted in terms of how they affect the relative standing of the candidates (Swanson, 1977). Moreover, the emphasis on candidate standing and media events often results in matters of substance being given short shrift. James McCartney (1977: 19) described the 1976 campaign coverage as junk news that, like junk food, "is mass-produced, has no flavor and little substance." McCartney (1977: 20) argues that there were issue differences between the candidates that merited coverage but that these were often overwhelmed by the media emphasis on gaffes and blunders. Such events as Ford's Eastern Europe comments or Carter's *Playboy* interview were certainly newsworthy, but not at the expense of other campaign stories.

The problem again arises from the definition of news. It is not news if a candidate goes through an entire campaign day without making mistakes. But should the candidate blunder, this gets elevated to a prominence that outweighs other activities and statements. From the perspective of the reporter, it is understandable why the rare gaffe receives so much attention. Reporters traveling with the presidential candidates are likely to have heard and written about the same speech before and may therefore be looking for new leads and angles. Hence, the candidate's occasional mistake provides an opportunity for a new story. This is only reasonable, but when it results in a heavy emphasis on less substantive matters, one can legitimately worry whether the needs of the media are helping to trivialize campaign discourse.

The horse race mentality carries over to reporting major campaign events. For example, "Who won?" is the first question asked about a presidential debate. And often the question is answered not in terms of the content of the candidates' statements but in terms of their style, appearance, and the like. ABC News embarrassed itself in 1980 by conducting a call-in survey after the Carter–Reagan debate. For fifty cents viewers could register their opinion as to which candidate had won the debate. Despite all the biases built into this procedure and despite the technical difficulties experienced with the telephone system, ABC announced that Reagan had been the winner of the debate by a two-to-one margin. Since this instant poll was the first assessment of public opinion about the debate, one might wonder how much ABC's reporting structured subsequent perceptions of who won the debate. Certainly the major campaign events of 1984 and 1988 were the presidential debates and, again, the initial media emphasis was on "who won" and much less on the substance of the debates.

Conclusion

It is clear that the role of the media, especially television, in presidential politics has increased markedly since 1952. This increased importance is due not only to the technological advances in electronic communication but also to structural changes in the nomination process, particularly the proliferation of primaries, that provide an opportunity for media influence. The media have become more active and influential participants in the presidential selection process, a factor that candidates must consider in their strategic planning. Hence, as the next chapter discusses the strategic aspects of seeking the presidency, keep in mind both the media environment discussed in this chapter and the campaign finance and nomination system constraints discussed in chapter 8.

Notes

1. For example, one study found that television news shows covered fewer of the key events in a major, ongoing news story than did three leading newspapers and concluded that the label of "electronic front page" often given to television news shows was quite appropriate. See Russel F. Harney and Vernon A. Stone (1969).

2. This is not to say that citizens unfailingly accept what television presents. For example, even though press and television coverage of the 1968 Democratic convention was largely sympathetic to the antiwar protesters beaten and arrested by the Chicago police, citizens tended to be far more favorable to the police and hostile to the demonstrators. See John P. Robinson (1970).

3. The assertion that partisan bias was absent does not mean that each candidate received the same amount and kind of coverage; in fact, Hofstetter uncovered a noticeable amount of structural and situational bias. McGovern received more coverage than Nixon, but Nixon's was more favorable. This in part reflects the deliberate strategies of the two candidates: McGovern seeking widespread coverage and being readily accessible to the media and Nixon avoiding the media.

More generally, it has been charged (by Spiro Agnew among others) that television network news emphasizes bad news at the expense of good news. This presumably occurs for a variety of reasons, including the supposed biases of the people who select the stories to be reported and the tendency to view bad news as newsworthy and good news as routine. An actual examination of the content of the network news shows found that only about 33 percent of the material reported could be considered bad news. While bad-news items were often reported in earlier segments of the news broadcast and received more visual emphasis, overall there was little evidence of any bias in favor of reporting bad news. See Dennis T. Lowry (1971). In support of the media, one might argue that if news is defined as that which is out of the ordinary, then "bad" occurrences should indeed be news, given their relative rarity. Of course, one might quarrel with this definition of news.

4. For information about Loeb and his newspaper, see Eric P. Veblen (1974). The *Union Leader* is an atypical paper; most major newspapers do not engage in such slanted reporting of campaigns. A 1968 study by Doris Graber (1971) on the campaign coverage of twenty newspapers found that there was widespread uniformity of press coverage despite the varying editorial policies of the papers. Likewise, an analysis of television, news magazine, and major newspaper coverage of the 1972 campaign found little evidence of partisan bias. There was a slight pro-Republican bias exhibited by news magazines, but newspaper editorial policies were not reflected in their coverage of the campaign. See Dru Evarts and Guido H. Stempel III (1974).

5. For a fascinating description of the *Union Leader's* biased coverage of the New Hampshire primary, see Jules Witcover (1972).

6. This is not to say that newspapers perform the information dissemination function entirely satisfactorily. In her study of coverage of the 1968 election, Doris Graber found that the press tended to focus on candidate characteristics rather than issue positions. Relevant facts were often left out of campaign stories, making it more difficult for the reader to make an informed choice. See Doris A. Graber (1974).

7. For a more detailed discussion of the broadcast media in American politics, see Edward W. Chester (1969).

8. It may be that cynicizing effects are not limited to television but can occur with other media. In a study analyzing newspaper content and public attitudes, Arthur H. Miller, Edie N. Goldenberg, and Lutz Erbring (1979) found that readers of newspapers more critical of government were themselves more distrustful, although the overall press coverage of government tended to be positive or neutral. Another study (Graber, 1976), which compared campaign news on television and in the press, found that press coverage of presidential qualifications was more negative than the coverage given by television.

9. Much of this discussion is from Herbert B. Asher (1977) with updated examples added. Because much of the following discussion emphasizes the sequential nature of the primaries, the reader may find it useful at this point to look at table 8.4, which presents the presidential primary schedule in recent elections.

10. David Broder (1979b) speculates that the horse race mentality may also be prominent among the White House staff. The ever-lengthening campaign required to seek the presidential nomination compels candidates to surround themselves with loyalists willing to make an indefinite commitment. If the candidates are successful, the faithful supporters may be rewarded with positions in the White House. Yet such staffers, usually young and relatively inexperienced in government, may be more interested and competent in

winning elections than in running the day-to-day affairs of government. Hence, their emphasis is on the next election and not on the current happenings in government, which works to the detriment of successfully formulating and executing public policy.

CHAPTER 10

Running for President

The presidential campaign can be analyzed and evaluated from a number of perspectives. From the perspective of the citizenry, the campaign can be viewed as an opportunity to inform and educate the electorate, and the success of the campaign may be evaluated by the extent to which this objective is met. This chapter, however, focuses on the campaign from the candidate's vantage point, assuming that the candidate and his or her organization have as their primary goal electoral success. Hence the focus will be on the strategies employed by presidential aspirants. *Strategies* are those plans and programs that are adopted to promote victory. Strategies should be distinguished from *tactics*—the means by which plans and programs are executed. Emphasis in this chapter is on strategies and not tactics, although it should be noted that the two are inextricably linked because certain strategies require specific tactics to have any chance of success. For example, Nelson Rockefeller hoped to win the Republican nomination in 1968 by convincing GOP delegates of his national popularity and electability while at the same time avoiding the primaries. Rockefeller obviously had to employ such means as nationwide radio, television, and newspaper advertising campaigns; had he relied on personal campaigning before small groups, his plans would have had no chance for success.

The analysis and evaluation of campaign strategies pose a number of difficulties. One is that the candidate may never announce a clear-cut statement of strategy. Even if such a strategy is publicly expressed, it may be modified repeatedly in response to the actual course of the campaign. Related to this problem is the availability of reliable information about strategies. One must often depend on third- and fourth-hand reports of campaign plans.

While a strategy generally deals with those features of the political environment that are manipulable by the candidate, recognize that many factors relevant to the election outcome—such as the existing distribution of partisan loyalties—are largely beyond the control of the candidate. Thus, evaluating a strategy makes sense only in the context of the constraints within which a candidate is operating. A sound political strategy must incorporate the realities of the current situation. However, in some instances the constraints and their consequences are not immediately apparent.

Finally, the evaluation of a strategy as successful or unsuccessful implies the existence of some baseline from which to judge the campaign. What baseline should be chosen? Some might argue that victory or defeat is the appropriate standard, that the candidate who wins has employed a wise strategy, and vice versa. Victory or defeat, however, seems too crude a basis for judgment; the minority party nominee who lost a very close election may in fact have employed the best possible strategy despite his or her loss. It has been argued that Nixon's strategy in 1968 was unsound despite his victory, since an apparent runaway election in September became a neck-and-neck race in November. Similar comments were made about Carter's 1976 performance.

Because it is difficult to discuss strategies in a detailed and thorough fashion, the focus will be on the scenarios that the candidates thought would lead to victory. William Cavala (1974: 33) describes a *scenario* as a factual description of the candidate's present state followed by a series of conditional statements as to what is likely to happen if certain conditions are met. Factors and conditions that rendered alternative plans realistic and unrealistic will be emphasized. Discussion will center around how various scenarios recognized or ignored the constraints upon the candidate. And wherever possible, those decisions explicitly made by presidential nominees that ultimately proved beneficial or harmful to their candidacies will be discussed.

Do Campaigns Matter?

Because of the finding reported in chapter 9—that very few citizens change their minds over the course of the campaign—one might argue that studying the general election period and the strategies employed therein is an uninteresting exercise since the election outcome is largely foreordained. Table 10.1 apparently supports this argument. It shows the proportion of citizens who decided on their vote choice at various junctures in the campaign. Note that about 66 percent of the citizens usually decide on their vote choice by the end of the national nominating conventions. The 1976 campaign was the major exception to the pattern. The highest percentage of voters deciding in the last two weeks occurred in 1980. This probably reflected a lack of enthusiasm for the choices and the fact that many citizens waited for the Carter–Reagan debate (which took place a week prior to the election) before making their vote choices.

Thus, it appears from table 10.1 that the campaign is not very effective in altering election outcomes. The table is misleading, however, for a number of reasons. One is that a significantly large bloc of voters does make its choice during the campaign period in response to unfolding events; the 33 percent of the electorate still undecided after the nominating conventions is an important battleground over which the election might be won or lost. Moreover, recognize that presidential contests are decided over a relatively narrow range of vote splits; seldom does the winner's share of the two-party vote much exceed 60 percent and the loser's share fall much below 40 percent, even in such landslide elections as 1964, 1972, and 1984. Thus, most election outcomes could have been reversed had only 10 percent or less of the voters changed their choice in the same direction. Finally, the table is misleading because it ignores the fact that presidential races are not directly popular vote contests but electoral vote contests. And the key, large electoral vote states tend to be politically competitive; this means that a change in the vote intentions of a small percentage of the electorate may spell the difference between victory and defeat in many crucial states. In 1976, for example, the difference between winning and losing was less than 6 percent in 27 states. Thus, candidates rightly view the campaign as an opportunity to affect their chances of victory even if a substantial majority of voters have already made up their minds.

The Major Constraints
on Presidential Candidates

Chapters 7, 8, and 9 discussed a number of constraints and conditions that the prospective presidential candidate must consider in formulating campaign strategy. For example, the voter's positions on issues, while not immutable,

TABLE 10.1

Time of Presidential Vote Choice, 1952–1988 (in percentages)

Decision time	Year									
	1952	1956	1960	1964	1968	1972	1976	1980	1984	1988
By the end of the conventions	68%	78%	62%	66%	59%	63%	54%	59%	70%	61%
After the conventions	21	12	25	21	19	23	22	15	17	22
Within two weeks of the election	9	8	10	9	15	8	17	17	10	12
On Election Day	2	2	3	4	7	6	7	9	4	5
Total	100	100	100	100	100	100	100	100	101	100

SOURCES: SRC/CPS election studies.

are one factor that the nominee must ponder. In fact, candidates commission extensive private polling throughout the campaign to ascertain the electorate's issue preferences and candidate perceptions. In 1988, the Bush campaign used focus groups to ascertain the potential effects of certain issues on the campaign. The availability of money and the services it can provide imposes obvious limitations on campaign activities; the shakily financed campaign of Hubert Humphrey in 1968 is an excellent example of a campaign whose conduct was severely handicapped by uncertainty about the availability of money. While numerous constraints impinge upon candidates, four are crucial to the conduct of any general election campaign: (1) the need to win the nomination, (2) the presence or absence of an incumbent president seeking reelection, (3) the majority versus minority status of the candidate's party, and (4) the impact of the Electoral College on campaign strategies.

STRATEGIC ASPECTS OF THE NOMINATION PROCESS

In order to run for president in the general election, the candidate obviously must first secure the party nomination. The process by which a candidate wins a presidential nomination imposes major constraints on the subsequent general election campaign. Donald Matthews (1974: 36) claims that the nominating process is the most critical stage of presidential selection since the major screening and elimination of candidates take place at this stage. The screening can occur at a number of points. Before the primary election season ever arrives, some potential candidates may have informally investigated the probable political and financial support that would be available to them if they declare a formal candidacy. They may drop out of the race without formally entering it if there is little likelihood of support for their candidacy. Similarly, other potential candidates may be deterred from seeking the presidency because of the rigors and sacrifices required.

The most important weeding out of candidates occurs as a result of the primary elections, and it is this aspect of the nominating process that I wish to emphasize, in part because of the recent pattern of selecting a substantial proportion of nominating convention delegates in primaries and the heavy media emphasis given to the primaries. Matthews claims that as a result of the presidential primary system, the preprimary front-runner has usually won the nomination. In analyzing the record of the primaries since 1936 as they have affected the party out of power, Matthews writes (1974: 36), "When the out-party has a single leading contender before the primaries, which is most of the time, the primaries rarely change the situation. When they do alter matters, it is more often to strengthen the claim of the initial leader than substantially to weaken it." This point is elaborated in the work by William R. Keech and Donald R. Matthews (1977) on nominations and convention decisions between 1936 and 1972; the authors appropriately downplay the importance of the primaries in affecting the selection of the nominee by noting that the preprimary favorite most often emerged victorious at the convention in that era.

However, this outcome is not inevitable, as witnessed by the failure of the front-runner Edmund Muskie to capture the Democratic nomination in 1972 and by the success of long-shot Jimmy Carter in 1976. The question is whether the Muskie and Carter examples are simply exceptions from the underlying pattern identified by Keech and Matthews or whether the 1972 and 1976 experiences signal the arrival of an era in which the primaries assume unparalleled importance. In an epilogue to the Keech and Matthews study, Keech seems to suggest that 1976 was more an aberration than a precursor of enduring change. But it seems that a stronger argument can be made for the position that the primaries have indeed become critically significant for the outcome of the nomination process, not least because of the high proportion of the delegates elected in the primaries. The heavy media emphasis on the primaries in conjunction with the democratic rhetoric surrounding primaries as a selection mechanism argues for their continued importance. Also, the horse race emphasis of the media and the economic necessity to attract an audience will probably result in a style of reporting detrimental to the preprimary favorite; after all, a horse race is less exciting to watch if the odds-on favorite leads the race from start to finish. Moreover, the success of Carter and McGovern resulted in increased competition as many prospective candidates said, "If they can do it, why not me?" Finally, the campaign finance and delegate selection reforms discussed in chapter 8 have reduced the power of the party brokers to deliver the nomination to the preprimary favorite. Candidates today have to compete more vigorously for delegates in the more uncertain environment of the primaries.

The fundamental decision that a presidential aspirant must make about the primaries is whether to enter them at all, although, as suggested earlier, it may be impossible today to skip the primaries and hope to win unless the convention is so split that a compromise choice becomes necessary. Adlai Stevenson in 1952, Senator Stuart Symington of Missouri in 1960, Nelson Rockefeller in 1968, and Hubert Humphrey in 1976, among others, all hoped to be their parties' presidential nominee without actively contesting the primaries. Only Stevenson was successful, his candidacy representing one of the few genuine drafts of a nominee. Symington in 1960 hoped that he would emerge as the dark horse, compromise candidate acceptable to all wings of the Democratic party. He envisaged Hubert Humphrey and John Kennedy knocking each other off in the primaries, Lyndon Johnson being unacceptable to the liberal and labor wings of the party, and favorite-son candidates posing no serious threat. Under these conditions Symington hoped that the convention would turn to him as the nominee. As mentioned earlier, Rockefeller's plan was to demonstrate his popularity through the public opinion polls, thereby bypassing the GOP primary electorate and appealing directly to the convention delegates, who, he hoped, would vote for the candidate mostly likely to win the general election. Humphrey's chances in 1976 depended on a convention in which no candidate was close to a first-ballot victory. In such a situation the party might turn to its former standard bearer as a compromise, yet popular, choice.

The decision not to enter the primaries is a strategic one that recognizes the constraints confronting the candidate. For example, Symington recognized that he had neither the political nor the financial resources to successfully contest the primaries; hence, a passive position may have been his only plausible path to the nomination. Likewise, Rockefeller was so unpopular with a substantial segment of the GOP rank and file, and Nixon so popular, that a challenge to Nixon in the primaries might have been electoral suicide. And Humphrey's formal entry in the primaries in 1976 might have reopened party wounds associated with the 1968 and 1972 conventions.

While skipping the primaries may be a reasonable response to the political environment within which the candidate is operating, it entails certain costs. A candidate may be considered less legitimate if he or she has never demonstrated popular support by the electorate. A deadlocked convention may be wary of turning to someone who avoided the primaries, especially in an age in which the media have elevated the primaries to such an exalted status. Of course, the other side to this argument is that nonparticipation in the primaries may make a candidate more acceptable to the warring factions battling in the primaries. Even if a candidate is successful in winning the nomination without entering the primaries, there is the potential cost of beginning the general election campaign with a lower level of voter recognition than the candidate would have had if he or she had contested the primaries. A difficulty confronting Stevenson's candidacy in 1952 was that he was relatively unknown at the outset of the general election campaign, in part because of the absence of extensive primary election campaigning. This was especially harmful to him since he was facing an extremely popular and well-known war hero in the general election. The fact is, however, that candidates who wish to become president generally enter the primaries, often because they have some weakness that can be overcome only by demonstrating electoral popularity. Once the decision to enter is made, there follows the critical choice of which primaries to contest. Should candidates run in all primaries or in a selected few? Are certain primaries unavoidable? Should candidates avoid challenging a specific opponent in his or her home territory? These questions will be addressed in the context of the 1972 and 1976 Democratic races.

Candidates must answer such questions on the basis of incomplete information: they may have to decide on which primaries to contest before knowing their competition or before resources are definitely available. For example, George McGovern announced his candidacy for the 1972 Democratic nomination in January 1971, at a time when not even the number of primaries was definite, let alone the identity of the contestants. The national campaign director for McGovern, Gary Hart, stated that the basic decision to run in New Hampshire, Wisconsin, and a number of other primaries was made in July

1970, six months before McGovern formally announced his candidacy (May and Fraser, 1973: 92). The McGovern camp gave serious thought to waging a strenuous campaign in the Florida primary. The decision was made not to contest Florida vigorously, which in retrospect proved to be a wise move, since George Wallace surprised a number of observers by conducting his 1972 presidential bid through the Democratic party and not his American Independent party. Making opposition to busing his major issue, Wallace swept the Florida primary. According to Ben Wattenberg, an adviser to Senator Henry Jackson, the Jackson campaign strategy in 1972 rested on a strong showing in Florida, a state that seemed congenial to a candidate of Jackson's persuasion (May and Fraser, 1973: 39). This strategy failed because of Wallace's presence in the Florida primary, a presence unanticipated earlier. Many of the decisions that must be made about the primaries are made in an aura of uncertainty.

Carter announced his 1976 candidacy in December 1974, again at a time when key pieces of information about the primaries, such as their number, scheduling, and contestants, were unknown. In fact, the basic Carter strategy was detailed in a document dated November 4, 1972, more than three years before the start of the 1976 primaries (Witcover, 1977: 119). The Carter plan was remarkably foresighted, except for its assumption that Edward Kennedy would be a candidate and thereby keep the field of challengers small. Instead, Kennedy decided not to run and the number of Democratic candidates ballooned.

While an early decision to enter the primaries has its costs, it also has important advantages. If a candidate anticipates that a number of contenders will be vying for the same supporters, it may be wise to enter the race early, thereby locking up some of these supporters and freezing out other competitors. Moreover, building an organization and collecting resources is a time-consuming process that must begin early. Jack Chestnut, national campaign manager for Hubert Humphrey in 1972, believed that the most damaging feature of the Humphrey primary campaign was its late start. Chestnut argued that the decision to run should have been made in July 1971 instead of the following December (May and Fraser, 1973: 74). Carter's success in 1976 and provisions of the campaign financing law encouraged the flock of contenders for the 1988 Democratic and Republican nominations to begin their campaigns early.

The decision about which primaries to contest is critical given the serial nature of the primaries. A strong early showing can give a candidacy a tremendous boost, just as a poor early showing can quickly end a candidacy. Yet some primaries may be considered unavoidable by the candidate even if they do not appear to be particularly hospitable. Candidates who fail to enter the New Hampshire primary, the nation's first, may be viewed as ducking the contest because of electoral weakness. This was one reason McGovern entered the New Hampshire primary despite the presumed invincibility of Senator Muskie, a New Englander, in that state. In reality, McGovern had little to lose in New Hampshire and much to gain. Prior to the New Hampshire primary, his support in the public opinion polls was only a few percent and his campaign was suffering from severe financial problems. Hence, a poor showing by McGovern in New Hampshire would have been interpreted as Muskie running well on his home ground, while a reputable showing would give new life to McGovern's candidacy and allow it to continue through a few more primaries. Gary Hart has explained that New Hampshire and Wisconsin were critical to McGovern's chances: the strong showing in New Hampshire helped bring in contributions and support and set the stage for the McGovern victory in Wisconsin (May and Fraser, 1973: 73). In contrast to Carter, Democratic U.S. Sen. Albert Gore chose not to compete in Iowa and New Hampshire in 1988, waiting instead for Super Tuesday and the southern and border states more likely to support his candidacy. Gore successfully avoided Iowa and New Hampshire, enjoyed some success on Super Tuesday, but dropped out of the race shortly thereafter. Overall most serious aspirants for the nomination have competed in Iowa and New Hampshire.

From the start the Carter strategy targeted New Hampshire and Florida as critical states, the goal being a respectable showing in New Hampshire and a victory in Florida; Carter achieved victories in both states. In New Hampshire, Carter profited from the lack of serious efforts on the part of Henry Jackson and George Wallace, who might have been expected to draw off some of Carter's moderate and conservative support, and from the presence of numerous liberal Democrats on the ballot, who divided the liberal vote. Jackson himself admitted that his failure to contest New Hampshire was a serious blunder that enabled Carter to emerge as a major challenger (Witcover, 1977: 203–204). In Florida, Wallace and Jackson were on the ballot against Carter, with the liberals staying out of the contest. The contrast with Wallace established Carter as the representative of the new South and left Carter as the heir to southern support. Overall, the Carter strategy, as laid out in the 1972 memo, had the following aims (Witcover, 1977: 123):

1. Demonstrate in the first primaries your strength as a candidate. This means a strong surprise showing in New Hampshire and a victory in Florida. [Carter won both.]
2. Establish that you are not a regional candidate by winning early primaries in medium-size states outside the south, such as Rhode Island and Wisconsin. [Carter won Wisconsin and lost Rhode Island, which held a late primary.]
3. Select one of the large industrial and traditionally Democratic states which has an early primary to confront all major opponents and establish yourself as a major contender. Pennsylvania and Ohio would be possibilities. [Carter won both states, Pennsylvania in the middle of the primary season and Ohio at the very end.]
4. Demonstrate consistent strength in all primaries entered.

The McGovern and Carter strategies clearly took advantage of the sequential nature of the primaries. What is fascinating about the McGovern campaign is that it picked its spots to maximum benefit. McGovern seriously contested only two (New Hampshire and Wisconsin) of the first four primaries in 1972 and won one (Wisconsin), while Muskie contested all four vigorously and won two (New Hampshire and Illinois), and Wallace won the Florida primary. Yet by the time the Wisconsin results were in, the McGovern campaign was on track and the Muskie effort derailed. Since McGovern did not view Florida and Illinois as serious targets, his sixth-place finish in Florida and his scant write-in votes in Illinois did not hurt him. Hence, the candidate's choice of primaries to contest and the media's designation of certain primaries as critical play an important part in determining the candidate's fate.

Thus, the present system of primary elections makes it possible for a relatively unknown and unsupported candidate to challenge successfully for the nomination by scoring early successes in carefully selected states; the institution of a national primary would eliminate this possibility. One empirical generalization about primary election results is that the winner of a primary inevitably jumps in the polls and usually receives an influx of campaign contributions. Hence, it is crucial to score a victory, the sooner the better, although Rockefeller's jump in the polls after his victory in the next to last primary, in Oregon, in 1964 suggests that the effect may be present throughout the campaign. Table 10.2 shows how McGovern's popularity among Democrats rose after his victory in Wisconsin and how Carter's fortunes soared after his successes in New Hampshire, Florida, and Pennsylvania. Traditionally, primary victories had been more important because of their impact on uncommitted delegates and less so in terms of the actual number of delegates won. For example, Eisenhower in his four contested primary victories in 1952 won only 99 delegates; the real impact of his successes was on the uncommitted delegates who became convinced of his popularity (Davis, 1967: 81). The larger number of primaries today and the Democratic rule changes requiring most delegates to announce their candidate preferences mean that there are fewer uncommitted delegates at conventions, so that primary victories are important for both psychological reasons and actual delegate acquisition.

The decision to run in all or only some of the primaries is based on multiple considerations. Acute resource shortage and foresight may explain McGovern's choice in 1972. In the case of Muskie, it has been argued that as the designated front-runner he felt the need to demonstrate his popularity by sweeping the primaries. Muskie wanted to establish his reputation as a national and not simply a regional candidate, a strategy that, if successful, would have given him a running start in the general election. Muskie's strategy entailed certain risks and possessed certain advantages. Obviously, spreading oneself too thin over a number of primaries can lead to disappointing performances, which can quickly convert a front-runner into an also-ran. In many of the states he entered, Muskie had been endorsed by the party leaders and the organization, which subsequently proved unable to deliver many votes. The weakness of his candidacy was quickly exposed by the effectiveness of the McGovern grass-roots organization. Yet consistent early success may lead a candidate's opponents to drop out of the race, resulting in an easy nomination victory and a unified party in the general election.

Like Muskie, Carter ran in all the primaries (except West Virginia); but unlike Muskie, this decision worked out well for Carter for a number of reasons. First, expectations of Carter's performance were initially low, so that he risked little in running widely. After Carter emerged as the front-runner

---

TABLE 10.2

Choice of Democrats for the 1972 and 1976 Nominations

	1972		
Survey date	*Humphrey*	*McGovern*	*Wallace*
March 3–6	31	6	15
	March 7—New Hampshire primary—Muskie wins		
	March 14—Florida primary—Wallace wins		
	March 21—Illinois primary—Muskie wins		
March 24–27	31	5	17
	April 4—Wisconsin primary—McGovern wins		
April 21–24	30	17	19
	April 25—Massachusetts primary—McGovern wins		
	April 25—Pennsylvania primary—Humphrey wins		
April 28–May 1	35	30	18
	May 16—Maryland primary—Wallace wins		
	May 23—Oregon primary—McGovern wins		
May 26–29	26	25	26

	1976			
Survey date	*Humphrey*	*Carter*	*Jackson*	*Wallace*
January 23–26	17	4	5	18
	February 24—New Hampshire primary—Carter wins			
February 27–March 1	18	12	5	14
	March 2—Massachusetts primary—Jackson wins			
	March 9—Florida primary—Carter wins			
March 10–13	27	26	15	15
March 26–29	30	29	7	13
	April 6—New York primary—Jackson wins			
	April 6—Wisconsin primary—Carter wins			
April 9–12	31	28	8	13
April 23–26	33	29	7	12
	April 27—Pennsylvania primary—Carter wins			
April 30–May 3	29	40	4	9

SOURCE: *Gallup Opinion Index,* June 1972, Report no. 84, p. 10; and *Gallup Opinion Index,* August 1976, Report no. 133, pp. 6–7.

and began to lose primaries to late entrants Jerry Brown and Frank Church, there was always at least one election on each primary day that Carter managed to win, which helped maintain his progress. For example, Carter lost two of three primaries held on June 1 and two of three held on June 8, but his single victories on those days kept his campaign rolling. And even when Carter lost a primary, he still captured a respectable share of the delegates, which brought his front-running total closer to the number needed for nomination. Hence, even as Carter faltered in the latter part of the primary season, his impressive delegate totals resulted in the media emphasizing how close he was getting to the nomination rather than how poorly he was doing at the polls.

As a general rule, candidates decide on the number of primaries to enter on the basis of their liabilities and assets. Underfinanced candidates of necessity must opt for only a few primaries, although most dark horse candidates look to the Iowa caucuses and the New Hampshire primary as the best places to try to score an upset. Other candidates face other constraints. For example, John Kennedy in 1960 had to demonstrate to party leaders that his Catholicism would not drag the ticket down to defeat in November. He accomplished this by entering and winning a large number of primaries. Similarly, Estes Kefauver in 1952 sought the Democratic nomination via the primary route because his support among party leaders was so weak. And Richard Nixon in 1968 had to enter the Republican primaries to dispel his image as a loser.

The primary election system usually weeds out candidates and results in a climactic primary, whose winner is likely to go on to secure the nomination. Gary Hart described the scenario the McGovern camp hoped for in 1972 (May and Fraser, 1973: 73):

> All the way through, our premise was that when you come to a nomination in the Democratic Party, there is, for all practical purposes, no center. Our strategy was always to co-opt the left, become the candidate of the liberal wing of the party, and then eventually get it down to a two-man race. . . . We always knew it would be a two-man race between a liberal and a conservative. There was, in fact, no center, and it was just a question of whether or not we could win on our side and who would win on the other.

While one can quarrel with Hart's liberal–conservative assessment, the race did narrow down to two men, and the California primary was climactic, just as it had been for the GOP in 1964. Many observers would argue that Pennsylvania was the climactic primary in 1976; Carter's victory there ended the Jackson candidacy and thrust Carter far ahead of the field. What makes Pennsylvania unusual as a climactic primary is that it was held midway through the primary season, with more than half of the convention delegates still to be selected. The 1984 Democratic primaries were somewhat unusual as Mondale and Hart took turns being the front-runner and enjoying momentum. Nevertheless, some would argue that Hart's failure to win the Illinois primary in late March set the stage for his ultimate defeat, even though he won seven primaries and numerous caucuses between April and June. Mondale effectively clinched the nomination on June 5 by winning New Jersey, even though Hart won three of the five primaries (including California) held on that date. In 1988, Bush's victory in New Hampshire followed by his sweep on Super Tuesday (March 8) ended the GOP nomination battle early. After the other Democratic challengers had faltered, Dukakis' victories over Jackson in Connecticut (March 29), Wisconsin (April 5), and New York (April 19) effectively ended the Democratic contest.

Obtaining the nomination is only the first step in the path to the presidency, and the strategies employed to secure the nomination can promote or hinder the candidate's prospects for victory in the general election. For example, if the candidate must appeal to an atypical segment of the party's constituency to win the nomination, then it may be difficult for the candidate to broaden his or her base and unify the party for the general election. This argument has been applied to the Goldwater and McGovern nominations. Both candidates were said to have appealed to fringes within their respective parties; both were nominated in conventions marked by sharp ideological conflict; both suffered substantial defection from their parties' loyalists; and both were overwhelmingly defeated in November. Candidates who appeal to an intense minority within their party may face an almost impossible situation in trying to achieve party unity. For example, if McGovern had strenuously tried to woo the labor leaders, party regulars, and others who had opposed his nomination, his supporters would have felt betrayed, and McGovern himself would have been viewed as just another self-serving politician. Yet failure to win over these groups spelled electoral disaster. In 1976 the primary election process served to enhance Carter's general election prospects. As Keech (Keech and Matthews, 1977) observes, a consensus candidate around whom all factions of the party could unite emerged out of the diverse field that began the primaries.

On the Republican side, unlike the Democratic side, the 1976 primary process did not produce consensus but instead generated divisiveness as Reagan challenged the incumbent Ford for the GOP nomination. Certainly intraparty challenges to an incumbent president run the risk of tearing the party apart—so the question becomes, "What strategic considerations go into a decision to challenge an incumbent president?" One obvious answer is that challenges to the incumbent are encouraged by the incumbent's political weakness and unpopularity; certainly Kefauver's challenge to Truman in 1952 and McCarthy's challenge to Johnson in 1968 (before both presidents decided not to seek reelection) were fueled by widespread dissatisfaction with the incumbents' performances. Likewise, Kennedy's decision in 1980 to challenge Carter's renomination was made at a time when Carter's public standing was very low. Kennedy could not have anticipated that the Iranian hostage crisis and the Soviet invasion of Afghanistan would revive for a time the political prospects of the Carter administration.

Incumbent weakness does not account very well for Reagan's decision to challenge Ford, because the polls showed Ford to be reasonably popular with Americans and to more than hold his own in trial heats with prospective Democratic candidates. Rather, Reagan's bid may have been encouraged by his having a natural and sizable base of support within the GOP; Reagan was prominent in national Republican politics long before Ford became vice-president in 1973. In general, incumbent presidents are more vulnerable when they do not enjoy a solid base of support within their party; certainly this is one problem that confronted Carter in 1980, because many components of the Democratic coalition, such as labor, liberals, Catholics, and Jews, seemed to have no special enthusiasm for Carter, as they might have had for Kennedy.

Taking on an incumbent is risky, of course, since presidents have tremendous resources at their disposal. Moreover, many party professionals shudder at the prospect of an intraparty contest. And should the challenger be successful in wresting the nomination from the incumbent, it may prove to be an empty victory if the party cannot achieve unity in the general election. Yet challenges to incumbents are enticing; after all, Truman and Johnson dropped out of the race and Reagan came very close to ousting Ford. Because party professionals no longer control presidential nominations, the would-be challenger can enter the primaries knowing that his or her effort to defeat the incumbent will be the subject of substantial media coverage.

Whether the primaries yield a definitive result, the formal selection of the nominee occurs at the national convention and is usually followed by an attempt to unify the party for the general election. However, the Republicans in 1964 and the Democrats in 1968 and 1972 left their conventions as seriously divided parties, and all three lost in November, while in 1976 the Democrats left their convention in uncharacteristic harmony and won on Election Day. In 1980, the harmony at the Republican convention was genuine, but the symbolic show of unity at the end of the Democratic convention was not very convincing for many observers. Thus, the national convention may have become less important in determining the identity of the nominee but may be extremely important in starting the nominee on a successful or unsuccessful path toward the presidency. Millions of citizens view the conventions, and the images they see may greatly influence their subsequent evaluations of the candidates and parties.

One final point about winning the nomination is how well placed the candidate is to expand his or her base of support in the general election. As mentioned before, Goldwater and McGovern appealed to intense ideological wings within their parties and were either unwilling or unable to moderate their positions to attract centrist or moderate support in the general election and to maintain the loyalty of their fellow party members. In contrast, Reagan in 1980 was very skillful in moving from his harsh conservative rhetoric of the primary season to a more moderate brand of conservatism in the general election. Reagan's success in doing this was aided by the fact that he was facing an incumbent president who was widely perceived as an ineffective leader.

Goldwater and McGovern, in contrast, were running against strong incumbents who fully recognized the importance of capturing the center of the political spectrum.

THE INCUMBENT–NONINCUMBENT,
MAJORITY PARTY–MINORITY PARTY STATUS OF THE CANDIDATE

Once the nomination has been secured, two considerations are of immediate importance in shaping campaign strategies. The first is whether there is an incumbent president seeking reelection, and the second is whether the candidate is from the majority or minority party defined in terms of the partisan allegiances of the electorate. In the situation where no incumbent president is running, a third consideration becomes relevant: "Is the nominee from the party that currently controls the presidency?"

An incumbent president seeking election seems to be in a formidable position. The very fact of being president, with its extensive media coverage, bestows upon the incumbent an aura of competence, experience, and familiarity that a challenger is hard-pressed to match. If being "presidential" is an important characteristic for voter acceptance, then the incumbent president possesses a tremendous advantage. Of course, as the elections of 1976 and 1980 indicate, incumbency also has its risks, particularly when the economy is not very robust. Yet even here, there are some things that presidents can do to alleviate or submerge problems in the short term. For example, if farm income is falling, the secretary of agriculture can channel money to farmers through a variety of means. More generally, if the economy is sagging, the president can take a number of steps, such as releasing funds and selling materials from government stockpiles, to provide a short-term stimulus so that by Election Day the economic situation will improve at least temporarily. And from the perspective of the electorate, movement toward the solution of such economic problems as unemployment and inflation may be just as important in its vote decision as actual success in solving the problems. The 1984 election exemplified the power of incumbency at its fullest; the national economy was healthy, and the incumbent president had a reputation for leadership, competence, and integrity.

While the president has some ability to alter the state of domestic affairs, his advantages become overwhelming in foreign affairs. An overseas trip to China or to the Soviet Union effectively blocks out media coverage of the opposition and further serves to emphasize presidential ability. Similarly, a vigorous defense of some American interest abroad will most often serve to rally the country behind the president. A cynic may justifiably question why major (and premature) announcements of significant moves toward peace in Vietnam occurred shortly before the 1968 and 1972 elections.

While presidents will be attacked for failing to accomplish certain goals, they can often outflank their critics by adopting some version of their proposals. The focus of media coverage is such that presidents' endorsements of a program will identify it as their own in the public mind even if the initiative for the program came from a congressional committee or elsewhere. A message to Congress or a speech to the public allows presidents to establish their credentials on an issue.

This emphasis on the power of incumbency should be hedged by recognizing that when the country really falls apart, as in the Great Depression, the incumbent will be in serious trouble, as witnessed by President Hoover's defeat in 1932. It has been asserted that Harry Truman in 1952 and Lyndon Johnson in 1968 did not seek renomination because domestic and foreign policy crises had made their reelection doubtful. It seems clear that both could have won their party's nomination, and it certainly could be argued that Johnson would have had a better than even chance to retain the presidency. Overall, incumbency seems to be a much more important factor than the majority–minority party status of the candidate.

The fact that Gerald Ford in 1976 and Jimmy Carter in 1980 lost may seem to belie the importance of incumbency. Yet only the power of incumbency can help explain how Ford was able to secure the nomination and run so strong a race in the general election, given the many strikes against him. Ford was an unelected president whose prior political base was his congressional district in Grand Rapids, Michigan. He was initially appointed vice-president by the disgraced president, whom he subsequently pardoned in a widely condemned action. During his brief presidency, the United States experienced high rates of unemployment and inflation simultaneously, while in foreign affairs North Vietnam successfully overran South Vietnam. Not the least of Ford's election problems was his being a member of the minority party. Yet despite all these disadvantages, Ford managed to run a very close race. Likewise, Carter's ability to ward off Senator Kennedy's challenge was enhanced substantially by the opportunities for presidential leadership provided by foreign policy crises.

The majority party–minority party distinction is too simple since it does not reflect whether the parties are united. McGovern and Humphrey were the candidates of a divided majority party, and Goldwater was the nominee of a divided minority party; all three lost. Likewise, this majority–minority factor assumes that there is indeed a majority party. If party ties continue to weaken, or if the Republican and Democratic parties reach parity in popular support, then the strategic importance of this distinction will change. Assuming that the parties are relatively unified, the majority–minority distinction has important implications for the kinds of strategies that are likely to be adopted. The majority party candidate will probably emphasize the importance of party, as did Kennedy and Carter, while the minority party nominee will stress the nominee and not the party, as did Nixon and Ford. Minority party candidates will want to de-emphasize partisan concerns, which they can accomplish by adopting positions close to those of the majority party or by nominating candidates with such immense popular appeal (for example, General Eisenhower) that party loyalties break down to a moderate degree. Further, minority party candidates can emphasize campaign themes and issues that will draw support from the majority party and win a large share of the independent vote.

The minority party may also attempt to win a majority of the vote by converting nonvoters to voters, recognizing that the vote difference between the candidates has been much less than the number of citizens who did not vote. The GOP employed this strategy in 1952 and 1964 with markedly different results. In a campaign plan written for the Republican party in 1952, Robert Humphreys (Lavine, 1970: 36) argued that the GOP in 1940, 1944, and 1948 had adopted unsuccessful "me-too" strategies to win the Independent vote, on the assumption that this vote was relatively liberal. Humphreys suggested that there was a fourth potential source of votes in addition to Democrats, Republicans, and Independents; namely, the stay-at-homes— "those who vote only when discontent stirs them to vote against current conditions." Humphreys asserted that the vote of the stay-at-homes heavily outnumbered that of the Independents and that the best way to win this vote was to attack the incumbent party for making a mess of things. As mentioned in chapter 5, the GOP slogan in 1952 was "Corruption, Korea, and Communism," three problems associated with the incumbent Democratic administration. Note that Humphreys' strategy assumed nothing about whether the stay-at-homes were liberal or conservative, only that they could be motivated to vote by sharp attacks on the incumbents. In fact, Humphreys was careful to advise the GOP not to try to rescind the New Deal or to take consistently conservative positions (Lavine, 1970: 36–37).

The premise of Barry Goldwater's campaign in 1964 was also that there were millions of stay-at-home voters, except that these were assumed to be conservative, Republican stay-at-homes. Hence, Goldwater argued that if the GOP would nominate a true conservative and offer a genuine choice rather than the me-too candidates of previous elections, these millions of stay-at-home conservative voters would flock to the polls and ensure a Republican victory. Goldwater's strategy was misguided since there were no millions of nonvoting conservatives; in fact, public opinion polls have consistently shown that the group with the highest turnout in presidential elections has consisted of strong Republicans of a conservative bent.

When the majority party is split, the minority party may still try to minimize partisanship in an attempt to win over disgruntled members of the majority; Nixon in 1972 scarcely mentioned his Republicanism, and many of his most effective television commercials were sponsored by Democrats for Nixon. At times, the majority party itself will minimize partisanship, especially when victory is assured. The division in the minority GOP in 1964 guaranteed Johnson's election, so that his major concern became the magnitude of his victory. Attempting to win over moderate and liberal Republicans upset over the Goldwater nomination, Johnson stressed his own moderate stances and played down his own partisanship.

When there is no incumbent president running, whether the candidate is from the party currently controlling the presidency becomes important. If so, the candidate faces a number of constraints, particularly if he or she is a part of the incumbent administration, such as the vice-president. For example, Richard Nixon in 1960 and Hubert Humphrey in 1968 were both caught in a dilemma. As vice-presidents in the outgoing administrations, they were responsible for defending their parties' records. Failure to do so might have led the president to undercut their candidacies and to deny them the kind of access to decision making that would be useful in demonstrating their presidential capabilities. Yet both Nixon and Humphrey, and particularly the latter, had to establish their own identities and to explain, without appearing to criticize the president, how they would improve the condition of the nation. This was a difficult task, and their opponents—Kennedy in 1960 and Nixon in 1968—went on the attack vigorously and successfully. Bush was in an easier position in 1988 because of the popularity of the Reagan administration. Nevertheless, Bush carefully distanced himself from the Reagan record on issues such as education and the environment. Even if the candidate is not formally a part of the current administration, he or she may still be saddled with the record of that administration; Adlai Stevenson in 1952 was handicapped by criticisms of the Truman administration even though he had not been a part of it. And Mondale in 1984 was attacked for his role as vice-president in the Carter administration between 1977 and 1981.

In summary, the constraints discussed in this section can be arrayed according to the flowchart depicted in figure 10.1. Note that the question of incumbency comes first; this has been done to suggest its paramount importance as compared to the other factors discussed. The flowchart should be read from the perspective of the candidate surveying the political environment in order to formulate a sound campaign strategy. Note that in four of six cases in which an incumbent president sought reelection, he was victorious (and by a landslide). Also note that Bush in 1988 was the only nonincumbent candidate of the party controlling the presidency who was victorious; Stevenson in 1952, Nixon in 1960, and Humphrey in 1968 were all unsuccessful.

THE ELECTORAL COLLEGE

Technically, Americans do not vote directly for the presidential nominees but for a slate of electors pledged, though not formally bound, to cast their votes for the candidate receiving a plurality of the popular vote in their state; these electors are collectively referred to as the Electoral College. To become president, a candidate must receive a majority of the electoral vote, a majority that can be achieved without achieving a majority of the popular vote. The number of electoral votes today is 538, so that a candidate needs 270 electoral votes to become president. The number of electoral votes of a state is equal to the number of U.S. senators and representatives from that state; in addition, the District of Columbia has three electoral votes. If no candidate receives a majority of the Electoral College vote, the U.S. House of Representatives selects the president from among the top three contenders, with each state delegation in the House having one vote and a majority of twenty-six votes needed to elect a president. State delegations with an equal number of Democrats and Republicans would probably deadlock and be unable to vote, thereby making it difficult to attain a majority of twenty-six states. Wallace's goal in 1968 as a third-party candidate was to win enough electoral votes to deny either major party candidate a majority of the electoral vote, thereby establishing himself as a potential kingmaker. Finally, electoral votes are almost invariably cast as

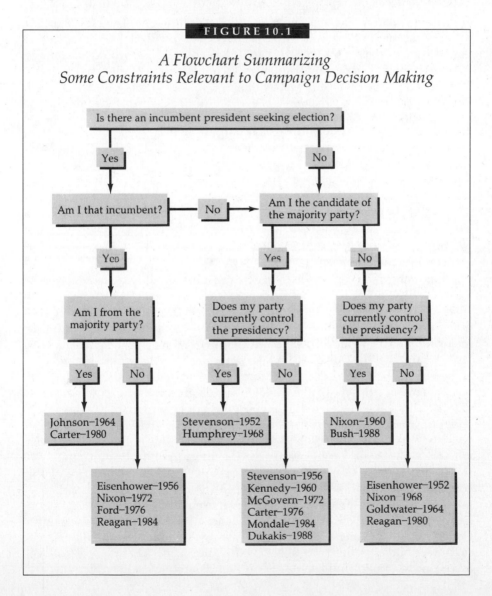

FIGURE 10.1

*A Flowchart Summarizing
Some Constraints Relevant to Campaign Decision Making*

a unit; that is, the candidate carrying a state wins all of its electoral votes, no matter how small his plurality. This means that the candidate who carries California (with forty-five electoral votes) by one vote and loses Vermont (with three electoral votes) by 50,000 votes is far ahead in the Electoral College even though he or she is trailing in the popular vote. Only the state of Maine, with four electoral votes, uses a method different from winner-takes-all. Instead, Maine allocates one electoral college vote for each congressional district a candidate carries, and two electoral votes to the candidate who carries the state at large.

Since the Electoral College system makes it possible to deny the presidency to the winner in the popular vote, the institution has been the object of major criticisms. For example, Lawrence D. Longley and Alan G. Braun (1972: viii, 3) point out that a shift of less than 30,000 votes in 1948 would have made Dewey the president despite Truman's lead of more than 2 million votes in the popular tally. In 1960 a shift of a total of 8,971 votes in Missouri and Illinois would have created an Electoral College deadlock because of the presence of unpledged electors, and a shift of a total of 11,424 votes in the five states of Illinois, Missouri, New Mexico, Nevada, and Hawaii would have made Nixon the president. In 1968 a shift of only 42,000 votes in three states would have sent the election to the House. And in 1976 a shift of only 5,600 votes in Ohio and 3,700 votes in Hawaii would have elected Ford, despite his trailing Carter by 1.7 million votes in the popular vote.[1]

These examples suggest why the state and not the individual voter becomes the focus of campaign strategies, especially in close elections. When candidates map out their strategy, they talk in terms of carrying states and not the popular vote. When a candidate is far ahead in the polls that measure popular vote strength, this advantageous position should also be reflected in an electoral vote landslide. Yet even here, candidates such as Humphrey in 1968 and McGovern in 1972, who trailed badly in the polls during the course of the campaign, still talked bravely of putting together an Electoral College majority by carrying the key states. In October 1988, when the polls showed Dukakis trailing, the Dukakis campaign announced that it would be targeting eighteen states plus the District of Columbia, which had a total of 272 electoral votes. In making this move, the Dukakis campaign was trying to demonstrate that it could still win the election and should not be written off by the media and the voters. And when the election appears close, the state results are watched very closely. Candidates commission statewide polls to supply them with critical information about the probable Electoral College outcome.

The Electoral College does overrepresent small states because of the constitutional provision that every state, no matter what its population, is guaranteed at least three electors (two for its senators and one for its at least one representative). Yet with respect to the focus of the campaign, the Electoral College and the winner-take-all rule for casting electoral votes favor the large, urbanized, industrialized states. And within these states the Electoral College, according to Yunker and Langley (1973), tends to give greater vote power to urban ethnic groups, although suburban residents tend to be more powerful than central city dwellers in terms of casting the decisive votes. As a result, the presidential constituency is more metropolitan than the nation as a whole. Black citizens are not as advantaged by the Electoral College since the black population is not concentrated only in the industrialized states but is also very prominent in the rural South and the District of Columbia.

Thus, the Electoral College system makes the large states the battleground of presidential elections, and this is reflected in the candidates' strategies, where they campaign, and where they spend most of their resources.[2] Even the Goldwater and Nixon strategies in 1964 and 1968, which have been labeled "southern" in orientation and which emphasized carrying the South, the border states, the mountain states, and the western states, still required winning some of the big industrialized states in order to secure victory. One of the best examples of the emphasis on the major states in presidential elections occurred in the 1960 Kennedy–Nixon race. Kennedy in 1960 stressed capturing the nine large states of New York, Pennsylvania, Michigan, Illinois, Ohio, New Jersey, Massachusetts, California, and Texas (Johnson's home state). If Kennedy had been victorious in all those states, he would have had 237 of the 269 votes needed for an Electoral College majority (White, 1961: 295). The rest of the votes needed for a majority were to come from the South because of Lyndon Johnson's presence on the ticket and from a scattering of votes won in New England and the Midwest. Table 10.3 shows that Kennedy's strategy worked largely as planned (California and especially Ohio were disappointments). Of the 269 votes needed for a majority, 237 came from either the South or the large industrial states. Nixon in 1960 focused on the same large states as Kennedy did, with the exception of Massachusetts (Kennedy's home state) and New Jersey (White, 1961: 318). Unfortunately for Nixon, his pledge to campaign in all fifty states had him campaigning in Alaska, with three electoral votes, when he might better have spent the time in Illinois, which he lost very narrowly.

In 1952, 1956, 1964, 1972, 1980, and 1984 the popular vote was so one-sided that the winner was assured of an Electoral College landslide. In 1968 the state-by-state planning was very detailed. Nixon conceded Alabama, Arkansas, Mississippi, Louisiana, and Georgia to George Wallace but challenged Wallace in the other six states of the Confederacy and won all except Texas, thereby receiving fifty-seven electoral votes from the South, which partially offset his losses in New York and Pennsylvania. Humphrey's strategy in 1968 was very clear: carry the major states. According to Lewis Chester, Godfrey Hodgson, and Bruce Page (1969: 795–796), one campaign plan called for Humphrey to confine his activities to twenty-seven states. Of the twenty-seven states, fourteen, such as New York, Michigan, New Jersey, Missouri, and Pennsylvania, were probable Humphrey states; nine, including Ohio and Washington, were genuine possibilities; four—California, Alaska, and the Carolinas—were outside chances; and Illinois was described as too big to ignore. Of his fourteen probables, Humphrey won all but New Jersey; but he lost Ohio, Illinois, and California, all in relatively close races, and that doomed his big-state strategy. While 132 of his 191 electoral votes came from the large states (see table 10.3), overall the best Humphrey could do was split the large states with Nixon. And given Nixon's strength in other areas, such as the border states, the plains states, the southwestern states, and the mountain states, Humphrey could not fashion an Electoral College majority.

In 1976, the Carter team developed a formula based on the size of a state, its Democratic potential, and the need to campaign in the state in order to determine how much of the campaign effort should be devoted to each state (Witcover, 1977: 551–552). According to Witcover (1977: 561–562), the Carter effort emphasized maintaining Carter's southern base, carrying traditionally Democratic states outside the South, and campaigning to some extent in Republican areas to keep the Ford effort on the defensive. The Carter team reasoned that if it could keep its southern base intact and add a few traditionally Democratic states, then only a few of the major industrial states would be required to assure victory in November. For Ford to be victorious, unless inroads could be made in Carter's southern support, a near sweep of the large states was required. Hence, as shown in figure 10.2, the key battleground of the election became the major industrial states, especially New York, Pennsylvania, Ohio, Illinois, and California; the South; and a few other states.

In 1980 Carter's strategy was similar: to run well in his home region and capture the bulk of the major industrial states. Yet even when the polls in 1980 were indicating a very close popular vote contest between Carter and Reagan, Carter's electoral vote strategy was flawed as statewide polls showed Reagan seriously threatening Carter's support in the South, while Carter was seriously challenging Reagan in very few states west of the Mississippi River. Hence, Reagan had a solid base of Electoral College votes upon which to build and had the advantage if the popular vote had remained close.

Table 10.3 helps illustrate some points about campaign strategy and the Electoral College. First, no candidate can afford to completely write off the major states. And in fact, most strategies, whether southern or whatever, still require carrying two or three large electoral-vote states. Nevertheless, the candidate who enters the election with a bloc of votes assured is freer to adopt any of a number of strategies to secure the remaining electoral votes needed for a majority. The distribution of the South's electoral votes since 1952 suggests how critical the region can be for Democratic and Republican prospects. If the South goes solidly for one party's candidate, then the candidate of the other party is of necessity forced into a large-state Electoral College strategy and the loss of only a few states will spell defeat.

In the six presidential contests from 1968 to 1988, the GOP has entered the general election with a solid bloc of Electoral College votes comprised mainly of states west of the Mississippi River. Indeed, in the last six elections the Republican candidate has carried twenty-two states with a (1988) total of 198 electoral votes all six times; sixteen of these twenty-two states with a total of 127 electoral votes are west of the Mississippi. In addition, the GOP has

FIGURE 10.2

Candidate Stops during the 1976 Presidential Campaign

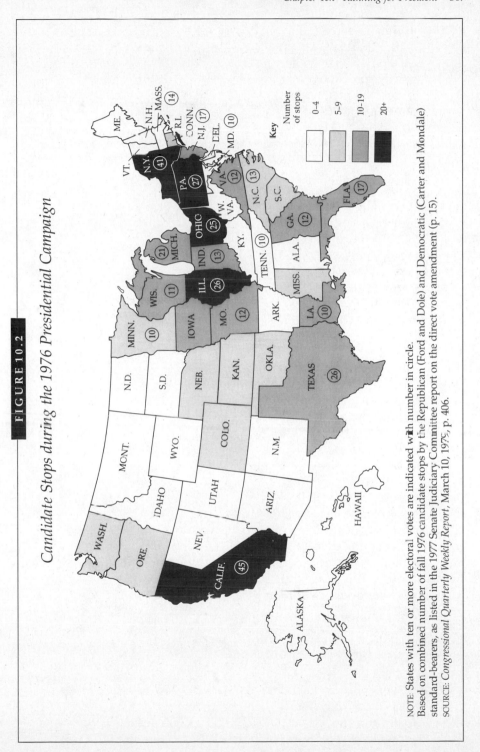

NOTE: States with ten or more electoral votes are indicated with number in circle. Based on combined number of fall 1976 candidate stops by the Republican (Ford and Dole) and Democratic (Carter and Mondale) standard-bearers, as listed in the 1977 Senate Judiciary Committee report on the direct vote amendment (p. 15).

SOURCE: *Congressional Quarterly Weekly Report,* March 10, 1979, p. 406.

TABLE 10.3

Large-State and Southern
Electoral Vote Allocation, 1952–1988

Election	Electoral votes needed to win	Total electoral votes won by candidate	Southern electoral votes won by candidate	Large-state electoral votes won by candidate	Large-state and southern electoral votes won by candidate
1952					
Eisenhower	266	442	57	247	270
Stevenson		89	71	0	71
1956					
Eisenhower	266	457	67	247	280
Stevenson		74	60	0	60
1960					
Kennedy	269	303	81	180	237
Nixon		219	33	67	90
1964					
Johnson	270	486	81	255	297
Goldwater		52	47	0	47
1968					
Nixon	270	301	57	123	166
Humphrey		191	25	132	132
Wallace		46	46	0	46
1972					
Nixon	270	521	130	245	332
McGovern		17	0	14	14
1976					
Carter	270	297	118	150	225
Ford		240	12	109	121
1980					
Reagan	270	489	118	259	334
Carter		49	12	0	12
1984					
Reagan	270	525	138	254	342
Mondale		13	0	0	0
1988					
Bush	270	426	138	205	293
Dukakis		111	0	49	49

NOTE: The large electoral vote states are the ten states with the largest number of electoral votes in 1984. With the exception of Florida, the same states ranked in the top ten throughout this period. Two of the ten large states are also southern (Florida and Texas), and this is adjusted for in the last column of figures presented above. By 1984 North Carolina had tied Massachusetts as the tenth largest Electoral College state. But to keep the classifications as comparable as possible over the 1952–1988 period, North Carolina was not included in the large-state category. In 1988, one elector in West Virginia cast his vote for Bentsen and not Dukakis.

SOURCES: Constructed from figures presented in *Nomination and Election of the President and Vice President of the United States* (Washington, D.C.: U.S. Government Printing Office, 1972), Table F, p. 7; *Guide to 1976 Elections* (Washington, D.C.: Congressional Quarterly, 1977), p. 25; and *Congressional Quarterly Weekly Report*, November 8, 1980, p. 3297.

carried an additional twelve states with a total of 133 electoral votes in five of the last six elections. In this same period the Democrats have carried only the District of Columbia with three electoral votes all six times and only Minnesota with ten electoral votes five of six times. Hence, the recent arithmetic of the Electoral College strongly points to the difficulty the Democrats have in winning the presidency, particularly when they are unable to win the South or cut into the Republican base in the West.

SOME FINAL CONSIDERATIONS ON ELECTION STRATEGIES

It is commonplace to assert that any candidate's major strategy in any election is to get his or her supporters to the polls and then to try to win support among uncommitted voters; efforts to convert the opposition to one's cause are usually viewed as futile. These maxims of campaigning are relevant for presidential elections. Certainly, nominees do not premise their campaigns on the assumption that all voters are equally likely to support them. Rather, candidates recognize that certain voters are predisposed to support them and that other voters are predisposed to oppose them.

The candidate's shorthand way of identifying probable supporters and opponents is to categorize voters into groups defined according to such demographic characteristics as race, religion, and occupation, and to determine how these groups voted in previous elections. Thus, while the Electoral College makes the state the critical unit over which the election is fought, candidates do not view that state as a single entity but instead divide it into distinct areas characterized by varying patterns of party support in the past. For this reason campaign strategists often make statements of this kind: "For the Democrats to carry Pennsylvania (or Illinois or New York), they must come out of Philadelphia (or Chicago or New York City) with a certain vote lead." Similarly, it is often stated that for the Republicans to carry California, they must build up a certain vote margin in Orange and San Diego counties and run strongly in Los Angeles County. These statements basically mean that a candidate must run well in his or her areas of natural support.

Statements about carrying Chicago or Orange County are further refined to identify the specific groups among which the candidate must run strongly to have a chance to carry the city or county by the necessary amount. For example, some observers argue that for the Democrats to carry Chicago by the needed margin, they will have to run well among such groups as blacks, Catholic ethnic groups, and union members—traditional sources of Democratic strength. In short, a presidential campaign tends to focus on groups that collectively add up to majority support in the electorate.

The existence of groups makes possible an economical way for a presidential candidate to appeal to the citizenry at large on the basis of a limited number of concerns important to groups. Obviously, it would be impossible for a candidate to direct individual appeals to millions of citizens. And, as Lewis A. Froman, Jr. (1966: 4) notes, the group serves as a mechanism of communication that provides its members with the standards by which political information can be evaluated.

John Kessel (1974: 116) observes that a focus on groups leads a "candidate to appeal to voters in a manner acceptable to the groups already supporting him." Kessel points out, however, that any successful campaign must do more than simply placate traditional party supporters. According to Kessel (1974: 117), a distinction must be made between activists and nonactivists; the former are probably very informed about politics and highly motivated by policy concerns and the latter less so. Thus, many of the candidate's activities and speeches are geared less to rank-and-file supporters and the general public and more to party activists. For example, Humphrey's 1968 Salt Lake City speech, in which he tried to move some distance from the Vietnam War policies of the Johnson administration, may be viewed as aimed primarily at those Democratic activists who were extremely upset by the war and seemed likely to withhold their critical resources and skills from the campaign unless some concessions were offered them. In retrospect, Humphrey's actual concessions in the speech seem quite minimal, but symbolically they were significant.

Hence, the candidate enters the campaign recognizing that most groups are not politically neutral, that they are in fact predisposed to support one party over the other because of traditional ties rooted in historical events and because of more contemporary policy concerns. Benjamin Page (unpublished paper, p. 27) found that in 1968 Humphrey and Nixon took different positions on a series of issues that reflected the differences in the issue preferences of the rank-and-file party identifiers. While the causal connection between the candidates' and the citizens' issue positions is ambiguous—candidates may be responding to citizens' wishes, or citizens may be formulating issue positions according to cues provided by their preferred candidate—it seems clear that the types of issue appeals emanating from candidates are to a large degree constrained by the preferences of party activists and party loyalists.

This means efforts by a candidate to appeal to a new coalition of supporters may be highly risky in terms of losing traditional support and failing to win sufficient new adherents. Goldwater in 1964 and McGovern in 1972 envisaged new support coalitions that failed to materialize. Goldwater's strategy was based on the myth of the stay-at-home Republican voters, and Goldwater paid heavily for succumbing to the myth. The coalition envisaged by the McGovern camp in 1972 seemed more plausible on the surface; it consisted of minorities such as blacks and Chicanos, liberal Democrats, progressive labor union members, and young people. This last group was particularly important since the enfranchisement of eighteen year olds plus the coming of voting age of the twenty-one to twenty-five year olds too young to vote in 1968 meant that there would be 25 million new young voters in 1972. McGovern hoped for high turnout and solid support among young voters and was disappointed on both counts. Young voters turned out at a rate noticeably lower than the national average of 56 percent, and they divided their votes almost evenly between Nixon and McGovern. Even among college students, those young people thought to be most heavily pro McGovern, vote preferences were almost evenly divided.

Thus, recent efforts to construct new and lasting coalitions of groups have apparently been unsuccessful. Robert Axelrod (1986) has charted the loyalty rates (see table 3.6) and the contributions that various groups have made to each party's vote support since 1952. Axelrod's analysis incorporates three elements in determining the importance of a group's contribution—the size of the group, its turnout, and its loyalty. Large groups that vote at a high rate and overwhelmingly favor one party can make a major contribution to that party's vote support. One of Axelrod's more important findings is that the contribution of blacks to the Democratic vote total has risen dramatically. In 1952, 7 percent of the Democratic vote came from blacks, while in 1972 and 1980 the proportion jumped to 22 percent, and in 1984 it rose further to 25 percent. Obviously, black citizens comprise a significant portion of the Democratic coalition. Note also that the percentage of the Republican vote coming from the North dropped from a high of 87 percent in 1952 to a low of 67 percent in 1976 and 1980; this is another way of stating that the South has become an increasingly important segment of the Republican presidential coalition. Table 10.4 summarizes the contributions made by various groups to the Republican and Democratic vote coalitions since 1952.

The 1972 Republican coalition is particularly striking since the GOP received the majority of the vote cast by poor people, union members, Catholics, and Southerners (see table 3.6). This unusual support does not stand out in table 10.4 since the GOP increased its share of the vote among all groups in 1972. The atypical GOP coalition in 1972 illustrates a number of more general points about the voting behavior of groups. First, group voting patterns change in response to specific campaign stimuli even as the underlying partisan attachments of the group remain fairly stable. Second, no group except blacks gives near-unanimous support to one party; this means that neither party can afford to write off completely any group, with the possible exception of blacks and the GOP. And finally, the notion of a typical party coalition is useful so long as one does not assume that the shape of the coalition is carved in stone. As group ties to a political party weaken, the group members will increasingly become susceptible to the opposition party appeals based on particular issues, attractive candidates, and the like.

One strategic ramification that Axelrod draws from his work is that if a party wants to improve its performance among a group, it must increase the turnout or the loyalty of the group, or both. The size of the group is essentially fixed except in situations where institutional changes expand the size of the electorate, as did the Voting Rights Act of 1965. The emphasis on increasing turnout and loyalty is another variant of the fundamental strategy of appealing to the candidate's supporters and probable supporters.

Therefore, the central task of a presidential campaign is to put together a coalition of support among groups already predisposed toward one's candidacy and to add to this coalition until victory seems assured. This emphasis

TABLE 10.4

The Contribution Made to Democratic and Republican Vote Totals by Various Groups, 1952–1988 (in percentages)

	1952	1956	1960	1964	1968	1972	1976	1980	1984	1988
Democrats										
Poor (income under $3,000, under $5,000 in 1980)	28%	19%	16%	15%	12%	10%	7%	5%	10%	6%
Black (and other nonwhite)	7	5	7	12	19	22	16	22	25	24
Union member (or union member in family)	38	36	31	32	28	32	33	32	30	26
Catholic (and other non-Protestant)	41	38	47	36	40	34	35	32	39	37
South (including border states)	20	23	27	21	24	25	36	39	32	30
Central cities (or 12 largest metropolitan areas)	21	19	19	15	14	14	11	12	7	14
Republicans										
Nonpoor	75	84	83	89	90	93	97	99	97	97
White	99	98	97	100	99	98	99	99	96	97
Nonunion	79	78	84	87	81	77	80	81	83	84
Protestant	75	75	90	80	80	74	76	74	69	74
Northern	87	84	75	76	80	73	67	67	72	72
Not in central cities	84	89	90	91	92	95	98	97	92	95

*The figures presented represent the percentage of the party's vote in any specific election due to the group in question.

SOURCE: Extracted from figures presented by Robert Axelrod, "Presidential Election Coalitions in 1984," *American Political Science Review* 80 (March 1986), pp. 281–284, 1988 CPS election study.

on specific groups, however, may not be the strategy of the future as the proportion of citizens within groups identifying with a political party shrinks and the number of Independents increases. If this trend continues, then there will be a shrinking base of citizens who enter the campaign as likely or latent supporters of a candidate, and group appeals may be less effective in generating support. Instead, issue-based appeals that may or may not have direct group relevance will become more prominent. The presence of large numbers of uncommitted Independents and apoliticals raises the possibility that a candidate might use unconventional appeals to win support from such voters. The pitfalls of this strategy are threefold. First, pure Independents, especially in recent elections (see table 3.7), have not voted at as high a rate as partisans and thus seem to be a risky group upon which to base a candidacy. Second, Independents are themselves a heterogeneous group, which makes it unlikely that the candidate can find one issue or one set of issues that will appeal to Independents en masse. And finally, substantial numbers of voters are still affiliated with the two major parties; a candidate receiving little support from partisans has major obstacles to overcome. Hence, the optimal strategy seems to be one in which a substantial share of the Independent vote is added to a core bloc of partisan support—a very traditional strategy in American presidential politics. The last chapter will consider whether the issue preferences of citizens will permit such a traditional strategy to succeed in the future.

Notes

1. Many reforms of the Electoral College have been proposed, including its abolishment in favor of direct (popular vote) presidential elections. Other reforms would keep the Electoral College but eliminate its winner-take-all feature by establishing a district plan that would give electoral votes to the leading candidate in each congressional district plus two votes to the statewide winner. Still other reforms would require that the electoral votes of a state be automatically cast for the candidate carrying that state, thereby eliminating the problem of the faithless elector. Finally, the Twentieth Century Fund recently developed a new proposal, labeled the *bonus plan*, which would add 102 electoral votes to the current 538. These 102 electoral votes would all go to the candidate winning the national popular vote, thereby almost assuredly ending the possibility that a candidate might win the popular vote but lose the Electoral College vote and the presidency.

Wallace S. Sayre and Judith H. Parris favor the existing system since it makes the more populous states more influential. In order to carry these states, a candidate must run well in the metropolitan areas with their large blocs of ethnic groups, such as blacks, Jews, Poles, and Italians. Presidential candidates must give attention to these groups, and this provides one way to meet the greater needs of these groups. According to Sayre and Parris, this gives a liberal bias to presidential campaigns, a bias they fear would be lost if Electoral

College reforms were adopted. Longley and Braun question whether the Electoral College will continue to produce this liberal bias and argue that the Electoral College system subverts the meaning of a popular election. For a discussion of the proposed alternatives to the Electoral College and their probable consequences, see Sayre and Parris (1970), Lawrence D. Longley and Alan G. Braun (1972), Yunker and Longley (1973), Yunker and Longley (1976), *Winner Take All* (1978), and *Congressional Quarterly Weekly Report*, March 10, 1979, pp. 405–410.

   2. For example, Stephen J. Brams and Morton D. Davis (1974) report that the Democratic and Republican nominees since 1960 have spent a disproportionate amount of their campaigning time in the large states. Stanley Kelley (1966: 64, 75) reports that in 1964 Lyndon Johnson spent 30 percent of his campaign time in California, New York, and Illinois. Nixon and Kennedy in 1960 campaigned most heavily in the same six states—New York, California, Illinois, Pennsylvania, Ohio, and Michigan. Even Barry Goldwater, whose strategy was not a large-state one, spent most of his scheduled campaign time in the large states, especially California, Texas, Ohio, Illinois, Pennsylvania, and New York.

CHAPTER 11

Toward the Future

A fter the presidential elections of 1964, 1968, 1972, 1980, and 1984, political commentators speculated whether the election outcomes signified fundamental shifts in the strength and sources of support of the Democratic and Republican parties. The Democratic landslide of 1964 led observers to wonder whether the GOP was dead. Gerald Pomper (1967) noted that the Democrats in 1964 ran strongest in the Northeast and weakest in the South, a reversal of traditional Democratic party support. This led Pomper to speculate that the Democratic coalition had been permanently transformed.

The Republican victory in 1968 put to rest the question of the viability of the GOP. Political journalists began to suggest that the Republicans were about to supplant the Democrats as the national majority party. This thesis received its most prominent statement in a book by Kevin Phillips entitled *The Emerging Republican Party*. Phillips described the new Republican majority as consisting of southern, Sun Belt, and heartland states, and California. He argued that the Northeast, which was formerly the strongest Republican area, had become much less important to GOP election prospects. And even within the Northeast, Phillips (1969: 465–466) saw certain groups, such as urban Catholics, trending toward the GOP in part because of dissatisfaction with the Democratic party's handling of race-related matters. Phillips described the upcoming cycle in American politics as one that was likely to match a majority GOP based on the heartland, the South, and California against a minority Democratic party based on the Northeast and the Pacific Northwest and relying heavily on northern and southern black votes. Phillips (1969: 467) asserted that the GOP did not have to appeal to such groups as young voters and blacks to win elections, despite what liberal Republicans said about broadening the base of the party.

The magnitude of the Republican landslide in 1972 at first glance seemed to confirm the emergence of the Republican majority. Nixon ran very strongly in the South and received a majority of the vote among such traditional Democratic supporters as union members and urban Catholics. Yet the 1972 GOP presidential victory was a very shallow one; the Democrats more than held their own in state and local races and in Congress. The subsequent revelations about Watergate crimes and the decline in the economy tended to dampen assertions about the inevitability of a GOP majority. And the partial reconstruction of the New Deal coalition by Carter in 1976 (see chapter 6) temporarily ended speculation about the imminence of the Republican majority and instead turned attention to the notion that the United States had a one and one-half-party system, with the GOP consigned to permanent minority status despite its strong presidential performances (Ladd, 1978c).

The 1980 election results once again fueled speculation that the Republican majority had finally emerged. Reagan's sizable victory along with the impressive Republican gains in congressional races seemed to indicate that a broad and deep conservative tide was sweeping the nation. Reagan's ability to make inroads into traditional sources of Democratic support such as Catholics and blue-collar workers was seen as evidence of a fundamental transformation of American political loyalties. But the 1982 elections temporarily dampened talk of a Republican era. With the economy in recession and the popularity of the president on the decline, the Democrats made strong gains in contests for the U.S. House and the nation's governorships. Traditionally Democratic groups that had been sympathetic to Reagan in 1980 returned home to support Democratic candidates in 1982.

With the economic recovery of 1983–1984, President Reagan's massive reelection, and polls showing that the GOP had narrowed the Democratic advantage in partisanship, speculation about realignment was once again prevalent. But the Democratic recapture of the U.S. Senate in 1986, polls showing the Democrats regaining their traditional lead in partisan loyalties, and the Iran–Contra arms scandal besieging the Reagan administration all served to temper claims about a realignment in favor of the Republicans. Bush's solid victory in 1988 and GOP gains in partisan allegiances in conjunction with the Democrats' strong performance in congressional and state races in 1988 and 1990 led some observers to speculate whether split control of government had become institutionalized in the United States with the GOP the majority party in presidential contests and the Democrats dominant in congressional and state elections.

Thus, discussions about the future shape of the American party system have occupied a prominent place in contemporary political discourse. The term used most often in analyzing potential changes in the parties' electoral fortunes is *realignment*. This refers to a major, permanent alteration in the partisan balance in the electorate. The type of change most frequently discussed is one in which the majority party becomes the minority, and vice versa, although other outcomes, such as the demise of the Republican and Democratic parties and their replacement by new parties, would also be classified as realignments. Another related phenomenon is the case in which the support coalitions of the parties change dramatically even as their relative strength in the electorate remains unchanged. This situation led Pomper to introduce the notion of a converting election (discussed in chapter 1). Thus, this chapter will focus on the possibility of partisan realignment in the United States. Some properties of realignment, as well as some characteristics of the present political scene that have encouraged speculation about change, will be considered first. Then some possible scenarios of realignment, followed by a summary assessment of their likelihood will be presented.

The Definition and Properties of Realignment

The basic definition of realignment as a durable change in the party balance comes from work by V. O. Key, Jr. (1955). Key focused on those "critical" elections that resulted in new partisan alignments, such as the elections of 1896 and 1928. While Key viewed a single election as critical or realigning, scholars have since argued that realignment is a process that occurs over time and have therefore shifted their attention to realigning eras rather than specific elections. For example, while in retrospect Roosevelt's 1932 election might be viewed as critical, the fact that the New Deal coalition did not achieve its peak strength until 1936 argues that important movements in the electorate were occurring throughout the period. Hence 1932–1936 might best be viewed as a realigning era.

One problem with the definition of realignment as a durable change is that only after the fact is it clear that realignment has occurred. There are, however, certain properties of past realignments that have led some contemporary observers to see a realignment as imminent in the United States. One characteristic of past realignments is that they have happened at regular thirty-six- to forty-year intervals. Since the last realignment was in 1932–1936, the cyclical nature of the phenomenon led some observers to believe that a new realignment was due in the 1972–1976 era. Possible reasons for the periodicity of realignments will be discussed later.

Walter Dean Burnham (1970: 6–7) states that past realigning eras were characterized by intense political feelings that at the elite level spilled over into disputes about party nominations and party platforms, as well as increased ideological polarization between the parties. At the mass level there was increased voter involvement and issue-related voting. All of these conditions, with the exception of higher voting participation, have been present in American politics since 1964. The Republican convention of 1964 and the Democratic conventions of 1968 and 1972 were characterized by intense conflict between disparate wings of the parties. The presidential elections of 1964 and 1972 were marked by an ideological polarization uncommon in recent American politics. And, as discussed in chapter 4, issue awareness and perceptions of party differences on the part of the citizenry increased sharply in the mid-1960s and the 1970s.

Additional changes at the mass and elite levels have further encouraged speculation about realignment. The sizable decline in partisanship and the growth in the number of Independents (see chapter 3) suggest to many observers that a citizenry exists that is readily mobilizable into a new party system. At the elite level, the switch in the 1970s to the Republican party by such former conservative Democrats as John Connally and Strom Thurmond and the switch to the Democratic party by such former GOP liberals as John Lindsay and Donald Riegle were viewed as forerunners of an eventual sorting out of elites into their ideologically compatible parties, which might produce substantial switches in partisanship by average citizens. A steady trickle of party switching continued in the 1980s and 1990s; most of it occurred in the South as conservative Democrats announced their conversion to the GOP. Although many of the switchers did not enjoy electoral success in their newly chosen party, some did, such as U.S. Sen. Phil Gramm of Texas and Governor Bob Martinez of Florida, both former Democratic officeholders. Despite such recent conversions, there has been no massive movement in recent years for prominent politicians to switch to the party with whose ideological position they are in agreement. Indeed, moderate and conservative Democrats in the South seem to be making a greater effort of late within the Democratic party so that it will continue to be a compatible home for their wings of the party.

A final characteristic of past realignments has been the presence of serious minor party candidates in the elections preceding the realignment. In 1968, George Wallace appeared as a third-party candidate, while John Anderson did so in 1980. Both attacked the major parties, accusing them of being incapable of handling the country's problems. Such candidacies fit well with past realignment situations. Nevertheless, a number of key conditions must be met if a realignment is to occur.

The Causes of Realignment

Realignment occurs when some issue arises that cannot be handled by the political parties because it cuts across the existing bases of support of the parties. Not just any issue can spark a realignment: rather, the issue must generate intense feelings in the electorate. Such issues are often symbolic and moral in nature rather than focusing on a specific policy area. When an issue cuts across the existing basis of a party's support, the party is effectively immobilized from coping with the issue since any action it takes will undoubtedly antagonize some segment of the party's supporters. Race is often viewed as such an issue, particularly with respect to the Democratic party. While the Democrats have come down largely on the pro-civil rights, pro-black side of many race-related matters, this has cost the party many of its traditional white supporters, particularly at presidential elections.

When a controversial, provocative issue arises, a number of outcomes are possible. James Sundquist (1973: 16–25) has discussed five possible outcomes, the first simply being maintenance of the existing party system as the issue recedes in importance or is successfully finessed by the parties. More dramatic outcomes are possible, including realignment of the existing parties through shifts in allegiances by current party supporters, realignment of the existing parties through absorption of a third party, realignment through the replacement of one major party, and realignment through the replacement of both old parties.

All of these outcomes have been mentioned in current speculation about the future shape of the party system. Some observers have argued that the present situation, in which both parties receive support from citizens who call themselves liberals and conservatives, is unstable and will eventually result in massive shifts in voters' allegiances. This would lead to the continued existence of the Democratic and Republican parties but with different sources of vote support.

Realignment of the existing parties through the absorption of a third party has received much attention given the success of the Wallace candidacy in 1968. While the majority of Wallace's votes came from people who called themselves Democrats, some observers believed that the American Independent party would serve as a way station for former Democrats on their way to becoming Republicans. According to this speculation, the bulk of the Wallace support would move to the GOP, thereby creating a national Republican majority. This did not occur.

Realignment through replacement of one of the major parties was discussed in the 1970s, most often in reference to the GOP. Some conservatives argued that control of the GOP was no longer their goal. Instead, many conservatives wanted to form a new national party because they felt that many citizens who might be attracted to the conservative cause would never be attracted to the Republican party, either because of their existing partisanship or because of perceptions of the GOP as the party of the privileged. (This last perception will be discussed later in the chapter.) Even with the election of a conservative Republican president in 1980, there were still voices calling for the creation of a new conservative party.

Realignment through the replacement of both parties has received less attention than the other possibilities. Some observers argue that the only way to get liberal and conservative citizens aligned in the proper way is to create two new parties. The attempt to make the Democrats the liberal party and the Republicans the conservative will be unsuccessful because of people's long-standing feelings about these parties. Hence, these observers claim that two new parties are required to effect a realignment.

While Sundquist has presented some thought-provoking scenarios, his discussion of the sources of realignment seems too limited. Sundquist sees realignment as resulting from the switching of partisan allegiances by adherents of the existing parties. However, the discussion of party identification in chapter 3 suggests that partisans are likely to be more immune to extraordinary political appeals than are citizens not identified with one of the two parties. Moreover, the principle that partisanship tends to become stronger the longer a person is identified with a party implies that older citizens will be less promising sources of realignment than younger citizens.

Hence, although Sundquist asserts that conversion—an actual switch in party loyalties—produces realignment, realignment may also be brought about by the mobilization into the electorate of young, Independent voters and former nonvoters, groups that are more susceptible to the prevailing political currents. There is a controversy as to whether the New Deal realignment was due to mobilization or conversion; undoubtedly, both processes occurred. Kristi Andersen (1976) opts for a mobilization explanation. Using recall data on past partisanship from national election surveys, Andersen reconstructs the electorate of the 1920s and 1930s and finds that the Democratic majority was forged from citizens of voting age in the 1920s who had not been party adherents and from voters first coming into the electorate in the 1930s. In response to the economic crisis and the appeal of Franklin Roosevelt, both groups of citizens were mobilized into the electorate in a heavily Democratic fashion. In contrast, Robert S. Erikson and Kent L. Tedin (1981) opt for a conversion explanation. Analyzing *Literary Digest* polls, they argue that the new voters were only slightly more Democratic than the existing electorate; hence, the mobilization of new voters would have produced no significant Democratic advantage and therefore no realignment. Instead, Erikson and Tedin argue that much of the Democratic gain came from Republican voters who began to vote Democratic and later began to think of themselves as Democrats. The research of Courtney Brown (1988) indicates that the New Deal realignment was a very complex phenomenon. Vote switching from the GOP to the Democratic party was the dominant process in the 1932 election, while in 1936 additional Democratic gains came mainly from the mobilization of new voters.

The fact that about half of Americans under thirty in 1988 were either pure Independents or Independent leaners (see table 3.1) means that there is a sizable group of voters who are highly susceptible to realignment pressures. Paul Beck (1974) states that the high incidence of Independents among young people today is caused by a party system based on New Deal cleavages that are not relevant to a younger generation that did not experience the Great Depression. Beck's argument raises some intriguing questions. If the New Deal party system is irrelevant to young people, what type of cleavage would attract young people to the political parties? Are young adults so homogeneous that it is possible to appeal to them as a bloc? Might any attempt to appeal to the young generation run the risk of mistaking certain segments of young people as representative of all young people? Might appealing for the youth vote backfire on the political parties if young adults are a negative reference point for many citizens? These questions are not easily answered, although they suggest that any youth-based realignment might be a highly unpredictable affair.

For scholars such as Walter Dean Burnham, the causes of realignment are reflected in their periodicity or cyclical occurrence. Burnham (1970: 9–10) views American history from a dialectical perspective, arguing that there is a fundamental contradiction between pluralist and incrementalist political institutions—that is, the institutions of a society that have many social groups and those that change by degrees—and a rapidly changing socioeconomic system. Normally, the tension between the political and economic spheres can be handled within the existing party system; but in times of great social and economic stress, the slow-reacting political institutions are incapable of handling crises. At such times, Burnham argues, tensions build, a flash point is reached, realignment occurs, a new party system develops that alleviates tensions, and a period of stability ensues for a while. However, the constantly changing nature of the economic system generates new tensions and sets the realignment process in motion again, thereby making realignment a periodic occurrence. Burnham's description is fascinating, although largely unsupported by solid evidence. Burnham's explanation makes the occurrence of realignment too automatic, although he does conjecture that the realignment currently due may not happen, for reasons to be discussed shortly.

Paul Beck (1974: 200–206) has developed a socialization theory of partisan realignment that dovetails nicely with the discussion of the learning and transmission of party identification in chapter 3 and that provides a plausible explanation for the periodic realignment of parties. Beck identifies three groups of individuals with respect to the learning of partisanship. Individuals in the first group acquired their partisanship as young adults during a realignment. Partisanship learned in this period, according to Beck, will be more firmly grounded in the issues and political realities of the era and as such will have a clear-cut rationale.

The second group includes those individuals who received their pre-adult partisanship from parents of a realignment generation. Beck refers to these people as *children of realignment* who, while lacking direct exposure to the realignment and its causes, did learn much about the realignment from their parents. Thus, the partisanship of these individuals is grounded in meaningful cleavages and should therefore be less susceptible to change.

Finally, there is a group of persons who learned their partisanship at least two generations removed from a realignment and hence may not have a clear understanding of the rationale underlying the party system. These citizens will have the weakest commitments to the existing parties and will be the most likely sources of realignment. Since the time interval between the socialization of adults during a realignment and the socialization of their grandchildren into partisanship is about forty years, the periodicity of realignments may reflect the presence of generations far removed from the original rationale of the party system. Thus, Beck's theory suggests that the presence of a generation distant from actual experience of the earlier realignment is a necessary condition for a subsequent realignment to occur. Note that Beck is not claiming that realignment will definitely occur, only that its likelihood is increased by the existence of such a generation.

The work of Norpoth (1987) and Rhodebeck (1990) examines generational replacement as a source of partisan realignment in the 1980s. Both authors found that the GOP had gained in the partisan allegiances of young citizens in the 1980s. Thus, as the older age cohorts depart the electorate to be replaced by their younger, more Republican compatriots, the GOP could expect to enhance its chances to be the majority party assuming the younger voters keep their Republican imprint. And this will depend to a large extent on how well the country fares under continued Republican presidential leadership and on the alternatives and choices provided by the Democrats. Norpoth and Kagay (1989) note that another source of growing GOP strength in the 1980s was the tendency of Independents to move more heavily toward the GOP. Hurley (1989), however, questions whether the pro-Republican movements observed in the 1980s will result in a Republican realignment. She argues that for these changes to be permanent, the Republican party will need to represent its existing supporters and new adherents on the issues. Instead, she finds that the issue congruence between Republican leaders (GOP members in the U.S. House of Representatives) and rank and file Republicans actually declined between 1980 and 1984, thereby lessening the prospects for a long-term realignment.

Possible Issue Bases of Realignment

As discussed earlier, if a realignment is to occur, it will be precipitated by the emergence of a new issue of sufficient intensity on which the existing parties take or are perceived to take differing positions. If the parties do not take contrasting stands on the new issue and instead try to straddle it, then a new party may emerge that offers a clear-cut alternative on the issue. The question arises as to what such an issue might be.

In the late 1960s political commentators (for example, Richard M. Scammon and Ben J. Wattenberg, 1970) wrote about a new phenomenon labeled the *social issue*, which they viewed as a potential source of realignment. The social issue was actually a cluster of issues dealing with such matters as race, campus unrest, law and order, and lifestyles. Presumably, white working- and middle-class citizens were upset by aggressive black demands for equality, angered by the violence perpetrated by a privileged college youth, concerned by the general breakdown in law and order, and threatened by the nontraditional values espoused by the drug culture and the advocates of sexual freedom. Since many of these angry white citizens were Democrats and since the Democratic party was presumably identified with the aspirations of blacks and college students and supportive of the new lifestyles, such observers argued that the party was about to lose many of its traditional supporters. Commentators asserted that many white citizens, alternatively referred to as the *center*, the *silent majority*, the *workingman*, and the *forgotten American*, were ripe for appeals based on the social issue.

The Republicans and Wallace exploited the social issue with some success in 1968, and the GOP, led by the histrionics of Vice-President Agnew, tried to capitalize on the issue in the 1970 congressional elections by branding the Democrats as soft on crime and violence and by associating the Democrats with elements of society feared by many white Americans. The Republican strategy failed as the Democrats refused to let themselves be portrayed as having a weaker commitment to law and order. Democratic candidates went on the attack by condemning lawlessness and violence. The social issue receded as a possible basis of realignment since there were no major differences between the parties on the issue. The association of the McGovern candidacy in 1972 with quotas for blacks and young people and with sympathy for the new lifestyles served to place the Democrats once again at a disadvantage with regard to certain aspects of the social issue.

Although the social issue did not produce a realignment in the 1970s, descendants of the issue continued to shape American politics in the 1980s. With the election of Ronald Reagan in 1980, the New Right social agenda gained a spokesman in the White House. Among the items on this agenda are opposition to abortion and the Equal Rights Amendment, support for prayer in public schools, and a general preference for "traditional" values in many aspects of social and political life. These issues, especially abortion and the Equal Rights Amendment, are controversial and may alter patterns of political support. It may be that one source of the gender gap (see chapter 6) has been Reagan's opposition to ERA and abortion. However, it seems unlikely that these issues will generate a realignment, for a number of reasons. First, although the parties tend to differ on these issues, they are by no means internally homogeneous in their positions. Hence, any nominee who pushes too hard in one direction or another runs the risk of antagonizing some party loyalists. Second, as long as the health of the economy remains a major concern, the New Right social agenda will receive less attention at the elite level (for example, in Congress) and among citizens. However, in a time of economic prosperity, such issues and others may enter the limelight, probably to the consternation of many party elites. Although the social issue has put the Democrats on the defensive and cost them support among white voters, especially in the South, the social issue is a mixed blessing for the GOP, particularly among younger voters who strongly supported the president in 1980 and 1984 and among more traditional GOP loyalists. Both groups tend to support conservative fiscal and defense policies, but this support does not carry over to the entire New Right social agenda. Hence, the social issue is a potential problem even for the GOP, particularly if the religious right wing seeks to gain a stronger voice in Republican party affairs.

The economic issue has also been considered a source of realignment, but it is unclear how it might bring about a change in the partisan balance. Economic issues have traditionally favored the Democrats, although the severe economic woes in the late 1970s during a Democratic administration eroded the usual Democratic advantage in this area. With the economic recovery of 1983–1984, the Republicans have been able to shed their negative economic image and profit at the expense of the Democrats. Thus, Gallup polls conducted from 1984 to 1986 increasingly showed the GOP to be viewed by Americans as the party of prosperity so that by March of 1986 the GOP enjoyed a 51 to 33 percent advantage over the Democrats on this topic, the first time since 1951 that a majority of Americans favored the GOP. Yet by early 1987 Gallup polls were showing that the newly won GOP advantage had eroded; as a result, Americans were evenly divided as to which was the party of prosperity. Moreover, the huge budget deficits run up during the Reagan administration have undermined traditional Republican advantages in the area of fiscal management. Hence, economic issues do not seem currently to be a likely basis for realignment, although they surely have short-run political benefits and liabilities, such as winning or losing control of the White House. Certainly the party in power during a time of economic recession or depression can expect to be punished at election time and in the distribution of partisan loyalties. Whether this will produce a realignment depends on the severity of the economic shock and on the skill and performance of political elites in responding to the economic crisis.

One issue frequently mentioned during the 1970s as a potential cause of realignment was race. Racial issues were viewed as a direct cause of the substantial Democratic decline in the South and as a likely source of continued Democratic losses among white ethnic groups in the North. Paul Abramson (1973: 7) has asserted that "the major Democratic liability is that blacks are an integral part of their coalition and that black votes are costly." Black votes are costly, according to Abramson, in the sense that association with the aims and aspirations of black people is likely to lose a party much white support. Abramson (1973: 1–8) declares that the Democrats are no longer the majority party (nor are the Republicans) because the Democrats cannot consistently carry the white working-class vote, which Abramson views as the heart of the New Deal coalition.

Walter Dean Burnham (1970: 142) observes that the mass migration of blacks from the South into the major cities of the North has nationalized the race issue and has led to hostile reactions by the segments of the white middle class most in competition with blacks for jobs, services, and the like. Public opinion surveys show that white attitudes toward certain aspects of the black movement for equality have become more negative in the past decade and that white attitudes have shifted toward the belief that blacks expect their conditions to improve too quickly.

Burnham (1970: 158) considers one possible realignment outcome—in which the Democratic party comes increasingly to be "the party of the technologically competent and technologically superfluous strata," while the GOP becomes "the partisan vehicle for the defense of white 'middle-America.' " In this scenario, the Democratic party would be a top–bottom coalition opposed to a middle-supported GOP. That is, the Democrats would attract the most- and least-advantaged groups in society and the Republicans the vast middle. While there is some evidence that the Democrats are running better of late among traditional Republican supporters, such as professionals, managers, and the highly educated, Burnham thinks that the top–bottom coalition will not materialize.

While it sounds plausible to say that race might serve as the basis for realignment, the fundamental question is, "Which specific race issue would produce realignment?" Is any particular racial issue of sufficient intensity to deflect many white Democrats from their traditional party allegiances? Certainly busing is an issue that has aroused intense passions, but it seems unlikely to result in realignment for a number of reasons. First, many liberal Democratic politicians have backed away from support of busing in response to the anger of their white constituents. Second, recent court decisions have given localities greater flexibility in handling the issue of school integration. In particular, a Supreme Court decision that ruled that busing across city lines into the suburbs was not required to solve the problem of school segregation should alleviate the fears of many suburban residents and defuse the busing issue. Moreover, it seems that second thoughts are developing among all segments of American society about the wisdom and practicality of busing, which may lead to its ultimate demise as a tool for integration. In addition, people who have no children or whose children have grown up are not likely to get aroused by busing. Finally, public opinion polls show that younger citizens with direct experience with busing are not as adamant in their opposition to it as once was thought. Thus, it appears that busing is not a likely source of realignment, although some cities still face the busing issue and it may yet intrude in presidential politics.

If busing is not the race-related catalyst for fostering realignment, what other racial issue might be? On a whole host of traditional civil rights matters, such as voting rights and public accommodations, there is practically a national consensus in support of the measures that have been taken, which means that these matters cannot serve as a basis for realignment. For example, Andrew Greeley (1974: 299–311) shows that whites overwhelmingly accept the goal of school integration today, a remarkable change from their attitudes of fifteen years ago. On many other issues, including the kinds of problems about which they are most concerned, blacks and whites exhibit similar attitudes (Greeley, 1974: 339–344).

There are other race-related issues in addition to busing that have upset many whites, but these also seem to be unlikely sources of realignment. For example, many white citizens (as well as many black citizens) are currently upset by a public welfare system that they see as giving unfair advantages to blacks at the expense of the white (and black) working class. Yet this seems unlikely to generate a pro-Republican realignment, especially when it was Democratic governors in such states as California and Massachusetts who tried vigorously to bring welfare expenditures under control. Moreover, the Republicans have not offered a serious alternative to the existing welfare program (notwithstanding the tentative steps that the Nixon administration took in this area), and running against "welfare cheats" does not seem to provide a sufficient basis for realignment.

The perception that the Democratic party supports preferential treatment for blacks and other minorities in the context of affirmative action programs and quotas could serve to promote realignment. For example, the quota system at the 1972 Democratic convention upset many longtime white Democrats who felt that they had been treated unfairly. Likewise, two election contests in 1990 demonstrated the potential political impact of preferential treatment. In North Carolina, Republican U.S. Sen. Jesse Helms blatantly claimed that affirmative action programs victimized white citizens; his opponent was black. In California, the GOP gubernatorial nominee, Pete Wilson, raised the issue in a more respectable form. In both cases, the Republican candidates won tough races. Some observers speculated whether the statement by a Department of Education official that race-based financial aid was illegal was perhaps a trial balloon to determine how this and related issues might play in the electorate in the 1992 elections. For preferential treatment to become a critical issue, the Democratic party and its candidates would have to advocate a set of measures that are seen as favoring minorities at the expense of whites. This seems unlikely to happen; it is more likely that future Democratic social programs and policies will emphasize improving the quality of life for all citizens in such areas as health insurance and jobs.

If the economy, the social issue, and race are unpromising sources of realignment, then what is left? Frederick Dutton (1971: 225) has speculated that the class cleavages of an earlier era may be replaced by a cultural cleavage exemplified by the competing slogans "Make the world safe for sex" versus "Support your local censor." While lifestyle concerns can certainly generate intense passions, they seem an unlikely foundation for realignment since parties are rarely on opposite sides on such issues, especially when the overwhelming majority of the population is on one side. Moreover, it appears that the more outrageous actions in support of and in opposition to alternative lifestyles have lessened since the early 1970s, perhaps indicating the decline in the issue's importance. Andrew Greeley (1974: 272–273) has identified a new issue, labeled *neopopulism*, that he thinks might produce realignment. Basically, the issue centers on the concentration of power in American society and on who is to participate in decision making. But it is difficult to specify the alternatives on the issue, where the parties stand, and the probable future shape of the issue. Phillips (1990) believes that the issue might revive the Democratic party if exploited properly. Greeley (1974: 274) himself argues that one of the tasks of leadership in the next decade will be to give shape and form to the issue. Along these lines, Ralph Nader called for the creation of a new political party that would focus on what he called the overriding issue of the times—corporate power—and would emphasize "the expansion of citizen access to all branches of government, the mass media, and corporate decision-making" (Broder, 1979a:). Nader envisaged a new party based on consumer groups, antinuclear organizations, some trade unions, and local citizens' organizations. Such groups, however, are far from consensual in their issue positions, so that unless the appropriate leadership and the critical issues emerge, the prospects for realignment are negligible.

A new cluster of issues focusing on such matters as energy and nuclear power as well as ecology and the environment has appeared on the political agenda. These issues are still in a formative stage and may not develop to the point of generating and sustaining new political cleavages. Nevertheless, it is easy to imagine how concerns about the environment can run headlong into concerns about jobs and economic security. The trade-off between economic expansion and job security versus environmental protection has already been a source of controversy in many localities, such as the coal mining region of Ohio when the Clean Air Act was extended in 1990. The Democratic party is most threatened by the potential conflict between jobs and environmental protection. The working-class and union component of the Democratic coalition is naturally more concerned about economic growth and job security, while the intellectual wing and many upper-middle class Democrats come down on the side of the environment. These issues have not yet developed to the point where existing party allegiances are threatened, and they may never reach this stage, especially as long as severe economic crises keep economic concerns paramount and make citizens more willing to compromise on environmental standards. Nevertheless, the Three Mile Island nuclear reactor incident provided impetus to antinuclear power and other ecology-oriented groups. The creation of an effective mass movement seems unlikely, although in a number of European countries the environmental movement has achieved notable political clout.

In the 1980s, the "war and peace" issue became more prominent in presidential politics. Citizen movements developed, focusing on such matters as a freeze in the construction and deployment of nuclear weapons and militarism in American foreign policy. Many states and localities had referenda on the ballot tapping citizens' opinions on these matters, and in the vast majority of cases the pro-freeze, pro-disarmament position won. Despite the greater attention given to these issues, they seem highly unlikely to generate a realignment, for the electorate's primary concerns deal with economic well-being—jobs and inflation—and not with foreign policy. Moreover, political elites are trying to position themselves so that they do not appear to be taking an extremist position on either side of this cluster of issues; this positioning will reduce the potential of these issues for generating long-term partisan change. Finally, the end of the Cold War, the restraints on defense budgets, and the successful prosecution of the Persian Gulf war have lessened the likelihood that military and national security issues will serve as the basis for realignment.

Thus, it appears that realignment is unlikely, given the absence of a critical issue and the leadership required to exploit that issue. But this conclusion begs the question of whether a realignment has already occurred, perhaps in response to a plurality of issues, each of which moved a number of citizens in the same direction. Thus, discussion will focus next on the two groups— Southerners and Catholics—most often discussed in conjunction with a pro-Republican realignment and examine what evidence there is about realignment on their part. Emphasis is on a pro-Republican realignment because that outcome received the greatest attention from political analysts until Watergate and the economy derailed the emerging Republican majority in the 1972–1974 period. Reagan's victory in 1980 once again generated discussion of a pro-Republican realignment.

Southerners and Catholics: Has Realignment Occurred?

THE SOUTH

The 1976 election may have seemed to belie the notion of a pro-Republican realignment in the South because Carter the Democrat carried the region handily. Yet from another perspective, Carter's southern performance shows how far the GOP has come in being a major force in southern presidential politics. Even though Carter was a native Southerner who belonged to the dominant religious group and had the reputation of being a political moderate, he received only about 54 percent of the total southern vote and less than half of the white vote. Indeed, white southern voters overwhelmingly supported the GOP presidential nominees in 1980, 1984, and 1988.

When attention is turned to party identification, the GOP is shown to have made substantial gains in the South among whites since 1952. Table 11.1

presents the distribution of partisanship in the South and non-South since 1952 for four age cohorts. The top half of the table places citizens who lean to the Democrats or Republicans under the category of Independents; the bottom half of the table assigns these independent leaners to the political party to which they lean. As shall soon be seen, this latter classification generates a picture of greater GOP gains in the South.

There are many points to be made about table 11.1. First, establish a baseline by examining the distribution of party identification in 1952. Note that in the South in 1952, every age cohort was heavily Democratic, topped by the 79 percent Democratic loyalty among citizens sixty years of age and older. In contrast, in the non-South in 1952, the oldest age cohort is more Republican while the two youngest are solidly Democratic. An examination of the sixty and over cohort since 1952 shows that it has always favored the Democrats over the Republicans, though by less of a margin in 1988 (49 percent to 20 percent) than in 1952 (79 percent to 14 percent). In marked contrast are the preferences of southern whites under thirty years of age. In 1952, this cohort was solidly Democratic, but by 1988 it favored the GOP over the Democrats by a 35 to 27 percent margin.

Hence the GOP is currently much stronger among younger Southerners than it was thirty years ago. This is important because as the older, more Democratic cohorts die off, the younger, more Republican cohorts will become numerically dominant. This growing Republican strength in the South is partially masked by looking only at the top half of the table. Upon closer examination, many more young southern Independents lean toward the GOP than toward the Democrats. For example, 39 percent of the youngest Southerners in 1988 claimed to be Independents (pure and leaners), but this 39 percent was comprised of 9 percent pure Independents, 9 percent leaning Democrats, and 21 percent leaning Republicans. When the leaners are assigned to their appropriate partisan categories, the GOP advantage over the Democrats among young white Southerners in 1988 jumps from 8 percent to 19 percent. By 1988, the two youngest southern cohorts are more Republican (when the leaners are classified as partisans), while the two oldest remain solidly Democratic.

Thus the GOP has made substantial gains in the South and is poised to become the dominant party in the region as the older, more Democratic cohorts pass on. Outside the South, the GOP has also made gains, though not of the same magnitude as in the South. In fact, among white non-Southerners in 1988, the GOP was preferred over the Democrats in all age cohorts. Hence, the Democratic party is not the majority party among white Americans; it is the heavily Democratic preferences among minorities, especially blacks, that enable the Democrats to maintain their national advantage.

In summary, the GOP has been highly successful in carrying the South in presidential elections and in increasing its partisan loyalties among white Southerners. Thus, the argument for a sectional realignment in the South seems compelling. Yet this realignment has not yet been fully felt in other

TABLE 11.1

The Distribution of Party Identification by Region and Age for Whites, 1952–1988 (in percentages)

	Non-South												South											
	Less than 30			30–44			45–59			60+			Less than 30			30–44			45–59			60+		
Year	D	I	R	D	I	R	D	I	R	D	I	R	D	I	R	D	I	R	D	I	R	D	I	R
1952	43	32	25	45	26	29	37	25	38	32	24	43	69	20	11	73	15	12	67	14	19	79	7	14
1956	35	39	26	39	29	32	34	26	40	34	21	45	57	33	10	69	16	15	67	14	19	67	7	26
1960	35	29	36	42	27	31	40	27	33	35	15	49	67	21	11	62	19	19	60	17	24	58	15	27
1964	43	34	23	47	29	24	49	21	30	36	19	45	61	27	12	53	26	21	68	17	15	71	6	23
1968	28	49	23	42	31	28	39	26	35	42	17	41	26	65	9	51	33	16	52	33	15	58	23	19
1972	28	56	16	29	46	25	40	29	31	39	23	38	34	48	17	41	37	22	61	18	21	52	17	30
1976	29	53	18	26	48	26	36	32	32	39	24	37	39	42	19	41	36	23	61	30	10	44	24	32
1980	26	50	24	32	42	26	37	36	27	38	28	34	29	45	26	36	35	30	43	38	19	54	20	26
1984	28	43	29	26	38	36	39	31	31	35	26	39	31	42	27	30	39	31	46	34	20	49	26	25
1988	20	47	33	24	44	32	28	34	39	36	24	40	27	39	35	28	44	28	40	41	19	49	31	20

SOURCES: SRC/CPS studies of 1952, 1956, 1960, 1964, 1968, 1972, 1976, 1980, 1984, and 1988.

offices. The Democrats continue to dominate local offices in the South and to control the state legislatures. Nevertheless, even at these levels, the GOP is making gains as more Republicans are elected to various statewide positions and improve their numbers in the state legislatures. Prior to the 1990 elections, the GOP controlled the governorship in both Florida and Texas, an important outcome from the perspective of building a strong grass-roots party structure. And even when the GOP lost the Texas governorship in 1990, it still won other statewide offices. Clearly, Florida and Texas are two key states in presidential elections that the GOP has swept in recent years. The process of building strong, two-party competition at all levels in these states is well under way.

The Republican gains in the South are attributable to a number of sources. One is the conversion of native Southerners from Democratic loyalty to Republican partisanship. Borrowing a term from V. O. Key, Bruce Campbell (1977: 749) has argued that a *secular realignment*—"a process which involves the more or less continuous conversion of party loyalties which accumulate in trends persisting over decades"—has occurred among southern whites. The secular realignment has been caused not by any one specific issue but by the continuous strain between white southern attitudes and various policies advocated by the national Democratic party. In the 1960s and 1970s, race-related matters were the major source of tension between the state parties and the national Democratic party. In the late 1970s and the 1980s, the GOP began to make gains among evangelical and fundamentalist citizens who found the GOP social agenda more in harmony with their own views. Indeed, the GOP explicitly appealed to such groups, since the leadership of the religious right worked closely with the GOP in fashioning the 1980 and 1984 Republican party platforms.

There are other reasons for Republican gains in the South that focus on population movements and generational replacement. In particular, the in-migration from the North of many citizens with Republican loyalties has lessened the Democratic coloration of the South, particularly in such rapidly growing areas as Florida. Likewise, the out-migration from the South of heavily Democratic citizens has resulted in a less Democratic South. Finally, as the older and more Democratic age cohorts depart the political scene, the South becomes less a Democratic territory.

GOP gains among white Southerners are not the only changes the South has experienced. Bruce Campbell (1977) argues that a pro-Democratic realignment has occurred among black citizens in the South. Prior to the 1964 election, between 40 and 50 percent of southern blacks identified with the Democratic party, with the second largest group of blacks classified as apoliticals and not as Independents or Republicans. Since 1964 about 70 percent of southern blacks have identified with the Democratic party and the percentage of apoliticals has dropped to about 1 percent (1977: 742). Thus, the South has witnessed a tremendous mobilization of blacks into Democratic partisanship, which has been critical to the Democrats' ability to dominate state and local office.

Campbell (p. 744) asserts that 1964 was a critical election (as defined by V. O. Key) for southern blacks. There was a sharp and durable alteration in the existing partisan preferences of blacks, as well as intense concern about the election outcome and a high degree of electoral involvement. According to Campbell (p. 745), the issue that brought about the realignment was civil rights. The 1964 election pitted a Democratic candidate with a firm commitment to civil rights against a Republican candidate who had voted against the Civil Rights Act of 1964.

Campbell (pp. 746–747) demonstrates that the blacks who favored federal government intervention in civil rights matters were the ones who shifted most toward the Democratic party. More generally, Merle Black and George Rabinowitz (1974: 17–18) show that images of the Democratic party changed dramatically among blacks from the 1950s to the 1960s. In 1956 and 1960, Democratic strength among southern blacks did not rest upon civil rights issues but upon bread-and-butter domestic welfare programs. In fact, southern blacks viewed the GOP very favorably with respect to civil rights, in part because it was a Republican president who sent troops into Little Rock to enforce the Supreme Court school desegregation decision. But by the mid-1960s, images of the parties among blacks had changed so sharply that they now clearly perceived the Democratic party as more sympathetic to civil rights.

In summary, while the South may not have undergone a realignment in the formal sense of the GOP replacing the Democrats as the majority party, there are two other ways in which realignment may be said to have occurred. The first is that there has been a shift in the partisan balance so that today the GOP has lessened its disadvantage with the Democrats with respect to partisan allegiances in the region. Second, there has been a shift in the demographic makeup of the Democratic and Republican coalitions in the South as black citizens solidified their Democratic loyalties at the same time as many white citizens have tended toward the GOP. And if many of the new Independents in the South are really nascent Republicans, then the GOP is well on its way to becoming the majority party. Even if the Independents are not nascent Republicans, a Republican presidential candidate can probably count on capturing the major portion of southern electoral votes unless the Democratic nominee is particularly attuned to southern preferences. Republican success in the South forces the Democrats into a large-state electoral vote strategy. Yet the GOP cannot afford to go too far in satisfying the South, particularly on racial and social matters, lest it guarantee Democratic victories in the industrial states by antagonizing more traditional elements of the Republican coalition. Finally, there remains one bright spot for the Democratic party in the South; namely, the black vote. Although black voters have overwhelmingly supported Democratic candidates, the black vote itself still has not been fully mobilized. An increase in black voting rates might enable Democratic nominees to carry some southern states, particularly in the Deep South, where black citizens comprise a larger share of the population than they do in the rim portion of the South, *if* the nominees can hold onto a respectable portion of the white vote. Democratic gubernatorial and senatorial candidates have been able to accomplish this; whether this can be achieved in the presidential contest depends on the identity of the Democratic nominee and the policies associated with the Democratic party.

CATHOLIC VOTERS

Traditional Catholic allegiances to the Democratic party rested, not on religious doctrine, but on historical circumstance. The waves of Catholic immigrants that settled in major American cities (with the exception of Philadelphia) encountered a Protestant-dominated Republican political establishment unsympathetic to the new arrivals. The Democratic party, on the other hand, welcomed the Catholic ethnic groups, effectively mobilized them into politics, and built urban political machines that were to last for decades. Successive waves of Catholic ethnic groups, such as the Irish and the Italians, gained political power largely through the Democratic party.

Conjecture about a pro-Republican realignment by Catholics has been common for a number of reasons. Some scholars have speculated that as Catholics moved up the economic ladder, they would increasingly leave the party of their parents and grandparents and move to the party that best embodied their middle-class aspirations. More recently, some observers have argued that working-class Catholic ethnic groups in major urban areas have become disenchanted with the Democratic party because of its increasingly close association with the goals of blacks and other minorities (Kevin B. Phillips, 1969: 140–175). Presumably, working-class Catholic ethnics are in greatest competition with blacks for political power and economic rewards, thereby heightening tensions between the groups and facilitating Catholic movement out of the Democratic party. Public opinion polls have indicated substantial animosity toward blacks and black aims on the part of Catholic ethnics. For example, a bare majority of all whites in the late 1960s were opposed to blacks moving into their part of town, compared to 60 percent opposition by Irish and Italian Catholics and 80 percent opposition by Polish Catholics (Frederick G. Dutton, 1971: 118). Finally, it has been claimed that recent Democratic party sympathy with the liberal position on a number of lifestyle controversies, such as abortion and birth control, has been particularly offensive to Catholic citizens, thereby furthering their departure from the party.

It therefore appeared that Catholic citizens were prime targets for a Republican realignment. In 1972, Catholics did vote heavily for Nixon, giving him 57 percent of their vote, while in 1980 Catholics supported Reagan over Carter by a margin of about 50 percent to 40 percent and Reagan over Mondale in 1984 by a 55 percent to 45 percent margin. Yet other indicators point to continued Catholic allegiance to the Democratic party, albeit at levels that are not as high as they were in the past. Most exit polls in 1988 showed Dukakis carrying the Catholic vote, albeit by relatively narrow margins. Moreover, throughout the 1980s, Catholics have preferred Democratic congressional candidates, although not by as great a margin as in previous decades. And though Catholic partisan loyalties to the Democratic party have declined sharply since 1960 (see figure 3.2), the Democratic party still enjoys a substantial advantage over the GOP among Catholic citizens.

Thus, substantial support for the Democratic party by Catholics in the future seems likely if the party and its candidates are perceived as sympathetic to the needs of white ethnic groups as well as blacks. It seems that the Democratic party should worry more about ethnic–racial–social tensions than about the possibility that Catholics' upward economic mobility will change them into Republicans. Joan M. Fee and Andrew Greeley (1975: 31) found that as Catholics rose in socioeconomic status between 1952 and 1972, their affiliation with the Democratic party did not lessen. Moreover, Catholics who moved to the suburbs seemed to be as strongly Democratic as Catholics in other areas.

Some Final Thoughts
on Presidential Elections and Political Change

Although a classic realignment such as the one that produced the New Deal Democratic majority has not occurred, substantial changes have taken place in political alignments and coalitions in the United States. Certainly the traditional Democratic coalition no longer exists with the departure of the South from the fold in presidential elections. And among the remaining components of the New Deal coalition, there are major tensions between black and white ethnic groups as well as liberal and conservative social groups that make the creation of a unified Democratic party difficult. Although Democrats still enjoy a slight advantage in partisan loyalties among the electorate in most polls, this advantage exists only because of the overwhelming identification of minorities, especially blacks, with the Democratic party.

Despite its advantage in citizens' party loyalties, the Democratic party has been markedly unsuccessful in recent presidential elections. It is the heterogeneity of the party's potential supporters that creates problems for the Democrats. Any party that depends upon black and conservative white votes faces an immediate problem in achieving unity. Indeed, some would argue that the issue of race and its various manifestations has dramatically shaped and altered contemporary American electoral politics. Civil rights issues, such as busing and affirmative action, certainly injected discord into the Democratic coalition as urban northern and rural southern Democrats felt threatened by the black agenda. The perception that fundamental economic and political power were at stake served to heighten competition and tension within the

Democratic coalition. The flight of whites from the cities and their associated urban ills enhanced the sense of conflict and competition among racial groups. Moreover, the GOP has been very skillful in tapping into white concerns and anger in such areas as crime, competition for jobs, reverse discrimination, and the like. Indeed, throughout the past three decades, as black political aspirations advanced, there was often a concommitant white response and counter-mobilization, as was evidenced in the voting rights struggle in the South in the 1960s or more recently in the reactions to Jesse Jackson's candidacy for president in 1984 and 1988.

There are other cleavages within the Democratic party. As shown in chapter 1, the political spectrum has become more complex, with the arrival of social or cultural or lifestyle issues that do not correspond to the traditional New Deal divisions. The Democratic party includes traditional liberals who are concerned with New Deal issues and new liberals who are more concerned with lifestyle and cultural matters and who at times may even be hostile to the philosophy of economic expansion and government activism espoused by New Deal Democrats. In addition, many of the New Deal liberals are overtly hostile to the values espoused by the party's lifestyle liberals. Hence, the Democratic party is potentially subject to severe ideological conflict; to the extent that lifestyle issues become prominent in a presidential campaign, the Democrats may be torn apart and may suffer at the polls. Likewise, if Democratic nominees and the Democratic party are not seen as sufficiently strong on national security and defense issues, then substantial numbers of Democrats, particularly in the South, may defect from the party at election time. The ideal situation for a Democratic victory is one in which traditional economic issues dominate, so that most Democrats can remain loyal to their party. This assumes, of course, that the Democrats are on the "right" side on economic issues, a situation that did not hold in 1980 and 1984. If, as many believe, the traditional New Deal issues and cleavages can no longer sustain the Democratic party in the 1990s, then the party must undergo intensive self-examination to decide what it can and does stand for.

Throughout the Reagan and Bush eras, and especially since the 1984 and 1988 Democratic debacles, the Democrats have conducted this examination in public and in private. Liberal factions within the party warn that there is no electoral future in abandoning the historical principles and positions of the party and becoming a clone of the GOP. Conservative Democrats retort that the electoral track record of the recent past demonstrates that the party needs to shed its image as a coalition of disgruntled groups and instead promote a positive program. As the 1992 election approaches, Democrats are increasingly focused on the related issues of America's competitiveness in the world and the security of jobs at home, as well as such concerns as health insurance and family care, issues around which the Democrats might be able to unite and win over the American public. One key question is how will the Democrats reassure the vast middle class that they—not the GOP—are the party of economic growth and opportunity, particularly since the party's emphasis on "fairness" was seen by many middle-class citizens as fairness for the poor and minorities at the expense of the middle class. And, of course, the Democrats must, in 1992, survive their often fractious nominating process. Would the nominating process yield a Democratic ticket and a Democratic platform that would have a chance to win in November? Could the Democratic party select as its presidential nominee a progressive with strong leadership skills who, in turn, would choose a moderate Southerner as running mate? Could the Democrats agree on a platform on which they might run rather than run from?

While the Democrats have greater schisms to confront, the GOP also has its problems. The Republican party is still the minority party. Furthermore, although it is more homogeneous internally than the Democratic party, the GOP has its own schisms. Moderates and some moderate conservatives within the GOP have come to terms with aspects of the New Deal, while some hard-line conservatives still yearn to repeal the New Deal. Ladd argues (1978b: 20) that the economic conservatism of the GOP—along with differences in class background between working-class Democrats and Republicans—hinders the development of a new party based on the following elements: Republicans and disgruntled working-class Democrats upset with their party's support for alternative lifestyles, and a de-emphasis of traditional economic issues. In 1990, open warfare broke out among GOP factions in the Congress and the White House over economic and tax policy.

A development holding both promise and problems for the GOP is the link between the Republican party and the religious right exemplified by Reverend Jerry Falwell and Reverend Pat Robertson. The advantages for the GOP of increased religious group involvement in the party are obvious. The religious right is large, reasonably well-organized with effective communications networks, and is tending toward the GOP with respect to partisan loyalties. The disadvantages are also obvious. The agenda of the religious right, particularly on social issues, may alienate other segments of Republican support, particularly among young people. Moreover, to the extent that the religious right is not content to be mere foot soldiers in the GOP, but instead seeks to gain leadership status, intraparty warfare may break out between Republican regulars and the Christian right.

Another problem for the GOP is that while recent polls indicate that many more Americans call themselves conservatives rather than liberals and while opposition in the abstract to a powerful federal government is high, these results do not signify widespread approval of the GOP's generally conservative stance. Many observers have noted that there is a paradox, even a contradiction, between citizens' preferences for political labels and their opinions about specific federal government programs. That is, while more people consider themselves conservatives in response to a general question about their political ideology, they simultaneously express strong support for a whole host of social programs traditionally espoused by the Democrats. Even at the height of the Reagan revolution, public opinion polls showed that Americans, including self-described conservatives, favored spending more money in such areas as health, education, and urban problems. This should not be interpreted as indicating support for all federal programs and government intervention, but it does indicate the problem that the Republican party faces in coming up with a program that will advance its electoral prospects in the post-Reagan era. Finally, the GOP suffers from long-standing image problems in the electorate. For decades many citizens saw the GOP as the party of the rich and big business, an image that has been reinforced somewhat during the Reagan administration. Concerns about the fairness and openness of the GOP threaten its ability to build a broader coalition.

Hence, the GOP has substantial obstacles to overcome in order to become the majority party. Yet the presence of a large number of Independents, particularly among young adults, leaves open the possibility of a partisan mobilization that could change the shape of the party system. Should the proportion of Independents in the electorate remain high, then future election outcomes will probably exhibit great volatility and the notion of realignment will become less meaningful because there will not be a stable baseline from which to evaluate partisan change. More generally, the political parties may continue to decline as meaningful political instruments. Walter Dean Burnham (1970: 173–174) talks of the decomposition of the party system, as shown by the decline in party-related voting. The decline of the parties in conjunction with the rise in cynicism toward governmental institutions and authorities (discussed in chapter 1) suggests a citizenry increasingly adrift on the political seas.

Robert Lane (1971: 293–294) talks of an era of "rootless politics" brought about by the decline in party identification, the transformation of the working class into the bourgeoisie, the enfranchisement of young voters with fewer economic and community ties and political experiences to guide them, and the relaxation of residency requirements. According to Lane (1971: 294), these developments have the effect of "reducing the weight of tradition, personal and communal, in voting, and increasing the importance of current stimuli." As party, community, and class cues become less important, the media and other sources of cues will become more important. And Lane fears that the kinds of cues provided by the media will be superficial slogans that will lower the quality of electoral decisions.

Lane's description seems unusually pessimistic, yet his notion of rootless politics is suggestive. In an era of rootless politics, how will interests be so organized that voters will be offered meaningful policy choices? In an era of rootless politics, might not a realignment occur on a scale far greater than that of past realignments, thereby threatening some fundamental democratic values? A massive realignment that resulted, for example, in a highly polarized party system—one in which the parties took very distinctive stands across a range of issues—might tremendously increase political stakes, thereby severely weakening the traditional processes of bargaining and compromise on matters of public policy and greatly increasing societal tensions.

Another outcome is continued dealignment to a point where the party in government and the party in the electorate become increasingly weak and fragmented. If the political party continues to decline as a key actor in the organization and expression of programmatic concerns, what institutional arrangements will perform the functions normally associated with political parties? Fortunately, there seems to be a growing recognition that an election process that puts a premium on the individual candidate rather than the political party may diminish the prospects for governing effectively. And Martin P. Wattenberg (1986) has shown that while Americans have become less positive about political parties, they have primarily shifted to a posture of neutrality rather than outright opposition to parties. Thus, Wattenberg argues that while it will be difficult to change citizens' views of political parties, the task is less difficult if citizens are simply neutral and indifferent to the parties rather than openly hostile to them.

There is some controversy as to whether the party system is in a period of inevitable decline. MacDonald and Rabinowitz (1987) assert that realignment occurs when there is a contradiction between the ideological and partisan positions of political elites. When such a disequilibrium exists, voters may cast ballots on the basis of ideology rather than partisanship, thereby giving the appearance of a weakening party system. But if the parties react to the partisan-ideological contradiction, there will once again be congruence between ideological and partisan positions with the result that the political parties will be reenergized as major actors in the political system. In a similar vein, Carmines, McIver, and Stimson (1987) see dealignment as an issue driven phenomenon. In particular, they focus on Independents who failed to acquire partisanship despite parental and other forces pushing them in a partisan direction. The authors argue that these citizens are Independent because their own issue preferences are not in harmony with the political party toward which they might be expected to align on the basis of family influence. Their independent status is a source of dealignment. But, as the authors point out, should these Independents move toward their natural (issue-based) party, then the party system would be strengthened and would be more compatible with the existing distribution of policy preferences in the mass electorate. At the elite level, this movement is already occurring, especially in the South. As Kweit (1986) and Nesbit (1988) have shown, there is a strong issue and ideological congruence between the views of party activists who have switched political parties and the positions of the political party to which they switched.

Thus, there is an ongoing debate about the future of political parties in the United States. As this debate continues, steps have been taken to strengthen the role of the political party and party officials in the presidential selection process. As seen in chapter 8, the Democratic party has created a group of "superdelegates" for its nominating conventions. These delegates consist of party and elected officials who are not committed to any candidate and who therefore can arrive at party-oriented judgments as to which candidate would make the strongest nominee. With respect to the campaign finance reforms discussed in chapter 8, a variety of steps have been taken to encourage contributions to the political parties and to foster state and local political party involvement in federal elections. For example, an individual can contribute up to $20,000 per year to a national party committee but only $5,000 per year to nonparty, multicandidate committees. In addition, the national party committees are permitted to spend on behalf of their presidential nominees.

There is ample evidence that the political parties at the national level have partially come to grips with the new technologies of campaigning and with the campaign finance laws. In particular, the Republican party has been highly successful in using computerized mail fund-raising techniques to raise millions of dollars in relatively small contributions from large numbers of donors. The GOP has used these monies to facilitate candidate recruitment and to provide candidates for office with such services as polling and media support. The Republican party has even sponsored nationally televised commercials for its entire slate of congressional candidates. Although the Democrats still lag behind the Republicans in harnessing the new technology, it is clear that both parties are continuing to move in this direction, which will probably further enhance their role in candidate recruitment and support. To the extent that the political parties can support their nominees, candidates will be less reliant on the resources of single-issue interest groups, PACs, and the like.

Certainly the nationalization and centralization of the political parties, especially the Democrats, has been furthered by the reforms adopted since 1968. Various political party and court decisions have supported the supremacy of national party rules. The other side of this, of course, is that many of the national party rules as well as the campaign finance reforms have done little to revitalize the local and state party organizations and have not provided much incentive for a cooperative, team approach to election campaigning.

Despite these changes, which suggest that the political party is not moribund, it is clear that the current nomination system is still more oriented to the individual candidate than to the political party. The selection process is still one in which the media play the major role in determining the credibility and viability of candidacies. The horse race mentality of the media rewards a candidate much more for a successful primary performance than for any particularly cogent stand on the issues or any demonstrated ability to govern.

Americans have traditionally been ambivalent about political parties. Much of our political rhetoric today extols the virtue of voting for the person, not the party. Citizen attachments to and support for the party system remain low. Yet political parties are much more than organizations for electing candidates. If that were all that parties did, then other organizations, such as PACs, could just as easily harness the new technology and contest elections. Political parties provide the critical links across and among levels of government. Political parties also foster the development of relatively broad coalitions out of which legitimate national public policy emerges. Hence, the prospect of politics without parties is troublesome. The candidate-centered campaigns that dominate today's presidential and congressional contests may be inevitable. Nevertheless, one must question whether such unbridled individual campaign entrepreneurship fosters effective governance by elected leaders willing and able to confront complex issues and make difficult decisions. At present, the prospects for change in the American political system seem unusually great given widespread concerns about campaign financing, political ethics, incumbency advantages, and the like. Yet the outcome of change need not be increased citizen satisfaction with political institutions and authorities and public policies. The end results of political change are unclear, and this should lead us all to view the future with both excitement and anxiety.

Constitutional Provisions Relevant to Presidential Selection

Article II

SECTION 1

[1] The executive power shall be vested in a President of the United States of America. He shall hold his office during the term of four years, and together with the Vice President, chosen for the same term, be elected as follows:

[2] Each State shall appoint, in such manner as the legislature thereof may direct, a number of Electors, equal to the whole number of Senators and Representatives to which the State may be entitled in the Congress; but no Senator or Representative, or person holding an office of trust or profit under the United States, shall be appointed an Elector.

[3] The Electors shall meet in their respective States and vote by ballot for two persons, of whom one at least shall not be an inhabitant of the same State with themselves. And they shall make a list of all the persons voted for, and of the number of votes for each; which list they shall sign and certify, and transmit sealed to the seat of government of the United States, directed to the President of the Senate. The President of the Senate shall, in the presence of the Senate and House of Representatives, open all the certificates, and the votes shall then be counted. The person having the greatest number of votes shall be the President, if such number be a majority of the whole number of Electors appointed; and if there be more than one who have such majority, and have an equal number of votes then the House of Representatives shall immediately choose by ballot one of them for President; and if no person has a majority, then from the five highest on the list the said House shall in like manner choose the President. But in choosing the President, the votes shall be taken by States, the representation from each State having one vote; a quorum for this purpose shall consist of a member or members from two thirds of the States, and a majority of all the States shall be necessary to a choice. In every case, after the choice of the President, the person having the greatest number of votes of the Electors shall be the Vice President. But if there should remain two or more who have equal votes, the Senate shall choose from them by ballot the Vice President.

[4] The Congress may determine the time of choosing the Electors and the day on which they shall give their votes, which day shall be the same throughout the United States.

[5] No person except a natural-born citizen, or citizen of the United States at the time of the adoption of this Constitution, shall be eligible to the office of President; neither shall any person be eligible to that office who shall not have attained to the age of thirty-five years, and been fourteen years a resident within the United States.

[6] In case of the removal of the President from office, or of his death, resignation, or inability to discharge the powers and duties of the said office, the same shall devolve on the Vice President, and the Congress may by law provide for the case of removal, death, resignation, or inability, both of the

President and Vice President, declaring what officer shall then act as President, and such officer shall act accordingly until the disability be removed or a President shall be elected.

[7] The President shall, at stated times, receive for his services a compensation, which shall neither be increased nor diminished during the period for which he shall have been elected, and he shall not receive within that period any other emolument from the United States or any of them.

[8] Before he enter on the execution of his office he shall take the following oath or affirmation:

"I do solemnly swear (or affirm) that I will faithfully execute the office of President of the United States, and will to the best of my ability preserve, protect, and defend the Constitution of the United States."

Amendment XII

(supersedes Article II, Section 1, para. 3)

[1] The Electors shall meet in their respective States and vote by ballot for President and Vice President, one of whom, at least, shall not be an inhabitant of the same State with themselves; they shall name in their ballots the person voted for as President, and in distinct ballots the person voted for as Vice President, and they shall make distinct lists of all persons voted for as President and of all persons voted for as Vice President, and of the number of votes for each; which lists they shall sign and certify, and transmit sealed to the seat of the government of the United States, directed to the President of the Senate. The President of the Senate shall, in the presence of the Senate and House of Representatives, open all the certificates and the votes shall then be counted. The person having the greatest number of votes for President shall be the President, if such a number be a majority of the whole number of Electors appointed; and if no person have such majority, then from the persons having the highest numbers not exceeding three on the list of those voted for as President, the House of Representatives shall choose immediately, by ballot, the President. But in choosing the President, the votes shall be taken by States, the representation from each State having one vote; a quorum for this purpose shall consist of a member or members from two thirds of the States, and a majority of all the States shall be necessary to a choice. And if the House of Representatives shall not choose a President whenever the right of choice shall devolve upon them, before the fourth day of March next following, then the Vice President shall act as President, as in the case of the death or other constitutional disability of the President.

[2] The person having the greatest number of votes as Vice President shall be the Vice President, if such number be a majority of the whole number of Electors appointed; and if no person have a majority, then from the two highest

numbers on the list the Senate shall choose the Vice President; a quorum for the purpose shall consist of two thirds of the whole number of Senators, and a majority of the whole number shall be necessary to a choice. But no person constitutionally ineligible to the office of President shall be eligible to that of Vice President of the United States.

Passed by Congress December 9, 1803.
Ratified July 27, 1804.

Amendment XX

SECTION 1

The terms of the President and Vice President shall end at noon on the 20th day of January, and the terms of Senators and Representatives at noon on the third day of January, of the years in which such terms would have ended if this article had not been ratified; and the terms of their successors shall then begin.

SECTION 2

The Congress shall assemble at least once in every year, and such meetings shall begin at noon on the third day of January, unless they shall by law appoint a different day.

SECTION 3

If, at the time fixed for the beginning of the term of the President, the President-elect shall have died, the Vice President-elect shall become President. If a President shall not have been chosen before the time fixed for the beginning of his term or if the President-elect shall have failed to qualify, then the Vice President-elect shall act as President until a President shall have qualified; and the Congress may by law provide for the case wherein neither a President-elect nor a Vice President-elect shall have qualified, declaring who shall then act as President, or the manner in which one who is to act shall be selected, and such persons shall act accordingly until a President or Vice President shall have qualified.

SECTION 4

The Congress may by law provide for the case of the death of any of the persons from whom the House of Representatives may choose a President whenever the right of choice shall have devolved upon them, and for the case of death of any of the persons from whom the Senate may choose a Vice President whenever the right of choice shall have devolved upon them.

SECTION 5

Sections 1 and 2 shall take effect on the 15th day of October following the ratification of this article.

SECTION 6

This article shall be inoperative unless it shall have been ratified as an amendment to the Constitution by the legislatures of three fourths of the several States within seven years from the date of its submission.

Passed by Congress March 2, 1932.
Ratified January 23, 1933.

Amendment XXII

No person shall be elected to the office of President more than twice, and no person who has held the office of President, or acted as President, for more than two years of a term to which some other person was elected President shall be elected to the office of President more than once. But this Article shall not apply to any person holding the office of President when this Article was proposed by the Congress, and shall not prevent any person who may be holding the office of President, or acting as President, during the term within which this Article becomes operative from holding the office of President or acting as President during the remainder of such term

SECTION 2

This article shall be inoperative unless it shall have been ratified as an amendment to the Constitution by the legislatures of three fourths of the several States within seven years from the date of its submission to the States by the Congress.

Passed by Congress March 21, 1947.
Ratified February 27, 1951.

Amendment XXIII

SECTION 1

The District constituting the seat of Government of the United States shall appoint in such manner as the Congress may direct:

A number of electors of President and Vice President equal to the whole number of Senators and Representatives in Congress to which the District would be entitled if it were a State, but in no event more than the least populous State; they shall be in addition to those appointed by the States, but they shall be considered, for the purposes of the election of President and Vice President, to be electors appointed by a State; and they shall meet in the District and perform such duties as provided by the twelfth article of amendment.

SECTION 2

The Congress shall have power to enforce this article by appropriate legislation.

Passed by Congress June 16, 1960.
Ratified March 29, 1961.

Amendment XXV

(supersedes Article II, Section 1, para. 6)

SECTION 1

In case of the removal of the President from office or of his death or resignation, the Vice President shall become President.

SECTION 2

Whenever there is a vacancy in the office of the Vice President, the President shall nominate a Vice President who shall take office upon confirmation by a majority vote of both Houses of Congress.

SECTION 3

Whenever the President transmits to the President pro tempore of the Senate and the Speaker of the House of Representatives his written declaration that he is unable to discharge the powers and duties of his office, and until he transmits to them a written declaration to the contrary, such powers and duties shall be discharged by the Vice President as Acting President.

SECTION 4

Whenever the Vice President and a majority of either the principal officers of the executive departments or of such other body as Congress may by law provide, transmit to the President pro tempore of the Senate and the Speaker of the House of Representatives their written declaration that the President is unable to discharge the powers and duties of his office, the Vice President shall immediately assume the powers and duties of the office as Acting President.

Thereafter, when the President transmits to the President pro tempore of the Senate and the Speaker of the House of Representatives his written declaration that no inability exists, he shall resume the powers and duties of his office unless the Vice President and a majority of either the principal officers of the executive department or of such other body as Congress may by law provide, transmit within four days to the President pro tempore of the Senate and the Speaker of the House of Representatives their written declaration that the President is unable to discharge the powers and duties of his office. Thereupon Congress shall decide the issue, assembling within 48 hours for that purpose if not in session. If the Congress, within 21 days after receipt of the latter written declaration, or, if Congress is not in session, within 21 days after Congress is required to assemble, determines by two thirds vote of both Houses that the President is unable to discharge the powers and duties of his office, the Vice President shall continue to discharge the same as Acting President; otherwise, the President shall resume the powers and duties of his office.

Passed by Congress July 6, 1965.
Ratified February 10, 1967.

Presidential Election Results, 1864–1988

APPENDIX B Presidential Election Results, 1864–1988

| Year | Republican | | | | Democratic | | | | Major third party | | | | Other | |
	Candidate	Popular vote	Percent of popular vote	Electoral College vote	Candidate	Popular vote	Percent of popular vote	Electoral College vote	Candidate and party	Popular vote	Percent of popular vote	Electoral College vote	Popular vote	Percent of popular vote
1864	Abraham Lincoln*	2,218,388	55.0%	212	George McClellan	1,812,807	45.0%	21					692	0.0%
1868	Ulysses Grant*	3,013,650	52.7	214	Horatio Seymour	2,708,744	47.3	80					46	0.0
1872	Ulysses Grant*	3,598,235	55.6	286	Horace Greeley	2,834,761	43.8	63					34,683	0.6
1876	Rutherford Hayes*	4,034,311	47.9	185	Samuel Tilden	4,288,546	51.0	184					90,244	1.1
1880	James Garfield*	4,446,158	48.3	214	Winfield Hancock	4,444,260	48.3	155					320,002	3.4
1884	James Blaine	4,848,936	48.2	182	Grover Cleveland*	4,874,621	48.5	219					326,197	3.3
1888	Benjamin Harrison*	5,443,892	47.8	233	Grover Cleveland	5,534,488	48.6	168					404,934	3.6
1892	Benjamin Harrison	5,179,244	43.0	145	Grover Cleveland*	5,551,883	46.0	277	James Weaver, Populist	1,024,280	8.5%	22	300,690	2.5
1896	William McKinley*	7,108,480	51.0	271	William Bryan	6,511,495	46.7	176					315,763	2.3
1900	William McKinley*	7,218,039	51.7	292	William Bryan	6,358,345	45.5	155					394,086	2.8
1904	Theodore Roosevelt*	7,626,593	56.4	336	Alton Parker	5,082,898	37.6	140					809,473	6.0

350

Year	Candidate	Popular vote	%	Electoral	Opponent	Popular vote	%	Electoral	Third party	Popular vote	%	Electoral	Others	%
1908	William Taft*	7,676,258	51.6	321	William Bryan	6,406,801	43.0	162					799,675	5.4
1912	William Taft	3,486,333	23.2	8	Woodrow Wilson*	6,293,152	41.8	435	Theodore Roosevelt, Progressive	4,119,207	27.4	88	1,142,271	7.6
1916	Charles Hughes	8,546,789	46.1	254	Woodrow Wilson*	9,126,300	49.2	277					861,933	4.7
1920	Warren Harding*	16,133,314	60.3	404	James Cox	9,140,884	34.2%	127					1,479,588	5.5
1924	Calvin Coolidge*	15,717,553	54.1	382	John Davis	8,386,169	28.8	136	Robert La Follette, Progressive	4,119,207	16.6	13	158,187	0.5
1928	Herbert Hoover*	21,411,991	58.2	444	Alfred Smith	15,000,185	40.8	87					378,188	1.0
1932	Herbert Hoover	15,758,897	39.6	59	Franklin Roosevelt*	22,825,016	57.4	472					1,165,969	3.0
1936	Alfred Landon	16,679,543	36.5	8	Franklin Roosevelt*	27,747,636	60.8	523					1,215,124	2.7
1940	Wendell Willkie	22,336,260	44.8	82	Franklin Roosevelt*	27,263,448	54.7	449					240,735	0.5
1944	Thomas Dewey	22,013,372	45.9	99	Franklin Roosevelt*	25,611,936	53.4	432					349,511	0.7
1948	Thomas Dewey	21,970,017	45.1	189	Harry Truman*	24,105,587	49.5	303	Strom Thurmond, State's Rights and Henry Wallace, Progressive	1,169,134 / 1,157,057	2.4 / 2.4	39 / 0	290,647	0.6
1952	Dwight Eisenhower*	33,936,137	55.1	442	Adlai Stevenson	27,314,649	44.4	89					300,332	0.5

(continued)

APPENDIX B Presidential Election Results, 1864–1988 (continued)

	Republican				Democratic				Major third party				Other	
Year	Candidate	Popular vote	Percent of popular vote	Electoral College vote	Candidate	Popular vote	Percent of popular vote	Electoral College vote	Candidate and party	Popular vote	Percent of popular vote	Electoral College vote	Popular vote	Percent of popular vote
1956	Dwight Eisenhower*	35,585,245	57.4	457	Adlai Stevenson	26,030,172	42.0	73					409,955	0.6
1960	Richard Nixon	34,106,671	49.5	219	John Kennedy*	34,221,344	49.7	303					500,945	0.8
1964	Barry Goldwater	27,177,838	38.5	52	Lyndon Johnson*	43,126,584	61.0	486					336,682	0.5
1968	Richard Nixon*	21,785,148	43.4	301	Hubert Humphrey	31,274,503	42.7	191	George Wallace, American Independent	9,901,151	13.5	46	242,568	0.4
1972	Richard Nixon*	47,170,179	60.7	520	George McGovern	29,171,791	37.5	17					1,385,620	1.8
1976	Gerald Ford	39,146,006	48.0	240	Jimmy Carter*	40,829,046	50.1	297					1,577,279	1.9
1980	Ronald Reagan*	43,904,153	50.7	489	Jimmy Carter	35,483,883	41.0	49	John Anderson	5,720,060	6.6	0	1,407,125	1.7
1984	Ronald Reagan*	54,455,075	58.8	525	Walter Mondale	37,577,185	40.6	13					620,582	0.7
1988	George Bush*	48,886,097	53.4	426	Michael Dukakis	41,809,074	45.6	111						

*Denotes winner.

SOURCES: Constructed from figures presented in *Presidential Elections Since 1789* (Washington, D.C.: Congressional Quarterly, 1975); *Guide to 1976 Election* (Washington, D.C.: Congressional Quarterly, 1977); *America Votes 14: Handbook of Contemporary American Election Statistics* (Washington, D.C.: Congressional Quarterly Inc., 1981); *American Votes 16: A Handbook of American Election Statistics* (Washington, D.C.: Congressional Quarterly, 1985); and *American Votes 18: A Handbook of Contemporary Election Statistics* (Washington, D.C.: Congressional Quarterly, 1989).

ABRAMOWITZ, ALAN I. "The Impact of a Presidential Debate on Voter Rationality," *American Journal of Political Science* 22 (August 1978), pp. 680–690.

ABRAMSON, PAUL R. "Why the Democrats Are No Longer the Majority Party," paper presented at the annual meeting of the American Political Science Association, New Orleans, September 4–8, 1973.

———. "Generational Change and the Decline of Party Identification in America: 1952–1974," *American Political Science Review* 70 (June 1976), pp. 469–478.

———. "Developing Party Identification: A Further Examination of Life-Cycle, Generational, and Periodic Effects," *American Journal of Political Science* 23 (February 1979), pp. 78–96.

ABRAMSON, PAUL R., and ALDRICH, JOHN H. "The Decline of Electoral Participation in America," *American Political Science Review* 76 (September 1982), pp. 502–521.

ABRAMSON, PAUL R., ALDRICH, JOHN H., and ROHDE, DAVID W. *Change and Continuity in the 1980 Elections* (Washington, D.C.: Congressional Quarterly Press, 1982).

ADAMS, WILLIAM C. "Media Coverage of Campaign '84: A Preliminary Report," *Public Opinion* 7 (April–May 1984), pp. 9–13.

ADATTO, KIKU. "Sound Bite Democracy. Network Evening News Presidential Campaign Coverage." research paper R-2, Harvard University, The Joan Shorenstein Barone Center, John F. Kennedy School of Government, June 1990.

AGRANOFF, ROBERT. *The New Style in Election Campaigns* (Boston: Holbrook Press, 1972).

ALDRICH, JOHN H., GANT, MICHAEL M., and SIMON, DENNIS M. " 'To the Victor Belong the Spoils': Momentum in the 1976 Nomination Campaigns," unpublished paper, 1978.

ALDRICH, JOHN H., SULLIVAN, JOHN L., and BORGIDA, EUGENE. "Foreign Affairs and Issue Voting: Do Presidential Candidates 'Waltz Before a Blind Audience?' " *American Political Science Review,* 83(1), March 1989.

ALEXANDER, HERBERT E. *Financing the 1960 Election* (Princeton, N.J.: Citizens' Research Foundation, 1962).

———. *Financing the 1964 Election* (Princeton, N.J.: Citizens' Research Foundation, 1966).

———. *Financing the 1968 Election* (Lexington, Mass.: D. C. Heath, 1971).

———. *Money in Politics* (Washington, D.C.: Public Affairs Press, 1972a).

———. *Political Financing* (Minneapolis: Burgess Publishing 1972b).

———. "Campaign Spending," in *Encyclopedia Year Book, 1973* (New York: Grolier, 1973).

————. *Financing Politics: Money, Elections, and Political Reform* (Washington, D.C.: Congressional Quarterly Press, 1976).

————. "Financing the Presidential Elections, 1988." Paper presented at the annual meeting of the International Political Science Association, September 8–10, 1989.

ALEXANDER, HERBERT E., and HAGGERTY, BRIAN A. *Financing the 1984 Election* (Lexington, Mass.: D.C. Heath and Company, 1987).

ALLSOP, DEE, and WEISBERG, HERBERT F. "Measuring Change in Party Identification in an Election Campaign," *American Journal of Political Science*, 32(4), November 1988.

ANDERSEN, KRISTI, "Generation, Partisan Shift, and Realignment: A Glance Back to the New Deal," in *The Changing American Voter* edited by Norman H. Nie, Sidney Verba, and John R. Petrocik (Cambridge, Mass.: Harvard University Press, 1976), pp. 74–95.

ARTERTON, F. CHRISTOPHER. "Recent Rule Changes within the National Democratic Party: Some Present and (Short Term) Future Consequences," paper presented at the annual meeting of the Social Science History Association, Columbus, Ohio, November 3–5, 1978.

ASHER, HERBERT B. "The Media and the Presidential Selection Process." in *The Impact of the Electoral Process*, Sage Electoral Studies Yearbook, vol. 3, edited by Louis Maisel and Joseph Cooper (Beverly Hills, Calif.: Sage Publications, 1977). Adapted by permission of the publisher, Sage Publications, Inc.

————. "Voting Behavior Research in the 1980s: An Examination of Some Old and New Problem Areas," in *Political Science: The State of the Discipline*, edited by Ada Finifter (Washington, D.C.: American Political Science Association, 1983).

————. *Causal Modeling*, rev. ed. (Beverly Hills, Calif.: Sage Publications, 1983).

AXELROD, ROBERT. "Where the Votes Come From: An Analysis of Electoral Coalitions, 1952–1968," *American Political Science Review* 66 (March 1972), pp. 11–20.

————. "Communications," *American Political Science Review* 72 (June 1978), pp. 622–624.

————. "Communication," *American Political Science Review* 76 (March 1982), pp. 393–396.

————. "Presidential Election Coalitions in 1984," *American Political Science Review* 80 (March 1986), pp. 281–284.

BAGDIKIAN, BEN H. "The Fruits of Agnewism," *Columbia Journalism Review* 11 (January–February 1973), pp. 9–21.

BALZ, DAN. "Democratic Strategists Warn Against Courting Special Groups," *The Washington Post*, May 23, 1983, p. A-2.

BALZ, DAN, and MORIN, RICHARD. "Poll Taps Public's Pessimism on Economy," *The Washington Post*, July 26, 1990, p. A-10.

BARBER, JAMES DAVID. *The Presidential Character: Predicting Performance in the White House* (Englewood Cliffs, N.J.: Prentice–Hall, 1972).

BASKIN, OTIS. "The Effects of Television Political Advertisements on Candidate Image," paper presented at the annual meeting of the International Communication Association, Portland, Oregon, April 14–17, 1976.

BEARDSLEY, PHILIP L. "The Methodology of the Electoral Analysis: Models and Measurement," in David M. Kovenock, James W. Prothro, et al., *Explaining the*

Vote, Part 1 (Chapel Hill, N.C.: Institute for Research in Social Science, 1973), pp. 1–42.

BECK, PAUL. "A Socialization Theory of Partisan Realignment," in *New Views of Children and Politics,* edited by Richard Niemi (San Francisco: Jossey-Bass, 1974).

———. "Partisan Dealignment in the Postwar South," *American Political Science Review* 71 (June 1977), pp. 477–496.

———. "Youth and the Politics of Realignment," unpublished paper.

———. "Realignment Begins?: The Republican Surge in Florida," *American Politics Quarterly* 10 (October 1982), pp. 421–438.

BENHAM, THOMAS W. "Polling for Presidential Candidates," in *The New Style in Election Campaigns,* edited by Robert Agranoff (Boston: Holbrook Press, 1972), pp. 213–231.

BENIGER, J. R. "Winning the Presidential Nomination: National Polls and State Primary Elections, 1936–1972," *Public Opinion Quarterly* 40 (Spring 1976), pp. 22–38.

BENNET, LINDA L. M. "The Gender Gap: When an Opinion Gap Is Not a Voting Bloc," *Social Science Quarterly* 67 (September 1986), pp. 613–625.

BENNETT, STEPHEN EARL, " 'Know-Nothings' Revisited: The Meaning of Political Ignorance Today," *Social Science Quarterly* 69(2), (June 1988), pp. 476–490.

BERELSON, BERNARD, LAZARSFELD, PAUL, and MCPHEE, WILLIAM. *Voting* (Chicago: University of Chicago Press, 1954).

BISHOP, GEORGE F. "Questions about Question Wording: A Rejoinder to Revisiting Mass Belief Systems Revisited," *American Journal of Political Science* 23 (February 1979), pp. 187–192.

BISHOP, GEORGE F., and BENNETT, STEPHEN E. "The Changing Structure of Mass Belief Systems: Fact or Artifact?" *Journal of Politics* 40 (August 1978a), pp. 781–787.

BISHOP, GEORGE F., MEADOW, ROBERT G., and JACKSON-BEECK, MARILYN, eds. *The Presidential Debates: Media, Electoral, and Policy Perspectives* (New York: Praeger, 1978).

BISHOP, GEORGE F., OLDENDICK, ROBERT W., and TUCHFARBER, ALFRED J. "Effects of Question Wording and Format on Political Attitude Consistency," *Public Opinion Quarterly* 42 (Spring 1978b), pp. 81–92.

BISHOP, GEORGE F., TUCHFARBER, ALFRED J., and OLDENDICK, ROBERT W. "Change in the Structure of American Political Attitudes: The Nagging Question of Question Wording," *American Journal of Political Science* 22 (May 1978c), pp. 250–269.

BLACK, MERLE, and RABINOWITZ, GEORGE. "An Overview of American Electoral Change, 1952–1972," paper presented at the annual meeting of the Southern Political Science Association, New Orleans, November 8, 1974.

BLUME, KEITH. *The Presidential Election Show* (South Hadley, Mass.: Bergin and Gravey Publishers, Inc., 1985).

BONE, HUGH A. *American Politics and the Party System* (New York: McGraw-Hill, 1955).

BOWEN, LAWRENCE, ATKIN, CHARLES K., NAYMAN, OGUZ B., and SHEINKOPF, KENNETH G. "Quality Versus Quantity in Televised Political Ads," *Public Opinion Quarterly* 37 (Summer 1972), pp. 209–224.

BOYD, RICHARD W. "Presidential Elections: An Explanation of Voting Defection," *American Political Science Review* 63 (June 1969), pp. 498–514.

———. "Popular Control of Public Policy: A Normal Vote Analysis of the 1968 Election," *American Political Science Review* 66 (June 1972), pp. 429–449.

———. "Structural and Attitudinal Explanations of Turnout," Paper presented at the Conference on Voter Turnout, San Diego, May 16–19, 1979.

———. "Electoral Change and the Floating Voter: The Reagan Elections," *Political Behavior* 8 (1986), pp. 230–244.

———. "The Effects of Primaries and Statewide Races on Voter Turnout," *Journal of Politics* 51 (August 1989), pp. 730–739.

BRAMS, STEVEN J., and DAVIS, MORTON D. "The 3/2's Rule in Presidential Campaigning," *American Political Science Review* 68 (March 1974), pp. 113–134.

BRODER, DAVID S. *The Party's Over: The Failure of Politics in America* (New York: Harper & Row, 1971).

———. "Political Reporters in Presidential Politics," in *Inside the System*, 3rd ed., edited by Charles Peters and James Fallows (New York: Praeger, 1976).

———. "Nader Says Time Nears for New Political Party," *The Washington Post*, May 8, 1979a, p. A-2.

———. "Carter's Staff Just 'Campaign Soldiers,' " *Columbus Dispatch*, May 27, 1979b, p. B-2.

———. "Rose Garden Visions," *The Washington Post*, August 5, 1981, p. A-23.

———. "Democrats Enter Final Round," *The Washington Post*, May 10, 1984a, p. A-l.

———. "The Start of the '88 Campaign," *The Washington Post National Weekly Edition*, August 27, 1984b, p. 4.

———. "First Impressions of Seven Hopefuls," *The Washington Post*, March 5, 1986, p. A-19.

BRODER, DAVID S., and PETERSON, BILL. "Hart Wins Narrowly in Ohio and Indiana," *The Washington Post*, May 9, 1984, p. A-l.

BRODY, RICHARD A. "Stability and Change in Party Identification: Presidential to Off-Years," paper presented at the annual meeting of the American Political Science Association, Washington, D.C., August 31–September 4, 1977.

BRODY, RICHARD A., and PAGE, BENJAMIN I. "Comment: The Assessment of Policy Voting," *American Political Science Review* 66 (June 1972), pp. 450–458.

BROWN, COURTNEY. "Mass Dynamics of U.S. Presidential Competitions, 1928–1936," *American Political Science Review* 82 (December 1988), pp. 1153–1181.

BUCHANAN, BRUCE. *Electing a President: The Markle Commission Report on Campaign '88*, (Austin, Texas: University of Texas Press, 1991).

BUCHANAN, PATRICK "How the Networks Fall Easy Prey to Political Manipulation," *TV Guide*, August 14, 1976, p. A-3.

BUCHWALD, ART. " 'Old' Nixon Has a Voice," *Newark Evening News*, September 17, 1968, p. 25.

BURNHAM, WALTER DEAN. "American Voting Behavior and the 1964 Election," *Midwest Journal of Political Science* 12 (February 1968), pp. 1–40.

———. *Critical Elections and the Mainsprings of American Politics* (New York: Norton, 1970).

CAMPBELL, ANGUS. "A Classification of Presidential Elections," in *Elections and the Political Order* by Angus Campbell, Philip E. Converse, Warren E. Miller, and

Donald E. Stokes (New York. Wiley, 1966a), pp. 63 77. Material reprinted by permission of publisher.

————. "Interpreting the Presidential Victory," in *The National Election of 1964,* edited by Milton C. Cummings, Jr. (Washington, D.C.: Brookings Institution, 1966b), pp. 256–281.

CAMPBELL, ANGUS, CONVERSE, PHILIP E., MILLER, WARREN E., and STOKES, DONALD E., *The American Voter* (New York: Wiley, 1960).

CAMPBELL, ANGUS, GURIN, GERALD, and MILLER, WARREN E. *The Voter Decides* (Evanston, Ill.: Row, Peterson, 1954).

CAMPBELL, BRUCE A. "Patterns of Change in the Partisan Loyalties of Native Southerners: 1952–1972," *Journal of Politics* 39 (August 1977), pp. 730–761.

CANNON, LOUIS. "Udall Complains 'Orgy of Publicity' Benefits Carter Drive," *The Washington Post*, April 17, 1976, p. A-4.

CARMINES, EDWARD G., MCIVER, JOHN P., and STIMSON, JAMES A. "Unrealized Partisanship: A Theory of Dealignment," *The Journal of Politics* 49 (May 1987), pp. 376–400.

CARMINES, EDWARD G., and STIMSON, JAMES A. "The Two Faces of Issue Voting," *American Political Science Review* 74 (March 1980), pp. 78–91.

CASSEL, CAROL A., and LUSKIN, ROBERT C. "Simple Explanations of Turnout Decline," *American Political Science Review* 82 (December 1988), pp. 1321–1330.

CAVALA, WILLIAM. "Changing the Rules Changes the Game: Party Reform and the 1972 California Delegation to the Democratic National Convention," *American Political Science Review* 68 (March 1974), pp. 27–42.

CHAFFEE, STEVEN H. "Are Debates Helpful to Voters?" paper presented at the annual meeting of the International Communication Association, Chicago, April 25–29, 1978.

CHESTER, EDWARD W. *Radio, Television, and American Politics* (New York: Sheed & Ward, 1969).

CHESTER, LEWIS, HODGSON, GODFREY, and PAGE, BRUCE. *An American Melodrama* (New York: Dell, 1969).

CLANCY, MAURA, and ROBINSON, MICHAEL J. "General Election Coverage: Part 1," *Public Opinion* 7 (December–January 1985), pp. 49–54.

CLYMER, ADAM. "Religion and Politics Mix Poorly for Democrats," *New York Times*, November 25, 1984, p. E-2.

————. "A Liberal by Any Other Name May Get More Votes," *New York Times*, November 24, 1985, p. E-5.

COHEN, RICHARD. "Time for Democrats to Rediscover Their Soul," *The Washington Post*, June 28, 1990, p. A-25.

COLLAT, D., KELLEY, S., and ROGOWSKI, R. "Presidential Bandwagons," paper presented at the annual meeting of the American Political Science Association, Chicago, September 2–5, 1976.

CONOVER, PAMELA JOHNSTON. "Feminists and the Gender Gap," *Journal of Politics* 50(4), November 1988.

CONVERSE, PHILIP E. "Non-voting among Young Adults in the United States," a data report to the American Heritage Foundation by the Political Behavior Program of the Survey Research Center, University of Michigan, Ann Arbor, June 1963, pp. 1–36.

————. "The Concept of the Normal Vote," in Angus Campbell, Philip E. Converse, Warren E. Miller, and Donald E. Stokes, *Elections and the Political Order* (New York: Wiley, 1966a), pp. 9–39.

————. "Religion and Politics: The 1960 Election," in Angus Campbell, Philip E. Converse, Warren E. Miller, and Donald E. Stokes, *Elections and the Political Order* (New York: Wiley, 1966b), pp. 96–124.

————. "Of Time and Partisan Stability," *Comparative Political Studies* 2 (July 1969), pp. 139–171.

————. "Attitudes and Non-Attitudes: Continuation of a Dialogue," in *The Quantitative Analysis of Social Problems*, edited by Edward R. Tufte (Reading, Mass.: Addison-Wesley, 1970a), pp. 168–189.

————. "Information Flow and the Stability of Partisan Attitudes," in *Political Opinion and Behavior*, 2nd ed., edited by Edward C. Dreyer and Walter A. Rosenbaum (Belmont, Calif.: Wadsworth, 1970b), pp. 407–426.

————. "The Nature of Belief Systems in Mass Publics," in *Public Opinion and Public Policy*, rev. ed., edited by Norman R. Luttbeg (Belmont, Calif: Wadsworth, 1974), pp. 300–334.

————. *The Dynamics of Party Support: Cohort-analyzing Party Identification* (Beverly Hills, Calif.: Sage Publications, 1976).

————. "Rejoinder to Abramson," *American Journal of Political Science* 23 (February 1979), pp. 97–100.

CONVERSE, PHILIP E., CAMPBELL, ANGUS, MILLER, WARREN E., and STOKES, DONALD E. "Stability and Change in 1960: A Reinstating Election," in Angus Campbell, Philip E. Converse, Warren E. Miller, and Donald E. Stokes, *Elections and the Political Order* (New York: Wiley, 1966), pp. 78–95.

CONVERSE, PHILIP E., CLAUSEN, AAGE R., and MILLER, WARREN E. "Electoral Myth and Reality: The 1964 Election," *American Political Science Review* 59 (June 1965), pp. 321–336.

————. "Electoral Myth and Reality: The 1964 Election," in *Political Opinion and Behavior*, 2nd ed., edited by Edward C. Dreyer and Walter A. Rosenbaum (Belmont, Calif.: Wadsworth, 1970), pp. 39–50.

CONVERSE, PHILIP E., and DEPEUX, GEORGES. "Politicization of the Electorate in France and the United States," in Angus Campbell, Philip E. Converse, Warren E. Miller, and Donald E. Stokes, *Elections and the Political Order* (New York: Wiley, 1966), pp. 269–291.

CONVERSE, PHILIP E., MILLER, WARREN E., RUSK, JERROLD G., and WOLFE, ARTHUR C. "Continuity and Change in American Politics: Parties and Issues in the 1968 Election," *American Political Science Review* 63 (December 1969), pp. 1083–1105.

COOK, RHODES. "Democrats Adopt New Rules for Picking Nominee in 1980," *Congressional Quarterly Weekly Report*, June 17, 1978, p. 1571.

————. "GOP Presidential Hopefuls Gave Plenty to Party Candidates in 1978," *Congressional Quarterly Weekly Report*, February 17, 1979, pp. 307–311.

COOMBS, STEVEN L. "Editorial Endorsements and Electoral Outcomes," in *More than News*, Michael B. MacKuen and Steven L. Coombs (Beverly Hills, Calif.: Sage Publications, 1981).

COSMAN, BERNARD, and HUCKSHORN, ROBERT J. "The Goldwater Impact: Cyclical Variation or Secular Decline?" In *Republican Politics*, edited by Bernard Cosman and Robert J. Huckshorn (New York: Praeger, 1968), pp. 234–244.

CRITTENDEN, JOHN. "Aging and Party Affiliation," *Public Opinion Quarterly* 26 (Winter 1962), pp. 648–657.

———. "Reply to Cutler," *Public Opinion Quarterly* 33 (Winter 1969–1970), pp. 589–591.

CROTTY, WILLIAM. *Political Reform and the American Experiment* (New York: Thomas Y. Crowell, 1977).

———. *Decision for the Democrats: Reforming the Party Structure* (Baltimore: Johns Hopkins University Press, 1978).

———. "Party Reform and Democratic Performance," paper presented at the conference on "The Future of the American Political System: What Can Be Done to Make It More Democratic and Effective?", sponsored by the Center for the Study of Democratic Politics, University of Pennsylvania, April 12–13, 1979.

CROUSE, TIMOTHY, *The Boys on the Bus: Riding with the Campaign Press Corps* (New York: Ballantine, 1973).

CUNDY, DONALD T. "Televised Political Editorials and the Low-Involvement Viewer," *Social Science Quarterly*, 70(4), December 1989.

CUTLER, NEAL E. "Generation, Maturation, and Party Affiliation: A Cohort Analysis," *Public Opinion Quarterly* 33 (Winter 1969–1970), pp. 583–588.

———. "Comment," *Public Opinion Quarterly* 33 (Winter 1969–1970b), p. 592.

DAVIS, JAMES W. *Presidential Primaries: Road to the White House* (New York: Thomas Y. Crowell, 1967).

Democratic State Central Committee of Michigan. Publication no. 92767-3, 1968.

Democrats: Striving to Avert a Midterm Blowup. (Washington, D.C.: Congressional Quarterly Weekly Report) 32:48, November 30, 1974, pp. 3209–3214.

DE NARDO, JAMES. "Turnout and the Vote: The Joke's on the Democrats," *American Political Science Review* 74 (1986), pp. 406–420.

DENNIS, JACK. "Support for the Institution of Elections by the Mass Public," *American Political Science Review* 64 (September 1970), pp. 819–835.

———. "Trends in Public Support for the American Political Party System," paper presented at the annual meeting of the American Political Science Association, Chicago, August 29–September 2, 1974.

———. "Some Properties of Measures of Partisanship," paper presented at the annual meeting of the American Political Science Association, New York City, September 3–6, 1981.

DENNIS, JACK, and MCCRONE, DONALD J. "Preadult Development of Political Party Identification in Western Democracies," *Comparative Political Studies* 3 (July 1970),pp. 243–263.

DEVRIES, WALTER, and TARRANCE, V. LANCE. *The Ticket-Splitter: A New Force in American Politics* (Grand Rapids, Mich.: Wm. B. Eerdmans Publishing, 1972).

DIONNE, E. J., JR., and MORIN, RICHARD. "Postwar Glow Has Faded, Poll Finds," *The Washington Post* (April 12, 1991), pp. A-1, A-4.

DOBSON, DOUGLAS, and ST. ANGELO, DOUGLAS. "Party Identification and the Floating Vote: Some Dynamics," *American Political Science Review* 69 (June 1975), pp. 481–490.

Dollar Politics, vol. 2 (Washington, D.C.: Congressional Quarterly Press, 1974).

DOWNS, ANTHONY. *An Economic Theory of Democracy* (New York: Harper & Row, 1957).

DREW, ELIZABETH. "A Reporter in Washington, D.C.: Winter Notes—I," *New Yorker,* May 17, 1976a, pp. 126–156.

———. "Winter Notes—II," *New Yorker,* May 31, 1976b, pp. 54–99.

DREYER, EDWARD C. "Media Use and Electoral Choices: Some Political Consequences of Information Exposure," *Public Opinion Quarterly* 35 (Winter 1971–1972), pp. 544–553.

———. "Change and Stability in Party Identification," *Journal of Politics* 35 (August 1973), pp. 712–722.

DUNN, DELMER D. *Financing Presidential Campaigns* (Washington, D.C.: Brookings Institution, 1972)

DUTTON, FREDERICK G. *Changing Sources of Power* (New York: McGraw-Hill, 1971).

ERIKSON, ROBERT S. "The Influence of Newspaper Endorsements in Presidential Elections: The Case of 1964," *American Journal of Political Science* 20 (May 1976), pp. 207–233.

ERIKSON, ROBERT S., and TEDIN, KENT L. "The 1928–1936 Partisan Realignment: The Case for the Conversion Hypothesis," *American Political Science Review* 75 (December 1981), pp. 951–962.

ENTMAN, ROBERT M. "How the Media Affect What People Think: An Information Processing Approach," *Journal of Politics* 51 (May 1989), pp. 347–370.

EVANS, KATHERINE. "Candidates and Their Gurus Criticize Coverage," *Washington Journalism Review* 2 (September 1980), pp. 28–31.

EVANS, ROWLAND, and NOVAK, ROBERT. "Inside Report," *Newark Sunday News,* October 27, 1968, p. C-2.

EVARTS, DRU, and STEMPEL III, GUIDO H. "Coverage of the 1972 Campaign by TV, News Magazines, and Major Newspapers," *Journalism Quarterly* 51 (Winter 1974), pp. 645–648, 676.

FARAH, BARBARA. "Convention Delegates: Party Reform and the Representativeness of Party Elites, 1972–1980," paper presented at the annual meeting of the American Political Science Association, New York City, September 3–6, 1981.

FEE, JOAN L., and GREELEY, ANDREW M. "Religion, Ethnicity, and Class in American Electoral Behavior," paper presented at the annual meeting of the Midwest Political Science Association, Chicago, May 1–3, 1975.

FELDMAN, STANLEY. "Structure and Consistency in Public Opinion: the Role of Core Beliefs and Values," *American Journal of Political Science,* 32(2), May 1988.

FIELD, JOHN OSGOOD, and ANDERSON, RONALD E. "Ideology in the Public's Conceptualization of the 1964 Election," in *Political Opinion and Behavior,* 2nd ed., edited by Edward C. Dreyer and Walter A. Rosenbaum (Belmont, Calif.: Wadsworth, 1970), pp. 329–346.

FIORINA, MORRIS P. "An Outline for a Model of Party Choice," *American Journal of Political Science* 21 (August, 1977), pp. 601–625.

———. *Retrospective Voting in American National Elections* (New Haven and London: Yale University Press, 1981).

FLANIGAN, WILLIAM. *Political Behavior of the American Electorate* (Boston: Allyn & Bacon, 1972).

FLEISHMAN, JOHN A. "Trends in Self-Identified Ideology from 1972 to 1982: No Support for the Salience Hypothesis," *American Journal of Political Science,* 30 (3), August 1986.

FRANKLIN, CHARLES H. "Issue Preferences, Socialization, and the Evolution of Party Identification," *American Journal of Political Science* 28 (August 1984), pp. 459–478.

FRANKOVIC, KATHLEEN. "Sex and Politics—New Alignments, Old Issues," *PS 3* (Summer 1982), pp. 439–448.

FROMAN, LEWIS A., JR. "A Realistic Approach to Campaign Strategies and Tactics," in *The Electoral Process,* edited by M. Kent Jennings and Harmon Ziegler (Englewood Cliffs, N.J.: Prentice-Hall, 1966), pp. 1–20.

FUNKHOUSER, G. RAY. "The Issues of the Sixties: An Exploratory Study in the Dynamics of Public Opinion," *Public Opinion Quarterly* 37 (Spring 1973), pp. 62–75.

GEER, JOHN G. "Rules Governing Presidential Primaries," *Journal of Politics* 48 (November 1986), pp. 1006–1025.

———. "Assessing the Representativeness of Electorates in Presidential Primaries," *American Journal of Political Science,* 32(4), November 1988.

GERMOND, JACK W., and WITCOVER, JULES. "Tax-Hike Politics and Class Warfare," *National Journal,* July 7, 1990, p. 1679.

GILENS, MARTIN. "Gender and Support for Reagan. A Comprehensive Model of Presidential Approval," *American Journal of Political Science* 32 (February 1988), pp. 19–49.

GLENN, NORVAL D., and HEFNER, TED. "Further Evidence on Aging and Party Identification," *Public Opinion Quarterly* 36 (Spring 1972), pp. 31—47.

GOLDBERG, ARTHUR. "Discerning a Causal Pattern among Data on Voting Behavior," *American Political Science Review* 60 (December 1966), pp. 913–922.

GRABER, DORIS A. "Press Coverage Patterns of Campaign News: The 1968 Presidential Race," *Journalism Quarterly* 48 (Autumn 1971), pp. 502–512.

———. "Press Coverage and Voter Reaction in the 1968 Presidential Election," *Political Science Quarterly* 89 (March 1974), pp. 68–100.

———. "Press and TV as Opinion Resources in Presidential Campaigns," *Public Opinion Quarterly* 40 (Fall 1976), pp. 285–303.

———. "Framing Election News Broadcasts: News Context and Its Impact on the 1984 Presidential Election," *Social Science Quarterly,* 68(3), September 1987.

GRABER, DORIS A., and KIM, YOUNG YUN. "Media Coverage and Voter Learning During the Presidential Primary Season," paper presented at the annual meeting of the Midwest Political Science Association, Chicago, April 21–23, 1977.

GREELEY, ANDREW M. *Building Coalitions* (New York: Franklin Watts, 1974).

———. "Catholics and Coalition: Where Should They Go?" In *Emerging Coalitions in American Politics,* edited by Seymour Martin Lipset (San Francisco: Institute for Contemporary Studies, 1978), pp. 271–295.

GREENSTEIN, FRED I. *Children and Politics* (New Haven: Yale University Press, 1965).

HADLEY, ARTHUR T. *The Empty Polling Booth* (Englewood Cliffs, N.J.: Prentice-Hall, 1978).

HARNEY, RUSSELL F., and STONE, VERNON A. "Television and Newspaper Front Page Coverage of a Major News Story," *Journal of Broadcasting* 13 (Spring 1969), pp. 181–188.

HARRIS, LOUIS. "Why the Odds Are against a Governor's Becoming President," *Public Opinion Quarterly* (Fall 1959), pp. 361–370.

HARTWIG, FREDERICK, JENKINS, WILLIAM R., and TEMCHIN, EARL M. "Variability in Electoral Behavior: The 1960, 1968, and 1976 Elections," *American Journal of Political Science* 24 (August 1980), pp. 553–558.

HERSHEY, MARJORIE RANDON. "The Campaign and the Media," in *The Election of 1988*, edited by Gerald M. Pomper (Chatham, New Jersey: Chatham House Publishers, Inc., 1989).

HESS, ROBERT D., and TORNEY, JUDITH V. *The Development of Political Attitudes in Children* (Chicago: Aldine-Atherton, 1967).

HIBBS, JR., DOUGLAS A. "President Reagan's Mandate from the 1980 Elections: A Shift to the Right?" *American Politics Quarterly* 10 (October 1982), pp. 387–420.

HOFSTETTER, C. RICHARD. *Bias in the News: A Study of Network Coverage of the 1972 Election Campaign* (Columbus: Ohio State University Press, 1976).

HOFSTETTER, C. RICHARD, ZUKIN, CLIFF, and BUSS, TERRY F. "Political Imagery in an Age of Television: The 1972 Campaign," paper presented at the annual meeting of the American Political Science Association, Chicago, September 2–5, 1976.

HOWELL, SUSAN E. "The Behavioral Component of Changing Partisanship," *American Politics Quarterly* 8 (April 1980), pp. 279–302.

———. "Short Term Forces and Changing Partisanship," *Political Behavior* 3 (1981), pp. 163–180.

HURLEY, PATRICIA A. "Partisan Representation and the Failure of Realignment in the 1980s," *American Journal of Political Science* 33 (February 1989), pp. 240–261.

IYENGAR, SHANTO. "Television News and Citizens' Explanations of National Affairs," *American Political Sciences Review,* 81(3), September 1987.

———. "How Citizens Think about National Issues: A Matter of Responsibility," *American Journal of Political Science,* 33(4), November 1989.

JACKSON III, JOHN S., BROWN, JESSE C., and BROWN, BARBARA L. "Recruitment, Representation, and Political Values: The 1976 Democratic National Convention Delegates," *American Politics Quarterly* 6 (April 1978), pp. 187–212.

JACOBSON, GARY C. "The Impact of Broadcast Campaigning on Electoral Outcomes," paper presented at the annual meeting of the American Political Science Association, Chicago, August 29–September 2, 1974.

JACOBY, WILLIAM G. "Levels of Conceptualization and Reliance on the Liberal–Conservative Continuum," *Journal of Politics* 48 (May 1986), pp. 423–432.

———. "Ideological Identification and Issue Attitudes," University of South Carolina, Autumn 1989.

JENNINGS, M. KENT, and LANGTON, KENNETH P. "Mothers Versus Fathers: The Formation of Political Orientations Among Young Americans," *Journal of Politics* 31 (May 1969), pp. 329–358.

JENNINGS, M. KENT, and MARKUS, GREGORY B. "Partisan Orientations Over the Long Haul: Results from the Three-Wave Political Socialization Panel Study," *American Political Science Review* 75 (December 1984), pp. 1000–1018.

JENNINGS, M. KENT, and NIEMI, RICHARD G. "The Transmission of Political Values from Parent to Child," *American Political Science Review* 62 (March 1968), pp. 169–184.

———. *The Political Character of Adolescence: The Influence of Families and Schools* (Princeton, N.J.: Princeton University Press, 1974).

————. "Continuity and Change in Political Orientations: A Longitudinal Study of Two Generations," *American Political Science Review* 69 (December 1975), pp. 1316–1335.

JOHNSON, LOCH K., and HAHN, HARLAN. "Delegate Turnover at National Party Conventions, 1944–1968," in *Perspectives on Presidential Selection*, edited by Donald R. Matthews (Washington, D.C.: Brookings Institution, 1973), pp. 143–171.

JUST, MARION R., NEUMAN, W. RUSSELL, and CRIGLER, ANN N. "Who Learns What from the News: Attentive Public Versus a Cognitive Elite," paper presented at the annual meeting of the American Political Science Association, Atlanta, Georgia, 1989.

KAGAY, MICHAEL, and CALDEIRA, GREG. "Public Policy Issues and the American Voter, 1952–1972," unpublished paper.

KATZ, ELIHU, and FELDMAN, JACOB J. "The Debates in the Light of Research: A Survey of Surveys," in *The Great Debates*, edited by Sidney Kraus (Bloomington: Indiana University Press, 1962), pp. 173–223.

KATZ, RICHARD S. "The Dimensionality of Party Identification," *Comparative Politics* 11 (1979), pp. 147–163.

KEECH, WILLIAM R., and MATTHEWS, DONALD R. *The Party's Choice* (Washington, D.C.: Brookings Institution, 1977).

KEETER, SCOTT. "The Illusion of Intimacy: Television and the Role of Candidate Personal Qualities in Voter Choice," *Public Opinion Quarterly* 51(3), Fall 1987, pp. 344–358.

KEETER, SCOTT and ZUKIN, CLIFF. *Uninformed Choice: The Failure of the New Presidential Nominating System* (New York: Praeger, 1983).

KEITH, BRUCE E., MAGLEBY, DAVID B., NELSON, CANDICE J., ORR, ELIZABETH, WESTLYE, MARK, and WOLFINGER, RAYMOND E. "The Myth of the Independent Voter," paper presented at the annual meeting of the American Political Science Association, Washington, D.C., September 4–7, 1977.

KELLERMANN, DONALD S., KOHUT, ANDREW, and BOWMAN, CAROL. "The Age of Indifference: A Study of Young Americans and How They View the News," *Times Mirror Center for The People & The Press*, June 28, 1990.

KELLEY, STANLEY, JR. "The Presidential Campaign," in *The National Election of 1964*, edited by Milton C. Cummings, Jr. (Washington, D.C.: Brookings Institution, 1966), pp. 42–81.

KESSEL, JOHN H. *The Goldwater Coalition: Republican Strategies in 1964* (Indianapolis: Bobbs-Merrill, 1968).

————. "Strategy for November," in *Choosing the President*, edited by James David Barber (Englewood Cliffs, N.J.: Prentice-Hall, 1974), pp. 95–119.

KEY, JR., V. 0. "A Theory of Critical Elections," *Journal of Politics* 17 (February 1955), pp. 3–18.

————. *The Responsible Electorate* (New York: Vintage Books, 1966).

KIM, JAE-ON, PETROCIK, JOHN R., and ENOKSON, STEPHEN N. "Voter Turnout Among the American States: Systemic and Individual Components," *American Political Science Review* 69 (March 1975), pp. 107–123.

KINDER, DONALD R., and ABELSON, ROBERT P. "Appraising Presidential Candidates: Personality and Affect in the 1980 Campaign," paper presented at the annual meeting of the American Political Science Association, New York City, September 3–6, 1981.

KIRKPATRICK, JEANE J. *The New Presidential Elite: Men and Women in National Politics* (New York: Russell Sage Foundation, 1976).

KIRKPATRICK, SAMUEL A., and JONES, MELVIN E. "Issue Publics and the Electoral System: The Role of Issues in Electoral Change," in *Public Opinion and Political Attitudes*, edited by Allen R. Wilcox (New York: Wiley, 1974), pp. 537–555.

KIRKPATRICK, SAMUEL A., LYONS, WILLIAM, and FITZGERALD, MICHAEL R. "Candidate and Party Images in the American Electorate: A Longitudinal Analysis," paper presented at the annual meeting of the Southwestern Political Science Association, Dallas, March 28–30, 1974.

KLAPPER, JOSEPH. *The Effects of Mass Communication* (New York: Free Press, 1960).

KLINGEMANN, HANS. "Dimensions of Political Belief Systems: 'Levels of Conceptualization' as a Variable. Some Results for USA and FRG 1968/69," preliminary handout prepared for the E.C.P.R. Workshop on Political Behavior, Dissatisfaction, and Protest, University of Mannheim (Germany), April 12–18, 1973.

KNIGHT, KATHLEEN, and LEWIS, CAROLYN. "The Growth of Conservatism in the American Mass Public: Measurement and Meaning," paper presented at the annual convention of the Southwest Social Science Association, San Antonio, Texas, March 19–22, 1986.

KRAUS, SIDNEY, ed. *The Great Debates, 1976: Ford vs. Carter* (Bloomington, Ind.: Indiana University Press, 1979).

KROSNICK, JON A., and KINDER, DONALD R. "Altering the Foundation of Support for the President Through Priming," *American Political Science Review,* 84(2), June 1990, pp. 497–512.

KROSNICK, JON A., and WEISBERG, HERBERT F. "Liberal/Conservative Ideological Structures in the Mass Public: A Study of Attitudes Toward Politicians and Social Groups," presented at the annual meeting of the American Political Science Association, Washington, D.C., August 1988.

KWEIT, MARY GRISPZ. "Ideological Congruence of Party Switchers and Nonswitchers: The Case of Party Activists," *American Journal of Political Science* 30 (February 1986), pp. 184–196.

LADD, JR., EVERETT CARLL. "The New Lines are Drawn: Class and Ideology in America," *Public Opinion* (July–August 1978a), pp. 48–53.

———. "The Lines Are Drawn: Class and Ideology in America, Part II," *Public Opinion* (September–October 1978b), pp. 14–20.

———. "The Shifting Party Coalitions—1932–1976," in *Emerging Coalitions in American Politics*, edited by Seymour Martin Lipset (San Francisco: Institute for Contemporary Studies, 1978c), pp. 81–102.

———. *Where Have All the Voters Gone? The Fracturing of America's Political Parties* (New York: Norton, 1978d).

———. "The Brittle Mandate: Electoral Dealignment and the 1980 Presidential Election," *Political Science Quarterly* 96 (Spring 1981), pp. 1–25.

LADD, JR., EVERETT CARLL and HADLEY, CHARLES D. "Party Definition and Party Differentiation," *Public Opinion Quarterly* 37 (Spring 1973–1974), pp. 21–34.

LADD, JR., EVERETT CARLL, with HADLEY, CHARLES D. *Transformations of the American Party System*, 2nd ed. (New York: Norton, 1978).

LANE, ROBERT E. *Political Life* (New York: Free Press, 1959).

———. *Political Ideology* (New York: Free Press, 1962).

————. "Alienation, Protest, and Rootless Politics in the Seventies," in *The Political Image Merchants*, edited by Ray Hiebert, Robert Jones, John Lorenz, and Ernest Lotito (Washington, D.C.: Acropolis Books, 1971), pp. 273–300.

LANG, GLADYS ENGEL, and LANG, KURT. "Immediate and Delayed Responses to a Carter–Ford Debate: Assessing Public Opinion," *Public Opinion Quarterly* 42 (Fall 1978), pp. 322–341.

LANG, KURT, and LANG, GLADYS ENGEL. *Politics and Television* (Chicago: Quadrangle Books, 1968).

LANGTON, KENNETH P., and JENNINGS, M. KENT. "Political Socialization and the High School Civics Curriculum in the United States," *American Political Science Review* 62 (September 1968), pp. 852–867.

LAVINE, HAROLD. *Smoke-Filled Rooms* (Englewood Cliffs, N.J.: Prentice-Hall, 1970).

LAZARSFELD, PAUL, BERELSON, BERNARD, and GAUDET, HAZEL. *The People's Choice* (New York: Columbia University Press, 1968).

LENGLE, JAMES I., and SHAFER, BYRON. "Primary Rules, Political Power, and Social Change," *American Political Science Review* 70 (March 1976), pp. 25–40.

LICHTER, S. ROBERT, AMUNDSON, DANIEL, and NOYES, RICHARD E. "Media Coverage," *Public Opinion* (January/February 1989), pp. 18, 19, 52.

LIPSET, SEYMOUR MARTIN, "Party Coalitions and the 1980 Election," in *Party Coalitions in the 1980s*, edited by Seymour Martin Lipset (San Francisco: Institute for Contemporary Studies, 1981).

LONGLEY, LAWRENCE D., and BRAUN, ALAN G. *The Politics of Electoral College Reform* (New Haven: Yale University Press, 1972).

LOWRY, DENNIS T. "Gresham's Law and Network TV News Selection," *Journal of Broadcasting* 15 (Fall 1971), pp. 397–407.

LUCY, WILLIAM H. "Polls, Primaries, and Presidential Nominations," *Journal of Politics* 35 (November 1973), pp. 830–848.

LUSKIN, ROBERT C., MCIVER, JOHN P., and CARMINES, EDWARD G. "Issues and the Transmission of Partisanship," *American Journal of Political Science*, 33(2), May 1989, pp. 440–458.

MACALUSO, THEODORE F. "The Responsiveness of Party Identification to Current Political Evaluations," mimeograph.

MacDONALD, STUART ELAINE, and RABINOWITZ, GEORGE. "The Dynamics of Structural Realignment," *American Science Review* 81 (September 1987), pp. 775–796.

MacKUEN, MICHAEL B. "The Press as Shepherd: A Fifteen-Year View," paper presented at the annual meeting of the Midwest Political Science Association, Chicago, April 19–21, 1979.

————. "Social Communication and the Mass Policy Agenda," in *More than News*, by Michael B. MacKuen and Steven L. Coombs (Beverly Hills, Calif.: Sage Publications, 1981).

MacKUEN, MICHAEL B., ERIKSON, ROBERT S., and STIMSON, JAMES A. "Micropartisanship," *American Political Science Review*, 83(4), December 1989, pp. 1125–1142.

MacRAE, DUNCAN, JR., and MELDRUM JAMES A. "Critical Elections in Illinois: 1888–1958," *American Political Science Review* 54 (September 1960), pp. 669–683.

MAGGIOTTO, MICHAEL A., and PIERESON, JAMES E. "Party Identification and Electoral Choice: The Hostility Hypothesis," *American Journal of Political Science* 21 (November 1977), pp. 745–767.

MAISEL, LOUIS, and LIEBERMAN, GERALD J. "The Impact of Electoral Rules on Primary Elections: The Democratic Presidential Primaries of 1976," in *The Impact of the Electoral Process*, edited by Louis Maisel and Joseph Cooper (Beverly Hills, Calif.: Sage Publications, 1977), pp. 39–80.

MARGOLIS, MICHAEL. "From Confusion to Confusion: Issues and the American Voter (1956–1972)," *American Political Science Review* 71 (March 1977), pp. 31–43.

MARKUS, GREGORY B., and CONVERSE, PHILIP E. "A Dynamic Simultaneous Equation Model of Electoral Choice," *American Political Science Review* 73 (December 1979), pp. 1055–1070.

MATTHEWS, DONALD R. "Presidential Nominations: Processes and Outcomes," in *Choosing the President*, edited by James David Barber (Englewood Cliffs, N.J.: Prentice-Hall, 1974), pp. 35–70.

MAY, ERNEST R., and FRASER, JANET, eds. *Campaign '72: The Managers Speak* (Cambridge, Mass.: Harvard University Press, 1973).

MAZMANIAN, DANIEL A. *Third Parties in Presidential Elections* (Washington, D.C.: Brookings Institution, 1974).

McCARTNEY, JAMES. "The Triumph of Junk News," *Columbia Journalism Review* 15 (January–February 1977), pp. 17–21.

McLEOD, JACK M., GLYNN CARROLL J., and McDONALD, DANIEL G. "Issues and Images: The Influence of Media Reliance in Voting Decisions," *Communication Research* 10 (January 1983), pp. 37–58.

McCLUHAN, MARSHALL. *Understanding Media* (New York: McGraw-Hill, 1964).

McCLURE, ROBERT D., and PATTERSON, THOMAS E. "Print vs. Network News," *Journal of Communication* 26 (Spring 1976), pp. 18–22.

McCOMBS, MAXWELL E., and SHAW, DONALD R. "The Agenda-Setting Function of the Mass Media," *Public Opinion Quarterly* 36 (Summer 1972), pp. 176–187.

McGINNISS, JOE. *The Selling of the President 1968* (New York: Trident Press, 1969).

McGRATH, JOSEPH E., and MCGRATH, MARION F. "Effects of Partisanship on Perceptions of Political Figures," *Public Opinion Quarterly* 26 (Summer 1962), pp. 236–248.

MENDELSOHN, HAROLD, and CRESPI, IRVING. *Polls, Television, and the New Politics* (Scranton, Pa.: Chandler Publishing, 1970).

MICHENER, JAMES A. *Report of the County Chairman* (New York: Random House, 1961).

MILBRATH, LESTER W. *Political Participation* (Chicago: Rand McNally, 1965).

MILLER, ARTHUR H. "Political Issues and Trust in Government: 1964–1970," *American Political Science Review* 68 (September 1974), pp. 951–972.

———. "Partisanship Reinstated? A Comparison of the 1972 and 1976 U.S. Presidential Elections," *British Journal of Political Science* 8 (April 1978), pp. 129–152.

———. "Normal Vote Analysis: Sensitivity to Change over Time," *American Journal of Political Science* 23 (May 1979), pp. 406–425.

MILLER, ARTHUR H., GOLDENBERG, EDIE N., and ERBRING, LUTZ. "Type-Set Politics: Impact of Newspapers on Public Confidence," *American Political Science Review* 73 (March 1979), pp. 67–84.

MILLER, ARTHUR H., HILDRETH, ANNE M., and SIMMONS, GRACE L. "The Political Implications of Gender Group Consciousness," paper presented at the annual convention of the Midwest Political Science Association, Chicago, April 9–12, 1986.

MILLER, ARTHUR H., and MALANCHUK, OKSANA. "The Gender Gap in the 1982 Elections," paper presented at the annual conference of the American Association for Public Opinion Research, Buck Hill Falls, Pennsylvania, May 19–22, 1983.

MILLER, ARTHUR H., and MILLER, WARREN E. "Partisanship and Performance: 'Rational' Choice in the 1976 Presidential Election," paper presented at the annual meeting of the American Political Science Association, Washington, D.C., September 1–4, 1977.

MILLER, ARTHUR H., MILLER, WARREN E., RAINE, ALDEN S., and BROWN, THAD A. "A Majority Party in Disarray: Policy Polarization in the 1972 Election," paper presented at the annual meeting of the American Political Science Association, New Orleans, September 4–8, 1973.

———. "A Majority Party in Disarray: Policy Polarization in the 1972 Election," *American Political Science Review* 70 (September 1976), pp. 753–778.

MILLER, ARTHUR H. and WATTENBERG, MARTIN P. "Throwing the Rascals Out: Retrospective Political Thinking in the American Public 1952–1980," paper presented at the annual meeting of the Midwest Political Science Association, Chicago, April 21–23, 1983.

MILLER, ARTHUR H., WATTENBERG, MARTIN P., and MALANCHUK, OKSANA. "Schematic Assessments of Presidential Candidates," *American Political Science Review* 80 (June 1986), pp. 521–540.

MILLER, WARREN E., and SHANKS, J. MERRILL. "Policy Directions and Presidential Leadership: Alternative Interpretation of the 1980 Presidential Election," *British Journal of Political Science* 12 (1982), pp. 299–356.

MITOFSKY, WARREN J. "1976 Presidential Debate Effects: A Hit or a Myth," paper presented at the annual meeting of the American Political Science Association, Washington, D.C., September 1–4, 1977.

MOORE, JONATHAN, ed. *The Campaign for President: 1980 in Retrospect* (Cambridge, Mass.: Ballinger, 1981).

MORIN, RICHARD. "The Public May Not Know Much, But It Knows What It Doesn't Like," *Washington Post National Weekly Edition*, January 23–29, 1989, p. 37.

———. "Margaret Thatcher? Wasn't She Gary Hart's Girlfriend?" *Washington Post National Weekly Edition*, December 18–24, 1989, p. 38.

NATCHEZ, PETER B. "Issues and Voters in the 1972 Election," in *University Programs Modular Studies* (Morristown, N.J.: General Learning Press, 1974).

NATCHEZ, PETER B., and BUPP, IRVIN C. "Candidates, Issues, and Voters," in *Political Opinion and Behavior*, 2nd ed., edited by Edward C. Dreyer and Walter A. Rosenbaum (Belmont, Calif.: Wadsworth, 1970), pp. 427–450.

NESBIT, DOROTHY DAVIDSON. "Changing Partisanship among Southern Party Activists," *The Journal of Politics* 50 (May 1988), pp. 322–334.

NEUMAN, W. RUSSELL, JUST, MARION, and CRIGLER, ANN. "Knowledge, Opinion and the News: The Calculus of Political Learning," paper presented at the annual meeting of the American Political Science Association, Washington, D.C., 1988.

NIE, NORMAN H., and ANDERSEN, KRISTI. "Mass Belief Systems Revisited: Political Change and Attitude Structure," *Journal of Politics* 36 (August 1974), pp. 540–587.

NIE, NORMAN H., and RABJOHN, JAMES N. "Revisiting Mass Belief Systems Revisited: Or, Doing Research Is Like Watching a Tennis Match," *American Journal of Political Science* 23 (February 1979), pp. 139–175.

NIE, NORMAN H., VERBA, SIDNEY, and PETROCIK, JOHN R. *The Changing American Voter* (Cambridge, Mass.: Harvard University Press, 1976).

NIEMI, RICHARD G., WRIGHT, STEPHEN, and POWELL, LINDA W. "Multiple Party Identifiers and the Measurement of Party Identification," *The Journal of Politics*, 49(4), November 1987, pp. 1093–1103.

NIMMO, DAN. *The Political Persuaders* (Englewood Cliffs, N.J.: Prentice-Hall, 1970).

NIMMO, DAN, and COMBS, JAMES E. *Mediated Political Realities* (New York: Longman, 1983).

NORPOTH, HELMUT. "Under Way and Here To Stay: Party Realignment in the 1980s?" *Public Opinion Quarterly* 51 (Fall 1987), pp. 376–391.

NORPOTH, HELMUT, and KAGEY, MICHAEL R. "Another Eight Years of Republican Rule and Still No Partisan Realignment?" paper delivered at the annual meeting of the American Political Science Association, Atlanta, Georgia, August 31–September 3, 1989.

NORRANDER, BARBARA. "Ideological Representativeness of Presidential Primary Voters," *American Journal of Political Science*, 33(3), August 1989a, pp. 570–587.

———. "Turnout in Super Tuesday Primaries: The Composition of the Electorate," delivered at the annual meeting of the American Political Science Association, Atlanta, Georgia, August 31–September 3, 1989b.

O'KEEFE, GARRETT J. "Political Malaise and Reliance on Media," *Journalism Quarterly* (Spring 1980), pp. 122–128.

O'KEEFE, M. TIMOTHY, and SHEINKOPF, KENNETH G. "The Voter Decides: Candidate Image or Campaign Issue?" *Journal of Broadcasting* 18 (Fall 1974), pp. 403–411.

PAGE, BENJAMIN I. "Presidential Campaigning, Party Cleavages, and Responsible Parties," unpublished paper.

PAGE, BENJAMIN I., and BRODY, RICHARD A. "Policy Voting and the Electoral Process: The Vietnam War Issue," *American Political Science Review* 66 (September 1972), pp. 979–995.

PAGE, BENJAMIN I., and JONES, CALVIN C. "Reciprocal Effects of Policy Preferences, Party Loyalties, and the Vote," *American Political Science Review* 73 (December 1979), pp. 1071–1089.

PAGE, BENJAMIN I., and SHAPIRO, ROBERT Y. "Democracy, Information, and the Rational Public," paper delivered at the annual meeting of the American Political Science Association, Washington, D.C., 1988.

PALETZ, DAVID L., AND ELSON, MARTHA. "Television Coverage of Presidential Conventions: Now You See It, Now You Don't," *Political Science Quarterly* 91 (Spring 1976), pp. 109–131.

PARRIS, JUDITH H. *The Convention Problem* (Washington, D.C.: Brookings Institution, 1972).

PATTERSON, THOMAS E. "Press Coverage and Candidate Success in Presidential Primaries: The 1976 Democratic Race," paper presented at the annual meeting of the American Political Science Association, Washington, D.C., September 1–4, 1977a.

———. "The 1976 Horserace," *Wilson Quarterly* 1 (Spring 1977), pp. 73–77.

———. *The Mass Media Election* (New York: Praeger, 1980).

———. "The Press and Its Missed Assignment," in *The Election of 1988*, edited by Michael Nelson (Washington, D.C.: Congressional Quarterly Press, 1989), pp. 93–109.

PATTERSON, THOMAS E. and DAVIS, RICHARD. "The Media Campaign: Struggle for the Agenda," in *The Elections of 1984*, edited by Michael Nelson (Washington, D.C.: Congressional Quarterly Press, 1985), pp. 111–127.

PATTERSON, THOMAS E., and MCCLURE, ROBERT D. *The Unseeing Eye: The Myth of Television Power in National Elections* (New York: G. P. Putnam's Sons, 1976).

PEABODY, ROBERT L., and LUBALIN, EVE. "The Making of Presidential Candidates," in *The Future of the American Presidency*, edited by Charles W. Dunn (Morristown, N.J.: General Learning Press, 1975), pp. 26–65.

PERRY, JAMES M. *Us and Them: How the Press Covered the 1972 Election* (New York: Clarkson N. Potter, 1973).

PETERS, CHARLES, "The Ignorant Press," *Washington Monthly* 8 (May 1976), pp. 55–57.

PETERSON, BILL and SAWYER, KATHY. " 'Expectations' the Big Foe," *The Washington Post*, February 21, 1984, p. A-1.

PETROCIK, JOHN. "An Analysis of Intransitivities in the Index of Party Identification," *Political Methodology* 1 (Summer 1974), pp. 31–47.

PETROCIK, JOHN R., "An Expected Party Vote: New Data for an Old Concept," *American Journal of Political Science* 33 (February 1989), pp. 44–66.

PHILLIPS, KEVIN B. *The Emerging Republican Majority* (Garden City, N.Y.: Doubleday, 1969).

PHILLIPS, KEVIN. *The Politics of Rich and Poor: Wealth and the American Electorate in the Reagan Aftermath.* (New York: Random House, 1990).

PIERCE, JOHN C., and HAGNER, PAUL R. "Conceptualization and Party Identification: 1956-1976," *American Journal of Political Science* 26 (May 1982), pp. 377–387.

PIVEN, FRANCES FOX, and CLOWARD, RICHARD A. *Why Americans Don't Vote* (New York: Pantheon, 1988).

POLSBY, NELSON W. *Consequences of Party Reform* (New York: Oxford University Press, 1983).

POMPER, GERALD M. "Classification of Presidential Elections," *Journal of Politics* 29 (August 1967), pp. 535–566.

———. *Elections in America* (New York: Dodd, Mead, 1968).

———. "From Confusion to Clarity: Issues and American Voters, 1956–1968," *American Political Science Review* 66 (June 1972), pp. 415–428.

———. *The Election of 1980* (Chatham, N.J.: Chatham House, 1981).

POOL, ITHIEL DE SOLA, ABELSON, ROBERT P., and POPKIN, SAMUEL. *Candidates, Issues, and Strategies* (Cambridge, Mass.: MIT Press, 1965).

PORTER, KIRK H., and JOHNSON, DONALD BRUCE, eds. *National Party Platforms* (Urbana, Ill.: University of Illinois Press, 1970).

POWELL, JR., G. BINGHAM, "American Voter Turnout in Comparative Perspective," *American Political Science Review* 80 (March 1986), pp. 17–43.

RABINOWITZ, GEORGE, PROTHRO, JAMES W., and JACOBY, WILLIAM. "Salience as a Factor in the Impact of Issues on Candidate Evaluation," *Journal of Politics* 44 (February 1982), pp. 41–63.

RANNEY, AUSTIN. "Turnout and Representation in Presidential Primary Elections," *American Political Science Review* 66 (March 1972), pp. 21–37.

————. *Curbing the Mischiefs of Faction* (Berkeley: University of California Press, 1975).

————. *Participation in American Presidential Nominations, 1976* (Washington, D.C.: American Enterprise Institute for Public Policy Research, 1977).

RANNEY, AUSTIN, ed. *The American Election of 1980* (Washington, D.C.: American Enterprise Institute for Public Policy Research, 1981).

RAPOPORT, DANIEL, "Campaign Politics—The Telltale Signs of a Regulated Industry," *National Journal*, January 20, 1979, pp. 92–95.

REITER, HOWARD L. "The Trend toward Presidential Non-Voting," paper presented at the annual meeting of the American Political Science Association, Washington, D.C., September 1–4, 1977.

RePASS, DAVID E. "Issue Salience and Party Choice," *American Political Science Review* 65 (June 1971), pp. 389–400.

————. "Levels of Rationality among the American Electorate," paper presented at the annual meeting of the American Political Science Association, Chicago, August 29–September 2, 1974.

RESTON, JAMES. "Mr. Nixon and the Arts of Evasion," *New York Times*, October 2, 1968, p. 38.

RHODEBECK, LAURIE A. "The Partisanship of Young Voters in the 1980s," paper delivered at the annual meeting of the American Political Science Association, San Francisco, Calif., August 30–September 2, 1990.

ROBACK, THOMAS H. "Dimensions of Republican Amateurism: Stability and Change among National Convention Delegates: 1972–1976," paper presented at the annual meeting of the Southern Political Science Association, New Orleans, November 2–6 1977a.

————. "Recruitment and Incentive Patterns among Delegates to the 1972 and 1976 Republican National Conventions: The Individual as the Strategic Factor in the Theory of Party Organization," paper presented at the annual meeting of the American Political Science Association, Washington, D.C., September 1–4, 1977b.

ROBERTS, STEVEN V. "Delegates 'Feel Good' About Candidate," *New York Times*, August 24, 1984, p. A-10.

ROBINSON, JOHN P. "Public Reaction to Political Protest: Chicago 1968," *Public Opinion Quarterly* 34 (Spring 1970), pp. 1–9.

————. "Perceived Media Bias and the 1968 Vote: Can the Media Affect Behavior after All?" *Journalism Quarterly* (Summer 1972), pp. 239–246.

————. "The Press as King-maker: What Surveys from the Last Five Campaigns Show," *Journalism Quarterly* (Winter 1974), pp. 587–594.

ROBINSON, MICHAEL J. "Public Affairs Television and the Growth of Political Malaise: The Case of the Selling of the Pentagon," Ph.D. dissertation, University of Michigan, 1972.

————. "An Idea Whose Time Has Come—Again," *Congressional Record*, June 19, 1975, p. E3336.

————. "The TV Primaries," *Wilson Quarterly* 1 (Spring 1977), pp. 80–83.

————. "TV's Newest Program: The 'Presidential Nominations Game,' " *Public Opinion* 1 (May–June 1978), pp. 41–45.

ROBINSON, MICHAEL J., and SHEEHAN, MARGARET. "How the Networks Learned to Love the Issues," *Washington Journalism Review* 2 (December 1980), pp. 15–17.

————. *Over the Wire and on TV: CBS and UPI in Campaign '80* (New York: Russell Sage Foundation, 1983).

ROBINSON, MICHAEL J., and ZUKIN, CLIFF. "Television and the Wallace Vote," *Journal of Communication* 26 (Spring 1976), pp. 79–83.

ROPER, BURNS W. "Distorting the Voice of the People," *Columbia Journalism Review* 14 (November–December 1975), pp. 28–32.

————. "The Effects of the Debates on the Carter/Ford Election," paper presented at the annual meeting of the American Political Science Association, Washington, D.C., September 1–4, 1977.

ROSENSTONE, STEVEN J., and WOLFINGER, RAYMOND E. "The Effects of Registration Laws on Voter Turnout," *American Political Science Review* 72 (March 1978), pp. 22–45.

RUBIN, BERNARD. *Political Television* (Belmont, Calif.: Wadsworth, 1967).

RUTHENBERG, RANDALL. "Politics on TV: Too Fast, Too Loose?" *The New York Times*, July 15, 1990, section 4, pp. 1, 4.

RYAN, MICHAEL. "View from the Losing Side." *TV Guide*, June 12, 1976, p. 8.

SANDOZ, ELLIS, and CRABB, JR., CECIL V., eds. *A Tide of Discontent* (Washington, D.C.: Congressional Quarterly Press, 1981).

SAYRE, WALLACE S., and PARRIS, JUDITH H. *Voting for President* (Washington, D.C.: Brookings Institution, 1970).

SCAMMON, RICHARD M., and WATTENBERG, BEN J. *The Real Majority* (New York: Coward, McCann & Geoghegan, 1970).

SCHNEIDER, WILLIAM. "The November 4 Vote for President: What Did It Mean?" in *The American Elections of 1980*, edited by Austin Ranney (Washington, D.C.: American Enterprise Institute for Public Policy Research, 1981), pp. 212–262.

SCHRAM, MARTIN. *The Great American Video Game: Presidential Politics in the Television Age* (New York: Morrow, 1987).

SCHREIDER, E. M. "Where the Ducks Are: Southern Strategy Versus Fourth Party," *Public Opinion Quarterly* 35 (Summer 1971), pp. 155–167.

SCHULMAN, MARK A., and POMPER, GERALD M. "Variability in Electoral Behavior: Longitudinal Perspectives from Causal Modeling," *American Journal of Political Science* 19 (February 1975), pp. 1–18.

SCHUMPETER, JOSEPH A. *Capitalism, Socialism, and Democracy* (New York: Harper & Row, 1950).

SEARS, DAVID O. "The Debates in the Light of Research: An Overview of the Effects," paper presented at the annual meeting of the American Political Science Association, Washington, D.C., September 1–4, 1977.

SEARS, DAVID O., and CHAFFEE, STEVEN H. "Uses and Effects of the 1976 Debates: An Overview of Empirical Studies," in *The Great Debates, 1976: Ford vs. Carter*, edited by Sidney Kraus (Bloomington, Ind.: Indiana University Press, 1979), pp. 223–261.

SEARS, DAVID O., and FREEDMAN, JONATHAN L. "Selective Exposure to Information: A Critical Review," *Public Opinion Quarterly* 31 (Summer 1967), pp. 194–213.

SHABAD, GOLDIE, and ANDERSEN, KRISTI. "Candidate Evaluations by Men and Women," *Public Opinion Quarterly* 32 (Spring 1979), pp. 18–35.

SHAFER, BYRON, and LARSON, RICHARD. "Did TV Create the 'Social Issue'?" *Columbia Journalism Review* 11 (September–October 1972), pp. 10–17.

SHAFFER, STEPHEN D., "A Multivariate Explanation of Decreasing Turnout in Presidential Elections, 1960–1976," *American Journal of Political Science* 25 (February 1981), pp. 68–95.

SHANKS, J. MERRILL and MILLER, WARREN E. "Policy Direction and Performance Evaluation: Complementary Explanations of the Reagan Elections," paper presented at the annual meeting of the American Political Science Association, New Orleans, August 29–September 1, 1985.

SHEATSLEY, PAUL B. "White Attitudes toward the Negro," *Daedalus* 95 (Winter 1966), pp. 217–238.

SHIVELY, W. PHILLIPS. "Information Costs and the Partisan Life Cycle," paper presented at the annual meeting of the American Political Science Association, Washington, D.C., August 31–September 4, 1977.

———. "The Development of Party Identification among Adults: Exploration of a Functional Model," *American Political Science Review* 73 (December 1979), pp. 1039–54.

SIGEL, ROBERTA A. "Effects of Partisanship on the Perception of Political Candidates," *Public Opinion Quarterly* 28 (Fall 1964), pp. 483–496.

SORAUF, FRANK J. *Party Politics in America*, 2nd ed. (Boston: Little, Brown, 1972).

SOULE, JOHN W., and CLARK, JAMES W. "Amateurs and Professionals: A Study of Delegates to the 1968 Democratic National Convention," *American Political Science Review* 64 (September 1970), pp. 888–898.

SQUIRE, PEVERILL, WOLFINGER, RICHARD E., and GLASS, DAVID P. "Presidential Mobility and Voter Turnout," *American Political Science Review* 81 (March 1987), pp. 45–65.

STANLEY, HAROLD, BIANCO, WILLIAM T., and NIEMI, RICHARD G. "Partisanship and Group Support Over Time: A Multivariate Analysis," *American Political Science Review* 80 (1986), pp. 969–976.

STANLEY, HAROLD W., and NIEMI, RICHARD G. "Partisanship and Group Support, 1952–1988," paper presented at the annual meeting of the American Political Science Association, Atlanta, Georgia, August 31–September 3, 1989.

STEWART, JOHN G. *One Last Chance* (New York: Praeger, 1974).

STIMSON, JAMES A. "Belief Systems: Constraint, Complexity, and the 1972 Election," *American Journal of Political Science* 19 (August 1975), pp. 393–417.

STOKES, DONALD E. "Some Dynamic Elements of Contests for the Presidency," *American Political Science Review* 60 (March 1966), pp. 19–28.

STOKES, DONALD E., CAMPBELL, ANGUS, and MILLER, WARREN E. "Components of Electoral Decision," *American Political Science Review* 52 (June 1958), pp. 367–387.

STRONG, DONALD S. "Further Reflections on Southern Politics," *Journal of Politics* 33 (May 1971), pp. 239–256.

SULLIVAN, DENIS G., PRESSMAN, JEFFREY L., PAGE, BENJAMIN I., and LYONS, JOHN J. *The Politics of Representation* (New York: St. Martin's Press, 1974).

SULLIVAN, JOHN L., and FELDMAN, STANLEY. "The More Things Change, the More They Stay the Same: The Stability of Mass Belief Systems," *American Journal of Political Science* 23 (February 1979), pp. 176–186.

SULLIVAN, JOHN L., PIERESON, JAMES E., and MARCUS, GEORGE E. "Ideological Constraints in the Mass Public: A Methodological Critique and Some New Findings," *American Journal of Political Science* 22 (May 1978), pp. 234–249.

SUNDQUIST, JAMES L. *Dynamics of the Party System* (Washington, D.C.: Brookings Institution, 1973).

SUSSMAN, BARRY. "The Public Hasn't Been Moving to the Right, the Politicians Have," *Washington Post National Weekly Edition*, January 5, 1987, p. 37.

SWANSON, DAVID L. "And That's the Way It Was? Television Covers the 1976 Presidential Campaign," *Quarterly Journal of Speech* 63 (October 1977), pp. 239–248.

TAYLOR, PAUL. "Shaky Front-Runners," *The Washington Post*, December 8, 1986, p. A-1

———. " 'A National Morale Problem': Americans Feel Increasingly Estranged from Their Government," *The Washington Post National Weekly Edition*, May 14–20, 1990, p. 6.

THAYER, GEORGE. *Who Shakes the Money Tree?* (New York: Simon & Schuster, 1973).

THIMMESCH, NICK. "The Editorial Endorsement Game," *Public Opinion* 7 (October–November 1984), pp. 10–13.

TUCKER, HARVEY J., VEDLITZ, ARNOLD, and DE NARDO, JAMES. "Does Heavy Turnout Help Democrats in Presidential Elections?", *American Political Science Review* 80 (December 1986), pp. 1291–1304.

VALENTINE, DAVID C., and VAN WINGEN, JOHN R. "Partisanship, Independence, and the Partisan Identification Question," *American Politics Quarterly* 8 (1980), pp. 165–186.

VEBLEN, ERIC P. *The Manchester Union Leader in New Hampshire Elections* (Hanover, N.H.: University Press of New England, 1974).

VEBLEN, ERIC P., and CRAIG, ROBERT E. "William Loeb and the *Manchester Union Leader*: A 1976 View," paper presented at the annual meeting of the American Political Science Association, Chicago, September 2–5, 1976.

VERBA, SIDNEY, and NIE, NORMAN H. *Participation in America* (New York: Harper & Row, 1972).

Voters' Time, Report of the Twentieth Century Fund Commission on Campaign Costs in the Electronic Era (New York: Twentieth Century Fund, 1969).

WALSH, EDWARD. "President Hopes to Offset Likely California Loss," *The Washington Post*, June 9, 1976, p. A-1.

WAMSLEY, GARY L., and PRIDE, RICHARD A. "Television Network News: Rethinking the Iceberg Problem," *Western Political Quarterly* 25 (September 1972), pp. 434–450.

WATTENBERG, MARTIN P. *The Decline of American Political Parties, 1952–1984* (Cambridge, Mass.: Harvard University Press, 1986).

WEAVER, WARREN. "Television and Politics: A Mixed Effect," *New York Times*, July 18, 1976, p. E-1.

WEISBERG, HERBERT F. "A Multidimensional Conceptualization of Party Identification," *Political Behavior* 2 (1980), pp. 33–60.

WEISBERG, HERBERT F., and ALLSOP, DEE. "Sources of Short-Term Change in Party Identification," paper presented at the annual meeting of the Midwest Political Science Association, Chicago, 1990.

WEISBERG, HERBERT F., and RUSK, JERROLD G. "Dimensions of Candidate Evaluation," *American Political Science Review* 64 (December 1970), pp. 1167–1185.

WEISBORD, MARVIN R. *Campaigning for President* (New York: Washington Square Press, 1966).

WHITE, THEODORE H. *The Making of the President 1960* (New York: Pocket Books, 1961).
———. *The Making of the President 1964* (New York: Atheneum, 1965).
———. *The Making of the President 1968* (New York: Atheneum, 1969).
———. *The Making of the President 1972* (New York: Bantam Books, 1973).
WICKER, TOM. "Republicans Get in Line for 1988," *Columbus Citizen Journal*, October 28, 1985, p. 6.
Winner Take All, Report of the Twentieth Century Fund Task Force on Reform of the Presidential Election Process (New York: Holmes & Meier, 1978).
WIRLS, DANIEL. "Reinterpreting the Gender Gap," *Public Opinion Quarterly* 50 (Fall 1986), pp. 316–330.
WITCOVER, JULES. "William Loeb and the New Hampshire Primary: A Question of Ethics," *Columbia Journalism Review* 11 (May–June 1972), pp. 14–25.
———. "The Trials of a One-Candidate Campaign," *Columbia Journalism Review* 11 (January–February 1973), pp. 24–28.
———. *Marathon: The Pursuit of the Presidency, 1972–1976* (New York: New American Library, 1977).
WOLFINGER, RAYMOND E., and ROSENSTONE, STEVEN J. "Who Votes?", paper presented at the annual meeting of the American Political Science Association, Washington, D.C., September 1–4, 1977.
YUNKER, JOHN H., and LONGLEY, LAWRENCE D. "The Biases of the Electoral College: Who Is Really Advantaged?", in *Perspectives on Presidential Selection*, edited by Donald R. Matthews (Washington, D.C.: Brookings Institution, 1973), pp. 172–203.
———. "The Electoral College: Its Biases Newly Measured for the 1960s and 1970s," in *Sage Professional Papers in American Politics* 3, 04-031, edited by Randall B. Ripley (Beverly Hills, Calif.: Sage Publications, 1976).
ZUKIN, CLIFF. "A Triumph of Form over Content: Television and the 1976 National Nominating Convention," paper presented at the annual meeting of the Midwest Political Science Association, Chicago, April 19–21, 1979.

BIBLIOGRAPHY

CAMPAIGN FINANCE

ADAMANY, DAVID W., and AGREE, GEORGE E. *Political Money,* Baltimore: Johns Hopkins University Press, 1975.

ALEXANDER, HERBERT E. *Financing the 1960 Election.* Princeton, N.J.: Citizens' Research Foundation, 1962.

———. *Financing the 1964 Election.* Princeton, N.J.: Citizens' Research Foundation, 1966.

———. *Financing the 1968 Election.* Lexington, Mass.: D. C. Heath, 1971.

———. *Financing the 1980 Election.* Lexington, Mass.: D. C. Heath, 1983.

———. *Money in Politics.* Washington, D.C.: Public Affairs Press, 1972.

———. *Political Financing.* Minneapolis: Burgess Publishing, 1972.

———. *Political Finance: Reform and Reality.* Philadelphia: Annals of the American Academy of Political and Social Science, 1976.

———. *Financing Politics: Money, Elections, and Political Reform.* 3rd ed. Washington, D. C.: Congressional Quarterly, Inc., 1984.

ALEXANDER, HERBERT E., and HAGGERTY, BRIAN A. *Financing the 1984 Election.* Lexington, Mass.: D. C. Heath and Company, 1987.

Dollar Politics. vols. 1 and 2. Washington, D.C.: Congressional Quarterly, 1974.

DREW, ELIZABETH. *Politics and Money.* New York: Macmillan, 1983.

DUNN, DELMER D. *Financing Presidential Campaigns. Washington,* D.C.: Brookings Institution, 1972.

HEARD, ALEXANDER. *The Costs of Democracy.* Chapel Hill: University of North Carolina Press, 1960.

MALBIN, MICHAEL, ed. *Money and Politics in the United States.* Chatham, N.J.: Chatham House Publishers, 1984.

MUTCH, ROBERT E. *Campaigns, Congress, and Courts: The Making of Federal Campaign Finance Law.* New York: Praeger, 1988.

NICHOLS, DAVID. *Financing Elections.* New York: New Viewpoints, 1974.

SABATO, LARRY. *Paying for Elections: The Campaign Finance Thicket.* New York: Priority Press Publications, 1989.

SORAUF, FRANK J. *Money in American Elections.* Glenview, Ill.: Scott, Foresman, 1988.

THAYER, GEORGE. *Who Shakes the Money Tree?* New York: Simon & Schuster, 1973.

Voters' Time. Report of the Twentieth Century Fund Commission on Campaign Costs in the Electronic Era. New York: Twentieth Century Fund, 1969.

ELECTORAL COLLEGE

DIAMOND, MARTIN. *The Electoral College and The American Idea of Democracy.* Washington, D.C.: American Enterprise Institute for Public Policy Research, 1977.

LONGLEY, LAWRENCE D., and BRAUN, ALAN G. *The Politics of Electoral College Reform*. New Haven: Yale University Press, 1972.

PIERCE, NEAL R. *The People's President: The Electoral College in American History and the Direct-Vote Alternative*. New York: Simon & Schuster, 1968.

SAYRE, WALLACE S., and PARRIS, JUDITH H. *Voting for President*. Washington, D.C.: Brookings Institution, 1970.

Winner Take All. Report of the Twentieth Century Fund Task Force on Reform of the Presidential Election Process. New York: Homes & Meier, 1978.

HISTORY OF PRESIDENTIAL ELECTIONS

Presidential Elections Since 1789. Washington, D.C.: Congressional Quarterly, 1975.

ROSEBOOM, EUGENE H. *A History of Presidential Elections*. New York: Macmillan, 1964.

TUGWELL, REXFORD G. *How They Became President: Thirty-six Ways to the White House*. New York: Simon & Schuster, 1964.

MEDIA AND CAMPAIGNING

AGRANOFF, ROBERT. *The New Style in Election Campaigns*. Boston: Holbrook Press, 1972.

BARBER, JAMES DAVID, ed. *Race for the Presidency: The Media and the Nominating Process*. Englewood Cliffs, N.J.: Prentice-Hall, 1978.

BARBER, JAMES DAVID. *The Pulse of Politics: Electing Presidents in the Media Age*. New York: Norton, 1980.

BENNETT, W. LANCE. *News: The Politics of Illusion*. New York: Longman, 1983.

BISHOP, GEORGE, MEADOW, ROBERT G., AND JACKSON-BEECK, MARILYN, eds. *The Presidential Debates: Media, Electoral, and Policy Perspectives*. New York: Praeger, 1978.

BLOOM, MELVIN H. *Public Relations and Presidential Campaigns: A Crisis in Democracy*. New York: Thomas Y. Crowell, 1973.

BLUMLER, JAY G., and McQUAIL, DENIS. *Television in Politics: Its Uses and Influence*. Chicago: University of Chicago Press, 1969.

BROH, C. ANTHONY. *A Horse of a Different Color*. Washington, D.C.: Joint Center for Political Studies, 1987.

CHAFFEE, STEVE H. *Political Communication: Issues and Strategies for Research*. Beverly Hills, Calif.: Sage Publications, 1975.

CHESTER, EDWARD W. *Radio, Television, and American Politics*. New York: Sheed & Ward, 1969.

CROUSE, TIMOTHY. *The Boys on the Bus*. New York: Ballantine Books, 1973.

DEVLIN, L. PATRICK, ed. *Political Persuasion in Presidential Campaigns*. New Brunswick, New Jersey: Transaction Books, 1987.

DIAMOND, EDWIN. *The Tin Kazoo: Television, Politics, and the News*. Cambridge, Mass.: MIT Press, 1975.

EPSTEIN, EDWARD JAY. *News from Nowhere: Television and the News*. New York: Random House, 1973.

GRABER, DORIS A. *Processing the News*. 2nd ed. New York: Longman Inc., 1988.

HESS, STEPHEN. *The Presidential Campaign.* Washington, D.C.: Brookings Institution, 1974.

HIEBERT, RAY, JONES, ROBERT, LORENZ, JOHN, and LOTITO, ERNEST, eds. *The Political Image Merchants: Strategies in the New Politics.* Washington, D.C.: Acropolis Books, 1971.

HOFSTETTER, C. RICHARD. *Bias in the News: Network Television Coverage of the 1972 Election Campaign.* Columbus: Ohio State University Press, 1976.

KEETER, SCOTT, and ZUKIN, CLIFF. *Uninformed Choice: The Failure of the New Presidential Nominating System.* New York: Praeger, 1983.

KELLEY, STANLEY, JR. *Political Campaigning: Problems in Creating an Informed Electorate.* Washington, D.C.: Brookings Institution, 1960.

KLAPPER, JOSEPH. *The Effects of Mass Communication.* New York: Free Press, 1960.

KRAUS, SIDNEY, ed. *The Great Debates, 1976: Ford vs. Carter.* Bloomington, Ind.: Indiana University Press, 1979.

KRAUS, SIDNEY, and DAVIS, DENNIS. *The Effects of Mass Communication on Political Behavior.* University Park, Pa.: Pennsylvania State University Press, 1976.

LANG, KURT, and LANG, GLADYS ENGEL. *Politics and Television.* Chicago: Quadrangle Books, 1968.

MacKUEN, MICHAEL B., and COOMBS, STEVEN L. *More than News: Media Power in Public Affairs.* Beverly Hills, Calif.: Sage Publications, 1980.

MacNEIL, ROBERT. *The People Machine: The Influence of Television on American Politics.* New York: Harper & Row, 1968.

MENDELSOHN, HAROLD, and CRESPI, IRVING. *Polls, Television, and the New Politics.* Scranton, Pa.: Chandler Publishing, 1970.

NIMMO, DAN. *The Political Persuaders: The Techniques of Modern Election Campaigns.* Englewood Cliffs, N.J.: Prentice-Hall, 1970.

———. *Political Communication and Public Opinion in America.* Santa Monica, Calif.: Goodyear, 1978.

NIMMO, DAN, and COOMBS, JAMES E. *Mediated Political Realities.* New York: Longman, 1983.

ORREN, GARY R., and POLSBY, NELSON N., eds. *Media and Momentum: The New Hampshire Primary and Nomination Politics.* Chatham, NJ: Chatham House Publishers, Inc., 1987.

PARENTI, MICHAEL. *Inventing Reality.* New York: St. Martin's Press, 1986.

PATTERSON, THOMAS E. *The Mass Media Election: How Americans Choose Their President.* New York: Praeger, 1980.

PATTERSON, THOMAS E., and MCCLURE, ROBERT D. *The Unseeing Eye: The Myth of Television Power in National Politics.* New York: G. P. Putnam's Sons, 1976.

PERRY, JAMES M. *The New Politics: The Expanding Technology of Political Manipulation.* New York: Clarkson Potter, 1968.

ROBINSON, MICHAEL J., and RANNEY, AUSTIN, eds. *The Mass Media in Campaign '84.* Washington, D.C.: American Enterprise Institute, 1985.

ROBINSON, MICHAEL J., and SHEEHAN, MARGARET A. *Over the Wire and on TV: CBS and UPI in Campaign '80.* New York: Russell Sage Foundation, 1983.

ROSENBLOOM, DAVID. *The Election Men: Professional Campaign Managers and American Democracy.* New York: Quadrangle Books, 1973.

RUBIN, BERNARD. *Political Television.* Belmont, Calif.: Wadsworth, 1967.

TAYLOR, PAUL. *See How They Run: Electing the President in an Age of Mediacrocy.* New York: Knopf, 1990.

WEISBORD, MARVIN R. *Campaigning for President*. New York: Washington Square
     Press, 1966.

POLITICAL REFORM

BICKEL, ALEXANDER M. *Reform and Continuity: The Electoral College, the Convention,
     and the Party System*. New York: Harper & Row, 1971.
CROTTY, WILLIAM J. *Political Reform and the American Experiment*. New York: Thomas
     Y. Crowell, 1977.
———. *Decision for the Democrats: Reforming the Party Structure*. Baltimore: Johns
     Hopkins University Press, 1978.
GRASSMUCK, GEORGE, ed. *Before Nomination: Our Primary Problems*. Washington,
     D.C.: American Enterprise Institute for Public Policy Research, 1985.
HEARD, ALEXANDER. *Made in America: Improving the Nomination and Election of
     Presidents*. New York: Harper Collins Publishers, Inc., 1991.
NELSON, MICHAEL. *A Heartbeat Away*. New York: Priority Press Publications, 1988.
POLSBY, NELSON W. *Consequences of Party Reform*. New York: Oxford University
     Press, 1983.
RANNEY, AUSTIN. *Curing the Mischiefs of Faction: Party Reform in America*. Berkeley,
     Calif.: University of California Press, 1975.

PRIMARIES, CONVENTIONS, NOMINATIONS, AND PRESIDENTIAL SELECTION IN GENERAL

BAIN, RICHARD C., and PARRIS, JUDITH H. *Conventions, Decisions, and Voting Records*.
     Washington, D.C.: Brookings Institution, 1973.
BARBER, JAMES DAVID, ed. *Choosing the President*. Englewood Cliffs, N.J.:
     Prentice-Hall, 1974.
BONE, HUGH A. *American Politics and the Party System*. New York: McGraw-Hill,
     1971. Selected chapters.
DAVIS, JAMES W. *Presidential Primaries: Road to the White House*. New York: Thomas Y.
     Crowell, 1967.
DAVID, PAUL T., GOLDMAN, RALPH M., and BAIN, RICHARD C. *The Politics of National
     Party Conventions*. Washington, D.C.: Brookings Institution, 1960.
FOLEY, JOHN, BRITTON, DENNIS A., and EVERETT JR., EUGENE B., eds. *Nominating a
     President: The Process and the Press*. New York: Praeger, 1980.
GRASSMUCK, GEORGE, ed. *Before Nomination: Our Primary Problems*. Washington,
     D.C.: American Enterprise Institute, 1985.
HEARD, ALEXANDER, and NELSON MICHAEL, eds. *Presidential Selection*. Durham,
     N.C.: Duke University Press, 1987.
KEECH, WILLIAM R., and MATTHEWS, DONALD R. *The Party's Choice*. Washington,
     D.C.: Brookings Institution, 1977.
KESSEL, JOHN. *Presidential Campaign Politics: Coalition Strategies and Citizen Response*.
     3rd ed. Pacific Grove, Calif.: Brooks/Cole.
KEY, JR., V. O. *Politics, Parties and Pressure Groups*. New York: Thomas Y. Crowell,
     1964. Selected chapters.
KIRKPATRICK, JEANE. *The New Presidential Elite: Men and Women in National Politics*.
     New York: Russell Sage Foundation, 1976.

LENGLE, JAMES I., and SHAFER, BYRON E., eds. *Presidential Politics: Readings on Nominations and Elections.* New York: St. Martin's Press, 1980.

MATTHEWS, DONALD R., ed. *Perspectives on Presidential Selection.* Washington, D.C.: Brookings Institution, 1973.

MILLER, WARREN E., and JENNINGS, M. KENT. *Parties in Transition: A Longitudinal Study of Party Elites and Party Supporters.* New York: Russell Sage Foundation, 1986.

Nomination and Election of the President and Vice President of the United States. Washington, D.C.: U.S. Government Printing Office, 1972.

PAGE, BENJAMIN I. *Choices and Echoes in Presidential Elections: Rational Man and Electoral Democracy.* Chicago: University of Chicago Press, 1978.

PARRIS, JUDITH H. *The Convention Problem.* Washington, D.C.: Brookings Institution, 1972.

POLSBY, NELSON W., and WILDAVSKY, AARON B. *Presidential Elections.* 5th ed. New York: Scribners, 1983.

POMPER, GERALD. *Nominating the President: The Politics of Convention Choice.* New York: Norton, 1966.

RANNEY, AUSTIN. *Participation in American Presidential Nominations, 1967.* Washington, D.C.: American Enterprise Institute for Public Policy Research, 1977.

SORAUF, FRANK J. and BECK, PAUL A. *Party Politics in America.* 6th ed. Boston: Little, Brown, forthcoming.

SULLIVAN, DENIS G., PRESSMAN, JEFFREY L., PAGE, BENJAMIN I., and LYONS, JOHN J. *The Politics of Representation: The Democratic Convention 1972.* New York: St. Martin's Press, 1974.

WATSON, RICHARD A. *The Presidential Contest,* 3rd ed. Washington, D.C.: Congressional Quarterly Press, Inc. 1988.

WAYNE, STEPHEN J. *The Road to the White House,* 3rd ed. New York: St. Martin's Press, 1988.

REALIGNMENT AND POLITICAL CHANGE

BASS, JACK, and DEVRIES, WALTER. *The Transformation of Southern Politics.* New York: Basic Books, 1976.

BRODER, DAVID. *The Party's Over: The Failure of Politics in America.* New York: Harper & Row, 1971.

BURNHAM, WALTER DEAN. *Critical Elections and the Mainsprings of American Politics.* New York: Norton, 1970.

CAMPBELL, BRUCE A., and TRILLING, RICHARD J., eds. *Realignment in American Politics: Toward a Theory.* Austin, Texas: University of Texas Press, 1980.

CHAMBERS, WILLIAM NISBET, and BURNHAM, WALTER DEAN, eds. *The American Party Systems: Stages of Political Development.* New York: Oxford University Press, 1967.

CLUBB, JEROME M., and ALLEN, HOWARD W., eds. *Electoral Change and Stability in American Political History.* New York: Free Press, 1971.

DELLI CARPINI, MICHAEL X. *Stability and Change in American Politics: the Coming Age of the Generation of the 60's.* New York: New York University Press, 1986.

DUTTON, FREDERICK G. *Changing Sources of Power.* New York: McGraw-Hill, 1971.

GREELEY, ANDREW M. *Building Coalitions.* New York: Franklin Watts, 1974.

KNOKE, DAVID. *Change and Continuity in American Politics.* Baltimore: Johns Hopkins University Press, 1976.

LADD, JR., EVERETT CARLL. *Where Have All the Voters Gone?* New York: Norton, 1978.

LADD, JR., EVERETT CARLL, and HADLEY, CHARLES D. *Transformation of the American Party System.* 2nd ed. New York: Norton, 1978.

LIPSET, SEYMOUR MARTIN, ed. *Emerging Coalitions in American Politics.* San Francisco: Institute for Contemporary Studies, 1978.

————. *Party Coalitions in the 1980s.* San Francisco: Institute for Contemporary Studies, 1981.

LUBELL, SAMUEL. *The Hidden Crisis in American Politics.* New York: Norton, 1971.

PHILLIPS, KEVIN B. *The Emerging Republican Majority.* Garden City, N.Y.: Doubleday, 1969.

SCAMMON, RICHARD M., and WATTENBERG, BEN J. *The Real Majority.* New York: Coward, McCann & Geoghegan, 1970.

SEAGULL, LOUIS M. *Youth and Change in American Politics.* New York: New Viewpoints, 1977.

STEWART, JOHN G. *One Last Chance.* New York: Praeger, 1974.

SUNDQUIST, JAMES L. *Dynamics of the Party System.* Washington, D.C.: Brookings Institution, 1973.

BOOKS ON THE CONTEMPORARY PRESIDENCY

BURNS, JAMES MACGREGOR. *The Power to Lead: The Crisis of the American Presidency.* New York: Simon & Schuster, 1984.

CRONIN, THOMAS E. *The State of the Presidency.* Boston: Little, Brown, 1975.

DUNN, CHARLES W., ed. *The Future of the American Presidency.* Morristown, N.J.: General Learning Press, 1975.

HARGROVE, ERWIN C. *The Power of the Modern Presidency.* New York: Alfred A. Knopf, 1974.

HIRSCHFIELD, ROBERT S., ed. *The Power of the Presidency: Concepts and Controversy.* 2nd ed. Chicago: Aldine-Atherton, 1973.

HUGHES, EMMET JOHN. *The Living Presidency: The Resources and Dilemmas of the American Presidential Office.* Baltimore: Penguin Books, 1973.

JAMES, DOROTHY BUCKTON. *The Contemporary Presidency.* 2nd ed. Indianapolis, Ind: Bobbs-Merrill, 1974.

KESSEL, JOHN H. *The Domestic Presidency: Decision-Making in the White House.* North Scituate, Mass: Duxbury Press, 1975.

KOENIG, LOUIS W. *The Chief Executive.* 3rd ed. New York: Harcourt Brace Jovanovich, 1975.

NEUSTADT, RICHARD E. *Presidential Power: The Politics of Leadership.* New York: Wiley, 1960.

NEUSTADT, RICHARD E. *Presidential Power and the Modern Presidents: The Politics of Leadership from Roosevelt to Reagan.* New York: Free Press, 1991.

PFIFFNER, JAMES P. *The Strategic Presidency: Hitting the Ground Running.* Chicago: Pacific Grove, Calif.: Brooks/Cole, 1988.

REEDY, GEORGE E. *The Twilight of the Presidency.* New York: World Publishing, 1970.

ROSSITER, CLINTON. *The American Presidency.* rev. ed. New York: Harcourt Brace Jovanovich, 1960.

SCHLESINGER, JR., ARTHUR M. *The Imperial Presidency.* Boston: Houghton Miftin, 1973.
SUNDQUIST, JAMES I. *Politics and Policy: The Eisenhower, Kennedy, and Johnson Years.* Washington, D.C.: Brookings Institution, 1968.
THOMAS, NORMAN C., ed. *The Presidency in Contemporary Context.* New York: Dodd, Mead, 1975.
TUGWELL, REXFORD G., and CRONIN, THOMAS E., eds. *The Presidency Reappraised.* New York: Praeger, 1974.
WILDAVSKY, AARON, ed. *Perspectives on the Presidency.* Boston: Little, Brown, 1975.

SPECIFIC PRESIDENTIAL ELECTIONS

1960

KRAUS, SIDNEY, ed. *The Great Debates.* Bloomington, Ind.: Indiana University Press, 1962.
POOL, ITHIEL DE SOLA, ABELSON, ROBERT P., and POPKIN, SAMUEL. *Candidates, Issues, and Strategies.* Cambridge, Mass.: MIT Press, 1965.
WHITE, THEODORE H. *The Making of the President 1960.* New York: Atheneum, 1961.

1964

COSMAN, BERNARD, and HUCKSHORN, ROBERT J., eds. *Republican Politics: The 1964 Campaign and Its Aftermath for the Party.* New York: Praeger, 1968.
CUMMINGS, JR., MILTON C., ed. *The National Election of 1964.* Washington, D.C.: Brookings Institution, 1966.
KESSEL, JOHN H. *The Goldwater Coalition: Republican Strategies in 1964.* Indianapolis, Ind.: Bobbs-Merrill, 1968.
LAMB, KARL A., and SMITH, PAUL A. *Campaign Decision-Making: The Presidential Election of 1964.* Belmont, Calif.: Wadsworth, 1968.
WHITE, THEODORE H. *The Making of the President 1964.* New York: Atheneum, 1965.

1968

CHESTER, LEWIS, HODGSON, GODFREY, and PAGE, BRUCE. *An American Melodrama.* New York: Dell, 1969.
KOVENOCK, DAVID M., PROTHRO, JAMES W., and ASSOCIATES. *Explaining the Vote: Presidential Choices in the Nation and the States, 1968.* Chapel Hill, N.C.: Institute for Research in Social Science, 1973.
McGINNISS, JOE. *The Selling of the President 1968.* New York: Trident Press, 1969.
WHITE, THEODORE H. *The Making of the President 1968.* New York: Atheneum, 1969.

1972

MAY, ERNEST R., and FRASER, JANET, eds. *Campaign '72: The Managers Speak.* Cambridge, Mass.: Harvard University Press, 1973.

THOMPSON, HUNTER S. *Fear and Loathing: On the Campaign Trail '72*. New York: Popular Library, 1973.
WHITE, THEODORE H. *The Making of the President 1972*. New York: Atheneum, 1973.

1976

POMPER, GERALD, ed. *The Election of 1976*. New York: David McKay, 1977.
SCHRAM, MARTIN. *Running for President*. New York: Stein & Day, 1977.
WITCOVER, JULES, *Marathon: The Pursuit of the Presidency, 1972–1976*. New York: New American Library, 1977.
WOOTEN, JAMES. *Dasher*. New York: Warner Books, 1979.

1980

ABRAMSON, PAUL R., ALDRICH, JOHN H., and ROHDE, DAVID W. *Change and Continuity in the 1980 Elections*. Washington, D.C.: Congressional Quarterly Press, 1982.
GERMOND, JACK, and WITCOVER, JULES. *Blue Smoke and Mirrors: How Reagan Won and Why Carter Lost the Election of 1980*. New York: Viking Press, 1981.
MOORE, JONATHAN, ed. *The Campaign for President: 1980 in Retrospect*. Cambridge, Mass.: Ballinger, 1981.
POMPER, GERALD. *The Election of 1980: Reports and Interpretations*. Chatham, N.J.: Chatham House, 1981.
RANNEY, AUSTIN, ed. *The American Elections of 1980*. Washington: American Enterprise Institute for Public Policy Research, 1981.
SANDOZ, ELLIS, and CRABB, JR., CECIL V., eds. *A Tide of Discontent: The 1980 Elections and Their Meaning*. Washington, D.C.: Congressional Quarterly Press, 1981.

1984

ABRAMSON, PAUL R., ALDRICH, JOHN H., and ROHDE, DAVID W. *Change and Continuity in the 1984 Elections*. Washington, D.C.: Congressional Quarterly Press, 1986.
BLUME, KEITH. *The Presidential Election Show: Campaign '84 and Beyond on the Nightly News*. South Hadley, Mass.: Bergin & Garvey Publishers, 1985.
BROOKHISER, RICHARD. *The Outside Story: How Democrats and Republicans Reelected Reagan*. Garden City, N.Y.: Doubleday, 1986.
CAVANAGH, THOMAS E. *Inside Black America: The Message of the Black Vote in the 1984 Elections*. Washington, D.C.: Joint Center for Political Studies, 1985.
MOORE, JONATHAN, ed. *Campaign for President: The Managers Look at '84*. Dover, Mass.: Auburn House Publishing Company, 1986.
NELSON, MICHAEL, ed. *The Elections of 1984*. Washington, D.C.: Congressional Quarterly Press, 1985.
POMPER, GERALD. *The Election of 1984: Reports and Interpretations*. Chatham, N.J.: Chatham House Publishers, 1985.
SANDOZ, ELLIS, and CRABB, JR., CECIL V., eds. *Election '84*. New York and Scarborough, Ont.: New American Library, 1985.

STEED, ROBERT P., MORELAND, LAURENCE W., and BAKER, TOD A., eds. *The 1984 Presidential Election in the South: Patterns of Southern Party Politics.* New York: Praeger, 1986.

1988

ABRAMSON, PAUL R., ALDRICH, JOHN R., and ROHDE, DAVID W. *Change and Continuity in the 1988 Elections.* Washington, D.C.: Congressional Quarterly Inc., 1990.

BLUMENTHAL, SIDNEY. *Pledging Allegiance.* New York: Harper Collins, 1990.

BUCHANAN, BRUCE. *Electing a President: The Markle Commission Report on Campaign '88.* Austin, Texas: University of Texas Press, 1991.

NELSON, MICHAEL (ed.). *The Elections of 1988,* Washington, D.C.: Congressional Quarterly Inc., 1989.

POMPER, GERALD M., BAKER, ROSS K., BURNHAM, WALTER DEAN, FARAH, BARBARA G., HERSHEY, MARJORIE RANDOR, KLEIN, ETHEL, and McWILLIAMS, WILSON CARY. *The Election of 1988: Reports and Interpretations.* Chatham, N.J.: Chatham House Publishers, Inc., 1989.

RUNKLE, DAVID R. *Campaigning for President: The Managers Look at '88.* Dover, Mass: Auburn House, 1989.

SIMON, ROGER. *Road Show.* New York: Farrar Strauss & Giroux, 1990.

TAYLOR, PAUL. *See How They Run.* New York: Knopf, 1990.

VOTING BEHAVIOR, POLITICAL PARTICIPATION, AND POLITICAL SOCIALIZATION

ABRAMSON, PAUL R. *Political Attitudes in America: Formation and Change.* San Francisco: W. H. Freeman, 1983.

AVEY, MICHAEL J. *The Demobilization of American Voters: A Comprehensive Theory of Voter Turnout.* New York: Greenwood Press, 1984.

BERELSON, BERNARD R., LAZARSFELD, PAUL F., and McPHEE, WILLIAM N. *Voting.* Chicago: University of Chicago Press, 1954.

BURDICK, EUGENE, and BRODBECK, ARTHUR J., eds. *American Voting Behavior.* New York: Free Press, 1959.

CAMPBELL, ANGUS, CONVERSE, PHILIP E., MILLER, WARREN E., and STOKES, DONALD E. *The American Voter.* New York: Wiley, 1960.

———. *Elections and the Political Order.* New York: Wiley, 1966.

CAMPBELL, ANGUS, GURIN, GERALD, and MILLER, WARREN E. *The Voter Decides.* Evanston, Ill.: Row, Peterson, 1954.

CAMPBELL, BRUCE A. *The American Electorate: Attitudes and Action.* New York: Holt, Rinehart & Winston, 1979.

CANTOR, ROBERT D. *Voting Behavior & Presidential Elections.* Itasca, Ill.: F. E. Peacock, 1975.

CONVERSE, PHILIP E. *The Dynamics of Party Support: Cohort-Analyzing Party Identification.* Beverly Hills, Calif.: Sage Publications, 1976.

CONWAY, M. MARGARET. *Political Participation in the United States.* 2nd ed. Washington, D.C.: Congressional Quarterly Press, 1991.

DEVRIES, WALTER, and TARRANCE, V. LANCE. *The Ticket-Splitter: A New Force in American Politics*. Grand Rapids, Mich.: W. B. Eerdmans Publishing, 1972.

DREYER, EDWARD C., and ROSENBAUM, WALTER A., eds. *Political Opinion and Behavior: Essays and Studies*. 2nd ed. Belmont, Calif.: Wadsworth, 1970.

DUNHAM, PAT. *Electoral Behavior in the United States*. Englewood Cliffs, New Jersey: Prentice-Hall, 1991.

FIORINA, MORRIS P. *Retrospective Voting in American National Elections*. New Haven, Conn.: Yale University Press, 1981.

FISHEL, JEFF, ed. *Parties and Elections in an Anti-Party Age*. Bloomington, Ind.: Indiana University Press, 1978.

FLANIGAN, WILLIAM H., and ZINGALE, NANCY H. *Political Behavior of the American Electorate*. 7th ed. Washington, D.C.: Congressional Quarterly Press, 1991.

GINSBERG, BENJAMIN. *Politics By Other Means: The Declining Importance of Elections in America*. New York: Basic Books, 1990.

GREENSTEIN, FRED I. *Children and Politics*. New Haven, Conn.: Yale University Press, 1965.

HESS, ROBERT D., and TORNEY, JUDITH V. *The Development of Political Attitudes in Children*. Chicago: Aldine-Atherton, 1967.

HILL, DAVID B., and LUTTBEG, NORMAN R. *Trends in American Electoral Behavior*. Itasca, Ill.: F. E. Peacock, 1980.

JENNINGS, M. KENT, and NIEMI, RICHARD G. *The Political Character of Adolescence: The Influence of Families and Schools*. Princeton, N.J.: Princeton University Press, 1974,

————. *Generations and Politics: A Panel Study of Young Adults and Their Parents*. Princeton, N.J.: Princeton University Press, 1981.

JENNINGS, M. KENT, and ZIEGLER, L. HARMON, eds. *The Electoral Process*. Englewood Cliffs, N.J.: Prentice-Hall, 1966.

KAMIENICKI, SHELDON. *Party Identification, Political Behavior and the American Electorate*. Westport, Conn.: Greenwood Press, 1985.

KEY, V. O. *The Responsible Electorate*. New York: Vintage Books, 1966.

LANE, ROBERT. *Political Life*. New York: Free Press, 1959.

LAZARSFELD, PAUL F., BERELSON, BERNARD, and GAUDET, HAZEL. *The People's Choice: How the Voter Makes up His Mind in a Presidential Campaign*. New York: Columbia University Press, 1968.

MAISEL, LOUIS, and COOPER, JOSEPH, eds, *The Impact of the Electoral Process*. Beverly Hills, Calif.: Sage Publications, 1977.

MILBRATH, LESTER W., and GOEL, M. L. *Political Participation: How and Why Do People Get Involved in Politics?* 2nd ed. Chicago: Rand McNally, 1977.

MILLER, WARREN E., and LEVITIN, TERESA E. *Leadership and Change: Presidential Elections from 1952 to 1976*. Cambridge, Mass.: Winthrop, 1976.

MULCAHY, KEVIN V., and KATZ, RICHARD S. *American Votes: What You Should Know about Elections Today*. Englewood Cliffs, N.J.: Prentice-Hall, 1976.

NIE, NORMAN H., VERBA, SIDNEY, and PETROCIK, JOHN R. *The Changing American Voter*. Cambridge, Mass.: Harvard University Press, 1976.

NIEMI, RICHARD G., ed. *New Views of Children and Politics*. San Francisco: Jossey-Bass, 1974.

NIEMI, RICHARD G., and WEISBERG, HERBERT F., eds. *Controversies in American Voting Behavior*. San Francisco: W. H. Freeman, 1976.

NIEMI, RICHARD G., and WEISBERG, HERBERT F., eds. *Controversies in American Voting Behavior.* 2nd ed. Washington, D.C.: Congressional Quarterly Press, 1984.

PIVEN, FRANCES FOX, and CLOWARD, RICHARD A. *Why Americans Don't Vote,* New York: Pantheon, 1988.

POMPER, GERALD M. *Voters' Choice: Varieties of American Electoral Behavior.* New York: Dodd, Mead, 1975.

SCHLOZMAN, KAY L., ed. *Elections in America.* Boston: Allen & Unwin, 1987.

SMITH, ERIC R. A. N. *The Unchanging American Voter.* Berkeley: University of California Press, 1989.

TEIXEIRA, ROY A. *Why Americans Don't Vote: Turnout Decline in the United States, 1960–1989,* New York: Greenwood Press, 1987.

VERBA, SIDNEY, and NIE, NORMAN H. *Participation in America.* New York: Harper & Row, 1972.

WATTENBERG, MARTIN P. *The Decline of American Political Parties, 1952–1984.* Cambridge, Mass.: Harvard University Press, 1986.

WATTENBERG, MARTIN P. *The Rise of Candidate-Centered Politics: Presidential Elections of the 1980's.* Cambridge, Mass.: Harvard University Press, 1991.

WOLFINGER, RAYMOND E., and ROSENSTONE, STEVEN J. *Who Votes?* New Haven, Conn.: Yale University Press, 1980.